INFANT MORTALITY, POPULATION GROWTH
AND FAMILY PLANNING IN INDIA

Other books by S. Chandrasekhar

India's Population: Facts, Problems and Policy
(Meerut: Meenakshi Prakashan, 1970). Second edition

Asia's Population Problems
(London: Allen & Unwin, 1967; New York: Praeger, 1967)

Problems in Economic Development
(edited) (Boston: D. C. Heath, 1967)

American Aid and India's Economic Development
(London: Pall Mall Press; New York: Praeger, 1966). Second printing

Red China: An Asian View
(New York: Praeger, 1964). Fifth printing

Communist China Today
(London: Asia Publishing House, 1964). Third enlarged edition

A Decade of Mao's China
(edited) (Bombay: The Perennial Press, 1962)

China's Population: Census and Vital Statistics
(Hong Kong: Oxford University Press, 1962). Second revised edition

A Report on South Indian Reading Habits
(Madras: Southern Languages Book Trust and Ford Foundation, 1960)

Infant Mortality in India, 1901–1951
(London: Allen & Unwin; New York: Humanities Press, 1959)

Population and Planned Parenthood in India
Forewords by Jawaharlal Nehru and Julian Huxley (London: Allen & Unwin, 1956). Second revised edition

Hungry People and Empty Lands
(London: Allen & Unwin; New York: Macmillan, 1955). Third edition

India's Population: Fact and Policy
(New York: John Day, 1950). Second edition

Census and Statistics in India
(Chidambaram: Annamalai University Press, 1948)

Indian Emigration to America
(Bombay: Oxford University Press, 1947)

India and the War
(New York: News-India, 1942)

INFANT MORTALITY
POPULATION GROWTH AND
FAMILY PLANNING
IN INDIA

by S. Chandrasekhar

London · George Allen & Unwin Ltd
Ruskin House   Museum Street

Printed in Great Britain
in 10 on 11 point Times New Roman
by Alden & Mowbray Ltd
at the Alden Press, Oxford

To my wife

HB

Preface

For a quarter-century India's population problem has been my major intellectual and professional concern, and high infant mortality is perhaps the most depressing feature of this problem.

This book is roughly divided into two sections. The first and major portion of the book is devoted to an examination of the two most important aspects of infant mortality in India. The first aspect deals with the availability of information about India's infant mortality and includes an historical survey of the census and vital statistical data (1901–71); the second deals with the known facts on the magnitude of the infant mortality rate and its components, as well as its causes. There is also a brief discussion on methods of calculating infant mortality rates, particularly in areas where all the needed data are unavailable or, when available, inaccurate and incomplete.

The second and more topical section of the book examines the interrelationship between population growth, infant mortality and family planning. Here, in the light of certain theoretical models, the problem of whether a reduction in mortality is a necessary prerequisite to a reduction of fertility or vice versa is examined and the accomplishments and failures of the family planning policy measures so far undertaken in reducing the Indian birth rate are reviewed. A policy and programme of action designed to reduce the high infant mortality rate is also outlined.

In any search for effective answers to the population problems of developing countries, some serious attention must be directed sooner or later to the problem of high infant mortality rates. When the close relation between high infant mortality and the dimension of the population problem is understood, the role of family planning as a long-range solution to India's population problem becomes obvious. Because many babies are born, many die in infancy, and the large

9

number of children born is apparently in response to the high number of infant deaths. Therefore, any attempt to evolve the small family norm in India must involve a serious policy to reduce the infant death rate.

I have been interested over the years in exploring various means of promoting family planning and reducing family size in India, and I am convinced that efforts to reduce the infant mortality rate, though difficult, will, along with other measures, eventually lead to a reduction in the high birth rate. And hence this study in some depth of India's infant mortality, particularly in its relation to India's overall population problem and the current family planning programmes. The humanitarian reason for saving infant lives is so obvious that it need not be enlarged upon.

Apart from its policy implications, this essay was undertaken because there is not a single study on the subject of infant mortality in India. As such, the book is addressed to various types of readers: first, as the subject of population explosion and India's illustrative case have become matters of topical and general interest, it is addressed to the intelligent layman and general reader who is interested in population questions or Indian problems. Secondly, it concerns undergraduate and graduate students pursuing courses on demography, public health, sociology, and statistics. It will also be directed at such professional groups as paediatricians, general physicians, and nurses, to government officials, both administrative and professional, in the municipal, state, and central governments who are in charge of implementing policy measures designed to reduce the relatively high birth and death rates in India and other developing countries.

I am indebted to Mr S. P. Jain, formerly of the Ministry of Health, Family Planning and Urban Development, Government of India, New Delhi, and Dr David S. Kleinman of the Battelle Research Center, for their many valuable suggestions. I am thankful to Messrs S. Krishman, R. V. Neelakantan and P. N. Chopra, my former secretaries in New Delhi, for typing the first draft, and to Mrs Marty Campbell and Mrs Susie Armstrong, my secretaries at the Battelle Research Center, who typed and checked parts of the manuscript. My thanks are also due to Dr Carl Sandler, Dr S. B. Mani, and Mrs Ruth Meier for their help with the graphs.

I am grateful to Dr R. S. Paul, Dr T. W. Ambrose, Mr. Kenneth B. Hobbs and other colleagues at the Battelle Research Center for valuable assistance in many ways in making my work and sojourn at the Center pleasant and stimulating.

Mr Charles Furth of George Allen & Unwin has, as always,

extended his cordial and warm co-operation in bringing out this book, and my special thanks go to him. I am also grateful to Mr Matthew Hodgson, Director of the University of North Carolina Press, for bringing out the American edition of the book.

More than anyone else, I am grateful to my wife, my severest and most constructive critic, for perusing the manuscript and seeing it through the press.

Some material from this study was presented sometime ago as the Sir William Meyer Endowment Lectures at the University of Madras and I would like to record my gratitude to the Vice-Chancellor and Syndicate of the University for honouring me in inviting me to deliver these lectures.

S. Chandrasekhar
Battelle Research Center
Seattle, Washington
June 1971

Contents

Contents

Tables

Charts

Plates

Introduction

This study is primarily an attempt to survey the level, causes, and course of infant mortality in India during the last seventy years, 1901–71. Besides this historical survey which is really the Government's continuous search for better and more data on the subject, this book examines the various implications of high and low infant mortality on the country's major problem of population growth and the current population policy designed to reduce the birth rate through family planning.

Today, India's population has passed the 550 million mark. To this population, a baby is born every second and a half, 21 million births a year. Some eight million persons die every year. Of these deaths, more than two million are infants below the age of one year; that is, about a hundred infant deaths for a thousand live births in a year. This is the magnitude and challenge of the problem of infant mortality in India.

All of the available and acceptable material on infant mortality in India during the period under review has been assembled to evaluate the range and magnitude of infant deaths, their causes, and possible solutions. The nature, worth, and value of the source material for the study have been examined in some detail, largely in the light of official reports and evaluation. While this examination may appear to be too detailed, it has been found necessary to indicate what kind of tools are available for the task that has been undertaken. In a sense, this examination is most important, for the weaknesses and strengths of the sources are reflected in the study. The cleanliness and purity of the stream are largely conditioned by circumstances at the source. The variegated evolution of the source material and the barrage of official and unofficial criticism to which it has been subjected through the years have been outlined, much of it in the language of the reports of the various committees and commissions. If the resulting statistical record has not improved, it can only constitute a sad commentary both on the cussedness of Indian administration and the lack of civic consciousness and statistical sense on the part of the people.

Despite obvious limitations, much reliance has been placed on official material, supplemented whenever possible by unofficial data, where such data have been found to be reliable. And where there is no direct evidence, one can only rely on opinions in the hope that they are expert ones. But opinions on such demographic matters as fertility and mortality can sometimes be notoriously misleading. As for customs, habits and manners, and the entire cultural ethos and its abiding impact on matters of life and death, expert data have been more easily available, for here cultivated observation can be largely relied on.

The first seventy years of this century, 1901–71, have been chosen as a period of study for various reasons. First, it is a long and yet not-too-long period wherein trends can be observed better than in short intervals of time. Second, trends are important because of the defectiveness of the available statistical material, where specific annual totals and rates in births or deaths do not have much significance. While surveying and establishing trends, seventy years constitute a convenient and significant stretch of time.

Third, the political evolution of the country from complete dependence on an alien administration and rule to full political freedom, a nationalist government and responsible administration for nearly a quarter century (1947–71) fit into the chosen period. The political aspect is important, for the advance of public health, preventive medicine and economic development are to a large extent conditioned by the political status of a country. The population dynamics of a country are considerably affected by such factors as peace, political freedom and blessings these can confer, which in turn may provide an opportunity for economic advancement, social progress, and cultural regeneration.

Several causes, conventional and otherwise, contribute to high infant mortality in India. Some of these causes, major infantile diseases, have been conquered elsewhere but not yet in India. Only in recent years has the vital role of nutrition in infant morbidity and mortality been recognized. And only during the last few years it has been established by studies in India that apart from the lack of calories, the want of protein in infant and early child nutrition has indirectly contributed to infant disease and death, as well as leading to poor physical development and mental dwarfism.

22

The long fight, apparently never wholehearted, initiated under the British rule by a few dedicated and pioneering British (and later American) medical men and women down to the efforts of the present Ministry of Health in the Government of India against this unnecessary and tragic loss of infants has been outlined. And some suggestions – educational, economic, medical, and cultural – which are easier advocated than implemented, for an effective attack upon this high infant mortality, have been offered. An indication is given of the progress and achievements of certain advanced countries and some hope is expressed that what is possible elsewhere should be possible in India also, given more or less similar circumstances.

The importance of an inquiry into all vital losses up to the age of one year is obvious. First, the infant mortality rate is a refined and sensitive index of the total cultural milieu of a community or a country. It reflects the state of public health and hygiene, environmental sanitation, cultural mores about feeding and clothing, socioeconomic development and the stage of the arts, and above all, the people's attitudes towards the dignity and value of human life itself. In the advanced Western countries, infant mortality due to environmental factors has been largely controlled, but in developing countries, where these factors are still uncontrolled, no simple statistical index conveys so much so effectively as the infant mortality rate.

Second, the magnitude and range of infant mortality are equally important for their effect on the future growth of population in countries where the population numbers are problematic in the sense of too many or too few in relation to the total set of relevant economic and social factors. A country which is under-populated or has a stabilized birth rate cannot afford to lose more than the minimum and unavoidable number of infants. And countries which are faced with too many people, with the problem of pressure of numbers on the available, limited resources, are bound to look at high infant mortality, no doubt unconsciously, with a certain amount of detachment and want of concern. It is not an accident that countries with considerable population pressure and with under-developed economies have high infant mortality rates. And they are discovering that even a nominal reduction of such mortality levels is bound to add more to their net annual additions of population.

And here is an ethical delemma. Every infant's life which can be saved, and today about 95 per cent can be, must be saved. The right of a newborn baby to the longest possible life can never be questioned in any culture. But then, if more babies are born, more babies are likely to, and do, die. Therefore, an effective reduction of infant

23

mortality seems to imply and involve a reduction of total births. A purposeful control of infant deaths and mortality in other age groups unaccompanied by a conscious control of fertility seems to be meaningless in the economies of many under-developed countries. This neo-Malthusian approach is now widely understood in view of the current population explosion in the world. In other words, a fall in the birth rate must, in ordinary circumstances, lead to a fall in the first-year death rate, since infant deaths make a heavy contribution to total mortality. Thus, for these two reasons, a country must watch over its total number of births and also ensure that as many births as possible flower into healthy and active adult lives for their own sake, if for no other reason.

But there is another and equally important aspect of the problem of infant mortality which is often overlooked in countries like India with considerable population pressure. This, as distinguished from the neo-Malthusian, may be called the Humanitarian aspect. While recognizing the existence of an acute population problem and conceding the imperative need for family planning, it is maintained that every possible effort must be made to reduce the infant mortality rate to promote family planning. In India and other developing countries where social security systems and old-age benefits are absent, old people expect to be supported in their old age by one or two sons as a matter of filial and familial obligation. In traditional and agrarian societies with high infant and child mortality rates, couples tend to have several children to ensure the survival of one or two sons to support the parents in their old age. Therefore, an effective reduction in infant mortality will contribute to a lower birth rate through family planning.

Therefore, there is a compelling need, as this study concludes, for a nation's resources, albeit limited, to be invested in birth control as well as death control, to evolve an economy with low birth and death rates and an eventual high rate of economic growth.

Chapter 1
POPULATION CENSUS AND VITAL STATISTICS IN INDIA

The idea of conducting a periodical enumeration of people was not unknown in ancient times. Like other countries, all the way from Greece to Great Britain, India has a census history that goes far back into the mists of antiquity and offers a considerable variety in technique. It is but natural that in ancient India the rulers should have resorted to some kind of rough counting of the people or their households, if only to gauge the military strength of the country and possibly for purposes of taxation. We have some evidence to this effect. Kautilya's *Arthasastra* (*c.* 300 B.C.) gives us a glimpse of the high level reached in statistical matters in ancient India. The individual enumeration of occupation and production recorded by Kautilya was fairly advanced even by modern standards. Megasthenes, the Greek ambassador to India in about 300 B.C., came across men employed by Indian rulers to collect census and vital statistics.[1] In Mauryan times (325–188 B.C.) we are told that periodical enumeration of the people was common and that civic bodies regularly conducted such work.[2] There was also a system of registering births and deaths for the information of the Government. A few centuries later, when Indian civilization reached its heyday under the Guptas (A.D. 300–600), census operations were not merely periodical but had something in the nature of a permanent continuing activity.[3]

And some decades before the British gained supreme political control over India, several attempts were made to count the people of Madras, the then senior major presidency of India. In 1767, on the suggestion of the East India Company, which was rapidly becoming

[1] Narendranath Law, *Studies in Ancient Indian Polity* (London, 1914), p. 18.
[2] Vincent Smith, *Early History of India* (Oxford, 1924), p. 134.
[3] Ibid., p. 134.

25

a quasi-political body, a rough computation of the number of people in the Madras Presidency was undertaken. But all these earlier and pre-British attempts were irregular and more or less devoid of scientific content. It is even doubtful whether they can be called census in the strict sense of the term.

The first attempt at a regular enumeration of the people, however, after the firm establishment of the Company rule, was made in 1822 in the Madras Presidency. This was carried out on a form devised by the famous British administrator, Sir Thomas Munro. In fact, he devised this form as early as 1802, and between 1813 and 1815 three yearly counts were taken along with the determination of the land revenue. It was, however, in 1849 that the Government of the East India Company contemplated a census of the people in all their then scattered possessions in India, and this was the earliest idea of a census beyond the frontiers of the then Madras Presidency. The suggestion was made for holding quinquennial counts of the population, and the Madras Government was the earliest to adopt the suggestion and thus pioneered the way. At least four such enumerations were carried out in the Madras Presidency before the Central Government took up the work and the provincial government's work became merged in the Imperial Census. With the experience of earlier enumerations, the Madras Government was quite confident of success, for it reported in 1871: 'There is nothing novel in the idea of a census in this Presidency and there is no reason to anticipate any difficulty in carrying out the wishes of the Government of India.' All these earlier attempts at counting heads – the early census operations were no more than that – made whatever use they could of the existing administrative and other agencies, and this principle, to a greater or a lesser extent, has always characterized the Indian census.

The first 'all-India' but partial census took place in 1872, but the first regular, decennial census series began from 1881. The procedure and the machinery of enumeration in India have not changed very much since the first regular census of 1881 down to the decennial census of 1961, except to the extent made desirable by the accumulating experience that demands more and more data to meet the changing economic and social conditions, and the growing, complex administrative machinery of the government.

CENSUS ORGANIZATION

Today the census hierarchy in India begins from the top at New Delhi with the Registrar-General and Chief Census Commissioner.

The post of a permanent Registrar-General was created in 1951 to take the place of a temporary, decennial appointment of the Chief Census Commissioner. Under him are the census superintendents in the various states of the Indian Union (these census superintendents are drawn for the most part from the Indian civil and administrative services). These posts are at present temporary and are usually created on the eve of the decennial census. Recently, the Government of India has agreed to maintain a small permanent staff of key officials in the states for the census organization. Then, in descending order of importance, the district officer, the sub-divisional or the Tahsil officer, the revenue circle inspector, the Parghana and so on to, finally, the village chowkidar, Patwari or headman. Of this hierarchy, only the first two groups are whole-time census officers and the rest are either members of the already-existing administrative machinery or temporary employees. When we come to the district, the main unit of administration in India, the census chain fits in with the administrative chain. Both authority and economy counsel this; the first because the immediate authorities recognized by the people are brought into the census as administrative heads. It follows in the administrative order of the district collector (that is, head of the district), the Tahsildar (head of a tahsil) and so on. The second reason is that these officers serve as useful links in the census chain without any extra payment. Many of them are touring officers, who are expected to spend a certain portion of the year in travelling around the areas under their charge.

Thus, the census operation becomes a by-product of the existing administrative system, since the census department makes the maximum and best possible use of the tours and other activities of lesser administrative heads also. The principle of making the census chain coincide with the administrative chain is naturally extended to other fields. Thus Customs and Post Offices are in charge of dock enumeration and postal personnel; the Railway personnel furnish the census staff for railway premises; the Army and Navy authorities are in charge of enumerating soldiers and sailors, and so on. Special arrangements are made for the enumeration of the prisoners in jails, patients in hospitals, sanatoria and asylums and of travellers by boat, road, rail or air. There are a few exceptions, of course, but they affect only a very small proportion of the country's population; for example, in certain tribal areas, where administration rests lightly and no competent literate residents are found, enumerators are sent in from outside to count the people (of such tribal areas). These enumerators are paid, and are practically the only enumerating personnel who are. In the last Census, enumerators were paid a small amount, Rs 20 each, to meet out-of-pocket expenses. It is increasingly realized that enumerators will have to be paid more adequately in future.

The Indian Census used to be a *de facto* one-night count, but from 1941 it has aimed at counting persons at their normal place of residence, except for certain absentees who remain away from their normal place of residence throughout the enumeration period. The enumeration period was spread over a fortnight in 1951 and twenty days in 1961. Regionally, the Indian census units, in ascending order, are block, circle, charge, tahsil, district and province or state. At the fourth item, as observed already, the census chain coincides with that of the ordinary regular administrative unit. Each village and town is divided into a number of blocks, each block consisting of 100 to 150 households and sometimes more. Each of such blocks constitutes the 'beat' of an enumerator. And a number of such blocks constitutes a 'circle' which is in charge of a census supervisor. The houses in each block are numbered and visited by enumerators, and particulars are gathered by them with reference to the categories contained in the census schedule.

The 'circles' in their turn are combined into 'charges' which in rural areas correspond to a revenue firka, while each urban 'area' is constituted into a separate 'charge'. The work in each 'charge' is looked after by a superintendent. In those parts of India where the administrative system recognizes such a feature as a revenue inspector in charge of a particular area (this is so for example in the States of Madras and East Punjab) this revenue inspector or Kanungo, or whatever he is called, will be a 'charge' superintendent.

Thus the district is generally taken as the unit of the census, with the district collector (who is the administrative head) in charge. In the municipal areas, the Commissioner or the Chief Executive Officer is put in charge of the work. In the village the Patwari looks after the work. The whole system resembles a pyramid of which the base is the individual enumerator in his block, which often corresponds to the village or a well-defined part thereof or a town or a city, and the apex, of course, is the Registrar-General and Chief Census Commissioner in New Delhi.

The actual enumeration is a very elaborate and tedious process, for, as a village enumerator once put it, the aim of the census is 'to catch every man and catch him once'. The first step in the Indian Census (of which figures always relate to March 1) is the preparation of a list of villages and within each village a list of the houses. The exhaustive house list in each village is very important, for it serves as the basis for the enumerator when he goes on his counting rounds. This house list always causes some difficulty, for the houses, especially in rural India, are neither permanent little independent brick-built cottages nor huge cement and iron apartment buildings. In bigger cities, not an insignificant section lives in temporary makeshift hutments mostly in slums, which are liable to appear and disappear with a frequency that is irritating to the Census Department. The existence of this hut, home, house or habitation – it is called all these in census literature – is all the more uncertain when the decennial enumerator comes along.

However, this is not so bad as it sounds, for in each village there is always the nucleus of more permanent structures, and the rural community being fairly compact and existing in a well-defined geographical area, it is seldom that residential changes escape the notice of the village enumerator, who, as already pointed out, happens to be the permanent village Patwari. Pavement dwellers with literally no roof above their heads and the other homeless population are caught in the Census in a one-night count. Their figures are also shown separately. For census purposes, the 'house' in India is defined in two ways. 'Where a structural criterion is taken,' says the Census Commissioner for 1921, 'a house is ordinarily defined with minor qualifications as the residence of one or more families having a separate independent entrance from the common way. Where the social aspect is looked into, it is defined as the home of a commensal family with its residents, dependants and servants.'[1]

Again for census purposes, a house is defined as a structure or part of a structure inhabited or vacant, or a dwelling, a shop, a shop-cum-dwelling or a place of business, workshop, school, etc., with a separate entrance from the common way. It may be used as a dwelling and occupied by a number of households, which the census defines as a group of persons who commonly live together and usually take their meals from a common kitchen. The household may comprise related and unrelated persons. According to Yeatts:

'Every house where a human being may be found is given a number and that number has to be white-washed or painted on the door or displayed prominently in one way or another. Sometimes in the conical huts frequent on the Coromandel coast there is no surface that will take paint or wash and in such cases a number on a ticket is given to the occupant of the house. Each enumerator is given a

[1] *Census of India, 1921* (New Delhi: Government of India Press, 1923), p. 142.

list of the houses entrusted to him and it is these houses that he is to visit on his beat and these alone.'[1]

In the 1961 Census, all houses, whether used as dwellings or not, were numbered. The census house-listing was utilized to collect information on the purpose for which the house was used, as well as on certain items recommended by the United Nations for a housing census. This produced information about the number of small-scale and cottage industries and yielded useful data on the state of housing in the country.

Beginning with the 1951 Census operations, each enumerator's record (answers to census questionnaire) was taken down on slips supplied to him. This is a welcome departure, for in the previous censuses the enumerator had to take in all the details on a schedule as in the United Kingdom and the United States, which were later transferred to the slips. This departure from the conventional method saves time and labour. The enumerator is given a booklet in which instructions and questions to be asked appear in the enumerator's own language. And on the slips the numbers of the questions are printed with a blank space opposite for recording answers. This procedure minimizes to a considerable extent the difficulties presented by the lack of a single common language in India. In 1961 the questions were reproduced on the census schedule.

When all the slips are filled up, they are sorted with indications as to their local origin. To complete this operation and minimize the enumerator's scriptory effort, a code system has been devised (which is printed on the slips, and this reaches the enumerator in a permanent form). Under this code, the districts within each province or state are arranged with ascending serial numbers from one in the order of their usual citation. Similarly, within a district, the tahsils are numbered, and similarly within a tahsil, the 'charges', and within a 'charge', the 'circle'. Every state in India has a district 1 and every district has a tahsil 1, and so on; and thus slips carrying a particular code number have a particular significance in every state in India.

Questions in the Indian census schedule, like any other census questionnaire, elicit information on familiar points of interest. Age, sex, civil condition, means of livelihood, birth place, mother tongue and literacy have been the usual items on which information is sought. The census schedule of 1951 had widened the field by asking

[1] M. W. M. Yeatts, 'The World's Largest Census', *Asia*, New York, February 1941.

some twenty-two questions. The additions were devoted to information on means of livelihood, information on fertility such as the age of the girl or boy at marriage, age of the mother at the birth of the first child, the number born and the number surviving.

The 1951 Census standardized the schedule which carried fourteen questions in all. They were: (1) name and relationship to the head of the household; (2) nationality, religion and special groups (like backward classes); (3) civil condition; (4) age; (5) birth place; (6) displaced persons; (7) mother tongue; (8) bi-lingualism; (9) economic status (employment and dependency); (10) principal means of livelihood; (11) secondary means of livelihood; (12) literacy and education; (13) a question left for each state government to frame to elicit information on some subject of peculiar importance to the state concerned; and (14) sex.

Thus, the 1951 Census schedule departed from earlier schedules both in the number of questions asked and in the nature of the questions themselves. These changes were partly the result of the experience gained at the previous censuses. Some questions like information on caste have been deleted, thus reducing the total number of questions asked, and some questions have been made more precise. In view of the considerable illiteracy of the population and a lack of statistical sense even among the educated middle classes, a more ambitious schedule was found inadvisable.

Besides, the new schedule reflects the new political status of India. Free India is trying to evolve a democratic and secular state. As Free India's constitution is a democratic one, and since caste and democracy are incompatible, even the enumeration of castes has been dropped. It has been found that the mere labelling of people as belonging to this or that caste has been a factor in the perpetuation of the invidious system.[1] Cross-tabulation of characteristics such as age, marital status and mother tongue was previously done by religion, but in 1951 cross-tabulation was made by the economic characteristic of livelihood of classes instead of religion.

But the question as to the community to which a citizen belonged

[1] The late Sardar Vallabhai Patel, while inaugurating, as Minister for Home Affairs of the Government of India, a conference of census superintendents in 1951, observed: 'Formerly there used to be elaborate caste tables which were required in India partly to satisfy the theory that it was a caste-ridden country and partly to meet the needs of administrative measures dependent on caste divisions. In the following census this will no longer be a prominent feature and we can devote our energies and attention to the collection and formulation of basic economic data relating to the means of livelihood of the people and other economic activitie of the individual and the state.'

31

at the last minute was at this time wanting. Although the people did not consider the Census so objectionable in itself, the opportunity of harassing the Government was too good to be missed.'[1]

It must be added in fairness to the Mahatma that he was too busy with his celebrated March to the sea to break the Salt Law, to advise the people to co-operate with the Government Census officials. The failure to secure Gandhi's blessings on the part of the Census Department resulted in increased responsibilities for the enumerators. One of the commonest forms in which trouble arose was the effacement of the census numbers on houses. It was not without recourse to the penal provisions of the law that the census work was eventually completed.

In 1941, due to the individualist nature and much toned down character of the Civil Disobedience Movement (confined to a few thousands instead of millions), it did not hinder the census operations. Despite the war conditions and the political deadlock in the country, the census operations went off in a relatively peaceful atmosphere compared to those in 1921 and 1931, although the tabulation of census data was seriously curtailed because of preoccupation with the War. In 1951, the first census in a free India, the country offered the fullest co-operation with the census authorities in gathering the required data, except for returns on mother tongue which were considerably vitiated because of the raging controversy on language, particularly in the Punjab. The adoption of the criterion of language for the settlement of state boundaries seemed to have had some effect on the census returns on this item even in 1961.

Other minor obstacles that beset the census enumerators in India arise from the nature of the family, caste, community life and the general low standard of living of the people. The problems posed by mass illiteracy and the diverse and variegated pattern of Indian social life have been referred to already.

To appreciate these difficulties, it must be remembered that society in India, which is so fragmented and divided by so many limiting and divisive factors, is sociologically a fiction. Religion and language have created several cultural groups which in turn have been divided and subdivided. Progressive protests against these traditional divisive barriers have not been wanting. As far as the census is concerned, agitation against caste and the enumeration of the people according to caste has gone on for some years now, at least since the Census of 1901. This anti-caste agitation started in Madras with the growth of

---

[1] *Census of India, 1931* (New Delhi: Government of India Press, 1932), p. 82.

34

nationalist and to a limited extent rationalist ideals and subsequently spread to Bengal, Maharashtra and the Punjab. Certain sections of the population rightly labouring under a feeling that they were victims of an invidious social system, claimed to be enumerated as Brahmins or other high-caste groups, though they were differently regarded by virtue of their birth by Hindu society. In the 1931 Census, some two million Hindus returned that they had no caste at all.[1] While this action, demonstrating strong disapproval of societal and official attempts to list and approve of the caste system, may be praiseworthy from the point of view of social reform, it was deplorable from the point of view of the census, which seeks the facts reflecting the structure and dimensions of contemporary society. Caste is no longer asked in the census now; only religion is recorded.

In 1931, the impending constitutional reforms and the prospect of an extended communal franchise led to great activity on the part of religious organizations, and their anxiety to register as many adherents as possible to their religion was not concealed. This unhealthy zeal for numerical strength for particular castes, creeds and religions was visible all over India. Disputes arose in the Punjab, for instance, where the depressed classes, including the Harijans, claimed to be converted and classed as Adi-Dharmis, a supposedly high caste. Acute controversies arose over the question whether these Adi-Dharmis should be regarded as depressed classes or Sikhs. It is as though Protestant, Catholic and Jewish organizations in the United Kingdom or the United States of America vied with one another to return as many adherents as they could of their particular faiths and thus magnify artificially through census statistics the real strength of religious minorities in the country. Such a tendency would be dangerous not only because it suggests that numbers alone matter in a democracy but also because census figures would then lose their scientific value.

And last, there is a certain amount of prejudice and superstition regarding a census and, for that matter, any inquisitive edict that descends upon the villagers from the governmental hierarchy in distant New Delhi. In a country where even a modicum of elementary education is a privilege, the superstition that counting the number in a household forebodes evil is bound to exist. It is true that this kind of superstition is not peculiar to India, for purificatory ceremonies after every census in Ancient Rome were performed to rid them of a supposed evil. Even in the British House of Commons, as late as 1753, the fear was expressed that 'a numbering of the people will be

[1] Ibid., p. 430.

35

followed by some great public misfortune or epidemical distemper'.[1] The United States of America fared no better. In the early years of the American census history, the fear that the census forebodes evil was manifested and, in certain parts, considerable resistance was offered. In New York it was alleged that sickness followed a census operation and in New Jersey it was feared that some such penalty as that imposed on David might be repeated.[2] And in 1955, when a census of the Sudan was taken, the old fears of the census reappeared. According to a writer in the Sudan:

'The first population census ever to be held in the Sudan is now being taken. The main difficulties to be contended with in taking the census are the substantial number of nomads or persons living in scattered tukls (grass huts); the relatively difficult communications; the large number of languages – there are over 70 different languages and, although Arabic is the *lingua franca* it will be necessary to operate in five languages; the shortage of persons available to act as enumerators; and lastly – and most important of all – the superstition prevalent in many parts of the country, that it is unlucky for parents to disclose all their children. To do so, it is often believed, will cause the children to fall sick or even to die. . . . Of the various difficulties that the census confronts, the most serious of all is the tendency of the head of the household to understate the number of his children. In most of the Muslim parts of the Sudan, the enumerator will not be allowed to see the children and women, and so will have to obtain all information about the household from the head of the household.'[3]

(In India, too, the enumerator obtains the particulars of the members of the household from the family head or someone in the household whom he is able to contact.)

This prejudice takes at times acute and unexpected turns. On the eve of almost every census some kind of prejudice comes to the forefront. When it was proposed in 1931 to gather information about fertility, some opposed it on the ground that such a demand arose out of the desire of the authorities to vilify the Indian people.

In the same way, an attempt to collect statistics about the 'educated unemployed' proved unsuccessful due to the apathy and in-

[1] G. F. McCleary, *Population: Today's Question* (London: Allen & Unwin, 1938), p. 50.

[2] H. P. Fairchild, *People* (New York: Holt, 1939), p. 57.

[3] A correspondent, 'Tribes that Fear to Count Children', *The Times*, London, July 8, 1955.

difference of the educated unemployed themselves, who felt convinced that counting their numbers would not redress their grievances; they were not interested in their numbers being counted for the sake of statistics and a policy that could be based on or result from such figures. So the attempt to census the educated unemployed was abandoned and the Census Report observes:

'The reasons given for the failure of the returns were various. In Burma [which was then part of India] the educated but unemployed are largely Indians and most to be found in Rangoon. The reason given for their failure to make the returns was that they feared use would be made of it to repatriate to India those who were without employment. In Bengal the reason alleged was the fear on the part of the unemployed bhadrolok that all that was wanted was a list of them for the police as political suspects, while another rumour accused the Government of trying to win over the unemployed from the Congress Party by false hopes of employment. In Madras the attitude of the recipient was more sensible for the recipient of the unemployed schedule was described as saying, "You will not give me employment, why should I fill up your schedule?" and it seems likely that this feeling, together with a dislike of admitting failure to have found employment and general apathy towards the Census is to be taken as the most common cause of the schedule's failure.'[1]

Yet one more difficulty of the Indian census set-up during the last fifty years has been the absence of an all the year round active administrative set-up and the lack of inter-censal continuity. This continuity is important, for as Walter F. Wilcox points out:

'A Census Report should explain what errors may lurk in the figures, estimate, if possible, their trustworthiness and suggest such inferences as might be of more than local importance and would be accepted as trustworthy by competent students. Each successive report, like each observation of an eclipse, should confirm or correct the interpretation put on previous reports and suggest questions which only future reports can answer.'[2]

In the past, this absence of inter-censal continuity has not been left unnoticed by the Indian census authorities. For M. W. M. Yeatts, the Census Commissioner for 1941, pointed out that the Indian census is

[1] *Census of India, 1931* (New Delhi: Government of India Press, 1932), p. 383.
[2] Walter F. Wilcox, *Studies in American Demography* (New York: Cornell University Press, 1944), p. 9.

37

a kind of comet appearing once every ten years in the statistical firmament, attracting much attention at its culmination but passing away eventually unnoticed. The Indian census throws only one slender beam of light on a subject that should be under the watchful observation of the eye of a cine-camera.

However, to a limited extent, the absence of inter-censal continuity is in a way more apparent than real. The continuity is found at the base rather than at the apex of the census pyramid, as contrasted with the British and American systems. A thread of continuity runs through the Indian villages which embrace the major surface area sheltering a great majority of the Indian population. And the enumeration in rural India is entrusted to the heads of the village administration. Since they are also in charge of collecting revenue and the general administration, additions to and deductions from the village seldom escape their attention. In some parts of India these rural offices are hereditary and one may have in a village the whole of the All-India census series represented in actual experience in the successive generations of village heads. This is true but only in theory and as the reliability of the rural records is very much in question, this kind of inter-censal continuity is only a rough approximation.

With the passing of the Indian Census Act in 1949, the Census Administration has been put on a permanent basis under the aegis of the Registrar-General and Census Commissioner, on the lines of the office of the Registrar-General in the United Kingdom and the Bureau of Census in Washington, D.C. With the present permanent organization, there is no reason why the census operations should not be made quinquennial so as to make them as up to date and useful as possible.

This brief survey of the *modus operandi* of the census organization reveals the difficulties faced by the administration and the extent to which they have been overcome. When all the extenuating factors, including that of cost, are taken into consideration, the Indian census represents something of a triumph in organization; but it still has a long way to go before its results can achieve a readily acceptable measure of reliability.

There are many major defects in the Indian census figures. Apart from attempts to exaggerate or underestimate (more the latter than the former) figures on the part of certain individuals and communities for political reasons (this is now becoming, one hopes, a thing of the past), there are certain practical difficulties which arise in recording figures about age, sex, civil condition and infirmities of the individual. These are simply the results of ignorance, illiteracy and the social condition of the masses. Most illiterate persons in India have no idea of their correct age. There is no institution of celebrating birthdays and there are few occasions when a person has to recall his age. The Census Department has devised measures to assist such people to discover their own age. During the census period, each province prepares a calendar going back about eighty years of important landmarks that linger in the memory of the public. Well-known incidents, especially those which have local importance, like the great famine of 1880, the First World War of 1914–18, the influenza epidemic of 1918, the Moplah Rebellion of 1921, Mahatma Gandhi's Salt March in 1932, the Bihar Earthquake of 1934, the Quetta Earthquake of 1935, the Second World War and the Bengal Famine of 1943 – floods, fires, famines and political upheavals that have burnt deep into the memory of the individual – are marked out. When an individual does not know his age, he or his family are likely to remember some important incident of local or national importance. The earliest of such incidents that he remembers gives a clue to his probable age.[1]

Of course, ignorance of this type can only be combated by widespread education and the provision of a nation-wide service to register vital statistics. Memory has often proved to be a misleading guide in this matter and, as it is, the census age returns show heavy concentration at preferred ages. There is a marked tendency to return ages in multiples of 5. Distortions in the Indian age return are much more serious than those shown by the age data of Western countries. Legal restrictions on the marriageable age tend towards efforts at concealment of marriages and this is more common among females than males. In the case of infirmities of the individual, the extent of both ignorance and wilful concealment cannot be estimated. Infirmities such as leprosy, insanity or deaf mutes in a family cannot be easily detected by the census enumerator at sight as the enumerator does not meet every member of the family on account of the purdah system prevalent in certain sections of Indian society. Even where there is no purdah, the head or any other member of the family who gives the information to the enumerator is not likely to give the correct information about the incidence of leprosy as it may offend the status of the family in the community.[2]

[1] The first census of Communist China in 1953 encountered similar if not greater difficulties in obtaining the correct age of the citizen. See S. Chandrasekhar, *China's Population: Census and Vital Statistics* (Hong Kong: Oxford University Press, 1960), second edition, pp. 26–27.

[2] Such failure to report the truth occurs in some instances in reporting the causes of deaths. Instances of the failure to enter the true cause of death, even

The defects from the point of view of the needs of our analysis of infant mortality are: (1) under-enumeration of the total population in the census, and this is directed more towards females than males; there is a relatively greater under-enumeration of infants; (2) consequent and, to a certain extent, independent inaccuracy of the sex composition of the population; and (3) defective age returns of the population which vitally affect the calculations of the number of infants under one year. In most of the Indian states, population enumerated as aged one year last birthday is in sharp deficit when compared with that enumerated as aged two years last birthday. This factor vitiates the number of infants shown by the census.

These defects can theoretically be overcome and to a certain extent they have been in India. The ideal situation is the one in which the daily official registration of births, marriages and deaths is so accurate and complete that the exact decennial census figure can be foretold, and the actual census count can serve as a mere check up. But as this seldom happens in practice and as the actual situation in India is far from this ideal, sampling techniques have been pressed into use. But here, again, no matter what sampling technique is used, it can never take the place of complete vital registration and accurate census count. The sampling process, despite its numerous advantages such as economy in both time and money, is not the desirable ideal but only an unavoidable alternative.

VITAL STATISTICS: A HISTORICAL SURVEY

Long before Western contact, India had a complex and quasi-religious system of registering births, marriages and deaths in her self-sufficing rural communities, though we do not know how accurate such registration was or what use was made of such information by the state or the community as such.

when definitely known, are not wanting. 'In countries where a copy of a death certificate, including the medical certification of cause of death, may be obtained for legal or other purposes, a physician may not always record the complete diagnosis of the cause of death if this diagnosis is likely to offend the family or the memory of the deceased. It is rather commonly believed that where this condition exists the statistics of mortality from alcoholism, syphilis, epilepsy and even cancer and tuberculosis are in varying degrees understated. This is the main reason why more than half a century ago Switzerland, and later a number of other countries in Europe and in America, adopted a confidential method of reporting the cause of death which gave the health authorities information they needed and at the same time assured the preservation of professional secrecy.' *Foetal, Infant and Early Childhood Mortality* (New York: United Nations, 1954), p. 42.

Registration of births and deaths in its modern connotation was introduced in 1844 in Madras, in 1848 in Bombay, in 1870 in Bengal, and in the decade 1870–80 in most places that came in contact with and eventually under the central political authority.

Unlike the census which was under central authority, the vital registration system in India during British rule (up to 1947) was left to the British provinces (under British governors) and Indian states (under the Maharajas). The result was that each province and state evolved different procedures to ensure vital registration. The provinces had to enact their own individual legislation outlining the procedures and delegating powers to various local authorities as embodied, for instance, in the Madras Presidency Births and Deaths Registration Act XXI of 1889, with the result that neither universality nor uniformity of procedure was secured.

The development of Panchayat Raj (rural self-government initiated partly under the British rule) contributed a major change in the registration system. In several states, vital registration was made the responsibility of Panchayats. The Panchayat Secretary was expected to collect information about births and deaths during his tour of villages and to register the events in regular registers. In other states where the Panchayats were not given this power, the village Patwari, or headman or watchman (the rural agent is called all these in different parts of India) is required to pass this information – births or deaths as the case may be – to some local authority like the police who maintain regular registers. In the towns, the procedure is rather easy since vital registration comes under the routine jurisdiction of the municipalities. The sanitary departments of these civic bodies take care of this as it is obligatory by law.

At regular intervals, information from these registers is tabulated and forwarded to a higher officer in charge of public health records. These records are periodically checked by certain touring officers who belong to departments that have no connection with vital statistics. The rural and urban reports in prescribed tabular forms are usually sent direct to the state capitals for compilation into district and state figures for the State Public Health Report. In some states, there were intermediate stages of compilation but this has been replaced by central compilation at the state level. The state tabulations are then sent to the Registrar-General of India in New Delhi, who draws up all-India figures and publishes them annually as the *Vital Statistics of India* – the only official source material for vital statistics of the nation.

The historical record of the vital registration system in India begun

41

under the British rule in the 1850s down to the comprehensive all-India Registration of Births and Deaths Act of 1968 (enacted by the Indian Parliament in 1969) which came into force on April 1, 1970 – covering a period of 120 years of search for better and more complete registration – is not without interest. It reveals the system's countless drawbacks and weaknesses, the attacks and criticisms to which it was subjected throughout the years, and the reforms and reorganization which the system has undergone.

The entire procedure of vital registration, as in the census organization, resembles a pyramid and the worth and reliability of the nation's vital statistics rest entirely on the validity of the information supplied by the base, the village functionaries and the municipal sanitary departments. The system is not without its drawbacks. Rural India, which accounts for a majority of the country's births and deaths, has the weakest system of registration. The rural agent – the Patwari or Panchayat Secretary or the headman – for recording and reporting all vital occurrences is often illiterate, ill-paid and has to attend to his permanent and more important job of being the administrative functionary of the village and then, as a rule, has to travel a considerable distance to make his report. When we rely on the data gathered by such agents, we ought also to pay due attention to the part played by 'human nature' in these statistics.[1]

Apart from the carelessness and the indifference of the reporting agent, the villagers themselves have not developed enough civic consciousness or statistical sense (which is rare even in advanced countries) and even so are under no obligation to furnish the reporting agent with the necessary information. It is, however, not uniformly true that rural returns are less accurate than the urban returns which are under the care of the relatively more enlightened municipalities and corporations of towns and cities. This, in other words, means that urban returns are equally defective. The indifference and apathy on the part of the people, added to the insufficient and inefficient organization, result in under-registration.

[1] Sir Josiah Stamp, writing some forty years ago, tells us that the individual's source of the statistics may be the weakest link. Harold Cox, for instance, tells a story of his life as a young man in India. He quoted some statistics to a judge, an Englishman and a very good fellow. His friend said: 'Cox, when you are a bit older you will not quote Indian statistics with that assurance. The Government are very keen on amassing statistics – they collect them, add them, raise them to the nth power, take the cube root and prepare wonderful diagrams. But what you must never forget is that every one of those figures comes in the first instance from the Chowkidar (village watchman) who just puts down what he damn pleases.' Sir Josiah Stamp, *Some Economic Factors in Modern Life* (London, 1929), p. 62.

An effective way of obtaining social statistics in any country is for the Government to offer some worthwhile service to the citizen in return. If a child on reaching a certain age can have free educational facilities at the expense of the state, the citizen will obtain a birth certificate, the better to prove to the school authorities that the child has reached the appropriate age. Similarly with a rationing system. A citizen is likely to register with an official agency the number, sex and ages of his family members if he knows that his ration cards will be forthcoming only when this information is furnished to the state. Under normal circumstances, and in the absence of any tangible social service offered by the state to the citizen, the only way to remedy this is by the provision of a nation-wide rural and urban public health service, charged with the collection of vital statistics. There is a tremendous need for educating the public to report willingly, the officials to register accurately, and the departments to consolidate and analyse these vital statistics for the use of the government and the public.

The vital statistical information sought by these government agencies in India includes particulars of births (live and still) and deaths, by sex and religion. Attempts are usually made to obtain the following particulars from parents or guardians within a prescribed period of the vital occurrence. In case of births, the date of birth (sometimes according to the Hindu calendar, and calendars differ with different linguistic and religious groups), sex, name of the child (invariably a difficult proposition, for the children are not named immediately after birth as in the West), names of parents, age of parents, and their religious affiliation (sometimes caste, though this particular is rightly being given up, of late) are recorded. And the death registers have name, sex, date of death, religion, age, and occasionally the cause of death to the best knowledge of the informant.[1] These are the details, which in themselves are inadequate, as we shall presently show, of vital statistics that the law demands and the municipal and rural authorities try to enforce. As for information on other aspects such as

[1] In India most deaths occur outside hospitals, and when they do occur in homes they are largely unattended by doctors. In fact the death rate is so high because of the lack of rural medical facilities. Since there is no proper medical certification of death, the great majority of deaths are usually classified under cholera, smallpox, plague and the broad categories of fever, dysentery and diarrhoea, respiratory diseases and 'other causes'. The reporting agents or the informants cannot adequately diagnose the real cause of death. The cause is either not given or when given, as in adult cases, it is misleading. One Provincial Census Report refers to the recording of childbirth as a cause of death among men!

sickness, employment, income, marital status details such as separation or divorce, nubility, fertility, legitimacy, dependency, neither reliable nor worthwhile and detailed data are available for the total population even today.

Even in gathering information on the few items under the broad categories of births and deaths, the basic duty of recording the very births themselves, as already observed is sometimes lost sight of. It is generally true of most countries that statistics of deaths are more reliable than statistics of births. In the former there is always a body to dispose of, and death, being generally an unexpected, unwelcome and sad event, seldom escapes the notice of the community anxious to know the cause of the event so that it is more often recorded. As for births, they are natural and happy events, and nobody bothers to take notice of them in any special sense. And when it is a case of illegitimacy, the recording of the vital occurrence is understandably and intentionally avoided. This trend is exaggerated in India, for omissions in recording births are definitely greater than the omissions in recording deaths.[1]

The disparity is clearly demonstrated, as pointed out already, by the gulf between the population forecast based on vital registration and the population figures reached by the actual census count. The estimated intercensal population for 1930 is given by the Census Commission as 335,873,000 while the total population on the completion of the census count approximated to 350 millions. This disparity between the population enumerated in the census and the figure arrived at by vital statistics has been repeated in all the censuses, though the difference has been decreasing gradually over the years.[2] It is due not to any faulty calculations in the population fore-

---

[1] K. C. Ray for instance, in his article 'A Note on Omissions in Registration of Births in the City of Calcutta' (*Sankhya*, Calcutta, December 1938) points out how an estimate of intercensal registration, 1921–31, related to total population change and registered surplus of births over deaths indicates approximately 21 per cent under-registration of births.

A discussion of the inaccuracies in an official report like that of the Bengal Public Health Report 1934, can be found in M. Jatindra Dutta's 'On the Presentation of Official Statistics', *Sankhya*, Calcutta, December 1938.

[2] A few forecasts of India's population in 1941 were made before the 1941 Census was taken. K. C. K. E. Raja in his article 'Probable Trend of Population Growth in India' (*Indian Journal of Medical Research*, Calcutta, July 1935), thought that on the basis of the proportion of the married female population of India at the reproductive ages of 15–50 to the total population, India would reach 390,238,582 in 1941. He also estimated that the population in 1941 was likely to be 401,422,517, if the rate of growth in British India was applicable to the whole of India. This estimate proved incorrect by a very wide margin.

cast by the available methods, but to the incomplete registration of births and deaths. The want of uniformity, even in a defect, leads to various degrees of error between province and province. According to the Chief Census Commissioner, the error in vital registration for India as a whole in 1930 was about 20 per cent, ranging from half of 1 per cent in Madras to 60 per cent in Assam. The Census Commissioner points out:

> 'In Madras Province, the returns are accurate enough for the Department of Public Health to prognosticate the result of the 1931 Census with an error (on the excess side) of not more than 2 per cent. Bengal and the United Provinces in that order are believed to be the next most accurate in respect of their returns.'

The striking failure to register births leads to another difficult and rather embarrassing problem, that of deciding the age of an individual. Birth certificates in India are neither demanded by the people nor easily supplied by the local governments. It is true that the practice of preparing a horoscope whenever a child is born is widespread among the Hindu population. It is not known, however, how far this practice is common among the rural millions. In any case the horoscope, being primarily intended for private consultation for marriage purposes, is seldom consulted for the benefit of the official vital statistical record or the census enumerator, and the record of the age in consequence is merely the result of guess-work, the degree of accuracy or error depending on the intelligence of the guess and the shrewdness of the enumerator. As the vital statistical record, particularly of births, is incomplete, the age hunt of the individual during each census count would be almost amusing, were it not so tragic.

In the case of infant mortality one would expect a parent to remember the exact age of the deceased infant as the period to be remembered is at most not more than a year. But in actual practice, obtaining the age at death of the infant has proved to be a difficult problem. For instance, the Public Health Commissioner with the Government of India, in his Annual Report for 1924, observes:

> 'The persistent high mortality of infants may be ascribed in part to defective registration, not only of births but of infant deaths, through the inclusion of still-births, since a distinction between the two is not always made by the illiterate Patwari and police mahawar and partly to the tendency of the more illiterate of the population to underestimate the age of the deceased infants.'[1]

[1] *Annual Report of the Public Health Commissioner with the Government of*

If this were true, and probably it is so in certain parts of the country, the defect becomes one of over-registration as it were, instead of the supposed and sometimes proved under-registration. This contention is supported by the observation of the Director of Public Health for Central Provinces in his Annual Report for 1934. He points out that: 'A study of death registers maintained in urban areas leads one to conclude that more deaths are entered under one year of age than is actually the case. Information given as to the age of the children, when reporting their deaths, is usually vague, with the result that many deaths of infants over one year are registered as under one year. This is clearly shown by the discrepancy usually met with between vaccination–birth registers which are reliable as the date of death of the child is entered against the birth entries and the general death registers. The former invariably show a much smaller number of deaths of infants under one than are recorded in the general death registers.'[1]

It is generally supposed that this difficulty in arriving at the correct age does not prove to be of any serious import except when the age group of the population has to be decided. But there is another and a more serious aspect to this problem. The absence of any definite proof of the age of an individual nullifies attempts at social legislation. Children under a particular age, for instance, are forbidden from employment in factories and mines. Authorities have found it difficult to enforce the law-offending employers and ignorant parents for want of definite evidence of the exact age of the child worker.

This difficulty has been brought into bold relief in the recent past when the Sarada Act (the Child Marriage Restraint Act) was being enforced. In many cases offending parents who were marrying off their children below the minimum permitted age could not be prevented from, or punished for, doing so due to the difficulty in proving in a judicial court that the party accused was below the age prescribed by law.[2] The successful working of social legislation in India, as elsewhere, depends on the availability and accuracy of vital statistics.

India for 1924 (New Delhi: Government of India Press, 1925), p. 26. See also 'Testing Reliability of Age Data in Census', U.N. Population Bulletin, New York, October 1952.

[1] Annual Report of the Public Health Commissioner with the Government of Ind.a for 1934 (New Delhi: Government of India Press, 1935), p. 62.

[2] The Sarada Act, providing penalties for marriage of girls under 14 and of males under 18 which came into effect in April 1930, and corresponding legislation in certain princely Indian states like Baroda, Kashmir and Mysore, led to a definite decrease in the accuracy of the records of age and civil condition.

Nor is the registration of marriages compulsory or uniform all over India even today. More than 85 per cent of Indian marriages are religious ceremonies, often performed in the bride's home and occasionally in the Hindu temple. The prospective couple, with rare exceptions, do not walk into the Registrar's office and walk out after a few minutes as husband and wife, and, therefore, Hindu marriages do not get registered in any official sense. The absence of civil marriage and the want of any official status or responsibility for the Hindu priest or the temple comparable to the clergymen and the Church in Western countries leave marriages without a permanent record, or for that matter without any record at all.

This does not mean that the Hindu marriage is not perfectly valid; it is recognized by law. The registration of marriages in Western countries is primarily to provide a permanent record of the civil condition of the citizen for legal and quasi-legal purposes like legitimacy, succession, inheritance, separation, divorce, etc. As social legislation in India has not developed either in value or volume, these considerations have not gained importance. But they are bound to, as the cultural fabric becomes more complex and when it is realized that social legislation cannot be enforced without adequate statistical data on the demography of the people.

Apart from serving legal purposes in proving legitimacy of birth, succession and inheritance of property and division of the estate of the deceased, an equal need for accurate vital statistics is felt in formulating public health programmes. Unless it is known at what age men and women marry, their fertility, health and ailments, their deaths and their causes, no government can intelligently formulate an effective public health policy. The Public Health Department is severely handicapped for want of accurate records in their efforts to apply preventive methods, because they do not know what diseases account for the high rate of mortality which they are trying to control.

The Government of India have recently launched a nationwide programme of family planning, which is examined in some detail elsewhere in this study. Vital records could have been of immense use in assessing the impact of the programme on fertility reduction were they only available. The evaluation of the effect of family planning work has become difficult.

Fortunately, these defects and lacunae in the collection and compilation of the Indian vital statistical data have not gone unnoticed over the last half a century and more. Every commission and committee that has inquired into some aspect of the Indian economy has

47

emphasized the undesirable nature of the sectional, incomplete and inaccurate data and has forcibly pleaded for a reorganization of the system of vital registration. The lament over the inaccuracy, incompleteness and unreliability of vital statistics began from more or less the beginning of the century.

At the Third All-India Sanitary Conference held at Lucknow in 1914, the British delegate representing the Government of India spoke at length pleading for more accurate vital registration. He concluded:

'In India the only certain thing we know about vital statistics at present is that they are highly inaccurate. They are more inaccurate in some areas than in others. We do not know the extent of their inaccuracy. We can only guess.'[1]

The Royal Commission on Industries in India did not have much to do with population, vital or morbidity statistics, but they found it necessary while discussing Indian statistics in general to observe:

'There is very little statistical data that can be relied on regarding the incidence of occupational disease or of the effects of industrial occupation on the prevalence of the common forms of communicable disease. This is a matter that urgently calls for thorough investigation. . . . In spite of the admitted paucity of reliable statistical data it may be profitable to offer a few remarks as to the effects of these diseases on the efficiency of labour.'[2]

Discussing the incidence and effects of tuberculosis on Indian labour, they referred again to the want of statistics:

'As regards tuberculosis and its special prevalence in workshop and factory, we have very few statistical records to guide us. There is evidence, however, that the disease is more prevalent in the large industrial centres than elsewhere; that the disease is definitely on the increase in rural areas abutting on such centres from which labour is drawn and to which the victims of the disease go to die; and that sufficient precautions are taken in few factories to reduce the risk of such places affording facilities for the transmission of tuberculosis infection from the sick to the healthy.'[3]

In 1928 one more commission, the Royal Commission on Agricul-

---

[1] *Report of the Third All-India Sanitary Conference* (New Delhi, 1915).
[2] *Report: Indian Industrial Commission, 1916–18* (Calcutta: Government Printing, 1918), p. 460.
[3] Ibid., p. 462.

ture in India, in their Report, drew attention to the paucity and the unreliable nature of the available vital statistics. They said:

'Under the heading "vital statistics" are comprised the returns of births, and deaths, occurring annually among the community, the causes of death, the nature and the incidence of the diseases from which the community suffers, the numbers and descriptions of institutions available for the treatment of the disease, the extent of the preventive measures taken against small-pox and cholera, and the strength and distribution of the health and medical services. The statistics of disease and of the causes of death are liable to inaccuracies which are due, in the main, to the same influences which affect the accuracy of agricultural statistics. We are confident that the public health officers are alive to the need for improvement and the only suggestion we have to make is that the statistics under the various heads should always be shown separately for rural and urban areas. At present, this separation is only effected in the case of deaths. We think also that the number and distribution of institutions for treatment of disease and the strength and distribution of the medical and health services should be shown separately for urban and rural districts. We consider it very important that the extent to which rural areas still lack these essential services, and the progress which is made in supplying them, should be stated clearly in the returns. There is also much useful work to be done in correlating the data of the incidence of disease and the death rate in rural areas with those relating to the agricultural conditions which prevail in those areas and with changes in those conditions arising from such causes as the extension of irrigation, improvements in the drainage of deltaic tracts, and the like. Similarly, the correlation of the statistical data relating to health conditions with changes in diet and with the conditions under which the staple foods consumed in the tract under consideration are grown, whether for example they come from irrigated or "dry" land, should in time yield information of the greatest value.'[1]

In 1929, the Age of Consent Committee reported, recommending to the Government that the age of consent within marital relations be raised to fifteen years. While examining this question they could hardly ignore the unreliable aspect of Indian vital statistics, on whose accuracy and dependability any statutory age of consent could work.

[1] *Report of the Royal Commission on Agriculture in India* (London: H.M.S.O., 1923), p. 614.

The Committee reported at length on what has become by now a periodical lament and it is worth quoting in full:

'Registration of births and deaths: the Law of Marriage and the amendment of the Law of Consent, which we have recommended, depend on their successful working to a large extent on the facilities which may exist for the accurate determination of the age of the party concerned. During our inquiry we have given great prominence to the consideration of the question, whether there is an accurate method of recording births and deaths and what defects there exist at present in connection with such records. We have been impressed by the fact that these records are neither as accurate nor as complete as may be desired. In rural areas, in practically all the provinces, the record of births is admittedly deficient. Even in urban areas, though the improvement is noticeable, it is still far short of what is requisite.

Officers of the Department of Public Health in all the provinces have deplored this fact and have suggested various means to remedy the defect. Census operators and witnesses before us have repeatedly drawn attention to this fact. We are aware that within the last decade an advance has been made, particularly in some provinces where a fairly adequate health staff has been paying special attention to this problem.

We feel, however, that the time has come when steps may be taken to ensure a more accurate registration of births and deaths. In the different provinces under local Acts various authorities have been entrusted with this duty. The Imperial Act which governs the subject is the Act VI of 1886. It seems to us that a greater uniformity of laws in the provinces together with more rigidity in their enforcement is called for. It has been suggested that in addition to other persons who may be under an obligation to report the birth or death of a child, parents and guardians of the infant should invariably be under an obligation to report such cases within seven days from the date of the birth of the child. It has been further suggested that every Municipal Council, Taluk Board, District Board, Union Board, Village Panchayat or Notified Area should be under a statutory obligation to maintain an accurate register of births and deaths and required to take stringent steps to enforce registration and prosecute those who fail to do so. This power is now conferred on these bodies in some provinces only.

One great defect in the registration of births is the fact that the name of the child is not given. The identification of the child from the birth register becomes very difficult where there are several children born at comparatively short intervals and the date of birth of one child can, either wilfully or through mistake, be confused with that of the preceding or succeeding child. The suggestion has been made therefore that the order of birth of the child may be given. Even this, though helpful generally, will often fail in its purpose, especially where some of the issues die.

A further suggestion of a more helpful character is that the name of the child should be entered. The fact that the name of the child is not given till some weeks or even months after the birth of the child makes this impossible at present. A supplementary report within a specified period will therefore be necessary when the name of the child, if surviving, will be entered in the register. We find that in some municipalities the name of the child is given at the time of vaccination and with the help of the vaccination register the birth register is later amplified by the entry of the child's name. We recommend that in all urban and rural areas the father or other guardian of every child born shall, where not already required by law, report the birth of the child in such form as may be prescribed within a stated time to a prescribed local authority and to make a further report mentioning the name given to the child, if surviving, within a year of the birth, to the same authority. We further recommend that the prescribed authority be required to maintain a register of births within a given area under its control, and to take stringent steps to enforce registration and to prosecute persons who omit to send a report within the prescribed period.

It is essential that these birth and marriage registers should be permanently preserved and that they should not be destroyed after a short period. The proof of age being mainly dependent on these registers, their retention is essential. It is also desirable that certificates of birth should be issued to the parent or guardian when the name of the child is reported and that the members of the public should be in a position to secure copies of such certificates on payment of a prescribed fee. We recommend that the registers of births be permanently preserved and that birth certificates, giving the date of birth, sex, parentage and name of the child and such other particulars as may be prescribed, be issued free by the prescribed authority, to the person making the report when the name of the child, if alive, is reported to the said authority.

Registration of marriage: It has been urged by several witnesses that registration of marriages is essential to make the Laws of Marriage and Consent effective. At present, there is no provision for the registration of marriages generally. However, among Brahmos, marriages are registered under Act III of 1872. So is the case among Parsis by Act XV of 1865 and Indian Christians by Act XV of 1872. Among Muslims, marriages are in some places optionally registered by Kazis and in Bihar and Bengal by persons appointed by the Government for the purpose, and the Kazis register is generally used to corroborate the fact of marriage and to establish the terms of dower; but the registration of marriages is not declared obligatory by law. It has been suggested that the registration of marriages be made compulsory in all cases in the same manner as under several local enactments, births and deaths are required to be reported to the prescribed authorities. The registration will only be a record of the fact of marriage and will in no way affect the validity of the marriage. It will be extremely difficult to enforce the Law of Marriage unless the reporting of a marriage to a specified authority is made obligatory. The Law must require that every marriage should be duly reported by some person or persons made responsible by law to report, the report to be verified in such a manner as may be prescribed within a specified time to an authority specified by the local government. In the case of Purdanashin women, the report may be sent through an authorized agent. The report should contain the name, parentage, description, address, age, date and place of birth of the parties to a marriage. Such report can be sent by post and need not be personally presented to the authority concerned.

In addition to this, it has also been suggested that the village Munsif, Patel, Lambardar or Chowkidar of every village where a marriage is celebrated shall be under a similar obligation to submit a report of such marriage to the authority concerned, giving such particulars as may be ascertainable within a prescribed time. The object of these reports is to enable the officer concerned to register the marriages and to find out whether the law has in any way been violated. Where either on information received or on a comparison of the reports, the registrar has reason to believe that an offence has been committed, he may hold a preliminary inquiry and, if satisfied, report the case to the nearest magistrate competent to try the case. The suggestion has further been made that the obligation to report such cases may be laid on the registering officer by law where he is satisfied that an offence has been committed.

The question also what agency should undertake the work of registering marriages has been discussed by several witnesses. We have not, however, the material before us to make specific recommendations on the subject. It is possible that it may vary in different provinces and that some existing department of a local government may be empowered to discharge this duty. The number of marriages celebrated annually is so large and the work involved so heavy, that we do not think it will be useful to suggest any cut and dried scheme for the purpose. There will be the provincial head, perhaps the Registrar of births, deaths and marriages appointed by each local government under Act VI of 1886. Under him there will be district and taluk officers who will be authorized to register such marriages. In some provinces at least the registration department suggests itself as the most suitable for the purpose. But as already stated, the question of agency and such questions as the person who should be authorized to initiate prosecutions, whether a Sub-Registrar or a District Registrar, must be left to a more detailed examination by the government and the committee must content itself with putting forward the various suggestions made in this connection.

It may be pointed out that the Baroda Marriage Act makes the registration of marriages compulsory and that the extent to which prosecutions of breaches by the law have been successful in that state is due almost entirely to such registration. It is also obvious that the registration of marriages will be of substantial assistance both in preventing early marriages and providing a permanent record.

Where the age of marriage is publicly declared, the parties will naturally be careful not to consummate the marriage before the statutory age. Moreover, an inspection of the marriage register will considerably strengthen the hands of those individuals or associations which suspect that an offence has been committed and which would welcome an indisputable proof of age before instituting a prosecution. We recommend that an accurate marriage register in a prescribed form be kept through an administrative department of government containing details of marriages including the ages of couples, that it be made obligatory by law on parties to the marriage, either personally or through authorized agents, to report the same to a prescribed local authority.

That the officer keeping the register of marriages be empowered and also be charged with the duty to complain of any breach of the marriage law, or any omission to report a marriage or of a false entry in the details required in the registration of marriages, to the nearest magistrate having jurisdiction to try such cases, after such preliminary inquiry as he thinks fit to make.

53

We also recommend that the registers of marriage be permanently retained, and that certificates of marriage be issued to the parties concerned free of cost, when the marriage is reported.'[1]

In 1930, the Royal Commission on Labour in India was confronted with the same problem again. They examined at some length the value of Indian vital statistics and the nature of the population problem in India:

'Although more than one attempt was made to give us vital statistics for groups of individual workers, none of these gave a picture sufficiently accurate to demonstrate any relation between industrial activity and increased death rates. This is not a matter for surprise when it is remembered that even in the larger towns, few sick persons see a doctor and certification of death is usually a matter of guess-work on the part of a non-medical registrar. Moreover, deaths are registered under one or other of only six or seven heads, three of these being smallpox, cholera, plague, so that by far the largest number is entered under all other causes. Lack of appreciation of their value in public health and of training on the part of individuals responsible for their collection lead to the continuance of grave inaccuracies in such records. Again, in industrial areas the influx of large numbers of young males changes the age distribution to a marked extent, and the failure to apply the necessary correction factor, before comparing them with other areas where the population is distributed more normally over the different age and sex periods makes fair comparison very difficult. There is therefore little chance of obtaining reliable statistics for special groups such as industrial workers and, in consequence, we have been unable to make any estimate of the effect of industrial life, as distinct from urbanization, on the death rates of these communities. Curious variations prevail in the methods of registering throughout the different provinces. We recommend that still-births should be excluded from both birth and death registers and that they should be separately recorded. Only when this is done will it be possible to obtain the useful information which these figures should provide.'

Turning to morbidity statistics, the Commission pointed out:

'We met with even greater difficulties in connection with the incidence of sickness among industrial workers. Few employers

[1] *Report of the Age of Consent Committee, 1928–29* (Calcutta: Government of India Press, 1929), pp. 145–9.

know the rate of sickness among their workers, and little is known of the amount of sickness in the general population. The records of hospital outpatient departments and of dispensaries refer to the general population living in their vicinity. Even where a particular industrial concern maintains its own medical staff and dispensary, the Indian worker frequently absents himself from work without reporting to the factory doctor. In a number of industrial concerns, it is necessary to keep an additional 10 per cent of workers on the wage books as substitutes to fill the places of absentees but neither this figure nor the figures of absenteeism can be used as a basis for estimating sickness rates, since the Indian worker stays away from his work for many reasons besides sickness.

Inferences from available figures: Erroneous though they are, the registered statistics show that birth rates generally are extraordinarily high as compared with those prevailing in Western countries, and both general and infantile mortality rates are correspondingly high. The general death rate in India, on a conservative estimate, may be taken to be between 30 and 35 per 1,000. It is known that the average expectation of life at birth is only about 25 years as compared with over 54 years in Great Britain. These two figures, although approximate, make it certain that sickness rates for the general population are several times higher than the corresponding rates for Britain. This brings us no nearer an estimate of the actual rates among industrial workers but it is certain that sickness and disease exact a heavy toll and detract from their efficiency and earning capacity to a marked extent.

The necessity for improved vital statistics is generally recognized and in several provinces marked improvements have been effected within recent years by stricter supervision and more effective inspection. It is essential, however, that municipal councils and local bodies, who are primarily responsible for registration, should devote much more attention to the matter. In the larger towns and the more important industrial areas, at least the appointment of medical registrars should be compulsory since only then will it be possible to improve the classification of causes of death.'[1]

In 1933, the Government of India invited two British economists, Professor A. L. Bowley and Mr D. H. Robertson, to advise them on the question of obtaining more accurate and detailed general statistics than were then available in India. In 1934 they submitted a Re-

---

[1] *Report of the Royal Commission on Labour in India* (Calcutta: Government of India Press, 1931), pp. 249–50.

port on a scheme for an Economic Census of India. While population census and vital statistics were beyond the purview of the terms of reference, they found it difficult to ignore the role of population statistics in any plan for the economic development of India. They wrote:

'The vital statistics of India are well known to be defective (*Census of India, 1931*, Vol. I, Part I, p. 91). This is evident both by knowledge of the methods of recording births and deaths, and by comparison in total or detail with the population censuses. Thus, in the decade 1921–30 about 83,500,000 births and 63,500,000 deaths were recorded in British India, while the increase between 1921 and 1931 was according to the censuses 24,700,000 instead of 20,000,000 (the defect is more than 4·7 millions in 83·5 millions because deaths as well as births are unrecorded); while there is probably a deficiency in the record of deaths, it is evident that the error in the record of births is more considerable.

The only excuse for estimating birth and death rates at all on these figures lies in the hope that the error is constant and therefore the tendency towards higher or lower birth or death rates can be known. But since any improvement in the organization results in apparently higher rates, the evidence would only be valuable if a decrease was shown, whereas in 1921–30 there is no clear tendency in either direction. . . . It should be seriously considered whether these figures should be published at all, except for areas where there was reason to believe substantial accuracy is obtained since they lead to quite unjustifiable conclusions. They have their use, however, to Medical Officers of Health if these are aware of their limitations. If published, at least allowance should be made in the denominator for the growth of population.

Meanwhile, it is possible to make a fairly good, if hypothetical, estimate of the growth of population by the use of the life tables, given in the Actuarial Report of the Census. These tables do not depend on the records of deaths but on the study of the figures of the Censuses of 1921 and 1931. Their accuracy is reduced by the aberrations that are known to be present in the statement of ages, but the mathematician is able to smooth these away with reasonable accuracy. By applying the life table to the (amended) numbers in the 1931 Census it can be estimated how many at each age will survive for 1, 2 . . . 10 or more years. Thus, the population aged 10 years or more in 1941 can be forecast, apart from migration, on the hypothesis that the rate of survival in 1921 to 1931 is repeated in the following decade. This assumes that the average death rate, age by age, is the same in the second as in the first decade, and great aberrations from this will be evident even in the imperfect records of deaths.'[1]

In 1945 the Government of India appointed a Commission to inquire into the Bengal Famine of 1943 which resulted in an estimated loss of more than a million and a half lives. This Commission also could not avoid passing strictures on the value and validity of Indian vital and health statistics. They reported:

'All public health statistics in India are inaccurate. Mortality figures indicate trends in the death rate but can rarely be accepted as absolute. Even in normal times, deaths are not fully recorded and the number of births registered may be 20 to 25 per cent below the number of births that have actually occurred. The famine mortality statistics issued by the Bengal Public Health Department, it may be remarked, tell a sufficiently tragic story, as they stand. Many people have, however, maintained that they grossly underestimate the actual number of deaths. Thus, witnesses appearing before the members of the Commission in Dacca estimated deaths in the districts in 1943 as one million, whereas the figure recorded by the Public Health Department was 149,000. . . . While the Commission cannot accept popular views on mortality, it is nevertheless of the opinion that the official figures underestimate the total number of deaths.

In rural Bengal, as elsewhere in India, the primary collector of mortality statistics is a village functionary to whom deaths are reported by relations of the deceased in the village. The village Patwari reported deaths to the Union Board Office, where by several stages the records ultimately reached the office of the Director of Public Health. The Patwari also reports the cause of death. In normal times the system scarcely lends itself to scientific accuracy and in 1942 and 1943 other factors making for errors and omissions were introduced. In certain places the salaries of Patwaris were not paid and they deserted their posts to obtain work on military projects and aerodromes. During the famine, Patwaris were not immune from starvation and disease and some of them died. The replacement of dead and vanished Patwaris was no easy matter and several weeks or months might have elapsed before successors could be found, during which deaths presumably went

[1] A. L. Bowley and D. H. Robertson, *A Scheme for an Economic Census of India* (New Delhi: Government of India Press, 1934), pp. 31–32.

unrecorded. Further in the height of the famine thousands of people left their homes and wandered across the countryside in search of food. Many died by the roadside – witness the skulls and bones which were to be seen there in the months following the famine. Deaths occurring in such circumstances would certainly not be recorded in the statistics of the Director of Public Health.'[1]

In the same year, 1945, the Population Data Enquiry was appointed. They went into the question of the organization of the census and vital registration. Commenting on the nature of the available Indian vital statistics, they pointed out:

'There is knowledge about them. It is well known that the birth rates and death rates run much higher than in countries of the West. And that infantile and maternal mortality rates are very much higher. But there is a great difference between declaring that piece of undoubted knowledge and stating the actual rates themselves. There is then no real contradiction between the fact that the birth and death rates in India run consistently higher and the inability to say with confidence that they are precisely this and not that particular figure. Policies and departures in policy should, however, always refer to accurately recorded facts and now that population questions in India are receiving so much attention the time has come (is in fact long overdue) for the actual organization of the information itself to receive attention.'[2]

They went on to discuss the role of the apparently unavoidable Patwari and the extent of under-registration. They reiterated what has become common knowledge:

'Indian vital statistics are still collected in many cases at second or even third-hand and may have no stronger basis than the recollections of an illiterate Patwari. . . . To be absolutely satisfactory, vital statistics should be (a) a hundred per cent complete and, (b) a hundred per cent accurate. This being a world of imperfection neither of these will in practice be achieved but it is definitely within the power of any government to establish 98 or 99 per cent completeness, and although not so easily, a substantial uniformity and elevation of standards which will enable the information to be used with confidence in projection. . . . A close

---

[1] *Famine Enquiry Commission: Report on Bengal* (New Delhi: Government of India Press, 1945), pp. 108–9.

[2] *Report of the Population Data Committee* (Simla: Government of India Press, 1945), pp. 3, 20.

study of one of the better areas of registration shows that the lowest figure of underestimation of births is 40 per cent and that a more likely one is over 50 per cent. For underestimation of deaths the range is even greater, from 35 to 55, with probabilities again nearer fifty, nearer the top than the bottom. If the ages are taken into question the under-enumeration of deaths covers a span of 25 to 65 per cent.

The Government of India should take positive steps to bring about ultimately complete, regular and accurate vital statistics in India. The record should invariably show in the case of births, the age of the mother and the number of births and for all births and deaths should invariably show the community and means of livelihood of the parents of the child or of the deceased person.

It is essential that the Central Government enter the vital statistics field by prescription of standard, establishing a right of inspection of the provinces' and states' figures, and by financial or other assistance as indicated. There should be an officer or an organization at the centre definitely charged with the co-ordination of all information on population growth, covering, that is, not only the census but the vital statistics and all allied matters. . . .'[1]

But no steps were then taken about these recommendations and nothing emerged from the labours of this committee.

In 1946, the Government of India appointed yet another committee, this time to survey the country's health and allied problems, under the chairmanship of Sir Joseph Bhore. This Committee pointedly referred to the now familiar story of under-registration and the unreliability of the general health and medical statistics in the country. The formulation of a national public health policy presumes certain desired objectives and efforts to reach them; and such an effort can be possible only on the basis of a large body of reliable knowledge of births, sickness and deaths in the country. The government which is anxious to lower the death rate must know what conditions and diseases are responsible for the high death rate which they are seeking to reduce. A policy must be built on facts and as long as there is uncertainty as to these there must be some inevitable confusion and conflict regarding the aim. The Committee examined the nature and methods of registration of vital statistics and their defects. They observed:

'The term vital statistics can in its wider sense include informa-
[1] Ibid.

59

tion relating to a wide range of human activities, but it is usually applied to a narrower field covering births, deaths, marriages and the incidence of disease in the community. In India registration of marriage does not take place among the two communities, the Hindus and Mohammedans, who together form over 90 per cent of the total population. Such statistics as may exist in this country for marriages can therefore relate only to a small section of the population and we shall not therefore refer to them here. We shall confine ourselves to the statistics of births, deaths and morbidity. As regards the last, no country can claim reasonably accurate statistics for the population as a whole, except in the cases of certain diseases which are made notifiable by law. In India, the available statistics in respect of births, deaths and notifiable diseases are defective. Such defects are associated partly with the registration of these vital events and partly with their compilation. Before we deal with these defects, it may be of advantage to describe briefly the agencies employed in different parts of the country for the registration and compilation of vital statistics.

Agencies for Registration and Methods of Compilation: In towns and cities the municipal authority is responsible for the registration of vital statistics and this function is usually a part of the duties of the health department. In the rural areas the village watchman or the Patwari is usually the reporting agent. In Northern India generally, the registrar is the officer in charge of the thana, or police station, while in the province of Madras the village headman is the registrar. In those provinces in which the registrar is the police station officer, births and deaths are registered on specific days of each month, when the Patwari is required to report himself at the police station. The interval between such visits of the Patwari is in some areas a week and in others a fortnight. In areas where the village headman is the registrar the recording of these events takes place more promptly.

As regards infectious diseases, it is understood that in certain provinces, an outbreak of any of the common infectious diseases has to be reported by the village Patwari immediately to the police station concerned, although subsequent events are brought to notice only on the days on which he is required to visit the thana headquarters in connection with his routine duties. In the Province of Madras, daily reports are required to be sent, it is understood, by the village headman throughout the course of an epidemic. The procedure in regard to the compilation of vital statistics differs to some extent in the provinces. In Bengal, for instance, the figures for the different rural thanas in a sub-division are compiled in the office of the sub-divisional officer and then passed on to the District Health Officer who, after including those for municipalities, which he receives direct, submits the figures to the Director of Public Health. In those provinces in which a public health organization has not been built up in the districts, the Civil Surgeon is responsible for the compilation of the statistics for the district as a whole and for their submission to the Director of Public Health. The Province of Bombay, which belongs to this category, is an exception. Here returns from municipalities and talukas are submitted to the Assistant Director of Public Health of the range concerned and he sends a consolidated return for his range to the Director of Public Health. In the Province of Madras the compilation of all the returns from individual villages has been centralized in the office of the Director of Public Health, the return from each village passing through the Tahsildar of the Taluk, to the Director of Public Health. It has been the experience that the chances of error in compilation become greater when the number of intermediate stages of compilation is increased.

Defects in Registration: These are mainly: (1) omission to register appreciable numbers of births, deaths and cases of notifiable diseases and (2) incorrectness of the recorded cause of death.

Incompleteness of Registration: Some idea of the extent of error, for the country as a whole, through incompleteness of registration, may be obtained from a comparison of the recorded birth and death rates for British India and those derived by what is known as the 'reverse survival' method [Table 1].

The differences between the birth and death rates based on the registered figures and those obtained by the reverse survival method are appreciable in respect of every decade.

In brief, one of the causes for such incompleteness of registration is that, over large areas in the country, registration of births and deaths is not compulsory. Further, even in those limited areas where registration is compulsory, the provisions of the Acts are rarely enforced so that generally speaking vital statistics are deplorably defective. Another cause is that the village Patwari who is responsible for reporting these events in respect of the rural population, and the police, who are responsible for registration, are so overburdened with other work that the tendency is to regard

Table 1

RECORDED AND ESTIMATED BIRTH AND DEATH RATES IN
INDIA (PROVINCES) 1891–1961

	Birth Rate		Death Rate	
		Estimated		Estimated
		Rate (reverse		Rate (reverse
	Recorded	survival	Recorded	survival
Period	Rate	method)	Rate	method)
1891–1901	33	46	31	44
1901–11	37	49	33	43
1911–21	37	48	34	47
1921–31	33	46	25	36
1931–41	34	45	23	31
1941–51	28	40	20	27
1951–61	21	42	11	23

their duties in connection with vital statistics as of relatively smaller
importance.

Incorrectness of the Registered Cause of Death: A reasonable
degree of accuracy in the registered cause of death can be obtained
only by certification by a medical man who has had the opportunity of examining the patient before his death. The absence of an
adequate health service to meet the requirements of the people and
the fact that, for the rural areas as a whole, the reporting agent is
the illiterate Patwari, together help to render the recorded census of
mortality of little value from the point of view of assessing public
health conditions. No accurate estimate of the degree of error in
these recorded causes of death can be given. The results of a
scheme of verification of the cause of death in Delhi City carried
out by the Medical Officer of Health during 1937 may, however,
help to throw some light on this question. Of 9,660 deaths registered during the year, nearly 98 per cent were inquired into by
medical men and, from the history obtained, the probable causes of
death were deduced. Obviously such a method is defective as
compared with medical certification. Nevertheless, the "verified"
cause of death is likely to give a greater measure of accuracy than
the cause ordinarily registered. The following figures [Table 2] and
the comments on them are quoted from the 1937 Annual Report
of the Public Health Commissioner of the Government of India.

In some cases the discrepancies are very large. The combined
figures for pneumonias, for instance, show a difference of 1779;
infantile diarrhoea, premature births, phthisis and puerperal fever

Table 2

NOTIFIED AND VERIFIED CAUSES OF DEATH IN DELHI CITY, 1937

	Notified and registered cause of death	Verified cause of death
1. Malarial fever	5	236
2. Measles	123	123
3. Typhoid fever	395	388
4. Diabetes	10	13
5. Smallpox	575	575
6. Broncho-pneumonia	6	2,252
7. Pneumonia	1,035	568
8. Phthisis	516	882
9. Puerperal fever	1	50
10. Senile debility	29	661
11. Infantile diarrhoea	123	1,171
12. Premature birth	5	194

all show considerable variations, while for "senile debility", the number recorded is no less than 632 in excess of the registered number. If the assumption is made that the "verified" causes of death give a greater measure of accuracy than the "notified" and "registered" causes, then the striking differences in numbers under such headings as pneumonia, puerperal fever, infantile diarrhoea and "premature birth" signify certain directions along which preventive measures should be taken. In the absence of medical certification, even verification of the cause of death on the lines indicated above can be of great value from the point of view of health administration.

Errors of Compilation: In the Madras Province, when the compilation of all returns from individual villages was centralized in the Office of the Director of Public Health, a considerable improvement was recorded. Defaulters could be watched and appropriate action taken so as to ensure that the consolidated return for the Province was made as complete as possible. We have already pointed out that the general experience has been that, with an increase in the intermediate stages of compilation, the chances of error creeping in become greater. In recognition of this, the Central Advisory Board recommended that other provinces should also adopt the centralized form of compilation which has been in operation in Madras.

Notifiable diseases: The large omissions in the registration of births and deaths and errors in compilation apply also to notifiable diseases. The extent of error in regard to omission is, however, less in the case of the common epidemic diseases of cholera, smallpox and plague, than in respect of other infectious diseases. This is due to the fact that the signs and symptoms of the former are generally known to the people. Although it would not be correct to claim even a reasonable approach to completeness of registration for these three diseases, the recorded figures for them give a fairly clear indication of their varying incidence from year to year. Such an assumption is not permissible in respect of other communicable diseases. Indeed, many of them can be diagnosed only if medical aid and laboratory facilities are available. Examples are tuberculosis, cerebrospinal fever, typhus, typhoid and relapsing fever. These are now notifiable in both rural and urban areas in a certain number of provinces. In the absence of the necessary facilities for proper diagnosis it seems certain that no reasonable proportion of the actual occurrences of these diseases will be recorded, while the correctness of the registered events under each disease is open to question. The number of communicable diseases which are notifiable in the different provinces varies considerably. For instance, the 1937 *Annual Report of the Public Health Commissioner* gives 22 per cent for the Central Provinces and 20 per cent for the Punjab. The question of reducing the list of diseases notifiable in rural areas to the minimum possible and of increasing the number of such diseases in urban centres in proportion to the facilities for diagnosis which may be expected to be available will have to be considered when we put forward our proposals for the improvement of vital statistics. To sum up, the main defects of the existing system of registration and compilation of vital statistics in India are:

1. Registration is not compulsory over large parts of the country.

2. Even when registration is compulsory, failure to enforce the law against defaulters has resulted in no material improvement being effected in such areas.

3. Omission to register births, deaths and cases of notifiable diseases is appreciable in all parts of the country, a contributory factor being that the duties to be performed by village Patwaris and police officials in regard to vital statistics are not adequately discharged because of other important duties they have to attend to.

4. Gross inaccuracy in the registered causes of mortality in the absence of medical certification of death.

5. Large omissions in the recorded incidence of notifiable diseases and incorrectness in their diagnosis, mainly owing to the fact that many such diseases have been made notifiable in areas where no proper facilities for their diagnosis exist.

6. Errors in compilation, probably assisted by the fact that, in certain provinces, this work is carried out at a number of administrative levels.'[1]

In the light of this survey, the Committee recommended the creation of the Registrar-General and several provincial and district offices charged with the task of the collection and compilation of vital and population statistics. While pleading for more compulsory registration, they pointed out:

'Efforts to improve the administrative machinery and thus produce an increase in vigilance on the part of the governmental staff to secure better registration cannot eventually produce the same results as an awakening of the sense of responsibility of the people to themselves and to the state for recording the vital events that take place in their homes. While the efforts of the health staff through educative work will, no doubt, contribute to this awakening, an effective method of stimulating interest will be by creating conditions requiring, in an increasing degree, the production of proof of age, community, parentage, etc. If courts, schools, and other institutions could be induced to insist on the production of birth and death certificates, the public would begin to feel the necessity for registering births and deaths in their own interest.

There is little doubt that the more general introduction of compulsory registration would have considerable effect in the direction of improving vital statistics. Moreover, even in those areas in which little or no notice is taken of breaches of the law, a few judiciously selected prosecutions would have a salutary educational effect.

We consider that the enforcement of the law through the prosecution of offenders is essential if definite improvement is to be secured.'[2]

[1] *Report of the Health Survey and Development Committee, Vol. I, Survey* (New Delhi: Government of India Press, 1946), pp. 153–7.

[2] *Report of the Health Survey and Development Committee, Vol. II, Recommendations* (New Delhi: Government of India Press, 1946), pp. 278–80.

In the same year (1946) the inter-departmental Committee on Official Statistics of the Government of India submitted its Report for the central co-ordination of all official statistics. Commenting on the nature of public health and vital statistics, this Committee pointed out:

'There is sufficient information for British India in regard to the number of hospitals and dispensaries and patients treated. Figures of births and deaths are also regularly published but the present system of collection of basic data should be overhauled so that the time lag may be reduced and the quality of the material may be improved. The Births, Deaths and Marriages Registration Act of 1886 under which the figures are collected at present provides for only a voluntary registration of births and deaths. It should also be remembered that marriage is not necessarily registrable in the case of the two principal communities (Hindus and Muslims).

The position, however, is not unsatisfactory in the urban areas where special bye-laws have been passed by municipalities for the purpose of recording births and deaths. In regard to the rural areas, there exists in no province, with the exception of Madras, any machinery through which the provincial health authority can be readily acquainted with conditions in the districts. It seems to us that the first essential step would be to frame an All-India Act containing provisions of a mandatory nature. If the provincial governments can be convinced of the importance of such central legislation it will be possible to proceed (as envisaged under Section 103 of the Government of India Act, 1935) to regulate the registration of vital statistics throughout British India on a uniform basis.

The Central Government can also prescribe the qualification of Registrars, the period within which registration should be carried out, and the penalty for non-compliance. It is possible that special circumstances such as lack of adequate laboratory facilities may make it useless to notify particular diseases in certain areas. We would then suggest that although the Act should provide a uniform set of notifiable diseases for all provinces, the decision regarding the enforcement of the provisions in respect of a specified disease in any area should be left to the discretion of the provincial government. It is to be hoped that with the gradual expansion of health services, the areas over which individual diseases can be made notifiable will extend greatly and the degree of reliability of the registered figure will increase proportionately.

It is a fact that in rural areas public co-operation is not too readily forthcoming but if, for instance, the production of a birth certificate were made compulsory for admission to a primary school or for holding any appointment under an established authority, the position would, without doubt, improve greatly.

It has also to be considered how best the collection of vital statistics in Indian states can be arranged on lines similar to those obtaining in British India.'[1]

In 1949, two officers of the Indian Government reported on the statistical organization existing then in the provinces and the states. In their review of the vital statistical organization, they travel over what is now an old and familiar story. Though their observations are neither original nor novel they are reproduced here to complete the record of official and quasi-official evaluation of the nature and accuracy of the Indian population and vital statistical record. They write:

'Inaccuracy: The main feature about vital statistics in India is that figures of births and deaths are not reliable. The margin of error may be about 20 to 30 per cent or more in the case of births and perhaps somewhat less in the case of deaths, the error usually being on the side of underestimation. Objective evidence about defects in vital statistics is provided by the surveys conducted by the All-India Institute of Hygiene and Public Health, in Singhur Village in West Bengal, by the Poonamallee Health Unit near Madras, and in Travancore by the Department of Public Health. Personal opinion of experienced individuals is practically unanimous about the unsatisfactoriness of present figures. Madras is probably the province which is least faulty in respect of vital statistics but even in the case of Madras about 15 per cent of births and 20 per cent of deaths go unreported.

Registration: Registration of births and deaths is compulsory in all cities, municipalities and notified areas under municipal rules even where provincial Acts do not exist. In rural areas registration is voluntary except in West Bengal, Bihar, Madras and Travancore. But even in regions where registration is mandatory practically nothing is done to enforce the law in this respect. It is not considered expedient to undertake prosecutions so long as the civic sense in this respect is not keener than at present and so long as the

[1] *Report of the Inter-Departmental Committee on Official Statistics* (Simla: Government of India Press, 1946), pp. 11–12.

reporting and registering agency continues to be as indifferent to quality as at present.

Primary Agency: The reporting agency in rural areas is almost everywhere the village Patwari. These are mostly illiterate, ill-paid and have no incentive for conscientious performance of their statistical duties. In Madras, however, we were informed that the village headmen who are responsible for the reporting of births and deaths are given special training and are required to pass a test. In Travancore the work is being taken away from the existing agencies and a special staff under direct control of the Public Health Department is being employed. One of the reasons why the reporting is unsatisfactory and irregular is stated to be the ridiculously low salary of the primary reporting staff. We were told that if Patwaris were warned, they refused to do the job; if they are dismissed no replacements are found.

In most provinces the present arrangements necessitate the reports originating in the police (or revenue) departments, passing first to the civil surgeons in the Medical Department who transmit the same to the headquarters of the Public Health Department. Compilation is also done at successive stages at the police stations, district headquarters and finally at the provincial headquarters. This not only causes delay and introduces omissions and errors but also makes it impossible to have many of the detailed tabulations that may be of interest.

Central compilation: In Mysore this system was changed and what is called central compilation introduced some time back. In the Mysore system the village registrars send a copy of the primary registration form direct to the headquarters office for tabulation, though another copy of the same passes upward through the usual channels. These are filed in the headquarters office and used as a permanent record which forms the basis for the issue of birth and death certificates as and when required.

Improvement of registration: For an improvement of registration the first requirement is an adequate primary and supervisory staff. One whole-time Registrar for about 20,000 to 30,000 of population is considered adequate in most of the provinces. Uniform legislation in all the regions making the registration of births and deaths (and if possible also marriages) mandatory will have to be put into force. But more important than legislation is the development of a civic responsibility in the matter of registering vital events.'[1]

And last, the 1951 Census Report of India and the Paper on *The Estimation of Birth and Death Rates in India 1941–50* reveal that the matter of correct and complete registration of vital events is still not under control. The Census Commissioner for 1951 points this out in the simplest possible terms:

'If reporting is complete and the basic (vital statistical) records are correctly maintained, the changes in numbers recorded by the census at ten-yearly intervals should tally with the balance of births and deaths during the ten-year period, leaving a relatively small margin to be explained by the net balance of migration of people, in and out of the territory in question. . . . This incompleteness is also indicated by census results in another way. The births registered during ten years work out to a rate (in round figures) of 25 per 1,000 people per annum. We have already noted that the count of infants in the state (Madhya Pradesh) yielded 33 per 1,000. Maybe this number was somewhat swollen by counting 13-month-old babies also, as infants. But, even so, if we make allowance for the number of infants who must have died during the year preceding the census, the census count of infants is a clear indication that actual births must have exceeded registered births substantially.'[2]

In 1963, at the instance of the Evaluation and Planning Committee of the Family Planning Programme of the Government of India, a Panel of consultants was constituted by the Planning Commission for the purpose of independently assessing and evaluating the family planning work both in the states and in the centre. This panel of consultants submitted their Report in 1965 and was published in 1967. This Report is the latest Government document to harp again on the need for better vital registration from the point of view of measuring the nation's fertility. They write:

'Need for strengthening measurement of births in the states: The state teams were not in any case able to get precise estimates of the level of birth rates in the states. Only in a few small special study areas are adequate birth statistics available. This is a most frustrating gap in the whole programme, since lack of such in-

[1] N. T. Mathew and P. Pant, *Report on the Present Statistical Organization in Provinces and States* (New Delhi, 1949), pp. 22–25.

[2] *Census of India, 1951, Vol. I (India) Part I: Report* (New Delhi: Government of India Press, 1953), pp. 78–79.

formation prevents adequate diagnosis of exactly what the population trends are in various areas of the country. More importantly, it is virtually impossible yet to detect the extent of success as a result of programme efforts.

Unless it is possible to get some "feedback" about the impact of programme efforts, it will be impossible to learn efficiently from experience, and a great deal of time, effort and morale will be lost, needlessly.

The panel hopes that at the state level particularly, the Bureaux of Vital and Health Statistics will be strengthened as rapidly as possible, and headed by senior and well-trained statistical personnel, so as to give leadership to this heretofore neglected aspect of the family planning and health programme. These Bureaux have critically important statistical responsibilities and should not be combined with the functions of making epidemiological investigations, or with other special fields.

Improvement of Normal Registration System: The family planning programme is now in a position to make an extremely important contribution to the building up of the total system for regular and accurate transmission of vital and health statistics information, through computors posted at the block level, and statistical assistants at the district level. Central policy, as agreed to by the Registrar General and the Health Ministry, is that the computor may be utilized, on behalf of the Panchayat or other registration authorities, to collect and transmit basic registration data from the village registrars. He could also be used for some "feeding-in" of additional data on births and deaths detected by the health personnel. However, optimally, such additional data are "fed-in" directly to the local registrar by the health staff rather than sent for matching with the registrar's reports at the block level. At the time of the teams' visits, this system also had not generally been implemented except in pilot areas. The panel suggests that special encouragement be given, from the Central Health Ministry as well as Registrar-General's Office, to the states, so as to place the computors and give the district statistical assistants adequate training, and utilize them as a transmission system for basic vital statistics.

It is absolutely essential that family planning personnel function so as to improve and strengthen the normal system – not to try to conduct separate and parallel registration activities.

Sample Vital Statistics Registration Scheme: With the assistance of the Registrar General of India, a sample vital statistics registration scheme is being implemented in the states. Under this scheme a sample of villages are taken, and registration is rapidly upgraded through special efforts. This method, also, should be strongly encouraged as being an essential system for evaluating family planning programme efforts in the immediate future, pending adequate improvement of the normal registration system.

Special Fertility Study Methods: In the Family Planning Communications Research Centre, important pilot experience has been accumulated in the development of a "Standard Fertility Study" whereby, through sensitive survey research methods plus upgrading of registration, etc., it may be possible to detect early changes in patterns of fertility in a target population. The panel recommends that, with establishment of a Central Standard Fertility Study Committee to maintain a high quality of work, the Standard Fertility Study be gradually duplicated in various parts of the country, as a system of "listening posts", for the family planning programme.

Administrative Data for Progress Analysis and the Implementation Review: Attempts to consolidate the administrative progress data for an assessment of the state of implementation of the programme by the state teams showed a number of weaknesses. There obviously needs to be an immediate review of (1) the kinds of data which should be regularly reported; (2) the methods and modes of reporting; (3) the system for checking up on completeness of reporting; and (4) the nature and methods of analysis of such data, at various levels. Improvement in progress reporting and analysis is urgently called for, if the planning of the programme is to be done more systematically, and the review and follow-up of the programme by the state and the central governments are to be more effective.'[1]

The problem is – how can we have a reasonably close estimate of the actual number of births and the actual birth rate as against the registered birth rate? There is a similar problem about deaths and death rates.[2]

The following table (Table 3) gives an official estimate of the range

---

[1] *Evaluation of the Family Planning Programme: Report of the Panel of Consultants* (New Delhi: Ministry of Health, Government of India, 1967), pp. 69–70.

[2] *Census of India, 1951, Vol. I (India), Part I: Report* (New Delhi: Government of India Press, 1953), pp. 78–79.

of under-registration in the various Indian states for the decade 1951–60.[1]

Table 3
REGISTERED AND ESTIMATED BIRTH AND DEATH RATES IN INDIA, 1951–60

State	Mean decennial birth rate		Percentage of unregistered births to estimated total births
	Registered birth rate	*Estimated birth rate*	
Andhra Pradesh	19·5	39·7	50·9
Assam	9·8	49·3	80·1
Bihar	14·8	43·4	65·9
Gujarat	27·3	45·7	40·3
Kerala	24·2	38·9	37·8
Madhya Pradesh	15·5	43·2	64·1
Madras	27·2	34·9	22·1
Maharashtra	29·0	41·2	29·6
Mysore	22·6	41·6	45·7
Orissa	24·5	40·4	39·4
Punjab	36·1	44·7	19·2
Uttar Pradesh	16·0	41·5	61·4
West Bengal	21·3	42·9	50·3

As a result of delegating vital registration to the village Panchayats in several states and other political developments, vital registration in India has deteriorated even further. There is as yet no indication that it will improve in the near future.

This survey of the original and largely unverifiable source material, namely population census and vital statistical data during the last seventy years, reveals the value and validity of the material available to the student of Indian demography. In one sense, one is grateful that such a relatively complete series for a whole century (1872–1971) is available, and in another sense one despairs of its innate reliability even when all the possible adjustments and refinements have been effected. No matter what corrections are made and no matter what sampling technique is used, there is really no alternative to a complete, 100 per cent registration throughout the year and a full quin-

[1] *Census of India, Life Tables 1951–60* (New Delhi: Registrar-General of India, 1963). The various projections made by the Planning Commission and some scholars for the 1961 population of India proved to be incorrect by a wide margin in the light of the actual 1961 Census figure.

72

quennial or decennial census count. This is true despite the numerous advantages of sampling such as economy of money, time and energy. Thus India is still far from any ideal or even desirable vital statistical set-up.

As the present study covers series over the long period of seventy years (1901–71) it has been found necessary to trace the evolution of the relevant statistical data in India, their overall worth and the trends they can be made to yield. This is what is available in the general field of population census and vital statistical data.

SOURCES FOR INFANT MORTALITY STUDY

For a study of infant mortality in India during the last seventy years two kinds of direct statistical data are available: (a) official records, and (b) unofficial studies. Both by virtue of their content and methods of compilation they are of limited value.

The official sources are the series of Reports on Sanitation and Public Health issued by the authorities of the government of India. The first series are the Annual Reports of the Sanitary Measures Taken in India. These are principally concerned with the protection and promotion of the health of British and Indian troops, jails and ports and the civilian population. These Reports simply record the total number of births, deaths and infant deaths for the area under registration, an area that has been growing steadily from year to year. The only other detail that some of these Sanitary Reports give is the infant mortality rate by sex, namely, the number of male and female infant deaths per 1,000 male and female live births. The authors of these Reports (printed in England by the order of the House of Commons) express considerable diffidence as to the accuracy of the figures but a modern student of the subject is grateful to them, such as they are, for although defective and not really adjusted to the slowly growing registration area, they cannot be too wide of the mark.

This series of Reports on Sanitary Measures in India begins from the year 1864–65, as the Annual Reports of the Sanitary Commissioner with the Government of India. As new concepts of the role of a government in promoting the public health of a country began to emerge, the Government of India appointed in 1920 a Public Health Commissioner in the place of the Sanitary Commissioner and from that year the publication became the Annual Report of the Public Health Commissioner with the Government of India for the year concerned. With the advent of freedom in 1947, it was decided to integrate and centralize the medical and public health activities of the

73

Government of India (actually a recommendation of the Bhore Commission Report of 1943). The designation of the authority was changed to that of the Director-General of Health Services and the Annual Report became that of the Director-General with an accompanying volume of statistical appendices.

Pursuant to the decision of the Cabinet, the Registrar-General took over the work of registration and vital statistics from the Director-General of Health Services in 1960. He now publishes the registration data in an annual publication entitled *Vital Statistics of India* but, unfortunately, this volume does not appear regularly and the time lag is between three and five years. Realizing the inadequacies of registration data, two major projects – an annual sample census and an annual sample registration – have been launched. The annual sample census aims at obtaining by sample survey techniques estimates of birth, death and infant mortality rates by states, besides some data on other demographic characteristics.

The rates yielded by the sample census are considerably higher than the registered rates but in most cases are obviously much below the true rates. The non-sampling bias is much too high. In sample registration the aim is to ensure complete registration of births and deaths, as they occur, in a probability sample of about 200 villages and blocks of towns by means of special agencies and close supervision. It is a sort of miniature registration in a small manageable sample, where events are registered as they occur and this is supplemented by a half-yearly house-to-house survey. Theoretically, it should lead to a complete recording of all events in the sampled areas but in practice the different field agencies seldom perform their duties with the necessary efficiency. However, efforts are being made to perfect the arrangements so that sample registration may yield reliable estimates of birth, death and infant mortality rates.

We also have the National Sample Survey which conducts annual sample surveys and collects *inter alia* information on current birth, death and infant mortality rates. However, this source also has not proved to be reliable due to the effect of non-sampling errors, which are only too obvious in the results. In the wake of family planning activities, a number of locational studies on fertility have been carried out. Quite often, they suffer from deficiencies similar to those in national surveys, but the main difficulty is that they do not cover infant mortality.

There are also, as pointed out already, the comprehensive reports of India's decennial censuses, the Census Reports of India which began in 1872 and have been issued in a more or less uniform manner every ten years (except in 1941 because of the Second World War) down to 1971.

On the same lines, we have the Provincial Reports on Public Health and Population Census. There are the Annual Report of the Director of Public Health and the Decennial Report of the Census for the various provinces and states. In addition, there are the Annual Reports of the Executive Health Officer for certain major cities such as Bombay, Calcutta, Madras, etc. These are the official and unverifiable sources of primary demographic data for India.

As distinct from these Government Reports, a few studies by individual social scientists, government officials and medical personnel are available. These are in the nature of private and academic *ad hoc* studies. With reference to mortality in general and infant mortality in particular, their scope and objectives are very limited as they deal with random and select samples of population such as a village, a famine-affected area, patients of a particular hospital or some selected villages and towns in the country. Though these studies cover only small samples of population, they are of some value, for such facts and trends as they do establish may prove to be either corrective or corroborative of official figures. A comparison between these two sets of official and unofficial figures, where possible, proves instructive, if the limitations of such a comparison are not overlooked.

And lastly, the Government of India have taken the long-overdue measure of legislating a Birth and Death Registration Act, which applies uniformly to the whole country replacing the various state and local body enactments and executive orders. It gives adequate powers for enforcing compulsory registration of births and deaths. This Registration of Births and Deaths Act was passed by the Indian Parliament in 1969 and came into force throughout India on April 1, 1970, making the reporting and registration of births and deaths compulsory. A copy of the Act is given in Appendix 2.

It is a matter of some gratification that the long fight for better and more complete statistics, lasting over a period of more than a century, has resulted in this relevant and much-needed legislation. It is to be hoped that it will be properly enforced and that complete registration in the country will yield reliable data not only of the usual type but also such data as are required for making more sophisticated studies.

However, a decade will have to pass before the effectiveness of this legislation can be tested. It remains to be seen whether the births and deaths registered for the coming decade 1970–80 tally with the census figure of 1981.

To conclude, these then are the available data and their limitations. They indicate the nature of research needed to tackle a problem like that of infant mortality in an underdeveloped country. In brief, the problem before us can be expressed in the words of Professor Bradford Hill: 'One must seek more facts paying less attention to techniques of handling the data and far more to the development and perfection of methods of obtaining them.'[1]

Whether it is medical statistics or demographic data or both as in the case of infant mortality or the overall population problem the need is the same – 'mehr Licht'.

[1] Bradford A. Hill, 'Cutter Lecture at the Harvard School of Public Health', *New England Journal of Medicine*, 1953, pp. 995–1001.

Chapter II

MEASUREMENT OF INFANT MORTALITY

WHAT IS INFANT MORTALITY?

For demographic statistical purposes, all children under one year of age are considered 'infants' and so the term 'infant mortality' refers to mortality among children of less than one year of age.

IMPORTANCE OF THE STUDY

The importance of the study of infant mortality cannot be over-emphasized if we consider the fact that in many under-developed countries one out of every five, sometimes even one out of every four infants, dies before completing its first year of life. In fact, even in advanced countries where the health conditions for infants are the best in the world, the first year of life remains the most vulnerable period (barring very old age, say about 70 years).

Since infants, more than any other section of the population, depend to a large extent on the environmental conditions for their survival, it would not be far wrong to say that the death of an infant in most cases is due to a poor and insanitary environment. And environment being something that society can improve considerably, a high rate of infant mortality would indicate that all that the society can do to improve the environmental conditions has not been done. Hence the infant mortality rate may be taken as a reliable and sensitive index of the total health conditions of a community or a country.

DEFINITION OF THE INFANT MORTALITY RATE AND OTHER CONNECTED TERMS

The infant mortality rate may be defined as the number of infant deaths that occur per thousand live births in any population in one

77

calendar year. From the very definition it is obvious that the infant mortality rate does not take into account either foetal deaths or still-births, but only live births and infant deaths. But what do we mean by the terms 'live births', 'foetal deaths', 'stillbirths' and 'infant deaths'? The Third Assembly of the World Health Organization of the United Nations, early in 1950, recommended the following definitions for international use in this connection:

'*Live birth* is the complete expulsion or extraction from its mother of a product of conception, irrespective of the duration of pregnancy, which after such separation, breathes or shows any other evidence of life, such as beating of the heart, pulsation of the umbilical cord, or definite movement of voluntary muscles, whether or not the umbilical cord has been cut or the placenta is attached: each product of such a birth is considered live born.

Foetal death is death prior to the complete expulsion or extraction from its mother of a product of conception, irrespective of the duration of pregnancy; the death is indicated by the fact that after such separation the foetus does not breathe or show any other evidence of life, such as beating of the heart, pulsation of the umbilical cord, or definite movement of voluntary muscles.

All live-born infants should be registered and counted as such irrespective of the period of gestation, and if they die at any time following birth they should also be registered and counted as deaths.'[1]

So an '*infant death*' is the death of any live-born child before it completes its first year of life.

In addition, the Third World Health Assembly also recommended the 'tabulation of foetal deaths in the following four groups according to the length of gestation measured from the beginning of the last menstruation:

'Less than 20 completed weeks of gestation Group I
20 completed weeks of gestation but less than 28 Group II
28 completed weeks of gestation and over Group III
Gestation period not classified in Groups I, II and III Group IV.'[2]

The foetal deaths in Groups I, II and III above were called 'early foetal deaths', 'intermediate foetal deaths', and 'late foetal deaths' respectively, and 'stillbirths' were considered synonymous with 'late foetal deaths'.

[1] *Foetal, Infant and Early Childhood Mortality, Vol. 1* (New York: United Nations, 1954), p. 4.
[2] Ibid.

These definitions, though given as early as 1950, are yet to be implemented by the different countries with the consequence that international comparisons of infant mortality statistics suffer from the divergent usage of the terms 'live births', etc.

THE CONVENTIONAL INFANT MORTALITY RATE

From the definition of the infant mortality rate as given earlier it will be seen that for its proper calculation, the so-called Cohort Analysis Method has to be adopted. That is to say, we have to follow a 'cohort' of 1,000 live-born children through their first year of life and record the number of deaths among them during that period to arrive at the correct infant mortality rate. But since this procedure has been found difficult to follow due to administrative and other difficulties, a modified infant mortality rate called the 'conventional infant mortality rate' has generally been adopted. The conventional infant mortality rate is defined as the number of infant deaths that occur during a given period of time, usually a calendar year, per 1,000 live births during the same period, in a given population. In the 'correct infant mortality rate', the numerator and denominator refer to the same cohort, but in the 'conventional infant mortality rate' they do not do so – the numerator includes deaths among the births of the preceding year and excludes some of the deaths in the following year among the births of the current year. Since most infant deaths occur early in the first year of life, largely during the first month of life or the neo-natal period, the error is small. If inclusions approximately balance the exclusions, the two rates do not differ much and the conventional rate is a sufficiently reliable measure of infant mortality.

DATA NEEDED

'A detailed, serious and profitable study of infant mortality in any community or country, however (and particularly in a large and heterogenous country like India), must be based on an adequate knowledge of the complex biological, economic, social and cultural factors affecting the health, morbidity and mortality of infants.

We need precise and adequate information on no less than some twenty-five points. First, the mother's physical condition, the mother's age, the number of children she has borne (her parity), month and season of the birth; order of births; interval between births; employment, if any, of the mother during pregnancy and during the first year of the infant's life; sex of the infant; duration of marriage; if no marriage, the nature of the union (illegitimacy) such as common law marriage, temporary concubinage or casual affair, etc.; whether the birth was premature (infant weighing $5\frac{1}{2}$ lb or below), single or multiple.

Secondly, and more important, precise information is needed on the age of the infant at death; type of feeding such as breast-feeding, bottle-feeding and any cultural peculiarities in infant feeding; pathological cause of death; and whether the infant had received any medical aid. The last two items and even the age of the infant are often difficult to obtain in an under-developed country like India where the public health services particularly in rural areas are neither adequate nor efficient.

Thirdly, we must go beyond the pathological cause to ante-cedent and predisposing causes and causal factors. Hence we need some reliable information on the father's occupation, the family's income, and if possible, the educational status of the mother and preferably of both parents. As residential conditions matter a great deal in any country and particularly in India, where a majority of the population have sub-standard rural and urban housing, information on the housing conditions are needed, such as thatched hut or brick-built house, and the presence, if any, of sanitary conveniences; residence of the family, whether rural or urban, village, town or city; knowledge of the family's religion and language as indicative of the cultural mores will also be useful. If the infant death was a case of peri-natal or neo-natal mortality (and for all confinements for that matter) we need information on the nature of the confinement (normal delivery, instrumental delivery or caesarian section, etc.), whether the delivery was in the home or in a hospital; if at home, whether there were any medical helpers (doctor, midwife, etc.). Any other information of a clinical and case-history nature, besides a knowledge of the home and up-bringing, particularly of the mother, would be helpful.

And last but not least are health, welfare and survival of the mother herself. The sickness, disability or death of the mother within one year after confinement has an enormous influence on the survival of the infant.

If the study is to be a comprehensive inquiry into all vital losses up to the age of one year, social, medical and environmental details from conception should be ascertained; abortion (spontaneous or induced), period and the immediate cause; premature births (any viable infant weighing $5\frac{1}{2}$ lb or 2,500 g or less being specified as immature or premature); and stillbirths (any infant born after the 28th week of pregnancy who did not at any time breathe or show any other sign of life). And for an analysis of stillbirths, a knowledge of the following factors would be helpful; type and duration of delivery; primary medical cause of stillbirths; history of previous pregnancies; health of the mother; nutritional assessment of the mother's diet during pregnancy; mother's employment, if any, during pregnancy; and history of sexual intercourse during pregnancy.'[1]

However, conventionally, stillbirths and foetal deaths are not treated as a part of infant mortality in most countries. And therefore in this study, stillbirths and foetal deaths are not treated as a part of infant mortality.

DATA GENERALLY AVAILABLE

While data on the above categories may be considered as almost the requisite minimum, no information on most of these factors is available for India as a whole (undivided India as well as for the present registration area of the Indian Union) or even for the former British provinces (British India) which are usually taken as the regular registration area in all discussions of Indian demography.

However, apart from the general demographic data available from the decennial census and annual vital statistical reports as already described, some specific but incomplete data are available for some provinces as to the age, sex of the infant, rural or urban residence, sometimes the caste and religious affiliation of the family, and occasionally medical attestation of the cause of the death. But the latter information is given in a majority of cases (unattended by medical personnel) by someone such as a parent, a relative, village headman or police official who is not medically qualified to do so. Thus information on the cause of infant deaths can only be taken relatively seriously in certain cities where some effort is made to ascertain the cause, to the best of the ability of the registration personnel. In view of this deplorable situation, which has not improved in recent years despite India's valiant efforts at progress in many directions, a plea for complete reorganization of the machinery for vital registration all over India becomes necessary. It need hardly be added that mere vital registration as far as mortality is concerned without medical attestation will be to a great extent without any

[1] S. Chandrasekhar, 'Some Observations on Infant Mortality in India: 1901–1951', *Eugenics Review*, London, January 1955, p. 214.

value. Such a reorganization can only be achieved when the public health system embraces the majority of the population which lives in India's far-flung villages. The formidable cost of any such organization – public health personnel as well as registration agencies – is not minimized, but there appears to be no sense whatsoever in a government trying to fight the inordinate morbidity and mortality of a people and particularly of its most defenceless and vulnerable section, infants, when the authorities are largely ignorant of the exact number and the basic and pathological causes of sickness and death. Any worthwhile policy must be based on unquestionable facts. But in the absence of factual and acceptable data, the public health and related policies of the government are no better than the proverbial blind man searching in a dark room for a black cat which was not there.

And yet there is no point in despairing, for when the ideal is unattainable, we must manage with the available. We must make do with the next best or any workable alternative. This long list of desirable and unobtainable data is cited not with any defeatist purpose but to highlight the more or less ideal set-up we should eventually aim at and hope for in our country.[1]

COMPUTATION OF THE INFANT MORTALITY RATE:

TRUE INFANT MORTALITY RATE

The true infant mortality rate, defined earlier, would involve, apart from the live births in a given calendar year, the deaths of infants in that calendar year from among the live births in that same year plus the deaths of infants in the next calendar year from the live births in the previous calendar year. Let us consider this symbolically.[2]

Let b_x be the total number of 'live births' in the calendar year x

d_x^x be the total number of 'infant deaths' in the calendar year x from out of the live births in the same calendar year x

and d_{x+1}^x be the total number of 'infant deaths' in the calendar year $(x+1)$ from out of the 'live births' in the calendar year x.

Then the 'true infant mortality rate' I is given by:

$$I = \frac{d_x^x + d_{x+1}^x}{b_x}$$

[1] S. Chandrasekhar, *Census and Statistics In India* (Chidambaram: Annamalai University, 1948), passim.

[2] Adapted from *Foetal, Infant and Early Childhood Mortality, Vol. 1*, pp. 10–11.

The following two components, with deaths related to population at risk, are involved in this rate I:

$$I_1 = \frac{d_x}{b_x} = \text{proportion of infants born and dying in the same calendar year } x$$

and

$$I_2 = \frac{d_{x+1}^x}{b_x d_x^x} = \text{proportion of infants born in and surviving the calendar year } x, \text{ dying in the calendar year } x+1 \text{ as 'infants'}$$

therefore

$(1-I_1)(1-I_2)$ = proportion of 'live births' in the year x surviving their first year of life

therefore

$1-(1-I_1)(1-I_2)$ = proportion of 'live births' in the year x that die before completing the first year of life.

Thus the computation of the true infant mortality rate would require that deaths be tabulated by the year of occurrence, age at death and by the year of birth of the deceased, which is seldom done in any country. Even granting that death registration is done in such detail and that the registration is complete (which is not at all true of many countries of the world), for computing the true infant mortality rate for the current calendar year one will have to wait till the end of the next calendar year.

REFINED INFANT MORTALITY RATE

To obviate this difficulty, however, Dr Valaoras[1] has proposed the 'refined infant mortality rate'. Using the same notation as before, this 'refined infant mortality rate' consists of two components:

$$i_1 = \frac{d_x^x}{b_x}$$

and

$$i_2 = \frac{d_x^{x-1}}{b_{x-1} - d_{x-1}^{x-1}}$$

where d_x^{x-1} = deaths of infants in the year x out of live births in the year $(x-1)$

b_{x-1} = live births in the year $(x-1)$

and d_{x-1}^{x-1} = deaths in infants in the year $(x-1)$ from among the live births in the year $(x-1)$.

[1] Vasilios G. Valaoras, 'Refined Rates for Infant and Childhood Mortality', *Population Studies*, Vol. IV, No. 3, London, December 1950, pp. 253–66.

The 'refined infant mortality rate' is then given as:

$$I_R = 1 - (1 - i_1)(1 - i_2)$$

It would be observed that i_1 here is the same as I_1 of the 'true infant mortality rate'. The i_2 here is comparable to I_2 of the true rate, but is instead based on data belonging to the previous calendar year. This i_2 would be a close approximation to I_2 as long as infant mortality is not changing rapidly from year to year, irrespective of the trends in birth rate. The refined rate, it may be pointed out, uses in the numerator deaths of infants occurring in only one year, but requires births in two calendar years and infant deaths in the preceding year among births of that year. For calculating it, one needs data for the current year and the preceding year, which are available, and hence one does not have to wait till the end of the next calendar year as is necessary in the case of 'true infant mortality rate' discussed on the preceding page.

A clearer idea of the difference between the 'true' and the 'refined' infant mortality rates just described will be had from Table 4. In the notation adopted for infant deaths 'd', the subscript denotes the calendar year of infant death and the superscript the calendar year of births, from amongst which the infant deaths have occurred.

Table 4
BIRTHS AND INFANT DEATHS IN SUCCESSIVE YEARS

Year	Births	Infant deaths in the calendar year from births in the current year	previous year	Total infant deaths
$x-1$ 1965	b_{x-1} 203,200	d_{x-1}^{x-1} 24,384	d_{x-1}^{x-2} 8,128	32,512
x 1966	b_x 260,400	d^x 23,436	d_x^{x-1} 15,624	39,060
$x+1$ 1967	b_{x+1} 248,752	d_{x+1}^{x+1} 21,766	d_{x+1}^x 9,328	31,094

Hypothetical numerical values for each are also shown for purposes of illustration.

In both the infant death rates, the component arising out of infant deaths among the birth cohort of the year is common. For 1966, it is $I_1 = 90.0$ per thousand births. The difference lies in the second component. In the case of the 'true' rate, infant deaths that occur in the following year from amongst the survivors of the current year's birth cohort are taken into account. Thus $I_2 = 9,328/(260,400 - 23,436) = 39\cdot4$ per thousand births. Then, $I = 1 - 0\cdot9100 \times 0\cdot9606 = 126$ per thousand births.

In the case of the 'refined' rate, the second component i_2 is based on the infant deaths in the *current* year from amongst the survivors of the preceding year's birth cohorts. Thus $i_2 = 15,624/(203,200 - 24,384) = 87\cdot4$ per thousand births. Then, $I_R = 1 - 0\cdot9100 \times 0\cdot9126 = 170$ per thousand births. Normally the second component does not vary from year to year and hence the 'refined' rate closely approximates to the 'true' rate. This is not true in the case of the illustration, since the second components differ widely. In such a situation the conventional infant mortality rate diverges more markedly from the true rate, as is clear from the example too. The conventional rate for 1966 is 150 per thousand births.

MODIFIED INFANT MORTALITY RATE: SEPARATION FACTORS

As pointed out earlier, the 'true' as well as the 'refined' infant mortality rates require that the year of birth of the infants who have died be known and this information is not always readily available. However, an estimate of the proportion of infant deaths in a calendar year belonging to births in the same year to the total number of infant deaths in that calendar year can be made and this estimate is known as the 'separation factor'.

It may be recalled that in the case of the 'conventional infant mortality rate', the total infant deaths occurring in a given calendar year are taken to relate to the total live births during that calendar year. This conventional way of expressing the infant mortality rate would, however, be correct if all the infants who died in a particular year were also born in the same year. In fact, however, infants who died before completing their first year of age in 1951, for instance, are the babies born in 1950 who died in 1951 before completing their first year and those born in 1951 who died before the end of that year. The conventional way will be approximately correct if the number of births in the year before was more or less the same as that in the current year and the risk of death in infancy has not changed much. But if births in the previous year are considerably higher or lower, or the risk of death in infancy has fluctuated rapidly, the conventional infant mortality rate is apt to be misleading and will remain at best a crude one.

However, this drawback could be overcome by using the 'separation factor' and in fact several attempts have been made in the application of this device. The most exhaustive of these is the study of Moriyama and Greville[1] who proposed that the infant deaths of any year be reallocated to the corresponding cohorts of births, and the adjusted infant mortality rate be calculated as follows:

$$\text{Adjusted infant mortality rate} = \frac{d_x f}{b_x} + \frac{d_x(1-f)}{b_{x-1}} \times 1{,}000$$

where

d_x = number of infant deaths in the calendar year x.

f = proportion of deaths under 1 year of age which were deaths of infants born and dying in the same calendar year = (separation factor).

b_x = live births in the calendar year x.

b_{x-1} = live births in calendar year $(x-1)$.

It may be pointed out however, that the separation factor for a given area may not remain constant from year to year. It can be seen that if infant mortality goes on decreasing, an increasing percentage of infants dying during a calendar year would be drawn from the live births during the same year thus increasing the separation factor. Similarly if the live births in a given year are more than those in the previous year, the separation factor for the given year will increase. However, some test calculations, which have been made to check this, indicate that within the range of likely annual changes in the live births and infant mortality rate, the separation factor remains stable over a period of 5 to 10 years. The separation factor should be taken from the data of a community having a similar level of infant mortality. A small error, however, has only a minor effect on the mortality rate. If no data are available, it may be taken as 0·30 arbitrarily, but it is doubtful if a purely arbitrary adjustment such as this is preferable over the crude infant mortality rate.

CALCULATION OF SEPARATION FACTORS

Now let us consider the methods of calculating the separation factors. The three possible methods of calculating the value of separation factors are:

[1] I. M. Moriyama and T. N. E. Greville, 'Effect of Changing Birth Rates upon Infant Mortality Rates', *U.S. Vital Statistics Special Reports, Vol. XIX, No. 21,* November 10, 1944, pp. 401–12.

    (i) the method of analytical reasoning based on the assumption of a uniform distribution of deaths over the first year of life;

    (ii) the method of using past statistical data;

    (iii) the method of using regression lines.

(i) *Method of Analytical Reasoning*

The separation factor could be used either to allocate the deaths in the current calendar year to the live births in the previous and current calendar years appropriately, in which case it is known as 'numerator separation' or to calculate the related births to deaths at each interval of the first year of age in the current calendar year, in which case it is known as 'denominator adjustment'. These two procedures may be examined in some detail as they happen to differ slightly.

(a) *Numerator Separation.* The basic requirement before 'numerator separation' can be applied is that the number of live births in the current and previous calendar years are known separately in addition to the number of deaths in the current calendar year tabulated by age at death. Once this information is available the problem is to allocate the deaths in each sub-division of age to the births in the current and previous calendar years. For example, if the age at death is tabulated as under 1 day, 1, 2, 3, 4, 5, 6 days, 7–13 days, 14–20 days, 21–27 days, 28 days to 2 months, and by single months of life from 2 months to 1 year, the problem is to allocate the number of deaths in each of these age groups to the births in the previous and current calendar years. The finer the subdivisions of age at death the more accurate the separation factor becomes.

    The logic of this method can be illustrated as follows: let d_1 be the number of deaths of children aged a_1 to a_2 months in the current calendar year. Now it can be seen that *all such deaths* occurring in the first a_1 months of the current calendar year should belong to the births in the previous calendar year and all such deaths occurring *after* the $a_{2\text{nd}}$ month of the current calendar year should belong to the births of the current calendar year. It is the deaths of infants aged a_1 to a_2 months occurring between the $a_{1\text{st}}$ and $a_{2\text{nd}}$ months of the current calendar year that present a problem. But conventionally it is taken that *half* of these deaths belong to the births in the previous calendar year and the other half to births in the current calendar year. If it is assumed that the deaths of infants aged a_1 to a_2 months is uniformly distributed over the year, the proportion of such deaths assigned to the previous calendar year would be

$$\frac{a_1 + \frac{1}{2}(a_2 - a_1)}{12} = \frac{a_1 + a_2}{24}$$

and the proportion assigned to the current calendar year would be

$$1 - \frac{a_1 + a_2}{24}$$

That is, if the number of infant deaths in the current calendar year tabulated by age at death is available, these deaths – by a simple arithmetical procedure – can be allotted to the appropriate births in the previous and current calendar years. The procedure is to multiply the number of deaths in each sub-group of age by the appropriate proportions and add the resulting figures. The following table (Table 5) gives the actual working.

Table 5
CALCULATION OF INFANT DEATHS FROM PREVIOUS YEAR'S BIRTHS

Period	No. of infant deaths	Separation factor	No. of deaths from previous year's births
(1)	(2)	(3)	(4)
Below 1 day	10,529	0·001	11
1–7 days	5,516	0·011	61
7–28 days	2,013	0·048	97
28 days to 3 months	3,446	0·162	558
3–6 months	2,744	0·375	1,029
6–9 months	1,243	0·625	777
9–12 months	852	0·875	746
Total	26,343		3,279

Deaths of infants aged below one day cover the time interval of 0–1 day. Accordingly, $\frac{1}{2} \times 1/365 = 0\cdot001$ of such deaths are taken to have occurred from out of the births of the preceding year. Deaths of infants between 1 and 7 days comprise deaths of infants aged over 1 day but less than 7 days and hence cover the time interval of 6 days. Accordingly

$$\frac{7 + \frac{1}{2}(28 - 7)}{365}$$

$= 0\cdot048$ of the infant deaths aged 7–28 days are taken to have occurred from out of the births of the preceding year. The interval between 28 days and 3 months is taken to be 62 days and accordingly

$$\frac{28+\frac{1}{2}(62)}{365}$$

$= 0{\cdot}162$ of the deaths in the age interval 28 days to 3 months are taken to have occurred from out of the births of the previous year. The separation factor for the period 3–6 months, 6–9 months and 9–12 months are

$$\frac{3+6}{24} = 0{\cdot}375, \frac{6+9}{24} = 0{\cdot}625$$

and

$$\frac{9+12}{24} = 0{\cdot}875$$

respectively.

The product of column 2 and column 3 gives the number of infant deaths from out of the births of the previous year. Their total comes to 3,279.

It may be noted here that when there are only two subdivisions of infant deaths as neo-natal (infants below 28 days of age) and post neo-natal (infants aged above 28 days and below 1 year), the proportions assigned to the previous year are *zero* and *half* respectively. This is a rather simplified but less accurate method of 'numerator separation'.

(b) *Denominator Adjustment.* The problem here is not one of allocation of deaths in the current calendar year to the births in the previous and current calendar years, but one of calculating the related births to deaths at each age. That is to say, the 'crude' denominator – the number of births in the current year – is adjusted by increasing or diminishing it a certain amount so as to make allowance for a different number of births in the previous year.

Let the total number of live births in the xth and $(x+1)$st calendar year be b_x and b_{x+1} respectively. Consider the deaths of infants of age a_1 to a_2 months in the current, that is, $(x+1)$st calendar year. If now we assume that the births in the xth as well as the $(x+1)$st calendar years are uniformly spread over the years, then the number of births to which these deaths of infants of age a_1 to a_2 months in the current calendar year are related are:

$$\frac{a_1+a_2}{24}b_x+1-\frac{a_1+a_2}{24}b_{(x+1)} = b_{x+1}+\frac{a_1+a_2}{24}(b_{x+1}-b_x)$$

Now, dividing the deaths of infants of age between a_1 and a_2 months in the current calendar year by the related births given above, and multiplying by 1,000, we get the mortality rate for ages between a_1 and a_2 months. Similarly we can calculate the mortality rates for all sub-divisions of age under 1 year and the sum of all these rates will give us the required infant mortality rate. In general this may be written as

$$\text{I.M.R. for year } (x+1) = \frac{d_{x+1}}{rb_x+(1-r)b_{x+1}} \times 1,000$$

where 'r' is the adjustment factor for births.

(ii) *Method of Using Past Statistical Data*

The method of analytical reasoning described above, would be valid only on the assumption of a uniform distribution of deaths and births (occurring in a year) over the year. But it is too well known that births and deaths in a year are subject to considerable seasonal fluctuations and therefore it would be better if we could make use of the statistical data, if available, of a normal period. That is, if for any normal year we have the number of deaths of infants classified by age at death and year of birth, we can calculate the proportion of deaths in the current calendar year which springs from the births in the previous calendar year and this proportion could be used for allocating deaths in the future years.

(iii) *Method of Regression Lines*

If in any country, the crude infant mortality rates for a number of years and the corresponding separation factors are available, it is possible to fit an appropriate regression line taking the separation factor as the dependent variable Y and the crude infant mortality rate as the independent variable X. From this regression line, the separation factor can be estimated if the crude infant mortality rate is known for any year.

This method has been applied by Valaoras in the case of Scandinavia, where for a number of decades vital statistics have been carefully collected. The following was the regression line fitted by Valaoras:

$$\text{Log } (Y-50) = 1 \cdot 490173 - 0 \cdot 005153\ X$$

where Y is the separation factor and X the crude infant mortality rate. The regression line reflects the fact that the infant mortality rate registered a declining trend in that country. Actually, the infant mortality rate declined from about 85 to about 30 per thousand live births during that period.

The ready application of the regression line given above is possible only in countries where the level of infant mortality is more or less the same as that in Scandinavia and also only if it shows a declining trend. Moreover, the application of this method may give misleading results in countries where the age distribution of infant deaths at a given level of infant mortality rate does not conform to the Scandinavian pattern.

INFANT MORTALITY RATE IN LIFE TABLES

An essential element in the computations involved in the construction of life tables is the mortality rate in the first year of life denoted by q_0. The usual method of calculating the mortality rates for the construction of life tables is to employ both the census figures and the registered deaths. But on account of the unreliability of the numbers enumerated at infantile ages (0 to 5 years) by the census, it has become customary to discard the census figures at these ages as incorrect and to use the birth and death registration figures for the calculation of the mortality rates at these ages.

(a) English Life Table Methods

The basic assumption employed in the construction of English Life Tables 1 to 8 was that there was a uniform progression in the movement of the population over the year of age – i.e. it was assumed that deaths between the attainment of age 'x' and the end of the calendar year (Z) were equal to the deaths between the beginning of the calendar year ($Z+1$) and attainment of age ($x+1$). Allowance for varying births and deaths in the different calendar years was made by using the data of a number of calendar years. The method used to calculate the mortality rate in the first year of life was essentially the 'denominator adjustment' approach which has been discussed earlier. By this method: infant mortality rate for the year ($x+1$) =

$$\frac{d_{x+1}}{r \cdot b_x + (1-r)b_{x+1}}$$

where d_{x+1} denotes the deaths of infants in the year $x+1$ and b_x and b_{x+1} denote the live births in the years x and ($x+1$) respectively. In the case of the English Life Tables 1 to 8, r was taken to be equal to 0·5 and the infant mortality rates were calculated.

In the case of English Life Tables 9 and 10, however, there was some change. Since it was found that there were violent fluctuations in the number of births during and after the war of 1914–18, the earlier assumption of uniform distribution of births over the year was abandoned, and since as returns of births and deaths were available for each quarter of each calendar year, it was assumed that the births and deaths in each quarter were distributed uniformly. Again the method used for the computation of the mortality rate q_0 was essentially the 'denominator adjustment approach'.

From the available data, the probabilities were calculated that an infant

   (i) will die in the first quarter-year of life;
  (ii) will survive the first quarter-year of life but will die before the end of the second quarter;
 (iii) will survive the first half-year of life but will die in the third quarter;
 (iv) will survive the first three-quarters of life but will die in the last quarter of the first year of life.

The sum of these four probabilities yielded the required infant mortality rate, as shown in Table 6.[1]

(b) *American Life Tables*

In the United States, a survey of the registration of vital statistics carried out along with the census in 1940 revealed that the under-registration of births and deaths was more or less of the same order and so the infant mortality rate could be calculated by using the 'numerator separation' method described earlier. By this method, the 'infant deaths' in the year were allocated to births in the previous and current years and then the Valaoras method of calculation of the 'Refined Infant Mortality Rate' was used to arrive at the infant mortality rate.

(c) *Indian Life Tables*

In India, life tables have been constructed on the basis of a comparison of the enumerated figures at the successive censuses. To calculate the infant mortality rate, the following method has been adopted. The recorded births in each year of the intercensal period are compared with the surviving numbers enumerated in the second census, assuming the effects of migration to be negligible. The sur-

[1] W. P. D. Logan, 'The Measurement of Infant Mortality', *Population Bulletin*, *No. 3*, New York: United Nations, October 1953, pp. 55–6. I am indebted to Dr Logan's excellent article and this part of the chapter is largely based on his reasoning.

Table 6
DETAILS OF THE COMPUTATIONAL METHOD USED IN ENGLISH LIFE TABLES 9 AND 10
FOR THE CALCULATION OF THE INFANT MORTALITY RATE

Quarter period	Quarter year of age	Deaths D_t (Numerator)	Related births Bi (Denominator)
1	0-2 months	$_1d_0 + _1d_1 + _1d_2$	$\frac{1}{2} \times _4b_{-1} + b_0 + b_1 + b_2 - \frac{1}{2} \times _4b_2$
2	3-5 months	$_2d_0 + _2d_1 + _2d_2$	$\frac{1}{2} \times _3b_{-1} + _4b_{-1} + b_0 + b_1 + b_2 + _2b_2 + \frac{1}{2} \times _3b_2$
3	6-8 months	$_3d_0 + _3d_1 + _3d_2$	$\frac{1}{2} \times _2b_{-1} + _3b_{-1} + _4b_{-1} + b_0 + b_1 + _1b_2 + \frac{1}{2} \times _2b_2$
4	9-11 months	$_4d_0 + _4d_1 + _4d_2$	$\frac{1}{2} \times _1b_{-1} + _2b_{-1} + _3b_{-1} + _4b_{-1} + b_0 + b_1 + \frac{1}{2} \times _1b_2$

Now $q_0 = \dfrac{D_1}{B_1} + \dfrac{D_2}{B_2} + \dfrac{D_3}{B_3} + \dfrac{D_4}{B_4}$

and

S^{st} = deaths in the sth quarter of life in calendar year 't'.

n^{bt} = births in the nth quarter of calendar year 't'.

b_t = births in the entire calendar year 't'.

vival ratios are computed and compared with those in existing life tables of other countries and if any table is found which has nearly comparable survival ratios, then 'proportional factors are formed from the ratio of deaths in infancy to total deaths from birth to successive ages in this life table'.[1] If these ratios are multiplied by the differences between the census enumeration and recorded births, estimates of infant deaths in the intercensal years are obtained. Thus with the annual births available, the infant mortality rate is calculated by the conventional method. The rate so obtained is a crude one and is necessarily a rough approximation to the correct infant mortality rate.

BOURGEOIS-PICHAT MEASURE OF INFANT MORTALITY RATE

M. Bourgeois-Pichat,[2] the French demographer, found that deaths in the first year of age could not all be placed under the same category since part of them were caused by 'endogenic' and the rest by 'exogenic' factors. The deaths classified under the former category would consist of those cases in which the child 'bears within itself, from birth, the cause resulting in its death, whether that cause was inherited from its parents at conception or acquired from its mother during gestation or delivery'.[3]

The second category would comprise deaths of infants due to the effect of the environment in which they live. Bourgeois-Pichat's contention is that this classification is important from the medical point of view, since the preventive measures designed to reduce the endogenic causes of mortality are different from those that are effective against exogenic causes. Also, by this method of distinguishing the exogenic component from the endogenic component, the difficulty inherent in the total infant mortality rate as to whether any of the early deaths have been omitted or misclassified as stillbirths can be avoided.

Once we accept the above argument of the necessity for the classification of infant deaths into 'exogenic' and 'endogenic' deaths, we

[1] W. P. D. Logan, op. cit., p. 57.

[2] Jean Bourgeois-Pichat, 'De la mesure de la mortalité infantile', *Population*, Paris, January–March 1946, p. 53 f.; Jean Bourgeois-Pichat 'Analyse de la mortalité infantile', *Revue de l'Institut International de Statistique*, 1950, No. 1/2, p. 45 f. Jean Bourgeois-Pichat, 'La mesure de la mortalité infantile', *Population*, Paris, April–June 1951, p. 233 f.; *Population*, Paris, July–September 1951, p. 459 f.

[3] Jean Bourgeois-Pichat, 'An Analysis of Infant Mortality', *Population Bulletin, No. 2*, New York: United Nations, October 1952, p. 1.

have to adopt some method to effect this classification. The simplest way to achieve this would be to classify all infant deaths into these two groups according to age, rather arbitrarily, say deaths under 4 weeks of age and those over 4 weeks of age.

However, the method given by M. Bourgeois-Pichat attempts to provide a more accurate distinction between the two groups of deaths than can be achieved by a division of infant deaths arbitrarily at a selected age. His method is as follows: 'The "exogenous" rate is essentially a weighted average of the mortality rates for each month in infancy after the first; the "endogenous" rate is then the difference between the mortality rate for the first year of life and the "exogenous" rate.'[1] The weights used in this calculation according to Bourgeois-Pichat are invariant both with respect to space and time. The application of this method to the data of England and Wales in 1950 is shown in Table 7.

The Bourgeois-Pichat method of calculating the 'exogenous' and 'endogenous' components of infant mortality lends itself to criticism on a number of points. First, it is not known what objective tests

Table 7

CALCULATION OF 'EXOGENIC' INFANT MORTALITY RATE, ENGLAND AND WALES, 1950[2]

Age (months) (1)	No. of deaths (2)	Cumulated deaths (up) (3)	Rate per 1,000 live births in 1950 (697,097) (4)	(Weights) co-efficient (5)	(Rate) co-efficient (6)
1	1,614	7,900	11·33	0·801	14·14
2	1,398	6,286	9·02	0·654	13·79
3	1,067	4,888	7·01	0·550	12·75
4	862	3,821	5·48	0·459	11·94
5	702	2,959	4·24	0·381	11·13
6	551	2,257	3·24	0·312	10·38
7	458	1,706	2·45	0·249	9·78
8	374	1,248	1·79	0·189	9·47
9	328	874	1·25	0·139	8·99
10	296	546	0·78	0·089	8·76
11	250	250	0·36	0·044	8·18
				Av.	10·85

Exogenic rate = Average of Col. 6 = 10·85 per 1,000 live births.
Total Infant Mortality Rate = 29·86 per 1,000 live births.
Therefore, Endogenic Infant Mortality Rate = 19·01 per 1,000 live births.

[1] W. P. D. Logan, op. cit., p. 60.
[2] Ibid., p. 54.

have been used to ascertain how accurately the calculated 'exogenic' and 'endogenic' rates actually measure the concepts they define. Secondly, as pointed out by Dr Logan, if these rates are used for mechanical guidance, it is not known as to how these compare with the best that medical opinion has to offer, i.e. with the findings produced by careful clinical and pathological examinations. Thirdly, the two terms 'exogenic infant mortality' and 'endogenic infant mortality' have not been precisely defined. Lastly, the claim of universality of the weighting factors (or coefficients) used by Bourgeois-Pichat is yet to be demonstrated. In the words of Dr Logan: 'On the whole, it seems fair to say that Bourgeois-Pichat has offered a novel and ingenious method for measuring certain aspects of infant mortality but that from the point of view of "medical statistics", the method offers no practical advantage over the existing methods.'[1]

STANDARDIZATION OF INFANT MORTALITY RATE

A number of factors like sex, race, socio-economic circumstances, legitimacy, age and parity of mother, family size, etc., affect the infant mortality rate and so, for the purposes of comparison of infant mor-

Table 8
STANDARDIZATION OF CRUDE INFANT MORTALITY RATES[2]

| | Legitimate | | Illegitimate | | |
	Males	Females	Males	Females	Total
Standard births (e.g. National)	340,000	320,000	20,000	19,000	699,000
Distribution per 1,000 total births	486	458	29	27	1,000
Area A					
Births	40,000	35,000	800	700	76,500
Deaths	1,600	1,050	48	35	2,733
	Crude Infant Mortality Rate = 35·7				
Area B					
Births	20,000	17,000	1,600	1,380	39,980
Deaths	780	493	94	68	1,435
	Crude Infant Mortality Rate = 35·9				
Deaths in a standard 1,000 births					*Standardized Infant Mortality Rate*
Area A	19·44	13·74	1·74	1·35	36·3
Area B	18·95	13·28	1·70	1·33	35·3

[1] W. P. D. Logan, op. cit., p. 54.
[2] Ibid.,

tality rates, it is necessary to standardize them. For example, Table 8 shows the effect of the distribution of legitimate and illegitimate births on the crude infant mortality rate of area 'A' and 'B' and the method of standardizing them with reference to the distribution of legitimate and illegitimate births in a standard population.

In Table 8, a comparison of the crude infant mortality rates for areas A and B reveals that area A seems to have a slightly lower infant mortality experience. But on a comparison of the standardized infant mortality rates – which are crude infant mortality rates adjusted for the effects of legitimacy by using the distribution of legitimate and illegitimate children in the standard population – it is seen that area B experiences a lower infant mortality than area A.

APPLICATIONS OF INFANT MORTALITY RATE

(i) *Estimation of the Number of Births from Census Data*
A census count of the number of children under 1 year of age, on any date, reveals the total number of births during the one year previous to the date of the census minus the infant deaths that have occurred during that one year. That is, if a census count of the children under 1 year of age on December 31 of any year be L_0, then $L_0 = L - d$ where 'L' is the total number of live births during that calendar year and 'd' the number of infant deaths during the same year.

Dr Giorgia Mortara[1] has shown that from a knowledge of L_0, we can estimate 'L', by making use of the infant mortality rate prevalent in that population. According to Mortara, two-thirds of the infant mortality takes place in the same calendar year of birth and only the remaining one-third in the following calendar year. Therefore, if L_0 be the census count of children under 1 year of age on December 31 of any year, the number of live births during that calendar year can be calculated as:

$$L = L_0/(1 - \tfrac{2}{3} \text{ of infant mortality rate per unit}).$$

The merit of this method lies in the fact that since the infant mortality rate in most countries of the world is known to lie in the range of 0·3 to 0·016 per unit, it is possible to give limits to the total number of live births in any year. But, however, caution should be exercised in making use of the census figures in the age 0 to 1, since it is subject to two types of errors. First, the reporting of children under 1 year of age may be imperfect and second, there is always a tendency among

[1] *Methods of Using Census Statistics for the Calculation of Life Tables and other Demographic Measures* (New York: United Nations, 1950), p. 3.

D

people to overstate the ages of their children under 1 year of age so that the census count of children under 1 year of age is usually an underestimate.

(ii) *Estimation of Under-registration*

S. P. Jain,[1] the Actuary for the 1951 Census of India, has studied the extent of under-registration of births in India by a slight extension of the method described above.

Using Mortara's method, from the 1951 Census count of children under 1 year of age, the total number of live births in the year immediately preceding the census was estimated. Then

$$1 - \frac{\text{(Registered number of births in the year immediately preceding the census)}}{\text{(Estimated number of births in the same one year)}} \times 100$$

gave the percentage of under-registration of births during that year.

In this connection, Jain has shown that even if Mortara's assumption of the proportion of infant mortality taking place in the same calendar year as two-thirds, varied between seven-tenths and three-quarters, and the infant mortality rate varied from 80 to 250 per thousand, the relative error in the estimated number of births by this method would be small. Table 9 shows, 'the percentage by which the estimated births come out to be higher than the number obtained by taking $r = \frac{2}{3}$ and $I = 80$'.[2]

Table 9

PERCENTAGE INCREASE IN THE NUMBER OF ESTI-MATED BIRTHS FOR DIFFERENT VALUES OF 'r' AND INFANT MORTALITY RATE[3]

Infant mortality rate	$r = 2/3$	$r = 7/10$	$r = 3/4$
80	—	0·3	0·7
160	6·0	6·6	7·6
250	11·4	14·5	16·6

[1] S. P. Jain, 'Computed Birth and Death Rates in India during 1941–50', *Census of India, 1951, Part I-B*, Annex 2, p. 150.

[2] S. P. Jain, 'Birth Rates derived from Infants Enumerated', *Census of India Paper No. 6, 1954* (New Delhi: Government of India Press, 1954), p. 50.

[3] Ibid., p. 50.

CONCLUSION

The foregoing discussion reveals the difficulties in the calculation of infant mortality rate, particularly in under-developed countries like India where accurate and reliable vital statistics are not available. We do not have even the correct basic data like total number of births, total number of deaths of infants under 1 year of age and the exact age at which the infants are lost. Under the circumstances, it is difficult to calculate even the crude and conventional infant mortality rate, not to speak of any attempts at refining or standardizing it. The various methods of careful and minute refinement discussed in this chapter are, by and large, inapplicable in a country where even the mere total births and deaths are disputable. The inescapable conclusion is that steps should be taken as early as possible not only to ensure adequate vital registration but also to improve the quality of such vital statistics. Advanced and refined methods of demographic analysis may not be of great use when the basic data are inaccurate and unreliable.

Chapter III

INFANT MORTALITY IN INDIA
AND THE WORLD-FACTS

THE FACTS

A perusal of the evolution of infant mortality trends during the last seventy years of this century among certain selected countries and territories of the world reveals, on the one hand, the phenomenal progress made in certain countries in ensuring infant health and welfare,[1] and, on the other, India's and most of the developing countries' unenviable position. The choice of some thirty-five areas listed in Table 10 is based on both the availability of sufficient statistical services to yield official infant mortality rates and a certain degree of representativeness of the world's population. Indian figures are based on registration records and are incomplete. But these series do serve to show the trend even though the absolute rates should not be compared uncritically with rates from countries having more complete registration as in those of European descent. The most privileged position has been attained by Western and North-Western European countries and Australia and New Zealand. The present-day position (1965–67) of infant mortality rates in these advanced countries does not reveal any further development. They continue to maintain the advantageous position which they reached two or three decades ago. Though these most advanced countries appear to have approached the maximum possible success in cutting down their infant mortality, it is possible that these countries may yet register

[1] Dudley Stamp writes: 'We are more apt to forget our increasing control over disease – the number of diseases no longer fatal, the lowering of maternal and infant mortality and the consequent greater expectation of life. Queen Anne of England (1665–1714) happily married and enjoying the best medical skill of the day bore seventeen children, only one of whom survived infancy, and he died at the age of eleven! Such a record was by no means uncommon two centuries ago.' Dudley Stamp, *Land for Tomorrow* (Bloomington: Indiana University Press, 1952), p. 22.

100

Table 10

THE EVOLUTION OF REGISTERED INFANT MORTALITY RATES FROM THE BEGINNING OF THE CENTURY TO THE LATEST AVAILABLE YEARS IN SELECTED COUNTRIES

Countries	1901–1905	1911–1913	1921–1925	1931–1935	1946–1950	1951–1955	1956–1960	1961	1962	1963	1964	1965
Africa												
Egypt	—	—	—	208	175	168	121	108	134	119	—	—
Mauritius	—	—	142	151	120	81	68	62	60	59	57	64
Union of South Africa (European population only)	—	91	73	63	36	33	29	28	29	29	—	—
America												
Canada (excluding Yukon and N.W. Territory)	—	—	98	75 (1928–38)	44*	35	30	27	28	26	25	—
Chile	264	301	265	248	161	132	122	111	121	111	114	—
Mexico	—	—	—	132	—	89	76	70	70	69	65	—
U.S.A. (White)	—	—	71	54	30	24	24	25	25	25	25	25
Asia												
Ceylon	171	207	190	182	99	75	62	—	53	53	—	—
India†	215	206	182	173	131	114	95	83	80	76	74	65
Israel (prior to 1948 Palestine)	—	—	126	76	41	36	32	24	29	23	28	27
Japan	—	—	—	122	—	47	36	29	26	23	20	19
Taiwan	—	—	—	—	—	33	33	31	29	26	24	—

Europe												
Germany‡	199	164	122	74	71	48	36	32	29	27	25	24
Belgium	154	145	106	89	63	44	34	28	28	28	—	—
Denmark	119	98	82	71	38	27	23	22	20	19	19	—
Spain	172	—	149	118	77	59	49	46	41	41	38	17
Finland	131	112	96	72	52	32	25	21	21	18	17	22
France	139	—	—	78	62	44	32	26	26	25	23	25
Ireland	94	89	70	68	57	40	33	30	29	27	27	—
Iceland	101	72	53	51	24	21	16	20	17	17	18	36
Italy	167	141	127	105	77	58	47	41	42	40	36	35
Malta	—	—	270	277	108	70	39	32	35	34	34	—
Norway	80	65	52	45	31	23	20	18	18	17	17	14
Netherlands	136	105	70	45	31	22	17	17	17	16	15	—
U.K. (England and Wales)	138	111	76	62	36	27	23	22	22	21	20	19
Scotland	120	109	92	81	47	33	28	28	27	26	24	23
Sweden	91	71	60	50	24	19	17	16	15	15	14	12
Switzerland	134	104	65	48	36	43	23	21	21	21	19	—
Yugoslavia	—	—	—	153	117	119	93	82	84	78	76	72
Oceania												
Australia	97	71	57	41	27	23	21	20	20	20	19	19
New Zealand (excluding Maoris)	75	56	43	32	24	21	20	23	20	20	19	20
Maoris	—	—	—	98	76	69	53	—	—	—	—	—

Source: *Epidemiological and Vital Statistics Reports* (Geneva: World Health Organization, 1967).

* As from 1946 including Newfoundland.
† Up to 1932 Birth registration area.
‡ As from 1956 Federal Republic of Germany.

further advances reducing both reproductive and infantile wastage to the lowest possible point.

WORLD-WIDE GAINS IN INFANT MORTALITY REDUCTION

Africa and Latin America apart, the regions listed in Tables 11 and 12 reveal that the reduction in infant mortality during the last fifty years and more has been world-wide. Though these areas belong to different stages of technical and socio-economic development they have on the whole been able to reduce infant mortality by 50 to 70 per cent between 1900 and 1952. In 1900, out of every 1,000 children born alive, nearly 265 died before completing their first year in the least developed countries (among the 35 areas) and about 75 in the most favoured nations. By 1952, infant mortality had been reduced to 160 in the least developed countries and 25 in the most advanced countries.

In most cases, where the infant mortality rate had not yet touched the low level of 25, the rate was further reduced to about half by 1956–60. The process of decline in the rate continued in the subsequent years till the infant mortality rate touched the level of about 20 in the economically developed countries. The reduction in the last decade has been remarkable – the rate has been cut to half in less than 10 years in some countries. The decline was greater where the infant mortality rate was initially high.

The reduction has been greater in post-neonatal death rates with the result that unlike the situation in countries which still have a high infant mortality, post-neonatal mortality in countries with low infant mortality is much less than the neonatal mortality. In these countries, the rate of decline has slowed down in recent years. In the earlier periods, the annual decline was between 3·2 and 6·1 but from the early 1960s the range has been lowered to 1·0 to 2·6. This is due to the levelling off in the incidence of mortality caused by infectious diseases following improved environmental hygiene and antimicrobial therapy with much less change in the mortality caused by diseases of early infancy and congenital malformations. Quite possibly more pregnancies, which earlier were terminating in foetal deaths, are now resulting in live births as a result of the great progress in obstetrics. This would tend to keep up neonatal mortality.

In countries with good registration international comparison of infant mortality rates is affected, though to a small extent, by the difference in definitions and registration and statistical practices for

Table 11

REGISTERED INFANT MORTALITY RATES IN SELECTED COUNTRIES
FOR 1901–05, 1947–51, 1956–60 AND 1964

Countries	1901–05	1947–51	1956–60	1964
Australia	97	26	21	19
Austria	88†	79‡	43§	—
Belgium	154	61	34	—
Bulgaria	146†	124‡	64	—
Canada	98 (1921–25)	44 (1946–50)	30	25
Ceylon	171	90	62	—
Chile	264	159	122	114
Czechoslovakia	115†	94‡	32§	—
Denmark	119	34	23	19
Egypt	—	139	121	—
England and Wales	138	35	23	20
Finland	131	47	25	17
France	139	62	32	23
Germany (F.R.)	199	64 (Western)	36	25
Hungary	135†	104‡	60	—
Iceland	101	—	16	18
India	215	116 (1951)*	95*	74
Ireland	94	52	33	27
Israel (Jews)	62†	40	32	28
Italy	167	72	47	36
Japan	—	64	36	20
Malta	—	—	39	34
Malaya, Federation of	149†	95‡	77§	—
Mauritius	—	—	68	57
Mexico	132 (1931–35)	—	76	65
Netherlands	136	28	17	15
New Zealand	75	23	20	19
Northern Ireland	108	—	—	—
Portugal	144	101 (1947–50)	91	69
Scotland	120	—	28	24
Singapore	162†	86‡	42§	—
Spain	172	72	49	38
Sweden	91	22	17	14
Switzerland	134	34	23	19
Taiwan	145†	67‡	33	24
Union of South Africa (White)	56†	35‡	30§	—
U.S.A. (White)	71 (1921–25)	31	24	25
U.S.S.R.	184†	81‡	44§	—
Yugoslavia	—	125 (1952)	93	76

Source: *Population Bulletin* (New York: United Nations, No. 6, 1962).
    * Incomplete.   † For 1936–38.   ‡ For 1946–48.   § For 1956–58.

Table 12
REGISTERED INFANT MORTALITY RATES FOR SELECTED COUNTRIES FOR CERTAIN YEARS
BETWEEN 1900 AND 1965

Year	India	Ceylon	Japan	U.S.A.	England & Wales	Australia	New Zealand	Holland	Sweden
1900	232	178	151	—	154	104	71	153	94
1910	209	176	160	—	105	75	56	108	75
1920	195	182	168	—	80	66	48	50	65
1930	181	175	142	—	60	47	32	39	60
1940	160	149	124	—	57	38	30	39	39
1950	127	84	60	29	30	24	23	25	20
1960	86	—	31	26	22	20	23	18	17
1961	83	—	29	25	22	20	23	17	16
1962	80	53	26	25	22	20	20	17	15
1963	76	53	23	25	21	20	20	16	15
1964	74	—	20	25	20	19	19	15	14
1965	65	—	19	25	19	19	20	14	12

demarcating deaths occurring immediately before or after birth. In this connection, signs of life recognized in the definition of 'live birth' is of basic relevance. The League of Nations Health Committee in 1925 mentioned only 'breathing' as a criterion of live birth. It was only in 1950 that the Third World Health Assembly incorporated also beating of heart, pulsation of umbilical cord or movement of voluntary muscles as evidence of life in the definition of 'live birth', which is now internationally accepted. These additional signs of life classify certain products of conception as live births which under the old definition would have been taken as foetal deaths. (These live births would then enter in the denominator of infant death rate, and also as infant deaths in the absence of signs of breathing subsequently.) Because of the high level of mortality near the time of birth, these variations in criteria of signs of life have the greatest effect on the mortality rate within 24 hours of life.

Changes in the definition of live birth to conform to the international recommendation were not made by all countries simultaneously. For instance, Sweden did not recognize the additional signs till 1959. Denmark has not legally specified signs of life. Furthermore, the implementation of the law, even if made, depends on its understanding and interpretation by the informant, who may be the parents, other relations, the attending physician, or midwife. However, the effect of variations in this regard is relatively small. It was estimated from the British data for 1946–47 that if criterion of life is limited to breathing, infant deaths would be decreased by 1·5 per cent and still births would correspondingly increase by 3 per cent.

In a special study of Swedish data covering 1,800 stillbirths registered in 1956, it was found that 700 died at birth. Information on criterion of birth was available on 646 of them, among whom 83 per cent were born with no signs of life. The remaining 17 per cent breathed or showed some other sign of life and qualified for being considered as neonatal deaths according to the W.H.O. definition. It is estimated that this correction would decrease stillbirths by 7 per cent and increase deaths under 1 week by 10 per cent, neonatal deaths by 9 per cent and infant deaths by 7 per cent.

The effect of statistical practices on infant deaths may be illustrated by the example of the Netherlands, where as early as 1924 all live births were required to be registered but all those who were dead at the time of registration were counted both as live births and deaths. In 1950 this was changed. Live births of less than 28 weeks' gestation, who were dead by the time of registration, were excluded from tabulations of live births and deaths. In 1964, the earlier practice was again adopted. Data for 1962 showed the death rate for 'under 1 week' to be 9·6, for 'under 1 month' 11·1 and for 'under 1 year' 15·3, when live births with gestation under 28 weeks were excluded. When they were included, the rates were raised to 11·3, 12·8, and 17·0 respectively. The number of infant deaths in the latter case increased by 10·9 per cent, the number of neonatal deaths by 15·0 per cent and the number of deaths under 1 week by 17·4 per cent.

Every country was able to effect some significant improvement; even those countries which started the century with relatively low infant mortality rates were able to effect further and sizeable reductions, revealing how much further progress in this direction is possible in the under-developed countries. While the degree of success in ensuring child health and the rate of reduction in infant mortality is still very uneven among these countries, the available figures (Chart 1) demonstrate that the reduction has been uninterrupted in

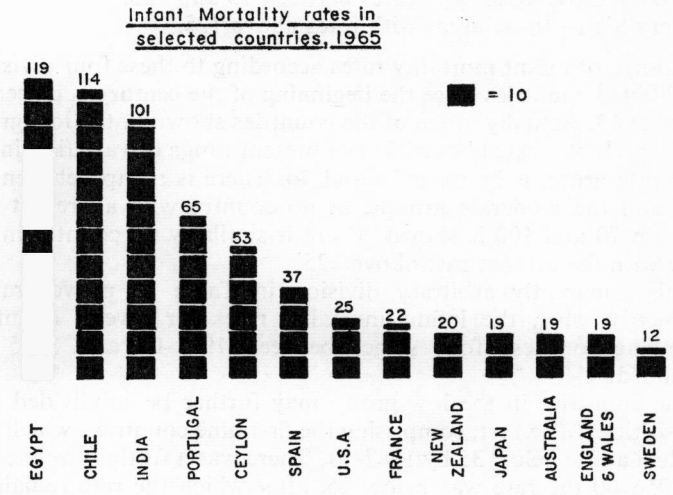

Chart 1

almost all the countries and there is practically no limit to the possible future reduction in infant deaths under certain conditions. The day is probably not far off when the great majority of infants born alive can complete their first and most dangerous year of life without any serious difficulty. Today the necessary knowledge in the social and medical spheres is available to achieve this end. But the major

107

difficulty seems to be in bringing this knowledge to every parent in the world, particularly the mothers, and in removing the cultural barriers in the path of the acceptance of the available knowledge.

INTERNATIONAL COMPARISON

For purposes of an international comparison of the present-day levels of mortality, different regions of the world which do report on infant mortality, irrespective of the range of under-registration and other errors involved (in 1951 these areas had a total population of 787 millions out of an estimated total world population of some 2,400 millions) can be divided into four major groups. They are:

1. Low – those areas with an infant mortality rate of 35 and below per 1,000 live legitimate births.
2. Moderate – those areas with rates between 35 and 75.
3. High – those areas with rates between 75 and 125.
4. Very high – those areas with rates above 125.

The range of infant mortality rates according to these four divisions for selected countries since the beginning of the century is presented in Table 13. Actually, none of the countries shown in the low group has at present a rate above 25. The present range of variation in the moderate group is between 35 and 70. There is a gap between the high and the moderate groups, as no country with a present rate between 70 and 100 is shown. There is similarly no country in the table with the present rate above 125.

This apparently arbitrary division in Table 13 proves rather instructive when the infant mortality rates for several countries belonging to these four stages between 1901–05 and 1965 are examined.

The countries in the low group may further be subdivided into two sections. The first, comprising the first nine countries, which had reached a rate below 35 by 1947–51. There was a further decline and by 1956–60 the rate was below 25, after which the rate remained, more or less, stationary. In this group England and Wales, Holland and Switzerland, which were once in the very high stage have advanced to the low stage involving considerable reduction in the rate of infant mortality in the last sixty years. Their present rate is 20 or even lower. The declines were greater where the rates were initially high, so that the earlier differences have been narrowed down. But such countries as the United States of America, Australia, New Zealand, Sweden and Norway, which began their demographic

Table 13
INFANT MORTALITY RATES IN SELECTED COUNTRIES FOR 1901–05, 1947–51, 1956–60, 1961, 1962, 1963, 1964 AND 1965

Present stage according to 1960–65 data	Infant mortality index	Country	Infant mortality rates							
			1901–1905	1947–1951	1956–1960	1961	1962	1963	1964	1965
Low	35 and below	Sweden	91	22	17	16	15	15	14	12
		Holland	136	28	17	17	17	16	15	14
		New Zealand	75	23	20	23	20	20	19	20
		England and Wales	138	35	23	22	22	21	20	19
		Norway	80	31	20	18	18	17	17	—
		Denmark	119	34	23	22	30	19	19	—
		Switzerland	134	34	23	21	21	21	19	—
		Australia	97	26	21	20	20	20	19	19
		U.S.A.	71	31	24	25	25	25	25	25
		Finland	131	47	25	21	21	18	17	17
		Belgium	154	61	34	28	28	28	—	—
		Scotland	120	—	28	28	27	26	24	23
		Canada	98	44	30	27	28	26	25	—
		Ireland	94	52	33	30	29	27	27	25
		France	139	62	32	26	26	25	23	22
		Germany (F.R.)	199	64	36	32	29	27	25	24
		Japan	—	64	36	29	26	23	20	19

Moderate	Between 35 and 75	Italy	167	72	47	41	42	40	36	36
		Spain	172	72	49	46	41	41	38	37
		Ceylon	171	90	62	—	53	53	—	—
		Portugal	144	101	91	—	—	73	69	65
		Mexico	132 (1931–35)	—	76	70	70	69	65	—
High	Above 75	India	215	130	†146* (1958–59)	106* (1961–62)	—	121*	115* (1964–65)	101* (1965–66)
		Chile	264	159	122	111	121	111	114	—
		Egypt	—	139	121	108	134	119	—	—

* Based on N.S.S. results.
† Rural.

histories sixty years ago with relatively low rates, have not registered comparable rates of progress, for possibly the factors that contribute directly to a reduction in infant mortality were brought under control some decades ago. The remaining 8 countries comprising the second section had a rate between 35 and 65 during 1947–51 but there was further improvement in subsequent years so that their rate by 1956–60 was between 25 and 36. The decline continued in the later years and by 1965 their rate was between 17 and 25. This group consisting of Finland, Belgium, Scotland, Canada, France, Germany, Italy and Spain, which began this century with high rates of infant mortality have shown no spectacular decline comparable to those countries which are today in the low stage despite their more or less identical European economies and cultural backgrounds.

The moderate group showed a comparatively smaller decline by 1947–51, when the rate was above 70. Again, comparatively smaller gains were achieved in subsequent years so that by 1956–60 the rate was between 50 and 75. The decline continued but the present rate lies in the moderate range. In the high group, the pace of decline in the rate has been much slower and the present rate is 100 or more.

The table also reveals India's unenviable position among the major countries in the world and even among the Asian countries. A precise assessment of the situation in India is made difficult due to the non-availability of reliable data. The first two rates of 215 and 130 for 1901–05 and 1947–51 are based on the registration data, which are undoubtedly incomplete. The deficiencies of registration increased in the later years and hence it is that instead of registration figures, those yielded by the National Sample Survey are given. These figures themselves cannot be held to be satisfactory. They can at best be taken to show the level of the rate at different times rather than its precise value. The conclusion, however, is irrefutable that India even today has, like Chile and Egypt, an infant mortality rate not less than 5 to 6 times that obtaining in the advanced western countries. It is a pity that information about the level of infant mortality in the different Asian countries is lacking but it is almost certain that it is high in all of them except Ceylon, Japan, Israel and Taiwan, where the rate is less than half of that of India.

The only Asian country found in the low stage today is Japan. Though reliable figures of her position in the first few years of this century are not available, they must have been high and therefore Japan's progress in this direction has been commendable. The other Asian country which is making rapid progress in lowering her infant mortality rate is Ceylon.

It is also noteworthy that the countries with the lowest infant mortality rates are the advanced and industrialized Western European ones and those with European patterns and levels of living such as Australia, Canada, New Zealand and the United States of America This distinction is not so much racial or biological as cultural and economic. The reasons for the decline in infant mortality in these areas will be discussed in some detail later, but it is obvious that these are the countries which have more or less low or stabilized birth rates and where babies cannot be had at bargain prices. This is true despite periodical spurts in the birth rates, as fashions in family-size change.

It is true that the infant death rate of 25 per thousand in the United States of America is slightly higher than the rates in several European countries and Oceania. Some of the difference may be explained by the variations in definitions and registration and statistical practices for demarcating deaths occurring immediately before or after birth, as explained earlier. However, the post-neo-natal mortality of 7 per 1,000 live births in 1962 in the United States is about twice the rate in Sweden and the Netherlands. Further, the perinatal mortality rate, which covers foetal deaths and deaths of live born during the first week of life after having completed 28 weeks of pregnancy and is thus not affected by the kind of definitional and other differences referred to above, was 27·6 per 1,000 live births in 1959 as against 20·9 in Czechoslovakia. The U.S. rate was higher than those recorded in seven countries showing that the U.S. does not have the most favourable experience. Moriyama has summarized the problem of low infant mortality countries very aptly, when he says that: 'No substantial progress in reducing infant mortality will be made until there is a break-through in dealing with congenital malformations and the diseases of early infancy, such as birth injuries, postnatal asphyxia and premature delivery of infants.'[1]

The knowledge and the technical means available which make substantial reductions in infant mortality possible in a short period of time have an obvious implication for developing countries.

The successful and widespread practice of contraception has led to smaller families with the consequence that a greater premium is put on the life of a baby. Smaller families on the average have a greater birth interval. In the Harvard–Khanna study (1956–59), it was found that the infant mortality rate was 135 when the average interval between the last two births was 24–48 months, but that it was 203 for

[1] I. M. Moriyama 'Infant Mortality in Countries of Low Mortality'. Paper submitted to World Population Conference, Belgrade, Yugoslavia, 1965.

the average birth interval of 0–24 months. The infant mortality rate was 175 in primipara cases.[1]

It is true that when more infants are born, more infants will die (Holland with a high birth rate and a low infant mortality rate is a notable exception) and by the same token more infants are likely to survive.

More infant deaths may be partly due to the fact that in overly large families resources are insufficient to take care of so many children. Families that have a large number of children and families that have high mortality have similar characteristics with respect to socio-economic status, lack of education, etc.

The converse is also true. The higher the infant mortality in a community, the higher the birth rate. It has been established that the average birth interval following an infant death is shorter compared to cases where the infant survives to childhood, particularly in communities where breastfeeding is common. This means a higher birth rate. This is due to a shorter amenorrhoea period following infant death when lactation is prematurely stopped.

John Knodel and Etienne van de Walle[2] in their analysis of German data for the late nineteenth and early twentieth centuries, bring out the interrelationship between breastfeeding, fertility and infant mortality.

Henry and Gautier[3] analysed a series of birth intervals recorded in the parish registers of Crulai in Normandy, recording marriages performed during 1674 to 1742. There was little evidence of fertility control practices in the community, which was rural. In the circumstances prevailing at that time it can be presumed that prolonged breastfeeding was the rule. The average birth interval in this community in cases where the child died in infancy was 20·7 months against 29·6 months in other cases. They attributed this to the effect of lactation on the amenorrhoea period. They also considered it possible that an early pregnancy caused interruption of breast-feeding, which in turn may have resulted in the death of the prematurely weaned child. Thus, mothers whose infants died young had

[1] John B. Wyon and John E. Gordon 'A Long-term Prospective-type Field Study of Population Dynamics in the Punjab, India', in Clyde V. Kiser, *Research in Family Planning* (Princeton University Press, 1962), pp. 24–30.

[2] John Knodel and Etienne van de Walle, 'Breast-feeding, Fertility and Infant Mortality: An Analysis of Some Early German Data', *Population Studies, Vol. XXI*, 2, September 1967, pp. 109–31.

[3] Louis G. A. Henry and E. Gautier, *La population de crulai, paroisse Normande* (Paris, 1958). See also Louis G. A. Henry, A. Girard and R. Nistri, *Facteurs sociaux et culturels de la mortalité infantile* (Paris, 1960).

113

a shorter birth interval. They were, however, able to show that the death of the child antedated the presumed conception time in an overwhelming majority of cases.

The following figures are given by T. E. Smith[1] for the Malay population of Cocos–Keeling Islands, where conditions regarding breast-feeding and contraception appear to be somewhat similar.

	Average birth interval (in years)
In case of stillbirth	1·43
Child died before 0·1 years	1·70
Child died between 0·1–0·2 years	1·57
Child died between 0·2–0·3 years	1·77
Child died between 0·3–0·4 years	1·78
Child died between 1·0–2·0 years	2·28
Child survives past 2·0 years	2·45

Knodel has given the results of two studies conducted to verify whether rates of infant mortality were associated with the absence of breastfeeding or early weaning. He found a strong negative correlation between breastfeeding index and infant mortality calculated from the data relating to the three German states. The analysis does not confirm an association between breastfeeding and fertility. Marital fertility appears to be more closely associated with infant mortality than with breastfeeding[2]. It is also clear that the low rates are related to the higher economic levels that these communities have attained. This relation becomes apparent when under-privileged economic groups in the same population or different ethnic groups in the same country register different rates of infant mortality. This is revealed when *per capita* national income figures and infant mortality rates of various countries and groups within countries are compared. Economic privilege is no doubt a significant factor in effecting a sizeable decline in infant mortality among different human groups when other factors remain more or less the same.

Perhaps more important than even the economic factor is the cultural, involving a scale of values in life which places a considerable premium on quality and not on quantity. The magnificent accomplishment of the Scandinavian countries, for instance, in cutting down their infant mortality rates to the present low levels reveals 'the wisdom of transferring part of the vital energy that women

[1] T. E. Smith, 'The Cocos–Keeling Islands: A Demographic Laboratory', *Population Studies* (November 1968). See also his *Population Growth in Malaya* (London: Royal Institute of International Affairs, 1952), pp. 54–55.

[2] John Knodel, Ibid.

formerly exhausted (and continue to exhaust in many parts of the world) in the biological process of bearing children to the proper care and feeding of the smaller number of babies which the average woman now brings into the world. Of course, there would be no room for optimism on this point if the advocates of natural selection could point to vigorous races and physical specimens produced in the parts of the world such as India, China or Egypt where infant mortality and other selective forces have held almost unbridled sway.'[1]

The advanced countries have reached a low point in infant mortality, and now the pace of further progress has slackened. Indication given by developing countries, which have a usually reliable statistical time series, is that rapid gains are being made by them. Thus there is a tendency towards equalization of infant mortality. It is difficult to know what is happening in developing countries with no or indifferent statistical records.

A study of infant mortality *vis-à-vis* total general mortality in the developed countries shows that the declines in the two are not closely associated. This indicates that the rapid decline in infant mortality in the recent decades is not wholly due to public health measures and medical facilities, which are mainly responsible for the decline in general mortality. Certain other important factors such as parity of birth, maternal age, social status of the family, ante- and post-natal care, etc. also influence infant mortality.

INFANT MORTALITY RATE AS A SENSITIVE INDEX OF SOCIO-ECONOMIC CONDITIONS

In the past, a decline in infant mortality usually accompanied economic improvement and this was so marked that the infant mortality rate has been looked upon as the most sensitive index of level of living and sanitary conditions. Sir Arthur Newsholme wrote at the beginning of the century that: 'No fact is better established than that the death rate, and especially the death rate among children, is high in inverse proportion to the social status of the population.'[2]

Further declines achieved by most of the Western countries seem to show that in a modern urban-industrial society a point may be reached when the significance of infant mortality as an index of socio-economic status is greatly minimized. In such a society, a majority of infant deaths occur during the first month of life. They

[1] Lynn Smith, *Population Analysis* (New York: McGraw Hill, 1948), p. 265.
[2] Arthur Newsholme, *Thirty-ninth Annual Report of the Local Government Board, Report Cmd. 5312* (London: Darling & Sons Ltd., 1910), p. 28.

115

are due to biological factors associated with processes of gestation and birth rather than socio-economic factors. The remaining infant deaths that occur between one month and one year of life are due to environmental factors and continue to be inversely related to socio-economic status. Successful public health measures and improved effectiveness of medical techniques go further to reduce post-neo-natal deaths, which fact greatly weakens the inverse relationship between the infant mortality rate and socio-economic status.

Infant mortality has been greatly reduced in the United States of America. The rate declined gradually from 100 per 1,000 live births in 1915 to 26 in 1956, and subsequently to 21·6 in 1968, the latest year for which figures are available. Between 1900 and 1957 the total death rate dropped by 55 per cent whereas the infant mortality rate declined during this period by 82 per cent. In the matter of saving infant lives the gains were much greater. Woodbury[1] in his study of infant mortality in the U.S. during the first quarter of the twentieth century recognized several variables such as race, physical condition of mother, age of mother, type of feeding, and length of interval between pregnancies affecting infant mortality, but found them to be highly correlated with the earnings of the father. He concluded that infant mortality rates were 'highest when the father's earnings were low and lowest when the father's earnings were relatively high'. In regard to the interrelationship between infant mortality, father's income and other causative factors he concluded:

'The analysis indicated that low earnings of the father exerted a potent influence over the prevalence of these factors and there-fore must be regarded as primarily responsible for greater mor-tality associated with them. The presence of intermediate factors in the chain of causation does not lessen the responsibility of low earnings as a primary cause.'

Since then the course of reduction in infant mortality in the dif-ferent socio-economic groups and areas within the urban population does not uniformly conform to the differences in socio-economic status. This raises the question whether infant mortality continues to be such a sensitive index of socio-economic status within such countries as the United States where mortality of infants has been fairly well controlled. Several workers have studied this problem with

[1] Robert M. Woodbury, *Causal Factors in Infant Mortality* (United States Department of Labour: Children's Bureau Publication No. 142), (Washington, D.C.: U.S. Government Printing Office, 1925), p. 8.

116

reference to selected local areas. For instance, Stockwell's[1] revealing study of infant mortality in Providence, Rhode Island, U.S.A., for the period 1949–51 is of relevance here both for its methodological contribution and the light it throws on the relation between infant mortality and socio-economic status.

Infant mortality rates were calculated for the different census tracts by the ratio of the average number of annual deaths during 1949–51 to the number of live births in 1950. To study the association between infant mortality and socio-economic status, two different methods of analysis were adopted – the first based on social area approach and the second on correlation approach. In the first approach, the arithmetic mean of the percentile scores for occupation, education and income for each census tract was taken as a composite socio-economic index for the tract. The census tracts were grouped into five social rank areas on the basis of the value of this index, so that each area covered approximately 20 per cent of the tracts. The various mortality rates for these areas were found to be as shown in Table 14.

Table 14

INFANT MORTALITY RATE AND ITS COMPONENTS BY SOCIAL RANK

Social rank area	Infant mortality rate	Neonatal mortality rate	Post-neonatal mortality rate	*Mortality due to* *Birth injuries &* *immaturity* *rate*	*Congenital malformation rate*
I (high)	31·5	27·2	4·3	18·0	6·6
II	30·3	26·7	3·7	24·6	3·7
III	24·0	18·2	5·9	15·5	3·3
IV	29·5	22·9	6·6	18·4	4·9
V (low)	25·9	19·9	6·0	18·2	2·6
All areas	28·2	22·8	5·4	18·9	4·2

There is no discernible pattern of association between socio-economic status and infant mortality. The neonatal mortality, i.e. deaths within the first month of life, approximates to a direct association but the post-neonatal death rates based on deaths of infants aged 1 to 11 completed months of life tend to increase as socio-economic status decreases. The effect is brought out more sharply

[1] E. G. Stockwell 'Infant Mortality and Socio-Economic Status: A Changing Relationship', *Milbank Memorial Fund Quarterly*, January, 1962, p. 101.

117

when the combined post-neonatal death rate for areas III–V which comes to 6·2 per 1,000 live births is compared with the combined rate of 4 per 1,000 live births for areas I–II. This clearly brings out the reduction effect, which is very likely due to the progress made by public health and medicine in controlling infections causing death. Table 14 shows that 65 per cent of infant deaths were due to birth injuries and immaturity and that the percentage is increased to 80 if congenital malformations are also included. Among the remaining, 6 per cent were due to infectious causes like enteritis, tuberculosis, pneumonia of the new-born and 14 per cent were distributed among a variety of causes, e.g. leukaemia, rheumatic heart disease, accidents, etc. The infectious causes have been largely controlled and hence the absence of any clear-cut association between socio-economic status and infant mortality. Birth injuries, immaturity and congenital malformations accounted for 75 per cent of all neonatal deaths, but only 38 per cent of post-neonatal deaths. This indicates the less significant role played by causes related to gestation and birth and the greater role of environmental factors in determining post-neonatal mortality. In this post-neonatal section, 40 per cent of the deaths were due to infectious causes such as acute bronchitis, pneumonia and diarrhoea of the new-born and 18 per cent due to accidental causes such as suffocating and poisoning. These causes are preventable. Success in prevention varies directly with the socio-economic rank of families; hence the level of post-neonatal mortality varies inversely with the socio-economic rank of the area.

In the second approach, rank correlation coefficient (Kendall's tau) between mortality rates and five indices of socio-economic status of 36 census tracts were calculated. The five indices were occupation, education, income, and two measures of housing characteristics, namely rent and crowding. They were defined as follows:

(1) Occupation: the number of craftsmen, operatives and labourers per 1,000 employed persons.
(2) Education: the number of persons per 1,000 aged 25 or over having less than 8 years of schooling.
(3) Income: census tract median income of families and unrelated individuals.
(4) Rent: the monthly contract rent of dwelling units.
(5) Crowding: the number of dwelling units containing 1·01 or more persons per room per 1,000 dwelling units.

The correlation coefficients that were obtained are given in Table 15.

All these socio-economic indices show a pronounced inverse as-

Table 15

RANK CORRELATION COEFFICIENT BETWEEN
INDICES OF SOCIO-ECONOMIC STATUS

	Total mortality	Infant mortality
Occupation	−0·25	+0·11*
Education	−0·39	+0·03*
Income	−0·45	−0·23
Rent	−0·29	+0·10*
Overcrowding	−0·36	−0·17*

* Not significant at 5 per cent.

sociation with total mortality of all ages but occupation, education and rent show a positive (though not statistically significant) association with infant mortality. Income and overcrowding show an inverse association but only income has a statistically significant value. The contrast in the associations shows that infant mortality differs distinctly from total mortality in its response to socio-economic differentials. The erratic variation of infant mortality with socio-economic status seems to be primarily due to the fact that a majority of infant deaths occur in the first few hours or days of life, and these are due to biological causes rather than socio-economic factors. A majority of post-neonatal deaths are due to causes other than physiological processes of gestation and births, and in this section, infant mortality continues to be associated inversely with socio-economic status. Recent studies emphasize the need to study separately the rate for neonatal and post-neonatal mortality, as the determinants of mortality in the two periods are different. It is obvious that in countries where post-neonatal deaths form a majority of infant deaths as is the case in most of the developing countries, infant mortality continues to be a sensitive index of socio-economic status.

We shall now examine the situation in some of the developing countries.

INFANT MORTALITY IN AFRICA

The lack of appropriate data for the native peoples of Africa with the exception of the Egyptians and the Europeans of South Africa constitute a serious omission. The infant mortality rates for most of the African peoples are not available for any long-time series to establish even rough trends. And such evidence as is available for small samples of population, the results of certain *ad hoc* studies in limited

119

areas, reveal abnormally high rates – the mortality under one year ranging between one-half and one-third of all live births. (Apart from economic, social and cultural implications of such high infant mortality, the most serious is its effect on the mothers.)

'Infant mortality data are only available in a very limited number of territories, only for small limited areas', writes an African student of the problem. 'When it is further kept in mind that both registration areas for death and infant mortality are likely to change from year to year and that the population for the calculation of the death rate and the registration of births for the calculation of infant mortality rates are of poor quality, it will readily be understood that the study of mortality trends in African territories presents a very difficult problem indeed.'[1]

Despite these obvious limitations certain observations and limited studies give a rough range of infant mortality rates for some of the African territories. At the First International Conference on the African Child (1931) figures for infant mortality were given ranging from 100 to 500 and even up to 820.[2] According to Jeliffe: 'It is my guess that, as noted by Blackhock (*Ann. Trop. Med. Parasit.*, 31, 3, 1956) the infant mortality rate is generally in the region of from 300 to 500 in most of Africa'.[3]

Only six small African territories have statistics of death registration covering the whole population. The available information on the infant mortality rate is given in Table 16.

It should be understood that the above data cannot give any idea of the level of mortality and its geographical and temporal variation in Africa in view of the great diversity of climate, culture, technology and level of economic development and other factors governing health in different parts of the continent.

Amongst smaller sample studies may be mentioned Lestrange, who found that 22·4 per cent of Coniagui children died in the first year of life while among the Bassari 44·4 per cent of the children died in French Guinea presumably out of 100 live births.[4] Harding found that a community in Sierra Leone (population 1,406) registered a

---

[1] Arne Barkhuus, 'Non-European Mortality and Infant Mortality in the Non-self-governing Territories in Africa South of the Sahara'. Paper presented at the U.N. World Conference on Population, Rome, 1954.

[2] E. Sharp, *The African Child: An Account of the International Conference on African Children* (Geneva: Weardale Press, 1931).

[3] D. B. Jeliffe, 'The African Child', *Transactions of the Royal Society of Tropical Medicine and Hygiene*, London, January 1952, p. 30.

[4] Monigue de Lestrange, 'La population de la region de Youkounkoun en Guinée Française', *Population Studies*, Vol. 5, No. 4, 1950, pp. 643–68.

Table 16
REGISTERED INFANT MORTALITY RATES FOR SELECTED
AREAS IN AFRICA, 1946–58

Country	Infant mortality rate				
	1946–50	1951–55	1956	1957	1958
Gambia:					
Bathurst	112	104	112	72	79
Ghana*	119	117	98	88	90
Mauritius except					
dependencies†	123	81	66	75	67
Rodriguez	128	99	90	122	87
Morocco:					
Centa†	84	77	62	52	58
Melilla†	73	45	46	35	35

Source: *Population Bulletin* (New York: United Nations, No. 6, 1962.)

  * Data are tabulated by year of registration and not occurrence and are limited to compulsory registration areas of 36 towns and townships, which comprise about 12 per cent of the total population.

  † Data are tabulated by year of registration and not occurrence. In the case of Centa and Melilla, deaths of infants occurring within 24 hours after birth are not included.

birth rate of 32·9 and a death rate of 32·9 with an infant mortality rate of 417.[1]

The latest infant mortality rates for certain African countries obtained from some demographic household sample surveys, in which information was collected retrospectively are presented in Table 17.

The accuracy of the data is doubtful. The wide differences are in fact due to various types of errors.

Nhonoli gives some relatively reliable figures for a Christian group of the Nyamwezi tribe in Tanganyika for the decade 1941–50. This tribal group with a population of about a million registered infant mortality rates ranging from as low as 145 to as high as 462.[2]

Thus political observers, travellers, historians and more recently medical and social scientists have borne testimony to the effect that the infant mortality rates for African peoples range between 150 to 450 per 1,000 live births during the last fifty years. The Registrar of

[1] R. D. Harding, 'A Note on Some Vital Statistics of a Primitive Peasant Community in Sierra Leone', *Population Studies*, Vol. 2, No. 3, 1948, pp. 373–7.

[2] A. M. M. Nhonoli, 'An Enquiry into the Infant Mortality Rate in Rural Areas of Unyamwezi', *East African Medical Journal*, Vol. 131, No. 1, 1954, pp. 1–12.

Table 17

INFANT MORTALITY RATES IN SELECTED AREAS IN
AFRICA OBTAINED FROM SAMPLE SURVEYS SINCE 1948

Area	Year	Infant mortality rate
Central African Republic (Ubangi-Chari):		
Bush	1959	188
Centres	1959	197
Congo (Leopoldville)	1953	148
Guinea:		
Bush	1955	218
Centres	1955	189
Ivory Coast:		
Bougouanou (Bush)	1955	157
1st Agricultural Sector	1958	138
2nd Agricultural Sector	1958	144
Mali:		
Bush	1957	320
Centres	1957	246
Senegal (Basse Vallee)		
Bush	1957	172
Centres	1957	152
Sudan:		
Zande East	1955–56	165
Zande West	1955–56	62
Fort Sudan Town	1955–56	131
Tokar	1955–56	108
Khartoum	1955–56	70
Ed Damer	1955–56	111
Rhodesia and Nyasaland, Federation of:		
Northern Rhodesia	1950	259
Southern Rhodesia	1948	123
	1953	120
Ruanda-Urundi	1952	129

Source: *Population Bulletin* of the United Nations, No. 6, 1962.

Births and Deaths for the Gold Coast (the present Ghana) writes for the year 1927:

'The explanation is not hard to seek, namely, that whereas there has been a considerable improvement in sanitary conditions in the past ten years or more, the weak spot in the armour, the ante- and neonatal condition of the mother and infant still remains to be strengthened and this should include the health of the expectant mother, the conduct of the delivery and puerperium and the neonatal care of the infant.'[1]

Nhonoli, referred to above, points out:

'Until very recently there prevailed the most unhygienic practices at childbirth and neither the mother nor the attendant old woman knew even the rudiments of asepsis. The umbilical cord would be tied with any piece of cord or string picked up at the moment and the distal portion be sliced off with any old knife that came handy.... I have used the past tense throughout here, but the occasions when a more hygienic procedure is followed are still unfortunately few compared with what has just been described. No wonder that tetanus is common and that most, if not all, premature babies fail to survive.'[2]

Table 18
INFANT MORTALITY RATES IN PARTS OF GAMBIA, 1953

Village	Rate per 1,000 live births
1. Depressed village (Kerewan)	525
2. Group of villages (trained nurses available)	207
3. Primitive village (Keneba)	462
Same village after the introduction of anti-malarial measures but with acute food shortage	351
4. Another village with adequate food supplies	166

Professor Platt in an inquiry into the relation between food intake and infant mortality in West Africa obtained some very high rates of infant mortality. He points out:

'Babies born to poorly fed mothers are generally underweight and they often die in infancy or childhood. Infant mortality data for poorly fed communities are unreliable; there is nevertheless evidence that in tropical countries rates are from ten to a hundredfold higher than in this country (United Kingdom). I have recently assembled some figures [Table 18] obtained for several villages in the Gambia (West Africa).'[3]

[1] Gold Coast, *Report on Births and Deaths* (1927), p. 6.
[2] A. M. M. Nhonoli, op. cit., p. 10.
[3] B. S. Platt, 'Food and Production', in A. Leslie Banks (Ed.), *The Development of Tropical and Sub-Tropical Countries with particular reference to Africa* (London: Arnold, 1954), p. 107.

However, it is interesting to note that the infant mortality rates in European enclaves in Africa approximate to those of the mother countries. Minorities of Asian and mixed stock in South Africa and most of eastern Africa hold a special position in the social hierarchy. Their standard of living is inferior to that of Europeans but markedly superior to that of the indigenous population. The available information from various sources on infant mortality rates for these different minorities are given in Table 19.

Table 19
REGISTERED INFANT MORTALITY RATES FOR EUROPEAN AND OTHER MINORITIES IN VARIOUS AREAS IN AFRICA, 1946–50 TO 1958–60

Country	*Infant mortality rate*				
	1946–50	*1951–55*	*1956*	*1957*	*1958–60*
Algeria:					
European population	78	53	45	40	43
Bechuanaland:					
Non-indigenous population	34	49	—	—	—
Congo (Leopoldville):					
White population	69	44	43	—	—
Morocco:					
Southern Zone, non-Moroccan population	64	47	47	—	—
Mozambique:					
Non-native population	58	39	31	35	—
Rhodesia & Nyasaland:					
Federation, European population	—	22	22	21	21
Northern Rhodesia:					
European population	33	28	23	19	21
Nyasaland:					
European population	33	28	23	19	21
Southern Rhodesia:					
European population	33	24	22	20	22
South-West Africa:					
White population	38	32	32	30	—
Tunisia:					
European population	74	49	47	38	—
Union of South Africa:					
Asiatic population	74	63	67	68	68
White population	36	32	31	29	29
Coloured (Native and White mixture) population	133	130	138	127	132

INFANT MORTALITY IN LATIN AMERICA

As far as reliable vital statistics are concerned, the position of many countries in Latin America is no better than in other developing countries. For many of these South American republics, infant mortality rates are available only for their capital cities and these only for recent years. If what is true of the capital cities is taken to be representative of the country as a whole, the infant mortality rates for many nations is unenviably high. It is probable that infant mortality rates for the total population with poor health facilities are bound to be higher compared to capital cities with a certain amount of public health facilities.

This region is not so much under-developed as unevenly developed. In some of the states, like Argentina and Uruguay, mortality has for a considerable time been at the same level as that of European countries. In others, like Costa Rica and Puerto Rico, there have been sharp declines recently and mortality levels now compare favourably with those of developed countries. But in others like Bolivia, Guatemala and Haiti mortality is considerably higher, according to the available evidence. On the whole, Latin America enjoys a middle position with considerably higher mortality rates than the advanced countries and distinctly lower rates than African or Asian countries.

There are even sharper variations in infant mortality rates between cities and rural areas and between areas surrounding cities. The health services and other amenities available to the more fortunate section of population in many of the principal cities are of a high order, but most of the elementary necessities are denied to a large section, particularly the migrants from rural areas who flock to these cities. From 10 to 30 per cent of the housing units lack piped water supply, electricity and sewage disposal. Even in the neighbouring rural areas, the living conditions are almost untouched by modern facilities. These conditions lead to marked differentials in the incidence of mortality particularly among infants. Health conditions in the countryside, as a whole, are improving as a result of the welfare activities of the various national governments in collaboration with international agencies, and as a result infant mortality rates are declining along with the reduction in general death rates.

Table 20 shows the infant mortality rates for certain representative Latin American countries for which data are available. Registration of births and deaths is defective and in these conditions registration

125

Table 20

REGISTERED INFANT MORTALITY RATES FOR SELECTED
LATIN AMERICAN COUNTRIES, 1935–39 AND 1955–58

| Country | Infant Mortality rate per 1000 live births | | |
	1935–39	1955–58	Percentage change
Costa Rica	142·7	85·5	−40·1
El Salvador*	125·4	80·7	−35·6
Guatemala†	103·8	98·6	−5·0
Mexico	127·6	78·8	−38·2
Barbados‡	209·9	100·3	−52·2
Jamaica	127·3	58·7	−53·9
Puerto Rico	122·9	53·8	−56·2
Trinidad and Tobago	103·7	62·8	−39·4
Argentina	98·8§	61·8	−37·4
Chile	240·8¶	121·6‖	−49·5
Uruguay	94·1	77·06**	−17·5
Venezuela	135·3	67·5	−50·1

Source: *Population Bulletin* (New York: United Nations, No. 6, 1962)

* Prior to 1955 rates are by year of registration rather than by year of occurrence.

† Prior to 1939, rates exclude deaths of infants occurring before registration of birth.

‡ Rates are by year of registration rather than by year of occurrence.

§ Registration incomplete outside Federal Capital and principal cities. 1938–39 excluding province of Santa Fe.

¶ Rates computed on live births registered within two years of occurrence.

‖ Rates computed on live births which have been adjusted for under-registration.

** 1955–56.

of infant deaths is likely to be more incomplete than in the case of total deaths. Some of the inter-country differences in the infant mortality rates shown above may be due to differential incompleteness of registration.

Latin America has yet to make effective gains in reducing her infant mortality rates. These countries, not unlike Asian countries, have yet to effectively organize and modernize their preventive and public health services and educate their women in mothercraft. Thus Latin America occupies a position between African territories on the one hand and European and North American countries on the other.

The most privileged position has been attained by Western and

North-western European countries and Australia and New Zealand. The present-day position (1970) of infant mortality rates in these advanced countries does not reveal any further significant development. They continue to maintain their advantageous position which they reached two or three decades ago. Though these most advanced countries appear to have reached the maximum possible success in cutting down their infant mortality, it is possible that they may yet register further advances reducing both reproductive and infantile wastage to the lowest possible point if *all* the people in these countries come to enjoy maximum welfare benefits that now a majority enjoy.

INFANT MORTALITY IN ASIA EXCLUDING U.S.S.R. AND INDIA

Considering the chronic insufficiency of housing, water supply, sewage disposal facilities and health services in most of the Asian countries, it is not surprising that the levels of mortality in Asian countries are relatively high. However, since the Second World War, as in Latin America, health, medical services and consequently mortality conditions have greatly improved. Mainland China, India, Indonesia, Japan and Pakistan together account for about 83 per cent of the population of Asia excluding the U.S.S.R. and

Table 21

REGISTERED INFANT MORTALITY RATES FOR SELECTED ASIAN COUNTRIES, 1935–39 AND 1955–58

| Country | Infant Mortality Rates Per 1,000 Live Births | | |
	1935–39	1955–58	Percentage
Aden Colony	—	147·0	—
Brunei	—	107·7	—
Ceylon	182·8	68·5	−62·5
		(1955–57)	
Taiwan	144·5	34·4	−76·2
Cyprus	122·7	31·0	−74·7
Federation of Malaya	149·6	77·2	−48·4
Hong Kong		59·3	—
Israel	60·6	37·8	−37·6
Japan	110·4	38·8	−64·8
Singapore	155·1	44·2	−71·5

Source: *Population Bulletin* (New York: United Nations, No. 6, 1962.)

127

Table 22

REGISTERED INFANT MORTALITY RATES IN INDIA, 1900–65
AND QUINQUENNIAL AVERAGES FOR REGISTRATION AREA
IN INDIA*

Year	Rate	Average during the preceding quinquennium	Year	Rate	Average during the preceding quinquennium
1900	232		1961	83	
1905	226	215	1962	80	
1910	209	218	1963	76	
1915	202	204	1964	74	
1920	195	219	1965	65	76
1925	174	182			
1930	181	178			
1935	164	174			
1940	160	161			
1945	151	161†			
1950	127	132‡			
1951	130				
1952	123				
1953	125				
1954	114				
1955	103	119			
1956	109				
1957	107				
1958	101				
1959	90				
1960	86	99			

* Registration throughout is officially stated to be incomplete. This is also true of the present States of the Indian Union. Comparability of these annual rates is adversely affected by different degrees of reliability. Second, there is the question of the validity of comparing the three parts of the time series – the period before 1921 relating to a scattered and growing area, the period 1921–46 relating to the former provinces of British India, and the period since 1947 relating to the registration area of the Indian Republic, that is, British provinces minus Pakistan and plus native states.

† Until 1946 the registration area comprised the British provinces in undivided India excluding the native states.

‡ For 1948 and subsequent years the figures are taken for the Indian Union as reconstituted after partition into India and Pakistan.

hence they determine the mortality trends in Asia. Except Japan, none of these countries has reliable mortality statistics and thus no

Table 23
REGISTERED INFANT MORTALITY RATES FOR CERTAIN INDIAN STATES, 1925–65

Year	Andhra Pradesh	Assam	Bihar	Madhya Pradesh	Madras	Maharashtra	Mysore	Orissa	Punjab	Uttar Pradesh	West Bengal
1925		174	138	204	181	162	128		188	176	179
1930		174	138	242	186	187	117		186	171	187
1935		163	129	224	179	164	144		155	157	159
1940		142	118	226	169	170	146	183	178	135	159
1945		131	100	257	169	161	101	178	145	123	143
1950*		101	80	196	130	127	93	158	100	104	126†
1951		90	89	194	119	117	87	189	123	129	110
1952		83	69	169	108	116	73	159	127	129	100
1953	129		71	169	114	118	79	153	132	122	94
1954	123	76	78	150	101	116	83	133	112	110	87
1955	123	85	62		103	100	73	127	106	99	79
1956	124	70	73	146	117	93	62	139	119	105	78
1957	93	91	62	139	111	106	61	175	100	97	86
1958	86	77	74	147	103	113	71	155	108	103	80
1959	83	89	73	99	91	97	70	120	96	85	70
1960	80	86	80	93	92	91‡	62	135	96	92	77
1961	75	86	87	95	89	90	62	124	92	90	64
1962	73	59	78	108	83	95	62	114	85	87	62
1963	73	40	76	101	81	93	55	103	79	84	64
1964	64	55	79	79	72	91	63	100	83	86	61
1965	65	51			66	80			71		56

* From 1950 and onwards figures relate to states as reconstituted from time to time.
† Prior to 1950 figures relate to West Bengal.
‡ Prior to 1960 figures relate to Bombay State.

E

reliable information on Asian mortality conditions. Middle Eastern countries excluding Israel suffer from a similar deficiency, but in their case also the infant mortality level is considered to be quite high. Japan and Israel have brought down their infant mortality levels to those of the advanced Western countries. Japan was able to achieve this privileged position even before the Second World War.

Table 21 shows the infant mortality rates in selected Asian countries with fairly reliable vital statistics. The table reveals substantial declines in infant mortality rates between 1935–39 and 1955–58, which mainly contributed to the decline in general mortality. Registered rates available for other Asian countries suffer from incompleteness, but some idea of the change may be attempted for them. In the Philippines, the registered infant mortality rate declined by 21 per cent from 141 in 1935–39 to 111 in 1955–57. In Burma the registered rate dropped from 202 to 170, 16 per cent. The recent infant mortality rates in Cambodia, Indonesia and Thailand are estimated to be well over 100 and in British Borneo, Burma, Laos and Pakistan around 200. According to a Sample Survey in 1950 of 173 villages situated to the south-west of Teheran in Iran, the estimated infant mortality rate was 217. The rate is believed to have declined in recent years.

INFANT MORTALITY IN INDIA

The difficulties in evaluating the deficiencies inherent in Indian vital statistics have already been examined in some detail. Here, for reasons already discussed, the figures and the official rates given by the provincial and central governments are accepted, such as they are, as revealing reasonable dimensions and trends. Table 22 gives the infant mortality rates in India between 1901 and 1965. Table 23 gives most of the available details of infant mortality in the different states in India between 1925 and 1965. Table 24 presents infant mortality as a percentage of total mortality in all ages in the then provinces and between 1920 and 1964. The percentage is declining.

Table 22 which gives the course of infant mortality in India from 1900 to the latest available year,[1] deserves a serious examination. It gives the official infant mortality for the provinces of British India up to the advent of freedom and in recent years for the area of the Republic of India, in annual rates and in quinquennial averages.

[1] Classification of infant deaths by age in months is not available for years before 1920, and these returns were discontinued from the beginning of the Second World War in 1939 until 1955.

130

Table 24

REGISTERED INFANT MORTALITY
AS PERCENTAGE OF TOTAL MORTALITY
AT ALL AGES IN INDIA, 1920–64

Year	Percentage
1920	23·8
1925	23·7
1930	24·0
1935	25·6
1940	24·2
1945	19·1
1950	19·8
1951	21·4
1952	21·2
1953	20·2
1954	21·3
1955	23·2
1956	22·8
1957	19·2
1958	19·3
1959	20·9
1960	19·9
1961	19·0
1962	19·0
1963	18·0
1964	17·9

How far are these figures correct? As pointed out already, the registration of both births and deaths is incomplete and defective, but it is probable that the registration of births is less reliable than that of deaths. As to the reliability of the entire record, there are three possibilities: some births are not registered; some infant deaths are not registered; when deaths are registered the recorded age of the deceased infant may be inaccurate.

This situation can be dealt with in many ways: the registration figures may be adjusted on the basis of the various decennial census figures, a procedure which presupposes the absolute reliability of the censuses, whereas it is known that they are not exact for there is always the problem of under-enumeration. Secondly, the magnitude of under-registration can be estimated on the basis of a sample study and the margin of error be taken as uniformly applicable to the entire area. Such sample studies should have been made for every year and for every region and preferably for every state in the Indian

Union to check the annual vital statistics rates and for every ten years to check the decennial census figures, but such corrections as these are not available. According to the Population Data Enquiry Committee Report, the magnitude of under-registration is estimated to be between 40 and 50 per cent but this is nothing more than a reasoned conjecture when a period as long as seventy years is considered.[1]

The Census Actuary estimated the birth and death rates for 1941–50 and by comparing them with the registration data found that births were under-reported by 31·3 per cent and deaths by 28·1 per cent. The range of variation in the states in the under-registration of births was 4·1 per cent in the Punjab to 64 per cent in Assam. For deaths the range was from 9·1 per cent in the Punjab to 64·1 per cent in Assam. The under-registration of births in the states varied from 20 to 80 per cent.

In general, and theoretically, birth registration is less complete than death registration for obvious reasons. This is particularly true in countries where burial is the rule and a permit for burial is issued only after registration of death, but not so in India, where the practice for the Hindus – an overwhelming majority of the population – is quick cremation because of climatic conditions. But even so, deaths are better registered than births because there is a body to be disposed of which comes under the scrutiny of the community.

And when deaths are registered the exact age of the deceased is uncertain. This error might be expected to be very minor in the case of infants, for a lapse of memory on the part of parents or relatives or the recorders could not arise in such a short time, but in practice the error is significant. A study of urban mortality statistics in India reveals that the information which is given about the age of the child when reporting the death is usually vague with the result that many deaths over one year of age are returned as under one year, thus swelling the infant mortality rate. The reverse of this situation – declaring a deceased infant of less than one year to be older – does not often arise. In view of these considerations, the official figures (Chart 2) are examined here as such without any attempt at correction or refinement. If we do not set much store by the actual figures and are guided only by the trends revealed in a period stretching over sixty-five to seventy years, we need not be misled by the various inaccuracies referred to.

In this connection, it may be of interest to describe a small

[1] *Report of the Population Data Committee* (Simla: Government of India Press, 1945), p. 6.

Infant Mortality rates in
Indian states, 1964

 = 10

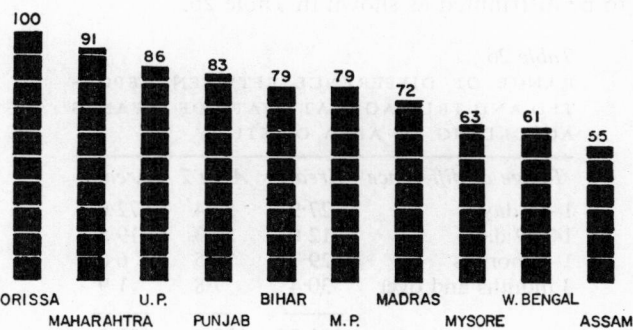

Chart 2

pilot study made in Egypt by Esmat I. Hammoud[1] on the discrepancy between reported and true age in cases of infant deaths in three areas with different registration facilities – one an urban area (area 3), another a rural area with a Health Bureau (area 2) and the third a rural area without a Health Bureau (area 1). He traced the age of the dead infant as reported at death to the birth date in the registration

Table 25

DIFFERENCE BETWEEN REPORTED AND
TRUE AGES AT DEATH OF INFANTS
ACCORDING TO AREA OF STUDY

Difference	Area 1	Area 2	Area 3
No difference	6·5	11·7	30·2
Over-reported	48·0	34·5	39·6
Under-reported	45·5	53·8	30·2
	100·0	100·0	100·0

[1] Esmat I. Hammoud, 'Effect of Misreporting Age of Infants at Death on Age-specific Mortality Rates – A Pilot Study', *The Journal of the Egyptian Public Health Association, Vol. 22*, No. 6, 1965.

records. The differences between the reported age and the true age as deduced from the registration records were found to be as shown in Table 25.

A higher percentage in the urban area reported age correctly. There was both under- and over-reporting. In areas 1 and 3 there was slightly more of over-reporting but in area 2 there was distinctly more of under-reporting. The magnitude of the difference was observed to be distributed as shown in Table 26.

Table 26
RANGE OF DIFFERENCE BETWEEN REPOR-
TED AND TRUE AGES AT DEATH OF INFANTS
ACCORDING TO AREA OF STUDY

Range of difference	Area 1	Area 2	Area 3
1–13 days	27·9	52·4	72·6
14–29 days	12·0	20·3	19·5
1–2 months	29·7	19·5	6·0
3 months and over	30·4	7·8	1·9
	100·0	100·0	100·0
No. of cases	169	145	308

It is evident from Tables 25 and 26 that correctness of age reporting decreased in the order of urban area, rural area with a health bureau and rural area without a health bureau. Among 622 cases studied, 417 were reported to be of infant deaths, whereas actually they included 441 deaths. Thus 5·4 per cent of infant deaths were reported to be of children above the age of 1. This means that infant deaths come to be under-reported to some extent due to misreporting of age.

Hammoud also made an interesting study of the effect of these mis-statements of age on the classifications by age, which determine the age-specific infant mortality rates. This effect was studied with reference to the usual four types of age-classification of infants. The first type (I) classified deaths into those of children above 1 year and of infants below 1 year, the latter being further subdivided into those occurring within 28 days of birth (neonatal deaths) and during the period 1–11 months after birth (post-neonatal deaths). In the second type (II) neonatal deaths were further classified into those occurring 7 days (hebdomadal deaths, namely the postnatal component of perinatal mortality) and during the period 7–27 days. In the third type (III) more refined subdivisions are adopted, namely, 1 day, 1–6 days, 1–3 weeks, 4 weeks to 2 months, 3–5 months, 6 months to 1 year. In the fourth type (IV) infant deaths are subdivided into daily for the first week, weekly for the first month and monthly thereafter. Table 27 shows the number of cases in which age was misclassified due to wrong reporting of age. It is evident that a misreported age that crosses the borders of one classification will necessarily cross the borders of all subsequent finer ones.

Table 27
EFFECT ON AGE CLASSIFICATION ACCORDING TO RANGE OF DIF-
FERENCE BETWEEN REPORTED AND TRUE AGES AT DEATH OF INFANT

Extent of difference between reported and true age	No. of cases where age was				No. of misclassifications in type			
	Correctly classified		Misclassified		I	II	III	IV
	No.	%	No.	%				
1–13 days	143	53·4	125	46·6	10	19	37	59
14–29 days	49	55·7	38	44·3	5	3	8	22
1–2 months	35	41·2	50	58·8	8	6	19	17
3 months and over	28	45·9	33	54·1	13	17	3	—
	255	50·9	246	49·8	36	45	67	98
Over-reporting	60	23·7	193	76·3	30	37	48	78
Under-reporting	195	78·6	53	21·4	6	8	19	20

Only in 121 cases, there was no difference between the reported and the true age. They are not included in Table 27. The conclusions of the study are reproduced below as they are of some interest to students of infant mortality problems in developing countries:

'1) There is a tendency to round the age at death of infants in reporting it in months and years, together with some preference of even over odd numbers. That rounding was observed less in the urban area, when the birth rate was correctly reported, and when the informer was one of the parents. There was no difference in relation to the infant's sex.

2) Relatives, neighbours, and health or civil officials volunteer to

135

report the death of infants more in rural than in urban areas, and with older than with younger infants (probably as a consolation to the parents). There was no significant difference regarding the type of informer in relation to the sex of the infant. As expected, almost three-quarters of the parents reported a correct birth rate of the deceased, while the corresponding proportion in the case of officials was less than 5 per cent.

3) Differences between the reported and true ages were present in 80 per cent of the deaths. That percentage was less in the urban area than in the rural area with health bureau, and greatest in the rural area without health bureau. It was somewhat less with males than with females, and was least when the informer was one of the parents.

4) It is disheartening to find that such a difference was observed in 71·9 per cent of the cases, for which a correct birth date was given. It seems that a tendency by the clerk in the health department to round the age in calculating it was responsible for most of them.

5) There was no specific tendency to over or under-report age.

6) The difference between the reported and the true ages was greater in the rural than in the urban area, with female than with male infants.

7) Such a misreporting of the age at death of infants did affect one or another of the age classifications in about two-fifths of the cases, and the finer the classification the more the effect. Even if we take the first year of life as a whole, infant mortality was found to be under-estimated by about 5·4 per cent (ranging between 3·5 per cent in the urban area and 8·2 per cent in the rural areas). Thus, some sort of a correction factor is needed to be applied to the reported infant mortality rates to adjust for such an under-estimation.'[1]

This study has a special interest for India, for general conditions in Egypt and India are not dissimilar and misreporting of age at death in India is also common. However, the rates registered in India during the last 10 years are seriously under-reported because of greater deficiency in registration. Nevertheless, four special Demonstration Health Units have been set up in India with special facilities for improving the health conditions in the area and one of their major objectives is to collect more reliable vital statistics in order to

[1] Esmat I. Hammoud, op. cit.

136

judge the impact of their health programmes. The infant mortality rates recorded by these Health Units are given in Table 28.

Table 28
INFANT MORTALITY RATES IN VARIOUS DEMONSTRATION HEALTH UNITS (INDIA)

Name of the Centre	1958	1959	1960	1961
Najafgarh (Delhi)	113	71	125	119
Poonamalle (Madras)	135	138	112	117
Singur (West Bengal)				
(Experimental Area)	—	—	122	118
Sirur (Maharashtra)	—	—	106	107

These figures and those given in Table 32 under the National Sample Survey suggest that the current infant mortality rate is between 100 and 125. Both the tabular material and chart 4 show that (a) the infant mortality rates throughout the period have been abnormally high in relation to rates in certain selected and, of course, advanced countries in Asia and the West, being four times as high as those of Sweden and New Zealand; (b) there were three peak years (1900, 1908–09 and 1918) when the rates were inordinately high – 232, 246 and 267 respectively; and (c) a declining trend is noticeable since the 1930s.

(a) During the last seventy years the infant mortality rates showed a wide range of variation from a figure well above 250 to one around 100. A comparison of the Indian rates with those of Japan and Ceylon in Asia, England and Wales, Sweden and Holland in Europe, the U.S.A., Australia and New Zealand even during the earlier years of this century, shows the difficult start India has had in the matter. She clearly began with a great handicap, for her public health and hygiene measures were (and unfortunately still are) in no way comparable to those existing in these countries. The causes for this excessive mortality, into which we shall inquire in some detail later, must be sought in the social, economic, cultural, religious and health background of India. The diseases and the pathological causes to which these infants apparently succumb are discussed below in the light of the available official information.

(b) Second, there are three peak years, 1900, 1908–09 and 1918, when the infant mortality rates (and mortality rates at all ages) were very high. Apart from what may be termed 'ordinary causes' from the Indian point of view, the high rate in 1900 was due to famine in the country as a whole with malnutrition leading to epidemics and

137

heavy loss of life. The year 1908 was also a bad one, due to a severe malaria epidemic over the whole of Northern India. While malaria is not always lethal in the case of an otherwise 'healthy' and normal adult, it often proves fatal to an infant.

The highest peak in infant mortality, in 1918, was caused by the world-wide influenza epidemic of that year which claimed in India some 12 to 13 million people of all ages.

Despite these peaks and variations a declining trend has been noticeable since the 1930s. The infant mortality rate has been on the decline since 1935 except for a slight rise in 1944 due to the severe famine in Bengal in 1943–44 which took an estimated toll of about 3 million (official figure 1·5 million) people of all ages. The infant mortality rate was exactly halved in the course of half a century from 232 in 1900 to 116 in 1952. The rate in England and Wales was reduced from 154 in 1900 to 30 in 1952. What England and Wales took twenty years to accomplish between 1900 and 1920, India took over fifty years to achieve. In the United States of America, which is perhaps more comparable to India in area and heterogeneous population, the infant mortality rate was reduced by half in about thirty years, from 99·9 in 1915 to 39·4 in 1944 and it was 122 in 1900 compared to 29 in 1950.

While the rate of decline in India during the period in question has not been impressive in comparison with that in certain other countries, the decline has begun which will be continued as a result of health improvements under the impact of successive Five Year Plans for raising the standard of living of the people. The evidence so far is that notwithstanding the declines, the Indian infant mortality rate is quite high, unlike the position obtaining in the advanced countries of the West, which have reduced their infant mortality rates to very low levels.

NEONATAL MORTALITY IN INDIA

As for neonatal mortality, figures are not available for the entire period under review. But the available limited data are presented in Table 29. They show that the neonatal mortality rate in India has remained around 45 for a long period.

That is, nearly 50 per cent of infant mortality in any year takes place in the first month of the infant's life. In Western countries, the marked decline in infant mortality in recent decades has taken place in the post-neonatal period covering the second to the twelfth month, while the first month has shown only a slight improvement.

138

Table 29

SOME DETAILS OF INFANT MORTALITY IN INDIA: 1920–1965
Neonatal mortality, mortality for 1–6 months, 6–12 months and respective ratios for 1,000 live births based on registration data

Year	Under 1 month per cent of total infant mortality	Ratio per 1,000 live births	1–6 months percentage of total infant mortality	Ratio per 1,000 live births	6–12 months percentage of total infant mortality	Ratio per 1,000 live births
1920	44·1	86	22·1	43	37·7	56
1925	49·6	86	28·2	49	22·2	39
1930	48·0	87	29·3	53	22·7	41
1935	47·0	77	30·0	49	23·0	38
1939	47·3	74	30·3	47	22·4	35
1956	46·6	37	27·4	22	26·0	21
1957	44·4	35	28·4	23	27·2	22
1958	44·3	32	28·7	21	27·0	20
1959	44·3	34	28·9	22	26·8	21
1960	43·2	41	28·3	27	28·5	27
1961	44·2	33	27·6	21	28·2	21
1962	43·5	33	28·7	21	27·8	21
1963	45·0	34	26·6	21	28·4	21
1964	45·0	33	26·0	19	29·0	22
1965	47·0	31	27·0	18	26·0	16

In these countries, neonatal mortality accounts for nearly 70–80 per cent of infant deaths. Table 30 shows the infant mortality and neonatal mortality rates in selected countries in 1962.

In India, the relative proportions of infant mortality under 1 month, 1–6 months and 6–12 months have remained practically steady; this goes to show that the decline in infant mortality is shared by all periods of infant life. It seems to be associated with the decline in general mortality.

The decline is marked in some provinces and it is striking in the composite State of Madras where the Director of Public Health, in his Annual Report for 1948, points out that the decline is real:

'The steady decline in infantile mortality in recent years in spite of the difficult food situation is due to improvement in environmental hygiene, expansion of maternal and child welfare services, health education and raising the age of marriage.'[1]

[1] Annual Report of the Director of Public Health, Madras, 1948 (Madras: Government of India Press, 1950), p. 9.

Table 30
INFANT AND NEONATAL DEATHS PER 1,000 LIVE BIRTHS IN SELECTED COUNTRIES OF THE WORLD BY CONTINENT, 1962

Continent and country	Under 1 year	Neonatal	Continent and country	Under 1 year	Neonatal
Africa			Europe		
Egypt (localities with health bureau)	155	31	Austria	33	21
			Belgium	28	18
Americas			Czechoslovakia	23	13
Canada	28	19	Denmark	20	15
Chile	121	37	England and Wales	22	15
Colombia	90	37	Finland	21	16
Costa Rica	63	20	France	26	17
Dominican Republic (1961)	102	35	Greece	40	20
El Salvador	71	30	Hungary	48	28
Guatemala	91	36	Ireland	29	19
Mexico	71	27	Italy	42	23
Panama	43	23	Netherlands	15	11
Trinidad and Tobago	36	22	Norway	18	12
United States	25	18	Poland	55	25
Venezuela	48	24	Portugal	79	27
			Sweden	15	12
Asia			Switzerland	21	16
Ceylon (1961)	52	32	Yugoslavia	84	34
Japan	26	15			
Philippines	68	33	Oceania		
			Australia	20	15
			New Zealand	20	13

In the face of the only available evidence, it must be assumed that some decline in infant mortality, as revealed in the official figures, must be taken to be nearer the truth. Various *ad hoc* inquiries over the years have yielded figures which though high when compared with those of Western countries are low in comparison with earlier official Indian figures.

SINGHUR (1943)

In 1943 the All-India Institute of Public Health and Hygiene in Calcutta conducted a general health survey of Singhur – a nearby rural area involving some 300 families and 307 live births. The Survey yielded an infant mortality rate of about 137. The Report points out:

> 'The sex specific infant mortality being 196 and 85 for males and females respectively, the former are again at a considerable disadvantage. The special reasons for higher rates amongst the former may also help to indicate lines along which endeavours could be made to reduce waste in early life. From the analysis of the causes of death so far carried out, it would appear that a multiplicity of causes are in operation but there are some indications of difficult labour as being one of the possible causes of infant mortality amongst the males.'[1]

NATIONAL SAMPLE SURVEY (1952–66)

The national sample survey, covering roughly about 1,000 villages, fifty towns and four cities, was set up in 1951 under the auspices of the Ministry of Finance of the Government of India and the Indian Statistical Institute at Calcutta. The second round of the national sample survey based on a sample of all-India rural households covering 1,106 villages taken in 1952 yielded the infant mortality rates set out in Table 31.

The figures for infant mortality rates given in the last column of Table 31 must be taken with considerable reserve and caution. The national sample survey is conducted by the interview method, and the limitations of such a method, in Indian conditions where the person interviewed is under no obligation to answer, much less to the best of his or her knowledge, are obvious. It is also possible that no serious distinction was made between stillbirths and live births. The figures in the last column point to the lapse of memory of couples about the deaths of their infants, increasing with the interval of

[1] *Report on the Singhur Health Survey* (Calcutta, 1945). Mimeographed.

Table 31

INDIA: NATIONAL SAMPLE SURVEY. INFANT MORTALITY RATES (1952)

Period of marriage	No. of couples	No. of infant deaths per 1,000 births
Before 1910	2,177	88
1910–19	2,415	102
1920–29	3,612	126
1930–39	4,652	134
1940–45	3,306	133
1946–51	3,714	181

time. This is not surprising for in villages the loss of an adult member is probably better remembered than the loss of an infant. There is also the further disadvantage of confusion over the age of the deceased infant. The death of a fifteen-month-old infant may be recalled as under one year. The last figure in the last column, the infant mortality rate of 181 per 1,000 births (presumably live) for the period of 1946–51 for rural India, is perhaps the only figure that merits some attention. These results are cited here only to show the approximate range of infant mortality rates for the five-year period. The mean average of official figures for the same five years yields the rate of 134 per 1,000 live births.

The National Sample Survey has been conducting yearly rounds of sample surveys to collect retrospectively, *inter alia*, information on birth, death and infant death rates by the interview method. Subject to the remarks already made about their reliability, the infant death rates obtained in these surveys for the latest available years are given in Table 32.

Table 32

INFANT MORTALITY RATES IN INDIA OBTAINED FROM NATIONAL SAMPLE SURVEYS (1958–66)

No. of Round	Reference period	Infant mortality rate Rural	Infant mortality rate Urban
14th	July 1958–June 1959	146	—
17th	September 1961–July 1962	111	81
18th	February 1963–January 1964	127	90
19th	July 1964–June 1965	121	85
20th*	July 1965–August 1966	108	67

* Provisional based on 2 samples out of four.

The urban rate seems to be substantially under-reported. It seems fairly certain that the current (1965–70) infant mortality rates in India are between 90 and 110.

MYSORE SURVEY (1952)

A general population survey of a sample of rural and urban families for the state of Mysore conducted in 1952 under the joint auspices of the Government of India and the United Nations yielded an infant mortality rate of 168·1 per 1,000 live births for rural (plains) and 110·9 for towns. This survey also revealed that infant mortality rates decreased with a rise in economic status. This, in the sense of a real increase in income, was reflected in better housing and in better domestic amenities (an elementary index adopted was the kind of lighting used, electricity, kerosene, etc.). The infant mortality rate for families in poor-class housing in urban areas was 100 per 1,000 live births but the rate dropped to 58 when housing conditions improved. In the rural areas the agricultural labour families had an infant mortality rate of 159 per 1,000 live births while the owner-cultivator families with better incomes had a rate of only 95.[1]

POONAMALLEE SURVEY (1953)

The object of this inquiry which was of a pilot nature was to assess the true infant mortality rate and the causes of such mortality in a rural area in Madras State (now Tamil Nadu). The plan involved following a cohort of births for a year in their own homes and ascertaining the causes of infant mortality by the inquiry method. (It may be recalled that rural births and deaths are registered by village headmen who are not medical men, and there is no medical certification of death.) This method is not 100 per cent correct but due to financial reasons and the want of laboratory facilities for performing autopsies and skilled medical personnel this method was adopted. The maternal and child health staff visited the infants periodically and made inquiries and recorded infant health conditions. When an infant died, the Woman Medical Officer and the Health Visitor visited the family and on the basis of an intensive personal inquiry and examination of health conditions already recorded during previous visits, the cause of death was finally determined by the Woman Medical Officer. No autopsy was carried out.

The inquiry was confined to infants born in the Poonamallee area

[1] United Nations: *The Mysore Population Study* (New York, 1961), p. 81.

143

between August 15, 1951 and August 14, 1952. The inquiry was completed on August 14, 1953, to complete one year of life for the latest baby born in the cohort.

The total number of expectant mothers who came under observation was 1,555. These women gave birth to 1,563 infants (838 males and 725 females) and included 8 twins. Of these, 1,506 were live births (807 males and 699 females) and 57 were stillbirths (31 males and 26 females). The number of infants who formed the cohort for observation was therefore 1,506. Of these, 186 infants were known to have died. Some infants moved out of the area and were thus lost for observation.

The inquiry yielded the following results: the infant mortality rates for the period under inquiry, August 1951 to August 1952, ranged between 137·59 and 387·84 per 1,000 live births. The true infant mortality rate was found to be 140·73 per 1,000 live births. The infant mortality rates in the age groups under one year were as follows:

Under 1 month	45·70 per 1,000 live births
1 to 6 months	63·40 per 1,000 live births
6 to 12 months	31·63 per 1,000 live births

Infant mortality rate 140·73

(1) As for the causes of this infant mortality, intestinal intoxication was the leading cause and accounted for 42 (22·6 per cent) infant deaths, 32 of those deaths (70 per cent) occurred between 3 and 12 months.

(2) Asphyxia was the next cause which claimed 26 infant deaths (14 per cent). Of these 26 infants, 21 died within the first month of life.

(3) The third important cause was prematurity, which was responsible for 23 deaths (12·4 per cent). Most of the deaths arising out of this cause occurred in the neonatal period.

(4) Bronchitis, pyogenic infection (skin) and nutritional maladjustments caused 14, 13, and 10 infant deaths, representing 7·5, 7·0 and 5·4 per cent of total infant deaths, respectively.

(5) Out of 66 neonatal deaths, 21 were caused by asphyxia and 16 by prematurity.

(6) In only 3 cases of infant deaths (1·6 per cent) the causes of death could not be decided.

This survey, carried out by the Department of Health Services of the Government of Madras, is the most detailed. Though the inquiry

144

was limited to a restricted rural area and could not be very scientific from the medical point of view, for reasons already explained, it gives a more or less true rate of infant mortality for the period in a well-defined area of the Indian Union.[1]

KHANNA STUDY (1956–59)

In this study,[2] the latest available, eleven villages near Khanna in Ludhiana district in the Punjab, with a population of about 12,000 were observed for four years with the aid of specially trained field staff. A resident woman village worker visited once a month all families where the wife was of child-bearing age, 15–45. A male worker interviewed husbands. Through long residence the village workers became a part of the community, a fact which greatly favoured collection of accurate information. A staff physician visited each village once a week, and thus a good proportion of serious illnesses was identified. He investigated every reported death. Deaths came to be known through observed activities at the cremation grounds and village gossip that came to the notice of the resident staff members. Four to eight men and women of the village, depending on its size, were appointed informants, who voluntarily assumed responsibility for reporting vital events for a specified group of 25 to 30 neighbourhood families. They reported to the village worker weekly once and additionally as events occurred. The data collected in this study may be taken to be reliable. Infant mortality rates obtained in the study are as shown in Table 33.

Table 33

INFANT AND NEONATAL MORTALITY RATES IN THE ELEVEN VILLAGES OF PUNJAB, 1956–59, OBTAINED FROM THE KHANNA STUDY

Year	Live births	Neonatal mortality rate	Infant mortality rate
1956	466	75·1	163·1
1957	457	74·4	142·2
1958	465	75·3	167·7
1959	480	70·3	172·9
All years	1,868	73·9	161·7

[1] H. M. Sharma, *Enquiry into Infant Mortality in the Poonamallee Health Unit Area* (Madras, 1955). Mimeographed.

[2] John E. Gordon, Sohan Singh and John B. Wyon, 'A Field Study of Deaths and Causes of Deaths in the Rural Populations of the Punjab, India', *American Journal of Medical Sciences, Vol. 241*, No. 3, March 1961.

Neonatal deaths were 45·7 per cent of total infant mortality; the officially recorded infant mortality rate for the Ludhiana district for 1952–57 is 112 and for the Punjab State 109. The data presented here amply show that post-neonatal mortality is still very important in India.

In this study, it was found[1] that the crude death rate of females exceeded that of males by a statistically significant difference of 26 per cent. (This feature of female mortality being higher than male mortality is observed in 7 countries out of 95 listed in the 1957 *Demographic Year Book* of the United Nations.) The study revealed the regularity of this phenomenon in different age groups. In infancy, there were 170 deaths per 1,000 male infants against 205·4 among females.

The study throws interesting light on the seasonal variation in infant mortality, which followed the same general pattern as the crude death rate, as could be expected from the fact that infant deaths constitute a large part of total deaths. Infant mortality rate during the hot dry season was the highest, being 239·6 per 1,000 live births per year against the annual average of 156·2. The hot wet months of July–September had a lower rate of 128 and the winter months of December–February an equally low rate of 128·9. The autumn months of October–November had a rate of 153·3. The hot dry summer is the most enervating period of the year with maximum temperatures running around 100° to 110° F. In the hot wet season the air is humid and loss of water through perspiration is less. Travel into and out of villages is inhibited by muddy and difficult road conditions with the reduced likelihood of infection reaching the village from outside sources. The months of October and November witness a rise in death rates. The colder months have favourable mortality, although the period is ordinarily rigorous for the village folk. The houses are built for tropical conditions and normal clothing is unsuited to cold weather.

INFANT MORTALITY RATES IN DIFFERENT COMMUNITIES

For certain years and for some provinces and cities, infant mortality rates have been recorded on the basis of caste and religion: Christians, Hindus and Muslims. An examination of these rates for the provinces

[1] John E. Gordon, Sohan Singh and John B. Wyon, 'Demographic Characteristics of Deaths in Eleven Punjab Villages', *Indian Journal of Medical Research*, *51*, 2, March 1963, pp. 304–12.

of British India up to 1939 reveals a very low rate for Indian Christians, a high rate for Muslims and the highest for Hindus. This order is maintained almost uniformly in seven provinces for ten years prior to the beginning of the Second World War.

The Indian Christian group form a small minority of the total population (see Appendix 5 for the religious composition of the Indian population) and while most of them belong either to the lower middle or low income groups they are educationally more advanced than the Hindus. Their fertility pattern, however, is not significantly different from that of the Hindus and Muslims. Their low infant mortality rates can only be explained by their better knowledge of child care and a higher percentage of educated women, and above all, their readiness to adopt, whenever economic factors permit, certain features of what is called the European way of life in India.

Even more interesting are the figures for Bombay City where infant mortality rates by communities show what reduction is possible under certain conditions. Bombay City is international in its population composition but the communities for which comparable figures are available are the Hindus (both the scheduled, that is backward, and the so-called high castes), Muslims, Indian Christians, Parsees and Europeans. While vital statistics in the City of Bombay are probably one of the most reliable series available, those for the Parsees are even more so, especially their mortality statistics, in view of their particular method of disposing of the dead (in the Tower of Silence) which necessitates full and unavoidable registration. Table 34 gives the comparative rates for the available years.

Table 34

INFANT MORTALITY RATES BY COMMUNITIES IN BOMBAY CITY, 1938–47

Period	Hindus (scheduled castes)	Hindus (other castes)	Muslims	Indian Christians	Parsees	Europeans
1938–39	332	272	247	236	111	174
1939–40	257	217	182	197	100	68
1940–41	232	209	187	169	95	39
1942–43	245	196	179	190	92	55
1943–44	261	193	181	193	84	53
1944–45	253	204	199	189	68	47
1945–46	286	186	166	164	80	26
1946–47	308	185	189	179	72	37

147

These rates are instructive, for the communal differentials in the infant mortality rates may be taken to be roughly comparable to the United Kingdom Registrar-General's five-fold social classification.[1] While all these communities, with the exception of the Europeans, are ethnically Indian, each has its own milieu easily distinguishable from the others. Socio-cultural patterns of living involving age-old habits, customs and traditions, affecting cleanliness, eating, clothing, child-care and almost every detail of daily living are conditioned by the communal mores.

These figures reflecting conditions in 1946–47 demonstrate how two Indian communities – the Hindus and the Parsees – living in the same city, can have such divergent infant mortality rates. The Hindus, who form an overwhelming majority of the population, have a rate of about 300, while the Parsees, who constitute the smallest minority, have a rate of about 70 per 1,000 live births. The Indian Christians, whose infant mortality rates in the provinces are much lower than those of the Hindus, have higher rates in Bombay City. This is probably the result of the heavy incursion of Catholics from Goa, most of whom belong to low educational and income groups and consequently are a high fertility group. The Parsees constitute an educated, advanced and relatively well-to-do group with a more or less Western way of life. While a majority of the Parsees live in relative ease and enlightenment they do not live in a geographical or social vacuum, for their infants are more or less exposed to the same environmental hazards as the infants of other communities. The real explanation here is probably one of income differentials as reflected in the different areas of residence, for Bombay has its Park Avenues as well as its East Ends. Another factor is the high percentage of educated mothers among the Parsees who know how to care for children in the sense of mothercraft.

The pattern of evolution of Parsee infant mortality during the last five decades is closer to certain European countries than to any Indian community. Table 35 presents the population numbers and the infant mortality rates of the Parsees for the last seven decennial years.

---

[1] The Registrar-General for the United Kingdom classifies the population into five social classes on the basis of occupation as follows: I class – middle classes, e.g. scientists, physicians, professors, etc; II class – intermediate class, e.g. farmers and farm managers, money-lenders, etc.; III class – skilled, e.g. foremen, watchmakers, nurses, etc.; IV class – semi-skilled, e.g. fishermen and hawkers, etc.; and V class – unskilled, e.g. manual labourers, porters, etc.

Table 35

INDIA: TOTAL PARSEE POPULATION AND THEIR INFANT
MORTALITY RATES AT CENSUS YEARS

Year	Population	Infant Mortality Rate
1901	93,617 undivided India	219
1911	99,412 undivided India	186
1921	101,075 undivided India	245
1931	108,988 undivided India	118
1941	114,890 undivided India	72
1951	111,791 (Indian Union)	51
1961	100,772 (Indian Union)	50

In the first quarter of the twentieth century the Parsee infant mortality rate was between 150 and 200 and in some years exceeded 200. In the next ten years the rate came down to about 100. Since 1945 the rate has declined considerably and today it is about 50. The present Parsee rate is far below those registered for other Indian communities (Chart 3).

The Parsees, who constitute only 0·03 per cent of the total Indian population, are predominantly urban, and more than half of them

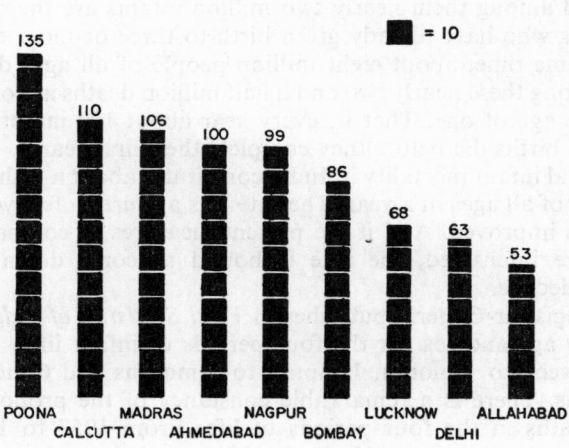

Infant Mortality rates in
major Indian cities, 1964

= 10

135 110 106 100 99 86 68 63 .53

POONA   MADRAS   NAGPUR   LUCKNOW   ALLAHABAD
  CALCUTTA   AHMEDABAD   BOMBAY   DELHI

Chart 3

149

live in Bombay City. The rest are distributed all over India, but most of them live in Maharashtra State. It should be possible for other communities to reach this low mortality record, given relatively high levels of income and education.

SOME CONCLUSIONS

The international data summarized in the preceding tables reveal that the variations in infant mortality rates are very great. They range from 20 to 500, all the way from Australia–New Zealand to parts of Africa. They vary from country to country, class to class and community to community. What is more, they vary between various ethnic, religious and cultural groups within the same country and also between rural and urban areas and between different income and educational groups.

As for India, certain obvious conclusions emerge from the limited available data and this necessarily incomplete analysis. The infant mortality rate and its component parts are high in contrast to the position in several advanced countries. But during the last few years, the trend of the rate is one of definite decline, despite an almost chronic food shortage, occasional epidemics and the all-too-visible low level of living of the Indian people. This marked decline in the infant mortality rate is real and not illusory.

During the last few years India's birth rate has been around 40 per 1,000. That is, every year about twenty-one million babies are born, and among them nearly two million infants are the offspring of parents who have already given birth to three or more children. At the same time, about eight million people of all ages die every year. Among these nearly two and a half million deaths are of infants under the age of one. That is, every year about 120 infants out of 1,000 live births die before they complete their first year.

The total infant mortality in India constitutes about a fifth of total mortality of all ages in a year. The rate was a fourth a few years ago but it has improved. And if the present measures to combat infant deaths are intensified, the rate is bound to come down further within a decade.

The Registrar-General publishes in *Vital Statistics of India* infant deaths by age and sex for the four periods of infant life – below 1 week, 1 week to 1 month, 1 month to 6 months and 6 months to 12 months. There is a remarkable constancy of the proportion of infant deaths in the four periods of life. From 1957 to 1960 the proportions in order were 23, 21, 29, 27 as against the figures of 24,

20, 28, 28, in 1961. The proportions in the different states do not differ much. These figures as well as those in Table 29 show that of the total infant deaths, nearly half (between 45 and 48 per cent) take place during the first four weeks – that is, the neonatal mortality is roughly half of the total infant mortality; and of this, about 60 per cent occurs in the first week – that is, the perinatal mortality is nearly three-fourths of the neonatal mortality. This provides a clue to the area of infantile morbidity which proves fatal and indicates the kind of measures to be taken to effectively reduce this abnormal rate (Table 29).

Table 36
REGISTERED INFANT MORTALITY RATES FOR INDIA BY SEX (FORMER PROVINCES AND PRESENT REGISTRATION AREA), 1900–65

Year	Male	Female
1900	—	—
1905	231	218
1910	217	201
1915	208	195
1920	210	188
1925	181	167
1930	189	172
1935	171	176
1939	163	147
1943	175	162
1948	152	140
1950	132	122
1951	123	114
1952	115	106
1953	116	108
1954	110	102
1955	99	91
1956	92	88
1957	98	94
1958	99	96
1959	90	83
1960	89	85
1961	85	81
1962	101	100
1963	78	73
1964	76	72
1965	67	64

According to official Indian vital statistics, 345,754 male infant deaths as against 298,462 female infant deaths were registered in 1961, i.e. 116 male deaths for every 100 female deaths. Some of this difference is because more female than male infant deaths escape registration. However, it appears that male infants have higher death rates than females of the same age. This is not only an all-India experience but it is also true of the various religious communities in India for which figures are available. As there is no male or female infanticide today, and the cultural bias, if anything, is in favour of the male, this fact confirms what is well known – that the female infants are biologically better fitted than male infants for survival. The sex distribution of infant mortality reveals the operation of a sexually select mortality removing far more males than females (Table 36).

Infant mortality rates in urban areas are invariably higher than

Table 37
REGISTERED INFANT MORTALITY RATES FOR RURAL AND URBAN AREAS IN INDIA (FORMER PROVINCES AND PRESENT REGISTRATION AREA OF THE INDIAN UNION), 1932–65

Year	Rural	Urban
1932	167	189
1935	158	213
1940	155	202
1945	148	177
1950	124	140
1951	122	124
1952	114	122
1953	118	119
1954	109	115
1955	100	100
1956	105	94
1957	107	96
1958	104	97
1959	89	84
1960	89	81
1961	85	77
1962	84	73
1963	81	70
1964	77	66
1965	67	63

those in rural areas. This is rather surprising, for in India a great majority of the general and maternity hospitals and nursing homes are located in urban areas where almost all general practitioners, gynaecologists and obstetricians practise. As a rule, more trained midwives operate in towns and cities as opposed to the untrained dias who work in the villages. If these figures are accepted (Chart 4),

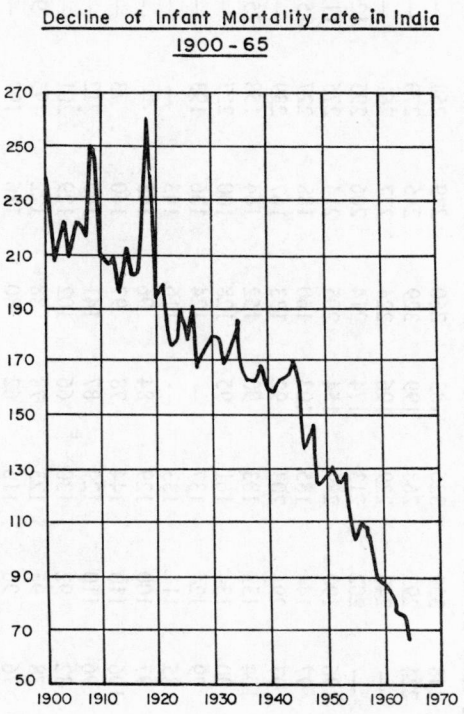

Chart 4

the prospects for a considerable decline in rural infant mortality appear to be bright if some health and medical services are extended to all the villages. The general lack of health and medical services in the villages is apparently compensated by more space, fresh air and less overcrowding in the rural areas, for there appears to be a direct correlation between higher infant mortality rates and over-crowded sections of urban areas. Urban overcrowding implies not

153

Table 38
REGISTERED INFANT MORTALITY RATES IN MAJOR INDIAN CITIES 1925 TO 1965

Year	Ahmeda-bad	Allaha-bad	Baroda	Bombay	Calcutta	Delhi	Lucknow	Madras	Nagpur	Patna	Poona	Surat
1925	323	236	248	359	326	183	260	279	258	—	611	330
1930	356	263	224	293	268	199	329	246	270	—	351	370
1935	280	194	—	248	239	196	224	227	261	—	320	272
1940	310	231	196	202	213	174	214	206	295	126	329	262
1945	187	191	97	190	289	154	205	214	275	115	320	308
1950	190	117	97	144	185	103	160	188	227	253	186	176
1951	169	99	104	294	203	92	133	167	239	—	154	156
1952	184	145	90	133	183	90	152	164	158	253	150	191
1953	162	102	79	134	161	95	128	100	227	—	165	150
1954	147	106	85	124	137	—	124	136	193	—	156	152
1955	145	86	97	111	133	—	116	143	—	—	123	145
1956	154	93	106	100	129	84	96	145	73	—	107	178
1957	149	84	96	110	144	78	97	140	212	—	101	140
1958	152	73	82	110	129	87	141	145	201	—	93	157
1959	117	77	78	92	130	66	102	129	195	98	99	141
1960	108	73	76	95	123	78	88	122	192	—	91	133
1961	119	66	72	96	116	62	80	116	96	44	88	143
1962	96	63	71	84	108	68	85	97	97	59	120	117
1963	101	—	66	81	127	59	77	108	90	33	106	110
1964	100	53	59	86	110	63	68	106	94	—	135	127
1965	86	—	—	96	111	55	—	100	—	—	94	95

Infant Mortality: number of deaths per 1000 live births in Japan: 1916-1965

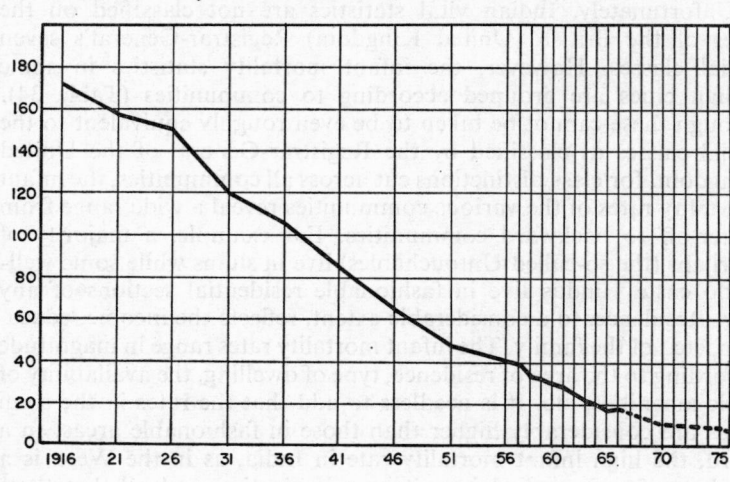

Chart 5

Infant Mortality Rates, United States

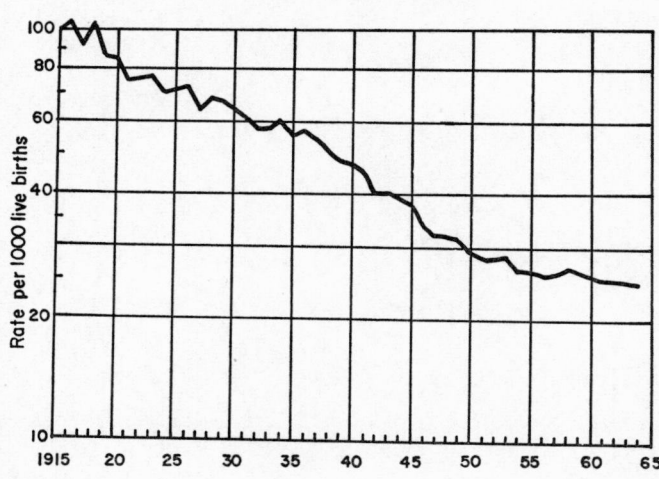

Chart 6

155

only so many adults per room but also poor or no sanitation and absence of personal and public hygiene in the urban slum areas.

Unfortunately, Indian vital statistics are not classified on the lines of the British (United Kingdom) Registrar-General's seven social classes. However, the infant mortality statistics in some Indian cities are grouped according to communities (Table 34). Though these cannot be taken to be even roughly equivalent to the social classes as classified by the Registrar-General of the United Kingdom, for class distinctions cut across all communities, the infant mortality rates of the various communities reveal a wide range from better-off to backward communities. For example, a majority of Harijans (the so-called Untouchables) live in slums while some well-to-do caste Hindus live in fashionable residential sections of any city. Residence, to a considerable extent, reflects the income, education, etc., of the family. The infant mortality rates range in magnitude according to the area of residence, type of dwelling, the availability of basic amenities, etc. It is needless to add that the rates in the slum areas are considerably higher than those in fashionable areas. In a word, the high infant mortality rate in India, as in the West, is a product of poverty and insanitary urbanization and all that these imply.

Chapter IV

CAUSES OF INFANT MORTALITY

'The termination of an individual's life,' writes Professor Titmus, 'is the product of an enormous number of complex and interrelated forces; from a Government's policy in international affairs to the local methods of refuse disposal and from a coal owners' decision to close the pits to a mother's intake of calcium. Reducing this diversity to identity, to find the causation of infant mortality, we can distinguish two main factors operating in the past to provide a high death rate. One can be summed up in the word poverty; the other in insanitary urbanization.'[1] There is no doubt whatever that a variety cf factors, some known and some unknown, some controllable and some uncontrollable in the present state of our knowledge of conditions, particularly in under-developed areas, accounts for such infant mortality as exists in many parts of the world.

Causes of infant deaths can be grouped roughly into two main classes each with a distinctive aetiology, namely those dying within one month of birth (neonatal mortality) and those surviving the first month of life but dying before the first anniversary of their birth (post-neonatal mortality).

The level and causes of infant mortality vary quite considerably in the early period of life and the later periods of the year. Accordingly, the W.H.O. have recommended that tabulations of infant deaths should be given for each day during the first week of life, the second week, the third and the fourth week, 28 days to 2 months and single months thereafter. Where such detailed tabulations are not practicable or desirable, the data should be shown for the first week, 7–27 days, 28 to below 3 months, 3 months to below 6 months, 6 months to below 1 year. Wherever such classifications are not

[1] Richard M. Titmus, *Birth, Poverty and Wealth* (London: Hamish Hamilton, 1943), p. 11.

possible, the data may be shown for under 28 days and 28 days to the rest of the year. However, few countries have reliable statistics of infant deaths according to the refined classifications and international comparisons are generally made for neonatal and post-neonatal periods.

Both exogenous and endogenous factors may lead to a given cause of infant mortality. Deaths among the first class, the neonatal deaths, are due principally to prenatal and natal influences, though susceptibility to exogenic and environmental hazards after birth also play a distinct part. The cause of many a neonatal death, in fact, is to be found far back in intra-uterine life, even at the earliest period of the individual's existence as a fertilized ovum.

These causes may be of genetic origin and traceable to the cellular growth of the organism and damage during gestation or due to birth injuries and hazards of delivery. Such endogenous natal and antenatal factors diminish in their importance after the first month.

The second group, the post-neonatal deaths, covers those who have succumbed in the main to causes arising from post-natal influences such as the various epidemic diseases, diseases of the respiratory system, faulty feeding, poor hygiene and other environmental factors.

The causes may be classified as (i) conditions arising from the type and extent of infant care, especially digestive diseases due to unhealthy feeding and (ii) infectious diseases determined by the general environment, including shelter, clothing and sanitary surroundings and exposure to the infectious agent.

In individual deliveries, it is often a matter of chance whether a foetus will die *in utero* shortly before delivery or whether it will be born alive and succumb within the first minutes or hours after delivery. Causes of foetal and early neonatal death are closely related. In certain cases a stillbirth may be saved only to end in a neonatal death. Perinatal rates, which cover foetal deaths of 28 or more weeks' gestation and early neonatal deaths, i.e. those under 7 days of age, permit consideration of foetal and early neonatal deaths simultaneously. Table 39 shows the perinatal mortality rates and its two components, late foetal deaths and early neonatal deaths for a number of countries.

Peller[1] is of the view that 'the real neonatal mortality is in the first week, not in the first month of life'. In view of its importance, he has proposed a separate term 'semanatal' mortality for mortality in the first week.

[1] S. Peller, 'Mortality, Past and Future', *Population Studies, 1943, Vol. I,* pp. 405–56.

Table 39

PERINATAL MORTALITY RATES PER 1,000 LIVE BORN
AND ITS TWO COMPONENTS IN 1955

A = *Late foetal mortality*
B = *Early Neonatal mortality*
C = *Perinatal mortality* = (A + B)

	(A)	(B)	(C)
1. Canada	15·6	15·8	31·4
2. United States	13·5	17·0	30·5
3. Japan	30·8	13·1	43·9
4. Germany			
(F.R.)	20·2	23·8	44·0
5. Austria	17·8	22·7	40·5
6. Belgium	18·4	17·0	35·4
7. Denmark	18·2	15·7	33·9
8. Finland	18·2	15·4	33·6
9. France	17·5	16·6	34·1
10. Italy	27·9	18·4	46·3
11. Norway	15·2	10·8	26·0
12. Netherlands	17·3	11·9	29·2
13. Portugal	32·8	14·6	47·4
14. England and Wales	23·7	14·6	38·3
15. Scotland	25.2	16·9	42·1
16. Sweden	17·0	11·4	28·4
17. Switzerland	14·5	16·3	30·8
18. New Zealand	16·0	11·8	27·8

Source: *Epidemiological and Vital Statistics Report* (*W.H.O.*) *Vol. 10*, Nos 11–12, 1957.

Infant mortality is linked to the standard of living and health conditions. Meerdink and Ramachandran[1] have, by using discriminant function technique, shown that of the five indices, the proportion of infant deaths occurring during 0–1 day of life, 0–1 week, 0–1 month, 0–5 months and total infant deaths, 'semanatal' mortality is the best discriminant of the standard of living and health conditions in the two groups of ten developed and ten developing countries examined by them. The developed countries examined were Australia, Canada, Denmark, England and Wales, France, New Zealand, Norway, Switzerland, the U.S.A., and Sweden and the underdeveloped countries were Ceylon, Colombia, Dominican Republic, Egypt, India, Federation of Malaya, Mexico, Peru,

[1] J. Meerdink and K. V. Ramachandran, 'Infant Mortality According to Social Status in Greater Bombay', *Journal of the Indian Medical Association*, *Vol. 38*, No. 9, May 1, 1962, pp. 477–82.

Philippines and Thailand. The value of the discriminant function D^2 based on all the five measures was found to be 46·1, which is significant at the 1 per cent level. This means that the five components of infant mortality can be used to discriminate between two groups of countries by applying the discriminant function technique. Separate values of D^2 and F that were obtained are given below:

$$\begin{aligned}
D^2 \text{ (0–1 day)} &= 10\cdot81 \; F_{1,\,15} = 45\cdot79 \\
D^2 \text{ (0–1 week)} &= 13\cdot78 \; F_{1,\,18} = 68\cdot91 \\
D^2 \text{ (0–1 month)} &= 7\cdot78 \; F_{1,\,18} = 38\cdot91 \\
D^2 \text{ (0–5 months)} &= 5\cdot39 \; F_{1,\,18} = 26\cdot93 \\
D^2 \text{ (0–1 year} = \text{I.M.R.)} &= 10\cdot43 \; F_{1,\,18} = 52\cdot15
\end{aligned}$$

For 36 countries of the world, which had reliable data on infant mortality, they obtained the following regression equations between infant mortality rate (y) and percentage of infant deaths in the first week in total infant deaths (x)

$$(1) \; x = 0\cdot5944y + 71\cdot45$$

and

$$(2) \; y = 1\cdot043x + 88\cdot28$$

A significant negative correlation of $-0\cdot79$ was found. This shows that the percentage of infant deaths up to a week of the total infant deaths is a good index for studying differences in levels of infant mortality based on social and hygienic conditions. They applied this result to the data on infant deaths recorded in 1958 in Greater Bombay, where registration of infant deaths is fairly complete.

The infants who died were classified into three social groups, high, medium and low, on the basis of father's occupation, as follows:

High Professional (engineers, doctors, lawyers, professors, etc.), higher administrative personnel, higher civil servants, managers of large enterprises, etc.

Medium Lower administrative personnel (clerks, etc.), lower civil servants (police, postmen, etc.), independent craftsmen, school teachers, shopkeepers, etc., and domestic servants if they reside in well-to-do residential quarters, etc.

Low Labourers, mill workers, daily workers, orphans, unemployed persons, hawkers, watchmen, etc., and domestic servants if they stay in slum areas or in *chawls* (slums) or in less well-to-do localities.

It was found that the percentage of infant deaths within one week in the total infant deaths was 45·9 in the high status group, 33·3 in the medium and 30·32 in the low group, giving an overall percentage of 31·4 in the three groups. An overall χ^2-test showed that the three groups differed significantly from each other at the 5 per cent level of significance. The differences in the high and the low and the high and the medium were found to be statistically significant, if they are taken as normal deviates, but the difference between the medium and the low was found to be near the significant value. Possibly, the latter difference was less marked due to difficulties of correctly classifying deaths between the medium and low social groups.

The leading causes of foetal and neonatal deaths in the advanced countries are placental and cord conditions in the foetus, and prematurity alone or in association with congenital malformations, birth injuries, postnatal asphyxia and atelectasis or pneumonia of the new born. Stillbirths, neonatal deaths and post-neonatal deaths are greatly affected by the standards of ante-natal and obstetrical care and the social and environmental conditions, which have a bearing on the health of the mother and the child before, during and after birth. These factors would seem to explain why in Table 39 the relative composition of perinatal mortality in terms of late foetal mortality and early neonatal mortality differ so markedly between different countries. In the U.S.A., Canada, Germany, Austria and Switzerland early neonatal mortality is greater than late foetal mortality. It is the other way round in other countries.

In the early neonatal period, congenital malformations and certain diseases or early infancy account for the bulk of infant deaths. Table 40 shows the relative incidence in 19 countries during 1953–55.

The composition of the fatality from the two groups of diseases is illustrated with reference to Sweden (1952–54) in Table 41.

Under congenital malformations, those of the circulatory system are the most important numerically. In the group of diseases of early infancy, intracranial and spinal injury at birth, post-natal asphyxia and atelectasis, immaturity and ill-defined diseases are the most important. 'All other causes' itself is a minor group.

Table 42 shows the break-up of early neonatal mortality by causes according to the number of days of infant life in the U.S.A. in 1955. It shows a heavy concentration of mortality in the first day and its tapering down as the number of days survived increases.

A study of the pattern of infant mortality by causes in the Western countries around the 1950s will help in understanding future trends in developing countries. By 1956 the Western countries had achieved a level of infant mortality which may be expected to be

Table 40

EARLY NEONATAL MORTALITY RATE PER 1,000 BIRTHS BY CAUSES DURING 1953–55

	Congenital malformations	Certain diseases of early infancy	Other causes	All causes
1. Canada	22	135	5	162
2. United States	19	142	9	170
3. Japan	6	120	11	137
4. Germany (F.R.)	21	222	3	246
5. Austria	19	—	—	236
6. Belgium	18	142	10	170
7. Denmark	17	135	3	155
8. Finland	20	133	2	155
9. France	15	96	13	124
10. Italy	19	165	5	189
11. Norway	12	88	4	104
12. Netherlands	22	92	10	124
13. Portugal (1955)	11	117	18	146
14. England	19	124	5	148
15. Scotland	23	143	4	170
16. Sweden (1952–54)	14	106	4	124
17. Switzerland (1952–54)	21	154	4	179
18. Australia	16	120	4	140
19. New Zealand	15	104	3	122

Source: *Epidemiological and Vital Statistics Report* (*W.H.O.*) *Vol. 10*, Nos 11–12, 1957.

Table 41

EARLY NEONATAL MORTALITY RATE PER 10,000 BIRTHS BY CAUSES DURING 1952–54 IN SWEDEN

	T	M	F
All causes	123·6	142·1	103·6
I. *Congenital malformations* (750–759)	14·0	15·5	12·1
(i) Monstrosity (750)	1·8	1·8	1·7
ii) Spina bifida and meningocele (751)	1·3	1·1	1·6
iii) Congenital hydrocephalus (752)	0·7	0·7	0·7
iv) Other congenital malformations of nervous system and sense organs (753)	0·2	0·2	0·1
v) Congenital malformations of circulatory system (754)	5·4	6·4	4·3
vi) Celft palate and hare-lip (755)	0·1	0·1	0·1

	T	M	F
vii) Congenital malformations of digestive system (756)	1·9	2·2	1·7
viii) Congenital malformations or genito-urinary system (757)	0·9	1·1	0·6
ix) Congenital malformations of bone and joint (758)	0·2	0·2	0·1
x) Other and unspecified congenital malformations (759)	1·5	1·7	1·3
II. *Certain diseases of early infancy* (760–776)	106·3	122·8	88·7
i) Intracranial and spinal injury at birth (760)	24·4	30·1	18·3
ii) Other birth injury (761)	2·2	2·7	1·7
iii) Postnatal asphyxia and atelectasis (762)	22·2	25·1	19·0
iv) Pneumonia of newborn (763)	2·2	2·6	1·8
v) Diarrhoea of newborn (764)	0·1	0·1	0·1
vi) Neonatal disorders arising from maternal toxaemia (769)	2·3	2·4	2·1
vii) Haemolytic disease of new born (erythroblastosis) (770)	2·7	3·3	2·1
viii) Haemorrhagic disease of new born (771)	1·3	1·4	1·1
ix) Ill-defined diseases peculiar to early infancy (773)	19·0	22·2	15·6
x) Immaturity with mention of any other subsidiary condition (774)	7·1	7·9	6·2
xi) Immaturity unqualified (776)	22·8	25·0	20·5
III. *All other causes*	3·3	3·8	2·8
i) All infective and parasitic diseases (1–138)	0·1	0·1	0·1
ii) Accidents, poisonings and violence (E800–E999)	0·4	0·4	0·3

Source: *Epidemiological and Vital Statistics Report (W.H.O.) Vol. 10,* Nos 11–12, 1957.

reached by the developing countries eventually. Table 43 shows infant mortality rates by broad groups of causes in 1956 for 25 countries which have fairly reliable statistics. It may, however, be borne in mind that comparability of these statistics is substantially affected by the varying standards of diagnosis of the cause of death, which differ from country to country. Even in the most advanced countries,

163

Table 42
EARLY NEONATAL MORTALITY RATES PER 10,000 LIVE BORN BY CAUSES ACCORDING TO AGE IN UNITED STATES IN 1955

	−1	No. of days of infant life survived						Total
		1	*2*	*3*	*4*	*5*	*6*	*Total*
1. All causes	100·00	28·9	18·4	9·3	5·5	4·3	3·2	169·6
2. Congenital malformations (750–759)	9·3	2·6	2·4	1·6	1·1	0·8	0·7	18·5
3. Congenital malformations of circulatory system (754)	2·4	1·5	1·5	1·0	0·5	0·4	0·3	7·6
4. Certain diseases of early infancy (760–776)	87·0	24·7	14·6	6·9	3·9	3·0	2·2	142·3
5. Birth injuries (760 and 761)	17·6	4·6	2·7	1·3	0·6	0·4	0·3	27·5
6. Post-natal asphyxia and atelectasis (762)	23·9	8·9	4·9	1·9	0·8	0·7	0·4	41·5
7. Ill-defined causes peculiar to early infancy	—	—	—	—	—	—	—	—
8. Immaturity (774 and 776)	36·1	8·3	4·6	1·9	1·2	1·0	0·8	53·9

Source: *Epidemiological and Vital Statistics Reports (W.H.O.), Vol. 10*, Nos 11–12, 1957.

varying emphasis is given to exogenous and endogenous factors in fixing the cause of death.

Causes of infant deaths in Table 43 show wide variations between countries. In countries with high infant death rates infective and parasitic diseases and the diarrhoeal group account for a high proportion of infant deaths. The table shows strikingly the control of mortality from diarrhoea and enteritis achieved in the advanced countries. The level of mortality from the diarrhoeal group is determined largely by the social and cultural environment, public health efforts and medical care. As regards infectious, parasitic and respiratory diseases, the initial immunity transmitted to the child by the mother is continued in the later period of life with the help of vaccination and serum. Further, effective curative medicines are now available to combat the infectious, parasitic and respiratory diseases. In the case of the last group, a variety of viruses may be involved. Further reduction in mortality may be made by the use of vaccines, control of cross-infection and development of antiviral drugs. The remaining exogenous causes have not yet been controlled so effectively.

In the endogenous group, 'infections of the new born' (B43) and 'other diseases of early infancy and immaturity unqualified' (B44) seem to be responsible in the main for the major differences in high and low-level mortality countries. The more important causes included in this group are (i) pneumonia and diarrhoea of the new born; (ii) neonatal disorders due to maternal toxaemia; (iii) haemolytic diseases of the new born (due to foetal-maternal blood incompatibility); (iv) haemorrhagic diseases of the new born; and (v) immaturity. Deaths from these causes have been greatly reduced by the discovery of new methods, such as foetal–blood exchange transfusion, use of incubators, etc., which require a high standard of medical attention and services. Advanced countries have naturally made greater use of these methods, which has resulted in a greater reduction in mortality from these causes.

There is not such a marked variation between countries in the incidence of mortality due to congenital malformations (B41) and injuries at birth, etc. (B42). In fact, the incidence is highest in the advanced countries, possibly because of better detection. The incidence of congenital malformations tends to rise as infant mortality decreases. The reason may be that in the advanced countries some of these congenital malformations would have been naturally aborted but for the application of advanced medical methods. In advanced countries, the first three most important causes of infant deaths in

165

Table 43

INFANT MORTALITY RATES BY BROAD GROUPS OF CAUSES OF DEATH FOR 25 COUNTRIES IN 1956. (RATES PER 100,000 LIVE BIRTHS)

Country	All causes	Infectious, parasitic and respiratory diseases (B1–B17, B30, B31, B32)	Diarrhoea and enteritis (B36)	Congenital malformations (B41)	(B42)*	(B43)† and (B44)‡	Ill-defined or unknown causes (B45)	Violent deaths (B47–B50)	Cancer (B18)	Cardiovascular diseases (B22, B24–B29)	Other
Chile	11,621	4,222	661	219	583	4,732	467	47	6	184	500
Portugal	8,782	1,701	2,356	225	281	3,093	647	36	4	17	422
Costa Rica	7,158	1,589	1,700	181	299	1,641	1,356	53	8	40	291
Mexico	7,099	2,402	1,485	196	270	2,385	154	65	8	6	136
Hungary	5,377	1,505	552	676	858	1,813	49	37	4	0	383
Puerto Rico	5,507	636	1,429	383	510	1,570	634	47	8	18	272
Italy	4,375	941	522	364	535	2,213	12	13	8	9	258
Austria	4,326	687	351	406	605	1,836	81	60	3	27	270
Japan	4,065	879	267	198	115	2,023	164	107	5	10	297
Belgium	3,937	528	93	497	405	1,551	447	53	13	52	298
Germany (F.R.)	3,842	464	39	503	512	1,968	62	68	5	9	212
France	3,635	451	44	436	424	1,543	289	60	7	29	352
Israel	3,589	514	495	574	493	1,090	39	64	0	40	280
Canada	3,195	505	109	512	708	967	56	112	6	7	213
Scotland	2,861	323	97	533	763	782	57	166	9	5	126
United States	2,599	266	67	377	711	839	61	87	7	12	17
Switzerland	2,584	198	68	428	798	905	8	71	10	1	13
Finland	2,567	349	161	483	514	809	13	52	9	9	16
Denmark	2,495	242	52	469	705	775	52	56	8	7	12

England and Wales	2,364	296	39	459	624	713	6	80	6	7	13
Australia	2,172	216	42	398	511	781	5	50	6	11	15
Norway	2,122	276	42	346	419	645	175	53	8	6	15
New Zealand	1,939	206	28	369	537	565	0	58	12	9	15
Netherlands	1,897	137	15	474	511	478	105	38	5	7	12
Sweden	1,733	132	22	339	539	546	7	39	8	6	9

Source: *Population Bulletin* (New York: United Nations, No. 6, 1962).

* Birth injuries, post-natal asphyxia and atelectasis.
† Infections of the new born.
‡ Other diseases peculiar to early infancy, and immaturity unqualified.

order of ranking are the group of diseases under B42 and B41 followed by pneumonia, B31. Only in France, B31 occupies the second place and B42 the third place. Moriyama has expressed the opinion that: 'No substantial progress in reducing infant mortality will be made until there is a breakthrough in dealing with congenital malformations and the diseases of early infancy, such as birth injuries, postnatal asphyxia and premature delivery of infants.'[1]

In most of the advanced countries respiratory deaths exceed those due to diarrhoea and enteritis. Cancer and cardiovascular diseases are not important as causes of infant deaths. Diseases of the digestive system other than enteritis and diarrhoea are the major ones under 'other causes'. A number of diseases of exogenous origin figure in this residual cause group.

A more refined study of causes of infant mortality was made by the national Centre for Health Statistics, Washington, D.C., U.S.A. Some of the conclusions reached are interesting and are discussed below.

Infant mortality in the U.S.A.[2] was compared with that in the six countries, Denmark, England and Wales, Netherlands, Norway, Scotland and Sweden. It was found that although perinatal mortality declined in all the countries, the rate for the U.S.A. was higher than those of the Scandinavian countries and the Netherlands, but lower than those of England and Wales and Scotland. In all these countries, the rate of decline since 1950 was lower than that of the earlier period. Available evidence shows that the U.S.A. occupies fifth position among these countries. It appears to have some advantage in foetal mortality but this is offset by higher mortality during the first 24 hours of life and the remainder of the first week. In the U.S.A. most registered foetal and infant deaths in the first 24 hours occur in hospitals, but death after the first week of life often occurs outside hospitals. Discharge from the hospital means a big change in the life of the infant, since the hospital and home environment differ greatly.

In addition to the effects of neonatal disorders like congenital malformations (particularly of the heart), pneumonia of the newborn, post-natal asphyxia and atelectasis, immaturity and accidents

[1] I. M. Moriyama, 'Infant Mortality in Countries of Low Mortality', *World Population Conference, 1965, Vol. II*, New York: United Nations, 1967

[2] *International Comparison of Perinatal and Infant Mortality: The United States and Six West-European Countries* (Washington, D.C.: U.S. Department of Health, Education and Welfare, Public Health Service; National Centre for Health Statistics, 1967).

168

begin to emerge as a more frequent cause of death than in the first week of life. However, mortality during the period 7–27 days is very much lower than that nearer birth. For instance, in the U.S. (1959–61) the mortality rate per 1,000 live births in the period under 24 hours was 10·3, as against 6·4 in the interval 1–6 days and 2·0 in 7–27 days and 7·2 in 28 days to 11 months.

Between the decade 1949–51 and 1959–61, perinatal mortality declined by 13 per cent, foetal deaths by 20·5 per cent and deaths in the interval 1–6 days by 16·9 per cent, but deaths in the interval 'under 24 hours' increased by 2 per cent. The decline in the mortality in the interval 7–27 days was by 28·6 per cent and in the interval 28 days to 11 months by 20 per cent. The slight increase in the mortality in the interval under 24 hours of life is intriguing, since over 97 per cent of live births occur in hospitals and other institutions and hence a high proportion of deaths in the first 24 hours of life occur there. There is a striking similarity in the trends in infant mortality by age, and the basic reason for the decelerating rates of change observed in all the seven countries compared may be identical. All of these countries achieved a low rate and it is of interest to study their picture of infant mortality by cause. Table 44 shows the percentage distribution of infant, neonatal and post-natal death by cause in 1959–61 in the selected countries.

Infant deaths are largely concentrated in the five general groups according to causes (cause-groups) post-natal asphyxia and atelectasis, immaturity, congenital malformations, influenza and pneumonia and the residual category of disease of early infancy. They together account for almost three-fourths of all infant deaths. The thread of prematurity and/or immaturity runs through a number of these causes. It may be noted that influenza and pneumonia account for 5 to 6·8 per cent of infant deaths in the case of Denmark, the Netherlands and Sweden but this proportion is nearly double in England and Wales, Scotland, Norway, and the United States. In contrast, the proportions of congenital malformations and birth injuries for the U.S.A. are lower than those for the Netherlands and Sweden. In the neonatal period, deaths are even more concentrated in the five cause-groups, which are the same as mentioned above in the case of infant deaths excepting that 'birth injuries', which figure prominently in neonatal deaths, replace 'influenza and pneumonia'. These five cause-groups account for nearly 90 per cent of neonatal deaths. Post-natal asphyxia and atelectasis, birth injuries and congenital malformations are strongly associated with low birth weight. Neonatal mortality from these causes among infants weighing

169

Table 44
INFANT, NEONATAL AND POST-NEONATAL MORTALITY RATES TOGETHER WITH PERCENTAGE DISTRIBUTION BY CAUSE OF DEATH IN 1959–61

Cause of death	Denmark			England and Wales			Netherlands		
	Infant deaths	Neo-natal deaths	Post-neonatal deaths	Infant deaths	Neo-natal deaths	Post-neonatal deaths	Infant deaths	Neo-natal deaths	Post-neonatal deaths
1. All causes rate per 100,000 live births	2191.7	1624.7	567.0	2181.0	1557.3	623.7	1622.8	1172.9	449.9
2. Percentage share of:									
i) Infective & parasitic diseases (001–138)	1.3	0.4	3.9	1.1	0.1	3.4	1.0	0.1	3.2
ii) Influenza and pneumonia including pneumonia of newborn (480–493, 673)	6.5	1.5	21.0	13.8	6.0	33.4	6.8	4.6	12.3
iii) All other diseases of respiratory system (470–457, 500–527)	1.8	—	—	2.7	0.4	8.3	0.8	0.1	2.4
iv) Gastritis (543, 571, 572, 764)	2.0	0.4	6.3	2.0	0.4	6.1	0.9	0.2	2.8
v) All other diseases of digestive system (530–542, 544–570, 573–587)	1.2	0.8	2.3	2.0	1.4	3.4	1.7	1.3	2.5
vi) Congenital malformations (750–759)	20.4	15.9	33.3	20.6	18.3	26.6	26.5	21.7	38.9
vii) Birth injuries (760, 761)	11.8	15.9	0.2	11.2	15.6	0.0	19.7	27.0	0.7
viii) Post-natal asphyxia (762)	22.0	29.4	1.0	15.7	21.8	0.5	7.9	10.8	0.3
ix) Haemolytic (770)	2.0	2.6	0.4	2.1	2.9	0.1	2.6	3.5	0.3
x) Immaturity (776)	11.9	—	—	16.8	23.4	0.2	11.6	15.9	0.3
xi) All other diseases (765–769, 771–774)	12.1	—	—	5.6	7.4	1.0	8.8	9.6	6.4
xii) Symptoms (780–793, 795)	1.7	0.4	5.2	0.2	0.1	0.2	3.9	2.5	7.6
xiii) Accidents (E800–E962)	1.7	0.2	5.8	2.7	0.8	7.5	2.1	0.4	6.7
xiv) All other causes (residual)	3.5	—	—	3.7	1.3	9.4	5.8	2.1	15.5
Total all causes	100.0	100.0	100.0	100.0	100.0	100.0	100.0	100.0	100.0

Cause of death	Norway Infant deaths	Norway Neo-natal deaths	Norway Post-neonatal deaths	Scotland Infant deaths	Scotland Neo-natal deaths	Scotland Post-neonatal deaths	Sweden Infant deaths	Sweden Neo-natal deaths	Sweden Post-neonatal deaths	United States Infant deaths	United States Neo-natal deaths	United States Post-neonatal deaths
1. All causes rate per 100,000 live births	1846·5	1214·3	632·2	2686·0	1850·4	835·6	1633·6	1317·7	315·9	2590·5	1871·4	719·1
2. Percentage share of:												
i) Infective & parasitic diseases (001–138)	1·8	0·0	5·1	1·2	0·0	3·8	0·7	0·2	3·0	1·3	0·3	4·1
ii) Influenza and pneumonia including pneumonia of newborn (480–493, 673)	10·5	4·2	22·5	13·2	4·9	31·5	5·0	2·2	16·7	12·0	4·6	31·2
iii) All other diseases of respiratory system (470–457, 500–527)	1·4	0·1	3·8	1·7	0·1	5·2	1·0	0·1	4·5	2·4	0·4	7·6
iv) Gastritis (543, 571, 572, 764	2·0	0·3	5·2	3·0	0·8	8·0	1·2	0·3	5·2	2·7	0·6	8·1
v) All other diseases of digestive system (530–542, 544–570, 573–587)	2·0	1·4	0·3	1·5	1·0	2·7	2·1	1·5	4·6	1·5	1·3	2·0
vi) Congenital malformations (750–759)	17·9	15·2	23·3	20·2	19·3	22·1	21·0	16·3	40·5	14·1	12·7	17·5
vii) Birth injuries (760, 761)	11·1	16·8	0·3	10·1	14·7	0·0	15·4	19·0	0·5	9·2	12·8	0·1
viii) Post-natal asphyxia (762)	10·4	15·4	0·8	20·1	28·9	0·4	20·4	24·9	1·6	17·6	24·1	0·9
ix) Haemolytic (770)	1·5	2·1	0·4	1·9	2·7	0·1	1·5	1·8	0·2	1·9	2·7	0·1
x) Immaturity (776)	19·5	29·1	1·2	13·4	19·4	0·1	17·7	21·8	0·7	17·5	24·1	0·4
xi) All other diseases (765–769, 771–774)	7·3	9·8	2·6	4·4	5·9	1·2	8·6	10·1	2·5	10·6	13·3	3·6
xii) Symptoms (780–793, 795)	7·5	4·6	13·0	1·3	0·2	3·8	0·1	—	0·4	2·2	1·3	4·7
xiii) Accidents (E800–E962)	2·1	0·2	5·7	5·0	1·0	13·9	1·2	0·2	5·6	3·4	0·7	10·3
xiv) All other causes (residual)	5·1	0·9	13·1	3·1	1·2	7·0	4·0	1·8	13·9	3·5	1·3	9·3
Total all causes	100·0	100·0	100·0	100·0	100·0	100·0	100·0	100·0	100·0	100·0	100·0	100·0

2,500 g or less at birth is many times the mortality among heavier infants. In fact, the overall infant mortality among low birth-weight infants is found to be about 20 times the mortality among infants of heavier birth weight. In the neonatal period, the adverse effects of prematurity and immaturity are specially pronounced.

In the post-neonatal period there are shifts in the level of mortality and infants' exposure to external risks, which lead to a realignment of important causes of death. Birth injuries, post-natal asphyxia and atelectasis, immaturity and other diseases of early infancy, which constituted three-fourths of neonatal mortality, are no longer important. They account for only one-twentieth of post-neonatal deaths. In the post-neonatal period, environmental causes assume much greater importance over developmental or biological causes.

Causes of death are now more dispersed. Influenza and pneumonia and congenital malformations figure as the two most prominent causes of death, the former cause group constituting the largest component. For instance, in the U.S.A. they account for 4·6 per cent of neonatal deaths but for 31·2 per cent of post-neonatal deaths. Accidents, which in the neonatal period account for below 1 per cent of neonatal deaths, assume a much greater importance in the post-neonatal period. Diseases of the respiratory and digestive systems and accidents, which are associated with environment and should be preventable, rank quite high in the post-neonatal period.

Enough has been said about the nature of census figures and vital statistics in India. However, the problem may be looked at from the point of view of causes of infant mortality. If Indian vital statistics in the sense of mere registration of births and deaths are inadequate and inaccurate, the registered causes of mortality, where they exist, are even more so. A majority of deaths, including those of infants, occur outside hospitals and clinics and, by and large, unattended by physicians or any medical personnel. While more than 70 per cent of the population live in villages which have no hospitals or clinics, about 80 per cent of the qualified medical personnel live in urban India. As death certificates, showing cause of death, are not issued by the medical authorities for the registration area as a whole, it is difficult to establish precisely the medical and pathological causes for the high infant mortality in India. Since death registration is incomplete, the numerous socio-economic–cultural factors contributing and leading to infant mortality cannot be adequately evaluated.

Though exact figures are not available it is known that a great majority of deliveries take place outside hospitals and maternity homes; births which take place in the home are not necessarily

172

attended even by trained midwives. While actual figures are not available to establish percentages an informed guess would put the number of home deliveries, unattended by medical personnel, at about 70 per cent of total births. Even small sample inquiries into the cause of infant deaths have been impossible on account of difficulties in performing post-mortem examinations.

Infant mortality figures as well as their causes are relatively more reliable in certain major Indian cities like Calcutta, Bombay, Madras and Delhi as medical certification of death is more or less obligatory on the part of municipal authorities. This limited data covering only a fraction of the country's population does throw some light on the major causes of infantile morbidity and mortality.

Vital Statistics of India issued by the Registrar-General gives causes of infant deaths by age and sex for Bombay, Madras, Calcutta and Nagpur. They are given in Table 45 for the latest available year.

For Nagpur, causes of infant deaths are given according to the International Detailed List, but to save space only the causes which account for a substantial number of deaths are shown in the table. Unfortunately the cause list is not uniform.

The list unmistakably shows that prematurity including immaturity, congenital malformations and respiratory diseases including pneumonia and bronchopneumonia are the major causes of infant deaths in India.

Dr B. C. Das Gupta[1] made an analysis of the material collected during September 1946–July 1947 from thirteen medical institutions in Bombay to show the bearing of premature and immature births on infant mortality, especially on the neonatal portion. Live births which had a period of maturity under 40 weeks were classified as premature. Those who attained full maturity but whose birth-weight was less than 4 lb 15 oz were termed immature, if the circumference of the head and weight of placenta was less than that of full-term mature infants and approximated more to premature infants. The averages by the period of gestation were found to vary as shown in Table 46.

It was found that 2,947, or 17·6 per cent, of the total births in the institutions studied were premature or immature. Immatures were 1,593 and were slightly in excess of prematures, who numbered 1,354, but mortality among prematures was found to be three times

[1] B. C. Das Gupta, *Report of the Inquiry into the Bearing of Premature and Immature Births on Infant Mortality in Bombay 1946–48* (New Delhi: Indian Council of Medical Research, 1951).

173

Table 45

CAUSES OF INFANT DEATHS BY AGE AND SEX IN BOMBAY, MADRAS, NAGPUR AND CALCUTTA

Cause of death	Sex	Total under 1 year	Weeks −1	1−	Months 4−	6−
		(1)	*(2)*	*(3)*	*(4)*	*(5)*	*(6)*
		I Bombay (1964)				
1. Tuberculosis of respiratory system	M	18	—	—	8	10
	F	9	—	—	1	8
2. Tuberculosis, other forms	M	57	—	—	11	46
	F	60	—	1	9	50
3. Dysentery	M	18	1	3	8	6
	F	16	—	—	8	8
4. Diphtheria	M	12	—	—	3	9
	F	7	—	1	1	5
5. Whooping cough	M	2	—	—	1	1
	F	2	—	—	1	1
6. Acute poliomyelitis	M	11	—	—	5	6
	F	5	—	—	—	5
7. Smallpox	M	19	—	—	8	11
	F	21	—	1	9	11
8. Measles	M	34	—	2	9	23
	F	29	—	—	9	20
9. All other diseases classified as infective and parasitic	M	162	35	98	21	8
	F	77	13	53	6	5
10. Anaemias	M	73	3	6	39	25
	F	61	6	4	18	33
11. Vascular lesions affecting central nervous system	M	24	12	2	8	2
	F	12	4	1	2	5
12. Non-meningococcal meningitis	M	47	2	7	20	18
	F	33	—	8	18	7
13. Diseases of heart and hypertension without mention of heart	M	16	2	3	8	3
	F	19	2	2	11	4
14. Pneumonia	M	1,179	—	—	680	499
	F	1,167	—	—	652	515
15. Bronchitis	M	21	4	2	5	10
	F	30	1	6	7	16
16. Intestinal obstruction and hernia	M	33	10	5	11	7
	F	10	1	4	3	2

174

17. Gastritis, duodenitis enteritis and colitis except diarrhoea of new born	M	602	—	—	344	258
	F	570	—	—	313	257
18. Congenital malformations	M	132	77	28	21	[6
	F	74	43	18	11	2
19. Birth injuries, postnatal asphyxia and atelectasis	M	366	344	15	4	3
	F	231	218	10	1	2
20. Infections of the new born	M	559	117	364	78	—
	F	423	95	267	61	—
21. Other diseases peculiar to early infancy and immaturity unqualified	M	2,339	1,541	517	207	74
	F	1,896	1,173	447	204	72
22. Psychosis, ill-defined and unknown causes	M	176	72	38	38	28
	F	138	31	35	39	33
23. Accidents	M	37	4	8	15	10
	F	23	2	2	7	12
24. Other causes	M	254	77	72	58	47
	F	251	67	64	71	49
All causes	M	6,191	2,301	1,170	1,610	1,110
	F	5,164	1,656	924	1,462	1,122
	Total	11,355	3,957	2,094	3,072	2,232

II Madras (1964)

1. Smallpox	96	—	11	26	59
2. Fevers other than enteric and malaria	185	24	55	46	60
3. Dysentery	475	4	120	202	249
4. Diarrhoea	758	6	58	302	392
5. Infantile debility and malnutrition including premature birth	1,630	1,068	380	161	21
6. Diseases of respiratory system	2,125	147	242	920	854
7. Convulsion	55	6	9	27	13
8. Other causes	2,419	700	317	520	804
All causes	7,803	1,955	1,192	2,204	2,452

III Nagpur (1964)

1. Tetanus	M	27	6	20	1	—
	F	9	4	5	—	—
2. Anaemia of unspecified type	M	17	—	—	10	7
	F	4	—	—	1	3

175

3.	Encephalitis, myelitis and encephalo- myelitis (except acute infectious)	M	34	1	—	9	24
		F	21	—	1	9	11
4.	Bronchopneumonia	M	28	—	—	19	9
		F	25	—	—	28	17
5.	Gastro-enteritis and colitis except ulcerative	M	47	—	—	19	28
		F	54	—	—	26	28
6.	Post-natal asphyxia and atelectasis	M	47	45	1	—	1
		F	38	36	2	—	—
7.	Pneumonia of new born	M	31	15	16	—	—
		F	19	10	9	—	—
8.	Diarrhoea of new born	M	13	—	13	—	—
		F	6	1	5	—	—
9.	Ill-defined diseases peculiar to early infancy	M	77	41	17	15	4
		F	73	27	25	16	5
10.	Immaturity with mention of any other subsidiary condition and immaturity unqualified	M	147	113	26	8	—
		F	147	111	32	4	—
11.	Convulsions	M	10	5	1	3	1
		F	2	1	1	—	—
12.	Other causes	M	172	46	28	52	46
		F	148	36	22	49	41
	All causes	M	650	272	122	136	120
		F	546	226	102	113	105
		Total	1,196	498	224	249	225

IV Calcutta (1962–63)

1.	Cholera	M	37	—	4	8	25
		F	27	—	5	6	16
2.	Smallpox	M	59	—	18	16	25
		F	74	—	18	19	37
3.	All bowel com- plaints	M	576	7	232	149	188
		F	550	17	211	132	190
4.	Respiratory system	M	980	191	492	133	164
		F	915	142	427	143	203
5.	Premature birth	M	994	792	191	4	7
		F	751	533	212	4	2
6.	Congenital debility	M	36	27	9	—	—
		F	40	31	9	—	—
7.	Marasmus	M	105	2	70	18	15
		F	100	3	53	29	15

8. Tetanus	M	118	37	74	3	4
	F	60	21	36	—	3
9. Infantile liver	M	9	1	3	1	4
	F	15	1	7	2	5
10. Other causes	M	1,280	404	408	173	295
	F	1,054	268	347	163	276
All causes	M	4,194	1,461	1,501	505	727
	F	3,586	1,016	1,325	498	747
	Total	7,780	2,477	2,826	1,003	1,474

Table 46

AVERAGE MEASUREMENTS OF INFANTS ACCORDING TO PERIOD OF
GESTATION

Period of gestation (weeks)	Average Birth weight (lb oz)		Length (in)	Circumference on the head (in)	Weight of placenta and cord (oz)
28	2	12	16	11¼	12
32	3	14	17	12	14
36	4	6	17½	12½	14½
40 & over	4	12	17½	13	16

as high as for immatures. Among the prematures, 48 per cent had died by the end of the period of inquiry, and only 16 per cent in the case of immatures. 75·8 per cent of the deaths occurred in the neonatal period and of these 81 per cent were those of prematures. In the post-neonatal deaths, 40·9 per cent were those of prematures. Thus, prematurity *per se* is an important cause of infant mortality, particularly in the neonatal period. Prematurity claimed 42·9 per cent of the total infant deaths. Congenital debility was the second most important cause of infant deaths and accounted for 20·8 per cent of the total. This cause was responsible for the largest number of deaths among the prematures and also the immatures of lesser weight.

The study ascribes prematurity and immaturity to the following conditions in the mother:

A – Pathological conditions in order of importance
   i) Severe anaemia.
  ii) Toxaemias.
 iii) Complications in pregnancy and labour.
  iv) Syphilis.
   v) Acute diseases.

177

B – *Other factors*
 i) Trauma following falls, journeys, etc.
 ii) Emotional strain.
iii) Over-work.

It has been the practice in the Western countries to treat infants weighing less than 2,501 g at birth as 'premature', but studies have shown that gestation – birth weight distribution in different population groups vary. It is, therefore, preferable to use the more accurate term 'low birth weight' but, of course, the primary criteria are the physical development and maturation of the infant. Birth weight is a more significant index of foetal maturity. Helen Chase[1] has given the following data relating to New York State (excluding New York City) for 1950–52.

Table 47
RELATIONSHIP BETWEEN FOETAL, INFANT AND EARLY CHILDHOOD MORTALITY RATES (PER 1,000 SURVIVORS AMONG SINGLE WHITE BIRTHS) TO INFANTS' WEIGHT AT BIRTH

| | *Infants' birth weight* | |
	2,500 g or less	*2,501 g or more*
1. Total no. of births studied	31,102	404,835
2. Foetal death rate	127·9	7·2
3. Death rate for the period of life		
i) under 28 days	169·9	5·9
ii) 28 days to 11 months	16·5	4·7
4. Death rate at ages 1–4 years	6·0	3·3

A similar study for the United Kingdom showed the estimated perinatal mortality to be 900 per 1,000 for infants weighing less than 1,000 g at birth and 10 per 1,000 for those in the optimum survival group 3,501–4,000 g. Mortality varies widely with foetal development. Overall rates will, therefore, be affected by small differences in the birth-weight distribution. It hardly needs reiteration that some differences in birth weight are due to actual racial differences but maternal malnutrition does lower the birth weight.

[1] H. C. Chase, *Relationship of Certain Biologic and Socio-economic Factors to Foetal Infant and Early Childhood Mortality* (Part II, 'Father's Occupation, Infant's Birth Weight and Mother's Age'), Albany, New York: New York Department of Health, 1962.

178

In view of the difficulties of the Indian situation, the general causes of mortality for the neonatal group are probably more easily ascertained than for the post-neonatal group. For the first group they are: ill-advised pregnancies, in view of the health of the potential mother; frequent and ill-spaced pregnancies; absence of antenatal care; malnutrition and low vitality of the expectant mother to begin with, and malnutrition during her pregnancy; insanitary surroundings; absence of trained health visitors and midwives; the damaging and meddlesome midwifery of the dai; and last, maternal mortality itself as a cause of infant mortality.

The causes of mortality in the post-neonatal group are more difficult to establish in the absence of statistics. However, statistics of a limited nature are available for some major cities where infant death returns by causes have been more or less obligatory. About nine cities have statistics for some of the years within the seventy years under discussion and there are some random sample studies of infant mortality.

Of the former, the statistics of causes of death provided by the Bombay City Executive Health Officer for a number of years appear to be reliable in that they represent continuity of observation. A composite list from such statistics for a period of twenty-five years, 1925–50, is given below in the order of the percentage of deaths of infants due to these various causes. However, the causes are rather vague and would not satisfy the needs of modern social medicine. But it must be remembered that even in a city like Bombay infant deaths are not necessarily certified by a qualified paediatrician. The list, however, does give an indication of the infantile ailments that prove fatal in India. They are: infantile debility, malformation and premature birth; respiratory diseases; convulsions; diarrhoea and enteritis; smallpox; dysentery; measles; fevers, particularly malaria.[1]

The Public Health Commissioner with the Government of India in his Annual Report for 1931 points out:

'In India, statistics of the causes of infant mortality are not recorded, but it is generally known that premature births, convulsions, fevers, malnutrition, respiratory diseases and bowel complaints are the main causative factors in the death rate under one year.'[2]

[1] *Annual Report of the Executive Health Officer of Bombay City* (Bombay, for various years, 1925–50).
[2] *Report of the Public Health Commissioner with the Government of India* (New Delhi: Government of India Press, 1932), p. 72.

179

In his Annual Report for 1934, the Public Health Commissioner states:

'The poor nutrition of the mother, overcrowding, a high birth rate and a high maternal mortality rate, frequent prematurity and the prevalence of respiratory diseases, convulsions, malaria and syphilis, combined with widespread ignorance of infant management – all contribute to the great loss of infant life in India. The birth rate as also the infantile death rate, is high among the poorer classes, owing to the inaccessibility to them of efficient medical service.'[1]

Thus, for former provinces which constituted the general registration area till 1947, we have no statistics beyond intelligent guesses based on general practitioners' knowledge of the people and their health problems in and outside their homes.

A more reliable picture of the cause of infant mortality is provided by an inquiry referred to earlier undertaken by the Government of Madras to assess for a selected rural area the true infant mortality rate and the causes of infant mortality. The unpublished report of this inquiry is the most recent one carried out for a cohort of infants born during a particular period until they completed one year. The causes of death in this survey were determined on the basis of a detailed inquiry. 'On the intimation of death of an infant – arrangements for its immediate reporting were specially made – the Woman Medical Officer and the Health Visitor visited the party and, on intensive personal inquiry and examination of health conditions recorded at the previous visits, noted the cause of death to the best of their knowledge. The principle of sampling by inquiry method was adopted. Although the results may not be as accurate as in an ideal method, the results of the inquiry secured in the field conditions obtaining in rural areas in the State (of Madras) are sufficiently reliable for practical purposes.

'The causes of infant deaths were determined as pointed out above by inquiry soon after the occurrence of death and on examination of records of previous and present illness. Generally, inquiry was made within seven days and in several cases on the same day of death. In a few instances, the inquiry was conducted later than a week. It may again be repeated that no post-mortem examination was made, and that a more intensive inquiry enabling each infant to be observed every day during the first year could not be carried out owing to the limitations set by funds made available.'

[1] *Report of the Public Health Commissioner with the Government of India* (New Delhi: Government of India Press, 1935), p. 73.

180

Table 48

CAUSES OF INFANT DEATHS CORRELATED TO AGE AT DEATH IN THE POONAMALLE AREA, 1951–52

Causes of deaths	0–24 Hours	1–7 Days	7–30 Days	1–3 Months	3–6 Months	6–9 Months	9–12 Months	Total
1. Birth injury	1	2	1	—	—	—	—	4
2. Prematurity	5	7	5	2	1	—	—	20
3. Congenital deformity	1	2	3	1	—	—	—	7
4. Gastro-intestinal infection	—	1	8	8	15	6	12	50
5. Respiratory infection	—	1	5	9	5	1	2	23
6. Pyogenic infection	—	—	1	3	2	—	2	8
7. Other infections	—	—	1	3	3	—	1	8
8. Asphyxia	1	8	3	2	—	2	—	16
9. Malnutrition	—	—	2	6	4	4	1	17
10. Accident	—	—	—	1	—	—	—	1
11. Infective hepatitis	—	—	—	1	—	—	—	1
12. Debility	—	—	1	—	—	—	—	1
13. Causes unknown	—	—	—	—	—	1	—	1
14. Virus infection	—	1	—	—	—	—	—	1
	8	22	29	36	30	14	18	157

An abstract of the causes of infant deaths is shown in Table 48.[1]

To these must be added poor mothercraft and the woeful lack of general education in the expectant mother. Reproduction and motherhood are held to be natural processes but when they are beset by so much morbidity and mortality there appears to be something unnatural about them.

MATERNAL MORTALITY

And last, the factor of maternal mortality itself as a cause of infant mortality is often ignored. But in an under-developed country like India where the incidence of maternal mortality itself is abnormal, its relation to infant survival must not be lost sight of. Perhaps the dominating factor affecting the health and welfare of the baby is the mother. In fact, in most cases, the very survival of the baby depends upon the mother. Her health, attitude, ability and understanding are directly concerned with the welfare of the baby. It is obvious that the death of the mother during labour or before the baby reaches its first birthday has a profound effect on its survival and welfare even in advanced societies; but in India the chances of adequate care and breast feeding for an orphaned baby are remote. Foster motherhood, even when it exists in the family home, can seldom take the place of the 'natural' mother with all her care, attention and instinctive affection (Table 49).

The problem posed by the causes of infant mortality is one of multiple causation. But because the problem is multifarious it does not mean that we cannot always isolate the major determinants. Isolation of the causes does not, of course, mean that we can be certain where one ends and another begins. They are, for the major part, overlapping and interrelated. However, it will be convenient for purposes of discussion to group these causes under four categories: (a) biological, (b) economic, (c) social and cultural, and (d) medical and pathological. This is at best arbitrary and cannot be taken as a mutually exclusive and hard and fast division, for it is not always easy to decide where the economic factor ends and the cultural factor begins. However, it is convenient to examine the causes of infant mortality in India under these four headings.

(a) BIOLOGICAL CAUSES

Before we can evaluate how far biological causes are responsible for

[1] H. M. Sharma, *Enquiry into Infant Mortality in the Poonamalle Health Unit Area* (Madras: Director of Public Health, 1955).

Table 49
CAUSES OF FOETAL AND INFANT MORTALITY

Stage	Period or approximate age	Causes
Prenatal	From 0 to 280 days	
Ovum	From 0 to 14 days	
Embryo abortion (spontaneous and induced)	From 14 days to 9 weeks	
Foetus	From 9 weeks to birth	
Premature infant	From 27 to 37 weeks	
Stillbirth	Average 280 days	Maternal toxaemia Asphyxia Cranial injury Maternal syphilis
Birth	Average 280 days	
Perinatal mortality (Post-natal component)	Under 1 week	
Neonatal mortality	Under 4 weeks	Prematurity Congenital debility Congenital malformation Birth injury Atelectasis Asphyxia at birth Melana neonatorum Other causes
Post-neonatal mortality	Second to twelfth month	Measles Whooping cough Diarrhoea and enteritis Bronchitis and Pneumonia Influenza Accidents Diphtheria Scarlet fever Gastric and intestinal disorders Respiratory diseases Communicable diseases Other causes
Total infant mortality	Under 1 year	All the above

183

infant mortality in India, a word must be said about a certain amount of infant mortality being outside human calculation. That is, in the present state of our knowledge, it is possible to contend that 'under the best circumstances a certain number of infants are bound to die in the first year of life, for the young of all species are subjected to special risks, and sometimes Nature herself does not build well enough to enable the tiny spark of life to survive'.[1]

We cannot determine precisely what this 'natural' death rate is, since we cannot study mankind under purely natural conditions. On the other hand, it may be contended that Nature's apparent failures are really man's and woman's unknown faults. If all pregnancies were medically advised and occurred under ideal conditions and an expectant mother had everything from the day of conception (and in fact from the day of her own conception) to a year after delivery, such as all conceivable prenatal care, balanced nutrition during pregnancy, expert gynaecological and obstetrical care during delivery, and all care for the infant during the first year, it is theoretically possible that the infant mortality rate, in such a community of cases, might be zero.

But even under these assumed ideal conditions some slips beyond human control may occur and some infants may die. 'Just as in every packet of seeds there are some that do not germinate and in the young of every flock some which do not survive, so it would appear that mankind must inevitably lose a certain proportion of his offspring, and with his present knowledge, he cannot hope to prevent this loss.'[2] A case in point is the birth of a blue baby to apparently healthy parents under what seem to be normal conditions, that fights a losing battle and fails to survive. This may mean, of course, that our knowledge is limited on why blue babies are born, and if it is the result of hormone disturbance, why such disturbance, and so on.

However, it appears *in the present state of our knowledge* of these matters, a certain amount of infant mortality is inevitable. It is difficult to surmise what this minimum rate of death for any community is likely to be. It may be 5, 10 or 15 per 1,000 live births. To begin with, this unaccountable factor must also be reckoned as one of the causes of infant mortality. It is, however, possible that in the foreseeable future this present 'unavoidable minimum' of infant mortality, if such can be assumed, can be reduced to nothing.

The United Nations' Report on infant mortality in the course of a

[1] William A. Brend, *Health and the State* (London: Constable, 1917), p. 62.
[2] Ibid., p. 102.

discussion of the biological factors associated with early wastage of life sums up the situation admirably:

'The following discussion of some of the most tangible biological factors which affect early mortality should not be misconstrued to mean that excess mortality found to be associated with these factors represents an inevitable wastage of life. Rather, the biological factors may at times be modified by changing social and economic conditions. For example, infant mortality has been found to vary with the order of birth, which is a biological factor, the highest mortality being found among first births and the highest orders of births. A reduction in the size of families and therefore in the proportion of births of higher orders may obviously have some effect upon infant mortality. The size of family, however, often varies inversely with the degree of social and economic advancement, the largest families being found in the under-developed areas of the world. In this situation, therefore, the degree to which the biological factor is permitted to operate seems to be to a large extent controlled by the social climate even though the ultimate size of the family is immediately determined by the balance of fertility and mortality.

Again, it is known that infants born in multiple births face a greater risk of death than do those in single births due in large part to the greater frequency of prematurity among the former. The incidence of multiple births is a purely biological phenomenon, which shows no class variations, but proper nutrition of the pregnant woman and careful prenatal medical care can somewhat reduce the incidence of prematurity among multiple births.

Even if it were possible to isolate the purely biological factors, it would be difficult to determine the exact nature of the relationships which exist. Knowledge on these points is still far too meagre to permit an exact evaluation of the degree to which any of these factors affect the infant's chances of survival since most investigations so far undertaken have been limited to fairly small samples.'[1]

These observations are particularly true of India. At the outset it may be pointed out that there appears to be no conclusive evidence to show that there is any genetic or inborn factor responsible for excessive infant mortality. If a generalization is permissible it may be said that the known causes of infant mortality are almost all environmental.

[1] *Foetal, Infant and Early Childhood Mortality, Vol. 2* (New York: United Nations, 1954), p. 2.

There are at least five biological factors connected with infant mortality. They are the general level of mortality, the general level of fertility, the mother's age, and the birth order, and length of intervals between births and the previous reproductive loss.

In general, in India, as in other countries, a large share in the reduction of general mortality can be credited to the control of infant mortality, though the degree of reduction is not as significant as in many advanced countries. In fact, the percentage decline in infant mortality has not been as great as in general mortality. 'If we take the years 1916, 1917 and 1920 as our base, we find that the average general mortality decreased 27·6 per cent by 1936–40, whereas infant mortality declined only 19·6 per cent. But despite its failure to drop quite as fast as general mortality, infant mortality has nevertheless been reduced substantially according to official returns.'[1] In other words, the available data reveal that high infant mortality rates are associated with high rates of mortality at higher ages and vice versa.

What about the relation between infant mortality and general fertility? It is well known that in most under-developed countries high fertility and high mortality rates go together, while in certain advanced nations low fertility rates are accompanied by low mortality rates. This simply means, as pointed out earlier, that if more infants are born more infants will die, though it is also true that more infants will survive. Exceptions, however, are not wanting. In Holland, for example, a high fertility rate is associated with low mortality and a particularly low infant mortality rate.

This apparently simple relation between high fertility and high infant mortality can be misleading. Large families do not necessarily imply a high rate of mortality. The obvious relation between a high birth rate and a high infant mortality rate is probably due to the fact that most large families occur among the poorest classes – classes that are subject to heavy infant losses on account of alterable socioeconomic factors.

The last set of biological factors that have direct bearing on infant mortality are the age of the mother, the order of birth and the time interval between successive births. Indian data for small samples confirm the definite conclusions reached by more detailed studies abroad on the relation between infant mortality and age of mother and parity. Very young mothers, as is the case in rural India even today, have an adverse effect on infant survival. Similarly, the infant mortality rate is higher when the mothers are older women approaching menopause.

[1] Kingsley Davis, *The Population of India and Pakistan* (Princeton University Press 1951), p. 34.

In a word, infant mortality rates are greater when the mother is either very young or relatively old.

Studies based on U.S. data show that the variation of neonatal and post-neonatal mortality with maternal age follows a 'U' curve. The optimum maternal ages are 20–30 years. Mortality rates in the older age groups (40 years and over) are only about 10 per cent higher than those for maternal ages below 20 years. Table 50 shows some available data.

Table 50

NEONATAL MORTALITY RATE PER 1,000 LIVE BIRTHS BY AGE OF MOTHER AND BIRTH ORDER: (UNITED STATES, JAN 1–MARCH 31, 1950)

Age of mother (in years)	Birth–Order				5 or more	All orders
	1	*2*	*3*	*4*		
15–19	21·2	28·1	35·3	—	—	23·8
20–24	16·6	18·2	22·0	24·9	35·8	19·0
25–29	17·3	14·3	17·7	19·6	25·5	17·6
30–34	24·1	16·1	16·9	18·8	25·5	20·0
35–39	28·7	20·3	19·8	21·5	26·1	23·6
40–44	30·9	25·3	26·4	23·6	28·0	27·2
All ages	19·1	17·8	19·7	21·1	26·9	20·0

The relation of birth order to infant mortality is nearly a corollary of the relationship between the age of the mother and the incidence of infant mortality. If the mother is very young, the chances of the first baby surviving are remote. The other side of the picture is also true – the risk for the fifth and subsequent babies is definitely greater. 'Too many births to the same mother lessen the chance of survival for the children born last. The lowest mortality rates usually occur among second children. Although the risk of death does not increase substantially until the fifth birth, it then rises sharply, so that tenth or later children have only half as much a chance of survival as do second children.'[1] The series of figures from Calcutta city and those from the Poonamallee Survey bear this out.

The history of reproductive loss in previous pregnancies has a bearing on the outcome of the ensuing pregnancy. The foetal loss rate is higher among women who have had a previous foetal loss or a

[1] *Foetal, Infant and Early Childhood Mortality*, op. cit., p. 9.

neonatal death. Further, compared with women whose current pregnancy results in neonatal death, women whose current pregnancy ends in foetal loss have a higher previous foetal loss rate. In their turn, the former group of women have a higher previous foetal loss rate than women whose newborn infants survive the neonatal period. There is a similar correlation between neonatal loss in the current delivery and death among prior live-born infants. These relationships are shown by all socio-economic groups, and hence cannot be due to this characteristic alone.

Certain studies have established the existence of a high-risk group of women, who, for reasons not adequately understood at present, are more prone to pregnancy losses in successive pregnancies in the form of foetal death, neonatal death or infants of low birth weight. For instance, Butler[1] has shown that stillbirth, a neonatal death, is more likely among women who previously had premature live births. Shapiro's study[2] indicates that women who had a low birth-weight infant or a foetal loss, had higher pregnancy loss rates in succeeding pregnancies. The reasons may be of genetic origin or may fall under constitutional characteristics of individuals or socio-economic factors. The observed association may or may not imply constitutional or biological defects in the parents and may be due partially or completely to external environmental factors, which may have been operating to affect the previous infant deaths as well.

And last, it has been established that the shorter the time interval between the termination of a gestation and the beginning of the next conception, the greater the risk to the survival of the baby. In other words, the desirable interval of three or four years between births ensures optimum survival rates. The time interval between successive births is conditioned by several factors such as patterns of sexual behaviour, traditional mores concerning lactation, family planning habits, if any, and such 'involuntary' social deviations as wars and epidemics. Whatever the reason, it is now conclusively established that the greater the interval between births, the lower the chances of infant deaths. Woodbury, Burns, Yerushalmy, Baird and a score of other investigators have demonstrated this interrelationship. Such data as are available in India for small samples lend support to these findings.

[1] N.R. Butler, and D. G. Bonham, *Perinatal Mortality* (Edinburgh and London: E. and S. Livingstone, 1963).
[2] S. Shapiro, L. J. Ross and H. S. Levine, 'Relationship of Selected Prenatal Factors to Pregnancy Outcome and Congenital Anomalies', *American Journal of Public Health*, 55, (2), 268–82, February 1965.

(b) ECONOMIC CAUSES

How far economic causes, in the sense of poverty, low income and consequent low standard of living, are responsible for infant mortality has been the subject of many inquiries. A few studies in the United Kingdom, the United States of America and several European countries have established that nearly 90 per cent of infant deaths occur among the poorest families. For instance, according to Woodbury, more than nine-tenths of all infant deaths in the United States occur among the poorest 30 per cent of the families. In the United Kingdom, Titmus has shown from official data that infant mortality rates gradually increase with the descent in the social scale, which is roughly equivalent to the gradations in income groups. The Thousand Families Survey in Newcastle upon Tyne shows that infant illness and deaths and bad housing go together. Other studies in France and Canada bear this out rather strikingly.

British data show an inverse relationship between parental status as determined from the father's occupation and foetal and infant mortality. Butler's[1] study suggests that even under the National Health Service in the United Kingdom when antepartum, partum and postpartum care had extended to the entire child-bearing population, relative differences between the classes did not decrease.

That poverty is the major factor responsible for high infant mortality does not need any statistical demonstration when it is realized that family income is the end-product of such factors as the kind of employment or occupation of the father (and sometimes the mother as well), the father's literacy and educational attainment, the family's general cultural level and social status, etc.

Based upon a highly suggestive scatter of infant mortality and *per capita* gross national product for 45 countries the regression line can be represented as shown in Chart 7.

Chart 7 shows that infant mortality declines sharply from 165 to about 35 as *per capita* income increases from $75 to $375. The decline in infant mortality is more gradual and small from 35 to 22 as *per capita* income increases from $375 to $775. Thereafter for further increases in income the decline in infant mortality is only nominal.

While we do not have in India adequate and direct evidence on this question on the basis of field studies, we do have sufficient indirect evidence to establish a direct correlation between low income and all that it connotes and high infant mortality.

[1] N. R. Butler and D. G. Bonham, *Perinatal Mortality* (Edinburgh and London: E. & S. Livingstone, 1963).

189

Regression Line for Per Capita Gross National
Product(in U.S. $) and Infant Mortality Rate

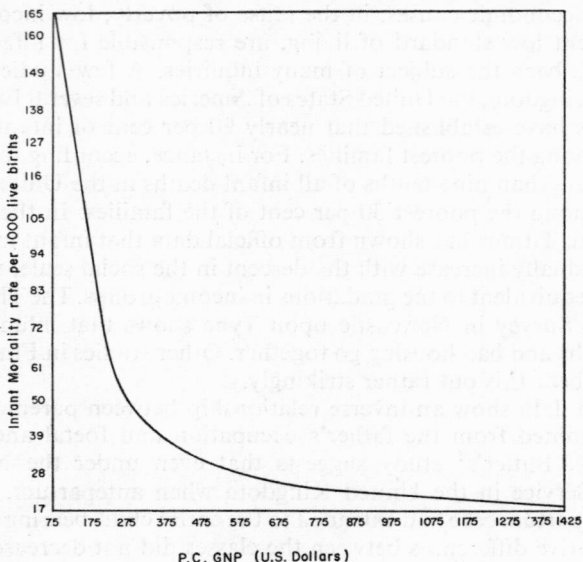

Chart 7

The monthly income of the father (and of the mother if the mother is an earner) conditions the nature of housing, diet and medical attention; the family income also reflects the occupation, class and social status of the family. The term 'economic class' in the sense of a particular income group and 'social status' in the sense of an arbitrarily evaluated hierarchy of jobs are more or less interchangeable, for in a majority of cases, the economic classification decides the social status.

That in India income, more than anything else, decides the kind of residential area and the nature of housing is clearly evident in cities. The poorest dwell in the blighted or slum areas where the city administration spends the least on amenities such as well-laid roads, potable water, and sanitary facilities such as conservancy, mosquito control, drainage, etc. The incidence of morbidity in these areas is always higher than in the better-class residential areas. For instance, in Bombay and Madras cities, the annual Municipal Administration Reports reveal that infant mortality rates are highest in the slums and cheries and lowest in the richer residential localities.

190

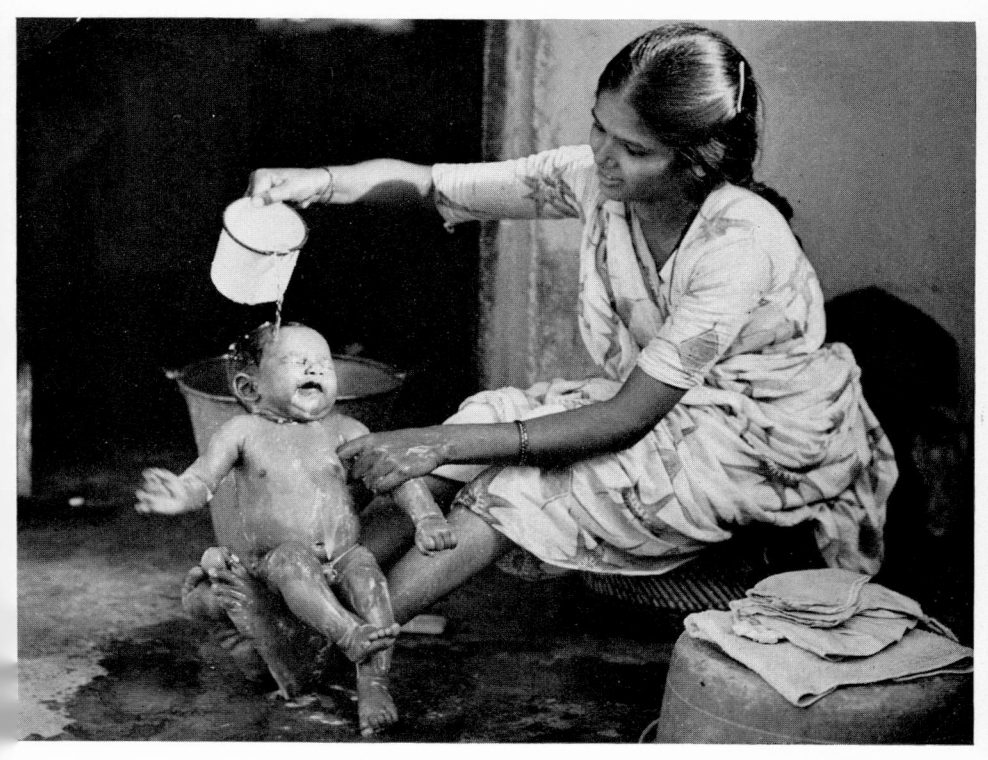

The Indian way of bathing an infant.

The Health Committee of the League of Nations started an international inquiry in 1926 into the causes of infant deaths from the medical, social and hygienic standpoints. The inquiry took into consideration the housing and social conditions of the family, the nature of work performed by the mother during pregnancy and the feeding of the child. It was carried out in Austria, France, Germany, Italy, Netherlands, Norway and Great Britain. It was found that where general conditions relating to housing and social conditions were favourable, a greater number of deaths occurred during the obstetrical period and in connection with respiratory diseases; while in districts where the conditions were unsatisfactory, the relative importance of these two causes was less marked, owing to a higher proportion of deaths due to infective diseases and digestive disturbances. The stillbirth rate tended to be lower in the higher social classes and to increase as the scale descended. As might be expected, unfavourable housing conditions appeared to have less effect on prenatal causes and neonatal causes of death than on post-neonatal causes. The point of interest which emerged from the inquiry was the absence of any one distinct factor in determining the infant mortality rate. Although the proportion of bad housing conditions to good was higher where the mortality was high than in those where the mortality was low, the discrepancy was not so marked as might be expected. The same was noted as regards antenatal care, so that lack of such care did not appear to be very much of a deciding factor. The mortality rate, therefore, seems to depend in every case on an interaction of various factors, any one of which may play a part in counteracting the other.

Income also decides the nutrition level of the family and particularly of the expectant and nursing mother.

The effect of economic conditions on mortality is so pervasive that in high mortality countries, infant mortality shows a high correlation with mortality in the later period of life. Krotki[1] obtained from the data relating to 38 territories of high fertility the following regression equation of infant mortality rate (y) on the mortality rate among non-infants (x):

$$y = 29 + 7 \cdot 7x$$

Here x is the number of deaths of persons aged 1 year or more per 1,000 persons aged one year or more. The value of the coefficient of correlation was found to be 0·65.

[1] Karol Josef Krotki, 'A Correction to Infant Mortality', *Sudan Notes and Records*, *Vol. 42*, Khartoum, 1961.

The regression equation of infant mortality rate (y) on z, total mortality rate (including infant deaths) for these territories was found to be as follows:

$$y = 17 + 6 \cdot 5z$$

The correlation coefficient obtained was 0·83. This value is higher due to auto-correlation between infant deaths and total deaths, which include infant deaths also.

Coale and Hoover[1] brought out a similar relationship based on the data from five special health units in India. The equation of the regression line obtained by them is given below:

$$y = 26 + 6 \cdot 5z$$

So vital is this association in their analysis, that they worked out alternative sets of population projections for the different values of infant mortality rate in 1951. They give the following estimates of birth rate, death rate and expectation of life at birth in 1951 for the different assumed levels of infant mortality rate:

Infant mortality rate	Birth rate	Death rate	Life expectancy (years)
200	40·6	28·4	34·1
225	43·2	31·0	32·2
250	45·7	33·5	30·2

Their argument is that an important component of total deaths is infant deaths, which would affect the estimated death rate and through it estimated birth and growth rates.

As for nutrition, infant feeding begins *in utero*. As Garry and Wood point out: 'At birth an infant is nutritionally 9 months of age. During pregnancy the mother requires nutrients for the 5–6 lb (about 2–3 kg) of developing infant and placenta; she also requires considerable quantities of calories, calcium and protein to store in her body tissues for the later production of milk.'[2] Foetal storage occurs mainly during the last three months of pregnancy, and unless the mother gets adequate nourishment during this period, infants born of malnourished mothers show a low birth weight as a result of failure of nutritional growth. It has already been shown elsewhere that low birthweight leads to higher infant mortality. At birth or during the first weeks of life the main manifestation of maternal malnutri-

[1] Ansley J. Coale and Edgar M. Hoover, *Population Growth and Economic Development in Low Income Countries* (Princeton University Press, 1958).

[2] R. C. Garry and H. O. Wood, 'Dietary Requirements in Human Pregnancy and Lactation: A Review of Recent Work', *Nutrition Abstract Review, Vol. 15*, 1946, p. 591.

tion is usually low birth weight. The mother supplies the best she can and the neonate usually has enough for his immediate needs. Sometimes later in the first year of life the rapidly growing infant has to draw to a considerable extent on his nutritional reserves; in such a case the effects of sub-normal foetal storage appear more prominently in the form of higher incidence of death. This situation underlines the greater importance of maternal and child-health centres where expectant mother's nutritional needs are attended to as against infant welfare centres.

Lack of stamina, to begin with, is aggravated by defective diet, qualitatively and quantitatively. Maternal malnutrition accounts for the high incidence of stillbirths and neonatal mortality. (Although poverty constitutes a menace to child health in many ways and particularly in the direction of malnutrition, poor nutrition may be prevalent in the homes of the wealthy as well as among the poor as a result of poor knowledge, faulty selection of foods, overfeeding, etc. as discussed later in this book.) When the inability to obtain adequate medical aid is taken into consideration, normal infantile ailments which can be controlled and cured when prompt medical attention is available, result in premature mortality. From the data available in the United States, where the material effects of class distinction are not so appalling as in India and other countries in Asia, Sydenstricker concludes: 'From data such as these, although they do not take into account heredity as a factor, it is difficult to escape the conclusion that the major determinants in the mortality of infants over one month of age is a complex of environment conditions among which the economic status of the family is a dominant factor.'[1]

According to Dr Leslie Banks:

'Studies at Toronto, Philadelphia and Harvard showed conclusively that the dietary habits of the mother affect her condition during pregnancy, labour and convalescence and also the health of the baby after birth. In the Toronto experiments, women whose diet was supplemented by milk, eggs, cheese, oranges and vitamins suffered less during pregnancy from anaemia and toxaemia, and women who had been on this diet for only a short period showed such a change in their outlook in the pregnancy itself and on life in general that an improvement in attitude and bearing was readily evident to those in charge of the clinics. These findings

[1] E. Sydenstricker, *Health and Environment* (New York: McGraw Hill, 1937), p. 84.

193

G

were supported by the Harvard and Philadelphia studies and especially noticeable was the decreased severity of nausea and sickness, toxaemia and fatigue.

The results of improved diets on labour were equally striking. In the Toronto group, the number of cases of prolonged or difficult labour was reduced, and premature births and stillbirths were fewer. The experience of the Philadelphia Lying-in-Hospital was similar, for premature births and stillbirths were both much more frequent in women on a poor diet.

It is an interesting point also that complications during labour are more marked in those on an inadequate diet in spite of the fact that the babies may be lighter in weight. This is of some importance in Eastern countries, where it is the custom to keep the expectant mother on a light diet so that she may have a small baby and an easy delivery. Here there is the danger of the vicious circle, for deprivation and seclusion may result in osteomalacia (adult rickets) with such deformity of bones that normal delivery may be impossible. The differences appear again when the nursing powers of the mother are considered, for those on a full diet can continue to breast-feed their infants whereas those on a low diet often stop after the first few weeks.

The advantages of breast feeding are so obvious that there is no need to enlarge upon them but the relationship between the state of nutrition of the expectant mother and the health of the infant is less well recognized. It is obvious that the relationship between infant and mother is so close that risks which affect the mother may endanger the child. Clearly premature births do so, but it is also true that infant deaths in the first few weeks of life and especially in the first week depend much on the health endowed by the mother. Such matters as slow progress and diminished resistance to infection are difficult to measure accurately, but expert opinion is agreed that infants of well-nourished women do better than those of mothers who are under-nourished. . . .

The precise nutritional requirements vary with each person but it is obvious that a patient with an adequate supply of first-class proteins and iron will, for example, stand less chance of anaemia than one who is not obtaining these in sufficient quantity. Similar considerations apply to the post-natal period, for adequate nutrition will help to safeguard against such conditions as anaemia and infection. The investigations in Britain of the Joint Committee of the Royal College of Obstetricians and Gynaecologists, the Population Investigation Committee and the Institute of Child Health published under the title of *Population Studies* in 1949 showed that during the first two years after delivery, 40 per cent of mothers suffer from some discomfort or disability following child birth. The complaints may not be serious but 26 per cent still had symptoms two years after delivery. The need for adequate ante-natal and post-natal care in addition to skilled attention during delivery is obvious.'[1]

The disadvantages of a new-born infant in a poor, insanitary and unhealthy environment and the family's poverty and consequent inability to afford even a modicum of adequate nutrition and medical assistance are obvious. But it is difficult to determine how far inheritance of physical constitution is associated with social class and income groups. Do the infants of the rich and professional classes inherit better constitutions than those of the poor and the working classes? While the available evidence is not decisive, the disadvantages of generations of poverty and substandard environments may be reflected in genetic endowments. This does not, of course, mean that the poor compared to the rich are constitutionally unfit, for, on the contrary, generations of exposure to undesirable circumstances might generate a better constitutional resistance to environmental hazards. Writing on the relation between poverty and infant mortality in the United Kingdom, Lord Boyd Orr observes:

'It used to be assumed that the poor represented an inferior strain of the population and that the high infantile mortality among the poor was Nature's method of eliminating the unfit. This view, which would absolve us from doing anything to abolish poverty, is not supported by facts. Where the infantile mortality rate is the highest, the survivors are of the poorest physique and vice versa. The factors which make for high infantile mortality seem to be the factors which make for ill-health and poor physique among the survivors. There is no doubt about the importance of heredity but we cannot dogmatize about inherited differences in health and physical fitness between the well-to-do and the poor until the environmental conditions affecting the health and physique are comparable in both classes. Of these environmental factors, nutrition seems to be of prime importance, because the results of the feeding tests show that when the diet of the children of the poorer classes is improved, making it more like that of the well-to-do, the rate of growth of the children approaches that of

[1] A. Leslie Banks, *Social Aspects of Disease* (London: Edward Arnold, 1953), pp. 281–3.

children of the well-to-do class, and there is a noteworthy improvement in health and physique.'[1]

In view of the importance of the practices in infant feeding and their relevance to infant malnutrition, mortality and morbidity in later life, the subject of infant feeding is examined in some detail in the next chapter.

Economic status in another sense influences the health of the mother. Inability to afford any domestic help, stretching the rupee to meet the needs of the husband, children, and last, herself, and constant worry, undermine the efficiency of the mother. While it is difficult to estimate precisely what part of infant mortality is due to maternal overall weakness, the direct relation between the overburdened mother and infant morbidity and death is obvious. 'A gradual deterioration in the mother's health would obviously react unfavourably on the infant particularly through the medium of maternal efficiency.' As Marjorie Spring Rice observes: 'It is of course a vicious circle . . . the husband and children must come first and as more of her (the mother's) energy and strength are consumed in this first care, she is obliged to omit the extra effort needed for herself.'[2]

It is a truism that poor-class wives have more children than the wives in the highest income groups. The amount of time a mother can devote to the care of her baby is determined partly by the size and range of the family. Too many children too badly spaced can only mean rationed care, not only to the children but also to the mother.

Even in a predominantly middle-class country like Sweden where extremes of wealth and poverty are largely absent, we have differentials in infant mortality on the basis of income. According to Mrs Alva Myrdal:

'When infants die, although medical knowledge knows how to prevent it, the technical development of a civilization has most cruelly out-distanced its humanitarian development. . . . The difference of infant mortality of 4·89 per cent and 1·43 per cent in the two income groups at the extreme ends of the scale is a grave accusation in a society that believes itself to be a democracy. There can be read in such figures what an uneven income distribution does to those who have nothing to do with its causes but all to do with the future of the country. Differences in family income mean

[1] *Nature* 1939, 144, 734.
[2] M. S. Rice, *Working Class Wives: Their Health and Condition* (London, 1939), p. 32.

differences in food, housing and medical care. A programme of population policy becomes a programme of humanitarian justice when it tries to equalize these very differences.'[1] It is now established, other factors being equal, that poverty is a potent cause of the high incidence of infant mortality. If this is true of relatively advanced countries such as the United States, Sweden and the United Kingdom, it is much more true of India. We have observed elsewhere how different residential areas register different rates of infant mortality in India, the lowest in the affluent and fashionable residential areas and the highest in disreputable slums. Only one factor – that of income – decides where a family lives, where in India or in England.

Along with housing go such other important factors as drainage, garbage and other refuse disposal, running water and general sanitation and hygiene. The availability of prompt, efficient and expert medical care is conditioned in India, where any kind of national health insurance is totally absent, by the ability of the family or the patient to pay. Low income sometimes connotes in India other factors such as lack of parental education and knowledge of child care and mothercraft. Thus the absence of material resources leads to a chain of related factors – all leading up to a greater incidence of infant illness and death.[2]

(c) CULTURAL AND SOCIAL FACTORS

Numerous cultural and social factors, ingrained in the traditional communal mores, affect adversely infant welfare and survival in any country, and India is no exception.

Before we discuss the cultural and social factors that have played in recent years and continue to play today a vital role in India, a factor of some historical importance – infanticide – may be referred to here. It is debatable whether infanticide can be called a social or cultural factor. But as the practice stemmed from the social mores of the people (the Hindus), and their attitude towards women, infanticide may be treated as an unhappy part of the cultural set-up of the country before the beginning of the present century.

During the last half of the nineteenth century, administrative, police, census and other official reports refer to the practice of infanticide in certain parts of India. We have also reports of the efforts

---

[1] Alva Myrdal, *Nation and Family* (New York: Harpers, 1939), p. 60.
[2] Muktha Sen, 'Maternity and Child Welfare Work in Singhur Health Centre', *Mother and Child*, London, December 1950.

of the British Government in India to put down this practice. This period is outside the limits of the present survey. However, even after the 1901 Census, occasional reference is made in certain official documents to infanticide as a cause of infant mortality. There are of course no statistics for no one is likely to voluntarily report a criminal act. There is no doubt that the practice did exist among certain groups like the Rajputs and the Gujaratis. But it is difficult to establish or deny the vogue of infanticide after the turn of the century.

According to the Indian Census Report of 1901:

'The Superintendent of Census in Bombay says that female infanticide was formerly in vogue among certain tribes in Sind and the Rajputs in Cutch. The common method of destruction was to drown the infants in vessels of milk in holes made in the ground and filled with the same liquid. Dudh Pilao given at the birth of a female infant was sufficient to secure its destruction. In other cases, female infants were either given opium or left uncared for until they expired. At the present day, says Mr Euthoven, the practice may be assumed to be of rare occurrence. The same view is held by Mr Burn in respect of the United Provinces where however a special law is still in force for the supervision of certain clans resident chiefly in the tracts adjoining the Punjab who were undoubtedly at one time addicted to the practice. In Baroda the Census Superintendent asserts that amongst the Lewa Patidars of certain Kulin villages, there are clear signs of female infanticide, and the figures which he gives certainly show an extra-ordinarily low proportion of females.

But if the practice of deliberately doing away with female infants is now confined to a limited area, and even there is perhaps somewhat rare, there is little reason to doubt that in most parts of India, female infants receive far less attention than males. It is almost universally the case that, whereas male offspring are ardently desired, the birth of a female child is unwelcome. It is especially so where the securing of a husband is a matter of difficulty and expense and where there are already several female children in the family. Consequently, even if there is no deliberate design of hastening a girl's death, there is no doubt that, as a rule, she receives less attention than would be bestowed on a son. She is less warmly clad, and less carefully rubbed with mustard oil as a prophylactic against the colds and chills to which the greater part of mortality amongst young children in India is due; she also probably is not so well fed as a boy would be, and when ill, her parents are not likely to make the same strenuous efforts to ensure her recovery. It seems clear therefore that even if they are constitutionally stronger than boys, girls in this country, especially amongst the Hindus, are less likely than in Europe to reverse the birth proportion of the sexes by a relatively low mortality during the early years of life.'[1]

Perhaps the most important factor affecting infant welfare is the societal attitude towards human reproduction in general and the role of the expectant mother in the home and the do's and don'ts that confront her during her confinement. Unfortunately, in Hindu culture as practised, and in other minority cultures influenced by the Hindu culture in India, confinement is considered ritually unclean and ceremonially impure. Therefore, several unhealthy taboos surround confinement, from the lying-in-room to infant clothing and feeding, taboos that are at variance with the available medical knowledge.

Dr K. C. Bose, a perceptive Indian medical practioner writing in 1912, presents what is really an accurate picture of the conditions attending the confinement of a woman in India. Though he is specifically describing the conditions among people in Bengal, particularly in Marwaris, some fifty-eight years ago, it must be admitted that the description is true of most other communities as well. The picture is depressing and those who know the average Indian home will note that the author has not exaggerated at all. It is sad to contemplate that conditions have not radically changed for the better during the last half a century and more in a majority of Indian communities and homes.

'From the description of their lying-in-rooms you will at once find that they of their own accord create factors of disease and death and their imprudent actions at times become culpable; with a little digression from the main subject, I would try to give you an outline of a model of a lying-in-room with its equipment to enable the conference to form an idea of the magnitude of evil they foolishly court to satisfy the whims and fancies of their elderly ladies who are supposed to understand the management of labour cases better than their medical advisers and qualified midwives.

There is no special site for the selection of a lying-in-room. In a moderately rich house the worst, the most ill-ventilated room,

---

[1] H. H. Risley and E. A. Gait, *Census of India, 1901, Vol. I, Part I: Report* (Calcutta: Superintendent of Government Printing, 1903), p. 115.

better if it stands near to a privy, is reserved to serve the purpose of a confinement room during emergency. Before the parturient woman is taken into it, the elderly ladies of the house carefully examine whether all its openings have been well covered with canvas purdahs to prevent the access of air, which kind God has given free of all charges to all creatures under the sun. After having satisfied themselves on all points, they allow the expectant mother to occupy her bed in the room. The room, in total disregard of its dimension, is unequally divided into two compartments by a screen made of old torn sacks impregnated with dust and germs of diverse kinds; the smaller compartment is reserved for the mother and the child, and the bigger one for the accommodation of the matrons and the maids of the house. A low and filthy class of women, vulgarly called "chammarnis", are engaged to discharge the function of midwives who are thought capable of doing anything necessary for the occasion and they are entrusted with the toilet of the child. You would, I doubt not, be disagreeably surprised to learn that the special function of the officious ladies of the house is to see that the mother does not fall asleep and they obstinately deny her this comfort for full five days. They consider sleep during the early period of confinement to be an evil which brings diseases and death to the mother. This practice has now been to a certain extent modified and the poor mother is allowed to sleep for a couple of hours during early morning. The mother after her delivery is laid on a charpoy with an old blanket to serve the purpose of a mattress and well covered with a quilt. All nourishment is denied to her and for five days she is to live upon a sluff made up of molasses, gum acacia and ajawan.

We now turn to consider the fate of the child. If the child is exhausted and does not cry after his birth, it is left aside and taken for stillborn. If it cries, the dai divides the cord with a split bamboo or with an old rusty knife as circumstances would allow and then ties it up with thread. The bleeding, if any, is stopped by putting a piece of cotton wool over the wound. The child is then hurriedly wiped with a piece of soft linen soaked in mustard oil and the "vernix caseosa", is thus partially removed. When the toilet of the baby is finished it is well covered up with old rags selected from the refuse of clothes used by its ancestors. The ancestral old rag is considered to be an emblem of longevity. The face of the child is also well covered with clothes and it is very nearly smothered; the poor little thing is allowed to breathe its own respired air which he gets from what is confined within the various layers of his ragged garments. A chirag is kept burning day and night and live charcoal is also kept within the room to keep it warm. The fire and the lamp consumes the greater portion of the oxygen of the room. Carbonic acid gas poisoning is not a rare accident of the lying-in-room of the Marwaris and Banias. I remember an instance where 13 women had to be dragged from the jaws of death and at this time whoever entered the room to rescue the inmates felt giddy and fell down unconscious and the whole thing was attributed to the doing of an evil spirit. The veranda of the room which forms its appendage is not void of its decoration; it is equally protected against the wind and forms the resting place of the confidential servants of the house, who stay there during the night. They are well supplied with their usual ration of ganja and bhang which they enjoy to their heart's content. Their duty is to keep the inmates of the room awake and they do this by firing Chinese crackers almost every five minutes. Their deafening sounds often prevent neighbours from enjoying rest during the night. I have a drawing of the lying-in-room and you can well imagine the amount of evil it does to the health of the mother and the child. One would be agreeably surprised to find a mother and her child come out safe after their period of confinement which generally extends to 40 days.

The Bombay Banias seldom use crackers nor do they keep the mother awake. The vagaries of these two classes of people do not cease with the conversion of the confinement room into a black hole. They also unconsciously and foolishly poison the infant by putting opium into its mouth as soon as it is ushered into the world. In rare instances the practice of giving opium to an infant as its daily ration is delayed till it attains the age of 40 days. Cases of opium poisoning often fall to the lot of medical practitioners who practise amongst these people. Amongst the well-to-do class of Mohamedans, the lying-in-room is often kept closed but not absolutely air-tight. They also put live charcoal into the room. The toilet of the infant requires special attention to enable the members of the conference to understand how far it is prejudicial to the interests of health. The "Mamens" and the "Soorties" who belong to the high-class Bombay Mohammedan domiciled in Calcutta, whose number is pretty large, bind their infants with several pieces of cloth to prevent free movement of the limbs. They take four square pieces of cloth each measuring 18 inches of the size and shape of a pocket handkerchief folded from corner to corner to form into a triangle with its base upwards and tied round the

201

infant in the following order, the first piece tied tight round the chest and upper arms of the infant, the second round the abdomen and the upper half of the forearms, the third tied round the waist and forearms and the fourth round the thighs and knees. The legs and feet are covered with a sufficiently broad piece of cloth but not likely tied up. All the knots are placed in front and they project upwards. In lifting up the child the mother or the nurse puts one hand under its neck and with the other holds one of the knots.

I would now pass on to consider infant feeding and its effects upon the health of the child. It is a popular belief that the child cries when it feels hungry and stops when it is put to the breast. Over-feeding and under-feeding are considered as relative terms having no intrinsic value of their own in the rearing of infants, and diseases and discomforts arising from these sources are often ignored. The majority of our people do not understand how the quality and quantity of a mother's milk are affected by the condition of her mind and body. A mother living under so many sanitary disadvantages cannot reasonably expect her child to be strong and healthy.

Amongst numerous diseases which infants are liable to, tetanus and convulsions deserve special mention. The one comes before the child has completed the first fortnight of its life, the other often after it. Both are preventable diseases and with a little care and attention they could be made things of the past, but the task of doing it is a problem which I fear will long remain unsolved. Cleanliness is next to godliness; but cleanliness of person is greatly at a discount in the Indian lying-in-room. With the exception of a limited number of the educated and enlightened class of people, the use of soap during the ablution of the child is almost unknown. Two baths are generally given to the child during the whole period of its confinement to the maternity room, and baths according to the ideas of the elderly ladies means sprinkling of tepid water over the head and body of the child. Head to foot bath is seldom given to the mother or the child.'[1]

Dr A. Lankester a British medical practitioner with the Government of India, writing in 1924, corroborates Dr Bose's observations. He points out:

'The practices which are found to exist are founded upon three

[1] K. C. Bose, 'Infantile Mortality: Its Causes and Prevention', *The Proceedings of the Second All-India Sanitary Conference held in Madras, 1912, Vol. II*, Simla Government Central Press, 1913, p. 324–5.

sets of ideas; firstly, the religious belief that a woman at the time of childbirth is ceremonially unclean, more defiling in fact than the lowest outcast; secondly, the belief that fresh air, whether warm or cold, is dangerously harmful for mother and child, being the usual cause of puerperal fever; and thirdly, a group of superstitious and oldfashioned theories as to medical treatment which naturally differ in various parts, but usually tend towards the extreme depression of the mother's physical strength during the lying-in period.

The belief that the woman at this time is unclean and a source of defilement to others determines the whole entourage of confinement. The room chosen must be not one which is used by other members of the household, and in actual practice it is very commonly a closet or outhouse with dung plastered mud floors and walls and the smallest possible doors and windows which are always kept ridigly shut. In some parts of Bengal a minute booth or shelter for the purpose will be constructed of matting in the backyard. The same idea dictates that it is an absurdity to use anything clean for one who is herself unclean, and so the oldest, dirtiest, coloured rags are often used, while as a matter of ordinary fact, the midwife in place of the spotless clothing protected by the sterilized "overall" of the West, delays to attend until she shall have exchanged her ordinary working costume for the dirty clothes suitable for the occasion, and used probably many times before without being washed.

Perhaps the hardest of all the consequences of this idea is the fact that it banishes the girl's own mother at the very time, if ever in a lifetime, a mother's help is needed. While, in some parts, it is permissible for the mother to enter the room on condition of her undergoing special ceremonial cleansing afterwards, special sets of clothing being reserved for the occasion; yet, in the vast majority of cases the presence of the mother is forbidden. This would matter less if the midwife was one in whom confidence might safely be placed. But this is far indeed from being the case. Dirty in habits, careless in work, and often callous to suffering, bold in treatment, with courage born of gross ignorance, and which causes untold mischief to her patients, the Indian dai belongs to a profession which, more than almost any other, is in urgent need of reform. Its very nature, as things are now, limits it to women of the lowest class while the fact that it is hereditary, one individual regarding it as her right to have the care of a limited group of families, removes the incentive of competition and rivalry. I have traced the course of a single woman of this sort for years amongst the respectable Hindus of a large city, her operations being continuously followed by a trail of puerperal fever and death. She and those like her would make frequent internal examinations, never using water to cleanse their hands until the end of the case.'[1]

The Dai

The second major social factor that is responsible for the high infant mortality in India is the role of the dai. The dai, usually a woman of the barber caste, is the traditional midwife in India. For nearly a century, Indian and foreign writers have drawn the most terrifying pictures of the person, equipment and doings of the indigenous dai. The government, medical authorities and social reformers have attacked her through the years and have pointed out her distressing role in the tragic and inordinate maternal and infant mortality in India.

The dai is an illiterate and an extremely ignorant woman, drawn from one of the most under-privileged castes in Indian society. She is divorced from any knowledge of basic and elementary rules of health, not to speak of any understanding of the rudiments of midwifery or gynaecology. Want of knowledge is one thing, but with the dai it is a worse case of rank superstition and old wives' tales. Her assistance in normal deliveries is bad enough but in abnormal cases the result is, more often than not, painful death. And yet, it is easy merely to criticize her. She has played a necessary, if damaging, role in assisting women in confinement through the centuries. Since a great majority of infants arrive in rural India where no medical personnel of any grade is available, not to speak of maternity hospitals or nursing homes, the dai has become indispensable.

The Bhore Commission pointed out that she has great influence over the common people and any plan to educate mothers on this question without the dai's active co-operation was bound to fail. Any plan to ban the dai without the provision of a suitable and trained substitute can only be disastrous. Undesirable as she is, she cannot be banished under the existing conditions. A reason underlying the hostility of the dai towards the health authorities is the fear that restrictions placed on her would deprive her of her work and the traditional emoluments she is entitled to. Secondly, a woman of her status cannot believe that her 'midwifery' is faulty and that the new methods suggested by the authorities are an improvement on her

---

[1] A. Lankester, *Lecture on the Responsibility of Men in Matters Relating to Maternity* (Simla: Government of India Press, 1924), p. 5.

own. One authority has pointed out that a mere washing of her hands before assisting in the confinements and the avoidance of interference with the normal course of delivery would improve the situation considerably. The meddlesome midwifery of the dai is as much a part of the cultural scene as the absence of trained medical personnel during labour. It is, of course, impossible to estimate how much the dai contributes to the present high infant and maternal mortality. On the basis of circumstantial evidence one may say that it must be considerable.

Illegitimacy
It is seldom recognized that illegitimate birth is a contributing social cause of infant mortality. Besides the general adequate nutrition of the mother and particularly through her pregnancy, and competent and trained supervision during confinement, a most important requisite for healthy motherhood is peace of mind and emotional stability. It is in this respect that the married mother has a great advantage over the unmarried mother. It is true that in India the problem of the unmarried mother is not of serious proportions. At least this is the popular assumption; no adequate or reliable statistics are available of the incidence of illegitimate birth for the country as a whole. When the registration of legitimate births is woefully incomplete, that of illegitimate births must be even more so. No matter what the magnitude, the problem is with us. It has been established in even fairly advanced countries – advanced in the sense of their progressive attitude towards the unmarried mother – that the death rate of illegitimate infants is much higher than that of legitimate children. This is true of the United States of America, Great Britain and several European countries. For instance, in Denmark in 1962 perinatal mortality was 24·1 per 1,000 for legitimate births and 34·1 for illegitimate births.

The reasons are obvious. The illegitimate child bears the burden of the parents' delinquency. And the child suffers from the unkind verdict that society puts upon the often unguarded, isolated and unprotected mother. While the attitude of the people and the governments towards the unmarried mother are undergoing a welcome change in recent years in most advanced and Western countries, the attitude in India still smacks of puritanical harshness and lack of sympathy. The usual difficulties are the desertion of the father and, when found, his denial of paternity. The unmarried mother has to conceal her pregnancy as far as possible. Parents and relatives of these mothers, especially when they are economically under-privileged, tend to be cruel and harsh. Then there is always the possibility of venereal disease. It is true that the rigour of these problems is sought to be mitigated by the work of such voluntary agencies as the Rescue and Vigilance Homes and Seva Sadans but the chances of an illegitimate infant surviving the first year are definitely less than those of a legitimate one.

When the baby does arrive numerous problems arise. Can the baby remain with the mother? Can she support it without any external financial aid and in the face of possible social stigma? If the baby is to be given in adoption, breast feeding will be out of the question. Even under the best possible circumstances, the illegitimate baby gets less than the conventional care that legitimate babies, even in under-developed countries, receive. Neither society nor government in India have sufficiently awakened to the need for tackling this problem.

Home Delivery
Some needless infant deaths can be attributed to the lack of hospitals' and physicians' care. In India, the reason behind this is largely economic as the country cannot afford in the present state of her development the needed hospitals, maternity homes and trained medical personnel. While this absence of hospitals and clinics is due to economic causes, the preference of the people for confinement at home, and going to the hospital only as a last resort, is a social factor. The average mother in India has an inexplicable distrust of the hospital where the atmosphere and set-up are so alien and far removed from her own home.

There is a familiar controversy in this connection on what constitutes the ideal place to have a baby – the home or the hospital. A hospital is undoubtedly the best place to have a baby, that is, if the hospital is properly staffed and operated. And though it is true that in India many hospitals, particularly the free, tax-supported, government general hospitals, provide a low grade of care, care in the home is infinitely worse because of the ignorance of the women who attend the delivery and, of course, the lack of any trained medical personnel as well as aseptic conditions. Professor Dugald Baird in the course of a discussion on the merits of home delivery versus hospital delivery points out:

'The argument that childbirth is a natural event and should take place at home does not guarantee that everything will be normal. It fails to take account of the fact that even in the most fit women

The Indian cradle hammock made out of a sari.

complications may still occur and that many women are of poor physique and health, and are far from well during pregnancy. Added to this, many homes are unsuitable for even a normal confinement and many doctors have had little training in obstetrics and in the past have learned largely by mistakes.'[1]

Western countries have advanced standards of medical education and medical care but there are notable differences in medical care and obstetric practices in cases of pregnancy, delivery and infancy. Some of them, e.g. preference for home delivery in the Netherlands, which nevertheless has a low level of infant mortality, or the use of anaesthetics in Great Britain or the U.S.A. may be due to tradition and others may be due to inertia to new ideas and to the need for accepting a compromise in view of the current conditions as in the case of length of hospital stay.

The relationships of infant mortality to medical care and obstetric practices are not clearcut. However, the general principles of maternal and child medical care are very similar in most important respects, e.g. early and continued medical care, reference of complicated cases to competent physicians or hospitals, hospitalization of complicated pregnancies and high risk groups and adequate postnatal attention of the mother and the child. India is still far away from realizing these standards. It is more than abundantly clear that in India infant mortality is substantially high due to the poor standard of medical care and unsatisfactory obstetric practices.

The Indian Cradle

Many infants die of asphyxia and this is often traced to the cloth cradle, a kind of hammock, in use in a great majority of Indian homes. The practice is to sling a sari or a bed sheet across a wooden rafter and tie the ends together. This makes a convenient cradle, for it is cheap and can be hung anywhere, including the branch of a wayside tree. The cradle is easy to operate, for all that the mother has to do is to give it a gentle push and it rocks the baby to sleep. But medical workers have pointed out from years of experience that the new-born and the young infant is sometimes turned over when the cradle is in motion and assumes the face-downward position; and when the cradle cloth is too thick, the baby experiences difficulty in breathing and, as it cannot turn over, it is gradually suffocated to death. This unhappy ending is usually prevented when the mother is

---

[1] Dugald Baird, 'The Future of Obstetrics', *The Transactions of the Edinburgh Obstetrical Society* (1952–53), p. 23.

around to push the cradle or look into it. But when working mothers leave their infants in such cradles for any length of time, they sometimes return to find babies who are no longer alive. The reasons for using this cradle are not primarily economic; it is used even in well-to-do homes. This is a part of the Indian cultural pattern and parents have to be educated out of this practice.

Mothercraft

And yet another important factor contributing to the high infant mortality rate is the ignorance of the average mother on how to take care of infants, especially when they are beset by infantile ailments which are easily curable. Mothers, unfortunately, have not the instinctive knowledge of a bird or a cat of how to rear their young. In our dirt-dominated and poverty-stricken slums, in our backward villages, and often even in well-to-do urban homes, mothers display an extraordinary lack of knowledge regarding the feeding, clothing and general care of the infant. Mothercraft is a difficult art and many a mother learns it by paying the dear price of the loss of one or two of her infants.

Absence of Family Planning

Though the relation between family planning and infant mortality is examined in a later chapter a brief reference to the absence of the family planning habit among rural and low-income urban families, as a cause of high infant mortality, may be made here. To put it more positively, the lack of both spacing and limiting births is a well-known factor in infant mortality. The urge and the ability to plan one's family is the product of economic, social, psychological and other factors but the absence of planned parenthood in India today is due more to cultural and social factors than to anything else. In India, few pregnancies are really planned. Almost all of them are accidental. Some of these unadvised pregnancies are really ill-advised in the sense that the mothers are either physically unfit to bear any more babies or the family cannot afford the necessary minimum care for another baby.

Fortunately, the country has of late become greatly conscious of the need for family planning. The Government of India as well as several state governments have recently undertaken vigorous measures to spread the family planning habit among the people through the available mass media. Knowledge of the mechanical, non-appliance and surgical methods of conception-control are being disseminated among the people. In a decade or two the total number of births in a family may become considerably less than the present number. The fewer the babies born, the fewer, of course, will be the infant deaths.[1]

(d) PATHOLOGICAL

The fourth and last category of causes of infant mortality are medical and pathological, that is, the exact physiological complication that renders prolongation of life impossible. These causes are important in the sense that they indicate the background of conditions of heredity and environment and all their attendant factors which lead to death.

Here it must be repeated again that we do not have medical certification of all infant deaths for the growing registration area, for reasons discussed earlier. Nor is there post-mortem examination and analysis available for even a small number or a representative sample of all infant deaths in India. Writing on the question of recorded medical causes of death, the Bhore Commission pointed out:

'For improving the accuracy of the registered cause of death medical certification is necessary. In our view, certification of the cause of death should be a by-product, if we may so put it, of the normal functioning of an adequate medical service for the community, because a reasonably correct diagnosis of the immediate cause of death can be given only by a physician who has attended the patient during his last illness, while recording of the remoter causes of death will require, in addition, information regarding his medical history. No short cut can, therefore, be devised for promoting the rapid growth of a reliable body of information regarding the true causes of mortality in the community.'[2]

This is all very well, but under the present circumstances nearly 70 per cent of deaths at all ages go unattended by physicians. Therefore, the medical certification of death will not be available until the country as a whole and particularly the rural areas obtain a modicum of medical services. Only then can the medical certification of death become a by-product of medical services.

In advanced countries, the pathological causes of infant mortality

---

[1] A discussion of this subject in some detail can be found in S. Chandrasekhar, *Population and Planned Parenthood in India* (London: Allen & Unwin, 1961), Second edition.

[2] *Report of the Health Survey and Development Committee* (New Delhi: Government of India Press, 1946), p. 276.

are reported on death certificates by physicians in attendance. These certificates therefore state the specific condition or disease that resulted in death. They are fairly reliable because the doctor has a statutory duty to supply a certificate and he has no special reason for making a vague or generalized statement. These may be malformation, congenital debility, enteritis, measles or any one of the infantile ailments which may prove fatal. But a plan to combat infant mortality cannot, of course, stop with mere pathological causes. The factors behind and beyond the pathological cause, that is, the predisposing and the antecedent factors, must be inquired into. These factors may range over a wide field, as pointed out already, from genetic qualities to customs and traditions affecting dress, diet and attitudes towards infants.

Difficulties, however, may arise in the statement of cause of death when vague concepts such as myocarditis or nephritis are used. This is particularly true when several factors have contributed to the death; it is rather difficult to establish the primary cause which is usually defined as that morbid condition which led directly to death. Besides this, doctors are sometimes led to be vague because they do not want to embarrass the relatives by the appearance in the public record of such conditions as syphilis.

In India, however, the situation is different. By and large, for all deaths, as already observed, medical certification of death is not available. In the case of infant deaths only a few major cities provide medical certification of death; even there the diagnosis is often perfunctory.

When diagnosed, how correct are these pathological causes? And can they be taken seriously? Even in relatively advanced countries such as the United Kingdom and the United States of America where adequate medical personnel, particularly paediatricians, are available, it has never been easy to establish the causes of infant mortality. On the basis of some experience gained in conducting an infant mortality survey in Newcastle upon Tyne, Dr F. J. W. Miller writes:

'The difficulty of diagnosing disease in infancy is so great that no opinion could be given in 15 per cent of the whole series of 272 cases. This difficulty must be recognized and it must be accepted that, in contrast with adult medicine, so little is yet known of the clinical symptoms of disease in infancy that even after the fullest clinical and pathological investigation, the cause of death in many cases may not be discovered. The remedy is the establishment of adequate facilities for research into the nature of disease in infancy, for even experienced physicians with extensive knowledge in disease in infancy are often at a loss to reach a diagnosis.

Inadequacy of training in paediatrics: the medical profession generally has undoubtedly received insufficient training in the care of the sick infant and the physiology and development of the healthy infant. This is because in England the subject has not been adequately supported by the teaching schools and there has been a lack of facilities both for training paediatricians and for giving adequate experience and post-graduate instruction to practitioners.

Failure to call medical aid: the first symptoms of illness in infants are often so slight that parents, especially in poor circumstances, frequently fail to call medical aid till their child is gravely ill, moribund or even dead. Indeed in 27 of the 272 cases a report to the Coroner was required and many of these children had been found dead in bed never having had medical attention. Only in 2 cases was an autopsy held.'[1]

Despite these difficulties, some effort should be made to demarcate the areas of infantile ailments which prove fatal. We do have a few random samples of intensive inquiries of infant mortality in some small areas like a village, a health unit area or a maternity and children's hospital for limited periods ranging from one or two years to ten years or more for certain cities like Madras and Bombay. Even these figures and causes must be taken more as near-approximation than the exact truth for reasons of the unavailability of clinical histories, expert diagnosis and laboratory facilities. But the available information is sufficient to indicate the broad areas of infantile diseases which prove fatal.

CONCLUSION

And last, the cultural base of an ancient society like that of India should not be overlooked. There are many ways in which family, caste, religion, and other social institutions, patterns of behaviour, ways of thinking, and attitudes towards children and family size and family planning are aetiologically related to infant mortality in India.

It is significant that cultural values and practices in India (no mat-

---

[1] F. J. W. Miller, 'Certification of Death in Infancy', *The Lancet*, September 5th, 1942, p. 269.

ter what their genesis or historical value or other specific significance) contribute to infant disease and death. And these centre around the three primal characteristics of all living matter: (a) The ingestion of nutrient (food supply); (b) the egestion of wastes (public hygiene and sanitation); and (c) the reproduction of the species (population growth).

(a) As pointed out elsewhere in this study certain Indian practices dilute or destroy nutrients, and interfere with absorption of nutrients in food (by frequent, routine and needless administration of castor oil or some potion as a purgative to infants) besides the undesirable custom of introducing solid foods at a relatively late age.

(b) As for the egestion of wastes, the distressing and unseemly promiscuous defecation and urination and (to a lesser extent) expectoration with the subsequent migration of pathogens to a new host via flies, water, dust, or food, constitute an important channel for the spread of disease in India affecting infant deaths.

This unfortunate situation has existed for centuries and Indian politics, economics, and public administration are such that this basic and fundamental need for modern sanitation and public hygiene has not so far received any priority in Indian development planning, either in significant financial allocation or administrative implementation. So filth continues to be characteristic of the countryside and the slums and underprivileged sections of the urban areas.

(c) As for the third factor covering the sexual mores and its cultural aspect, it is difficult to generalize in a country as vast and variegated as India. But, Dr Yankauer points out,

'A factor which seems to have received little attention in the literature is the relationship of the culturally defined purpose of the sexual act itself to fertility and family size. In Western society today, sexual intercourse, by and large, is apt to be consciously seen as the culmination of deeply felt love between two human beings and as an emotional experience whose achievement is an end in itself, even though some segments of society would consider such a purpose immoral. In India, its purpose, as formulated by the culture in which it exists, appears to be more directly related to the production of children, so that it is not apt to be viewed as an experience valuable in itself. The expressed desire of many Indian families to limit the number of children they produce, a fact revealed by various surveys, is in seeming conflict with such an observation. However, if this observation is correct, it would merely point up an ambiguity in motivation and add another cultural factor to the list of those interfering with a programme of population control.'[1]

In conclusion, the basic causes of the excess infant mortality in India are the poor nutritional status of the infants and their over-exposure to large doses of pathogenic micro-organisms and the community's excessive fertility. These three basic causes interact, supplement, and reinforce each other. Nutritional privation lowers resistance to infection and infection accentuates nutritional privation, and high infant and childhood mortality leads to excessive fertility which results, in view of limited family resources, in high infant mortality.

This complex of under-nutrition and over-infection, combined with high fertility and high infant mortality has both a material and non-material base. The material component arises out of Indian shortages of resources, capital, and technological know-how. The non-material component, which is perhaps more important, is the product of India's cultural patterns of behaviour, human relationships, motivations, and values.

The answer to the problem of high infant mortality in India is to be found both in an increase of the nation's resources, which broadly means an overall national economic and social development and a significant rise in the standard of living and level of consumption of the people, and a hastened cultural change in reproductive behaviour resulting in the acceptance of the small family norm and definitive decline in the nation's birth rate. This will be examined later in some detail.

Therefore, the problem of infant mortality in India must be viewed broadly as the product of both the material and non-material aspects of a total ancient society and not merely as the product of a group of infantile diseases which require only medical treatment and medically trained personnel for their prevention and cure.

[1] Alfred Yankauer, 'An Approach to the Cultural Base of Infant Mortality in India', *Population Review*, July 1959.

Chapter V

NUTRITION AND INFANT WELFARE

Of the many causes of illness and death among infants and children in India and other tropical developing countries, malnutrition is recognized to be most important. It is well known that malnutrition, apart from its direct effects on general health, also exerts an indirect deleterious effect by lowering resistance to infectious diseases. However, the exact magnitude of the contribution of malnutrition to total infant mortality is difficult to assess in view of other interrelated factors. Poor families in India, who constitute a vast majority of the population, are not only undernourished but live under incredibly unhygienic and insanitary conditions. While these and other factors are responsible for the high infant mortality in India and other developing countries, there is no doubt that malnutrition is a highly important factor.

A W.H.O. Expert Committee in their report on *Nutrition in Pregnancy and Lactation* (1965) points out: 'Reports from many parts of the world have illustrated a general association between low birth-weights, high foetal and infant mortality rates, and diets of poor nutritive value; and it seems reasonable to conclude that under-nutrition and malnutrition among mothers, especially in the developing countries, contribute towards impaired maternal, foetal and infant health and vitality.'[1]

These and similar considerations led an earlier committee, the joint F.A.O./W.H.O. Expert Committee on Nutrition (1962), to plead as follows:

'Expectant and nursing mothers, infants and children constitute vulnerable groups of a population from the nutritional standpoint and merit special consideration. The usual diets of women in most

[1] *Nutrition in Pregnancy and Lactation* (Geneva: W.H.O., 1965), p. 5.

214

of the developing countries have been found nutritionally inadequate, and the special needs of pregnancy and lactation seem to have received little consideration. Hence the states of physiological stress may aggravate chronic dietary inadequacy and thus adversely influence the course and outcome of pregnancy, foetal growth and the health and growth of the infant. It must be emphasized, therefore, that a high priority should be given to a study of maternal and infant malnutrition and of possible preventive measures.'[1]

The problem of the relation between nutrition and infant mortality may be examined under three convenient headings:

1. The available facts regarding infant nutrition in India.
2. The problem they pose in terms of sickness and death.
3. What can be done to solve them under the existing conditions.

Also, our knowledge of milk and food consumption habits can be reviewed from the point of view of (a) the pregnant woman, (b) the lactating mother, and (c) the infant up to the age of twelve months.

NUTRITION DURING PREGNANCY

It is well known that pregnancy is a period of great anabolic activity when the most rapid rate of growth takes place. Popular and traditional opinion has long held that the foetus develops at the expense of the mother, but this idea is incorrect: both mother and infant are likely to suffer if the prenatal diet has been poor.

Nutritional needs during pregnancy include the normal requirements of the mother, those of the developing foetus (including the uterus and the placenta) and the building up of reserves for both labour and lactation.

There is considerable evidence to show that the nutritional status of the woman before conception may be of as great importance in determining the success of her pregnancy as is the food consumed while she is pregnant. The well-nourished woman is much better able to meet the demands which pregnancy makes on her body than is a woman whose body stores of needed nutrients are inadequate either because of poor nutrition and an unbalanced dietary pattern, or a succession of unspaced pregnancies, or because her own body has not attained its full maturity as in the case of early marriage. It is unfortunate that many parents in India do not realize that girls who marry early and conceive in their teens before they have fully com-

[1] *Nutrition* (Geneva: W.H.O., 1962).

215

pleted their own growth bear the strain of the demands of pregnancy and adolescence at the same time.

The state of nutrition of the expectant mother is one of the important environmental factors influencing the course of pregnancy. Both the growth of foetal tissues and other products of conception and the metabolic alterations associated with pregnancy make increased demands on the expectant mother's nutritional requirements. Students of nutrition and maternal and child health have established through studies conducted in many countries that those women who enjoyed superior physical conditions and good diets during pregnancy brought forth babies in excellent condition. The expectant mothers who were on poor diets had a higher number of such complications as miscarriages, premature births, stillbirths, etc., and the conditions of babies delivered at full term was far from satisfactory.

The foetus growing for nine months from conception to birth depends entirely on the mother for its nutritional needs. Therefore, the mother's diet should supply not only her normal needs but those of the growing foetus as well. The quality of her food is more important than mere increase in quantity. The growth of the foetus is most rapid during the last month when it may increase its size as much as threefold and so the need for most nutrients is particularly great at this time. During this period there is a marked increase in the basal metabolic rate. The caloric need is also increased. The total energy replacement is also affected by the energy needed for the activities and movement of a larger body. The increased energy cost is about 150 calories per day during the second half of pregnancy. The Indian Recommended Daily Allowance for calories for the latter half of pregnancy is 2,300 as compared to 2,000 for the non-pregnant woman.

As for protein needs, there is no doubt that the expectant mother requires additional protein for foetal growth and maintenance. The protein has to be synthesized by the mother from the protein foods in her diet. It has been estimated that an average pregnancy needs 900 to 950 g of protein in addition to the amount normally needed by the woman before she becomes pregnant.

Concerned agencies have made varying recommendations regarding protein allowances in pregnancy. The variations are traceable to the safety factor allowance made by different agencies as well as differences in the biological value of protein foods available in the country. In the United States, the United Kingdom and much of Europe, as much as 12 per cent of the calories in the diet may be supplied by animal protein of high biological value. Many people in

India and other developing areas which are largely vegetarian obtain only 8 per cent of the calories in their diet from proteins and that too of vegetable origin.

DIET OF THE PREGNANT WOMAN IN INDIA

Several questions may be raised on this subject. What does an average pregnant Indian woman eat? Does she alter her diet as pregnancy progresses and during lactation? How does the consumption vary between urban and rural women, rich and poor women, illiterate and educated women, and women of different castes and religions? Does her diet during this period differ quantitatively and qualitatively from that during the non-pregnant state?

Further and more important, do overall socio-economic conditions, beliefs and cultural patterns, traditions and taboos, and advice from her mother, mother-in-law, midwife or physician, if any, influence her, and if so, for better or worse?

Unfortunately, data of this kind based on carefully supervised scientific dietary surveys are not available in India and one has to rely on fragmentary evidence and perceptive observations.

While the diets of pregnant women in developed countries show an average intake of above 2,000 kcal, usually 2,400–2,700 kcal, the average intake in such poor countries as India ranges between 1,500–2,000 kcal. In one survey in Calcutta, pregnant women in the richer classes showed an intake of 2,760 kcal, comparable to conditions in affluent countries.[1]

But another study, involving low-income pregnant women in Hyderabad, Andhra Pradesh, showed an intake of 1,390, 1,520 and 1,650 kcal during the first, second and third trimesters of the pregnancies, respectively.[2] And in a study of the diet of pregnant women of low socio-economic groups in South India, the average daily intake of protein was 38 g (animal protein 6 g), calcium 315 mg and iron 18 mg. The total caloric intake was as low as 1,408 whereas the recommended figure was 2,300 calories. Other nutrition surveys of groups of pregnant women in various parts of India have also revealed high incidence of nutritional deficiency and anaemias.[3]

In a study of trends of infant mortality rates in Calcutta by Mitra

---

[1] K. Bagchi and A. K. Bose, *American Journal of Clinical Nutrition II* (1962), 586.

[2] K. Shankar, *Indian Journal of Medical Research 50* (1962), 113.

[3] P. S. Venkatachalam, *Bulletin of the World Health Organization 26* (1962), 193.

217

et al., the obstetrical history of 1,502 Hindu women was analysed. It revealed that poor maternal nutrition had an adverse effect on the physical condition and development of the foetus and was largely responsible for the high incidence of prematurity which is a major contributory factor, as pointed out earlier, to the high infant mortality rate.[1]

NUTRITION OF THE NURSING MOTHER

It is well known that breast-feeding has several advantages over artificial feeding and it is perhaps the most essential step in establishing an emotional link between the mother and the child. However, breast-feeding involves a greater strain on the mother than pregnancy because the woman nourishes a fully developed and rapidly growing baby whose food needs increase day by day. If the mother's diet during pregnancy is satisfactory, she will have accumulated a store of nutrients in readiness for satisfactory breast feeding. If, however, the mother has gone through pregnancy successfully on a faulty and deficient diet, it means that she has freely drawn upon her own tissues to build her baby and she will continue to do so as long as she nurses her child. In such cases, it is imperative that the defects in the maternal diet are rectified forthwith in order that she and her baby may be saved from malnutrition and its consequences.

The diet consumed by the average nursing mother in India is far from adequate. For the majority of nursing mothers, particularly in rural India, the problem is one of poverty and lack of adequate purchasing power. Among middle-class mothers, the problem is one of ignorance of what constitutes a desirable diet. Only a small proportion of nursing mothers have the advantages of both money and knowledge and enjoy proper nutrition.

The food consumed by nursing mothers in poor Indian communities – in quality as well as quantity – does not differ appreciably from that consumed by them during pregnancy. With the exception of slightly increased quantities of rice or wheat, there is often no other change in the diet. A diet survey of nursing mothers in the low-income groups has revealed that only a small percentage of them was consuming milk.

If the mother is to breast-feed her infant successfully and without any undue strain on her own body, she must eat an adequate and balanced diet to meet the requirements of lactation. The woman who

[1] D. M. Satur and S. Bhatia, *A Review of the Work Done on Infant Mortality* (New Delhi: Indian Council on Medical Research, 1957) passim.

is breast-feeding her baby requires not only larger quantities of body building and protective foods than she needs during pregnancy, but also additional energy-giving foods to facilitate the abundant formation of breast milk. Unfortunately, the prevalent diet of nursing mothers in a majority of communities is not adequate even for a woman who does not have to meet any nursing demands.

There is an additional reason why a diet of good quality is especially important during nursing in India. Unlike in affluent and sophisticated societies, it is customary in India to breast-feed infants for prolonged periods, from six months to two or sometimes even three years. One of the reasons for this custom is the widely accepted belief that prolonged lactation is a barrier to conception.

(This belief and custom have wide repercussions which will be examined elsewhere. But it may be pointed out here that available evidence indicates that high infant mortality leads to short intervals between successive births. This is explained by the widely accepted notion just referred to that during the period of lactation the fecundability of the mother is greatly reduced, resulting in the low probability of subsequent conception of the mother. If the infant or child dies, the mother ceases to lactate and she regains normal fecundability. Thus, in a culture such as India's with high and near universal incidence of breast-feeding, infant mortality becomes a crucial factor affecting the interval between successive births. Even in a sophisticated society with a low incidence of breast feeding, the importance of the relation between infant mortality and the interval between births is not basically affected. It is plausible that parents, in the event of the loss of a child, are likely to be motivated to replace it, particularly in their early years of family building.)

The Indian mother, therefore, continues to nurse her baby into the second and often into the third year, hoping that she will not become pregnant though she has resumed normal conjugal relations with her husband without contraceptive aid. But the average mother frequently becomes pregnant again. Nevertheless, she continues to nurse the first baby until the new one arrives and occasionally even after the birth of the new baby. The Indian woman is thus in an almost continuous state of lactation – however meagre – throughout the child-bearing period of her life.

It is well known that when nursing mothers are given extra amounts of body-building foods they produce larger amounts of breast milk for their infants. At the same time, the health of the mothers also registers marked improvement. Possibly some of the body-building nutrients from the additional foods are diverted to replenish the maternal

219

tissues which have been depleted by pregnancy and nursing.

It is, however, fortunate that despite a faulty and insufficient maternal diet, the quality of breast milk does not suffer. On the contrary, it compares well with that of nursing mothers consuming excellent diets in other parts of the world. This strange fact can be explained only by the assumption that the Indian nursing mother keeps up the quality of her milk by withdrawing nutrients from her own bone, blood and muscle. Hence the need to check the drain on the maternal tissues by providing the needed raw materials from a nourishing diet to assure both optimum health for the mother and adequate breast milk for the infant.

While preparations for lactation begin during pregnancy and are dependent upon the nutritional status of the expectant mother, the period of lactation is a time of even greater nutritional stress for the mother than pregnancy. The growth and development of the mammary gland and the process of milk production in general are known to increase the need for such nutrients as calories, proteins, vitamins and water. The extent of the increase depends to some extent on the adequacy or otherwise of the mother's previous diet, the stores of nutrients built up in her body during pregnancy, her general dietary pattern and her normal physical activity.

The energy needs of the nursing mother are determined by her daily work, the glandular activity of milk production and the energy value of milk secreted. It is estimated that 1,000 food calories are required to produce 600 calories of breast milk. The fact that many Indian mothers in low-income groups have been observed to lose weight while nursing a baby may indicate that their caloric and protein needs have not been adequately met. Some evidence is available to suggest that poor Indian lactating women are in a greater state of hydration than non-pregnant, non-lactating women.[1]

While the volume and quality of mother's milk are affected by a variety of factors, the single most important one is the mother's nutrition. The W.H.O. Expert Committee points out, 'The energy in milk must be derived ultimately from the diet, but may at any time be subsidized by catabolizing maternal tissues. The energy exchanges of lactation, of course, form part of the total maternal energy metabolism. . . . It may therefore tentatively be assumed that energy supplied in the diet may be used for milk production with an efficiency of at least 80 per cent.'[2]

[1] P. S. Venkatachalam and C. Gopalan, *Indian Journal of Medical Research* 48 (1960), 507.
[2] *Nutrition in Pregnancy and Lactation* (Geneva: W.H.O., 1965), pp. 25–26.

NUTRITION AND BIRTH WEIGHT

The available evidence shows that the birth weight of most American and European babies is about 3,300 g. In most other cases, the mean birth weight is around 3,000 g, but for Indian and Ceylonese babies, the average weight is around 2,700 g.

Among homogeneous national or ethnic groups, there appears to be a simple and direct correlation between birth weight and socio-economic status; that is, the well-to-do mothers tend to have bigger babies than the poorer mothers. It is possible that differences in birth weight between two different national and ethnic groups such as British and Indians are due to both genetic and socio-economic as well as environmental factors but no evidence to separate the contributions of the factors is available.

While the influence of nutrition on birth weight and prematurity (based on either foetal growth or period of gestation) is obvious, a meaningful exploration of the relation must take into consideration such factors as age of mother, maternal size, parity, duration of pregnancy, nutritional status, ethnic origin and overall socio-economic status. Unfortunately, no such study of Indian infants is available to the knowledge of the present writer. However, the available data of the variations of birth weight from some sample populations in India is presented in Table 51.[1]

Table 51
MEAN BIRTH WEIGHTS ACCORDING TO SOCIO-ECONOMIC STATUS

Place	Population	Mothers' socio-economic status	Mean birth weight (g)	Source
Madras	Indian	Well to do	2,985	Achar and
		Poor	2,736	Yankauer (1962)
South India	Indian	Wealthy	3,182	Venkatachalam
		Poor	2,810	(1962)
Bombay	Indian	Upper class	3,247	Udani (1963)
		Upper middle class	2,945	
		Lower middle class	2,796	
		Lower class	2,578	
Calcutta	Indian	Paying patients	2,851	Mukerjee and
		Poor class	2,656	Biswas (1959)

Several epidemiological and experimental studies have yielded sufficient evidence to show that the major factor contributing to low

[1] See *Nutrition in Pregnancy and Lactation* (Geneva: W.H.O., 1965), p. 14.

221

birth weights and a high incidence of prematurity in India and other developing countries is maternal malnutrition.

A study of over 16,000 obstetric cases in South India[1] showed that the evidence of premature birth (using the criterion of a body weight of 5 lb (2·2 kg) as normal) was 8·1 per cent among the poor general ward patients as against 1·6 per cent among affluent patients admitted to the special wards.

Another study using a birth weight of 2·5 kg as the criterion found that the incidence of prematurity among infants of the low socio-economic group was nearly 30 per cent while the corresponding figures among the high socio-economic group was about 14 per cent. If a birth weight of 2·0 kg was used as the criterion, the incidence of prematurity was less than 2 per cent among infants born to mothers in the high socio-economic group as compared to 10 per cent in the poor socio-economic group.[2]

In brief, birth weights of tropical babies are usually somewhat below the standards considered to be 'normal' in Western countries. Reasons for this may vary from one region to another but include maternal malnutrition and overwork during pregnancy, malarial infection of the placenta, inadequate prenatal care, and inherited (genetic) differences in diverse human groups. However, it is probable that genetic differences are less important than previously considered, as the birth weight of the babies of well-fed, upper socio-economic groups corresponds much more closely with Western standards.

BREAST-FEEDING

The extent of lactation varies from country to country and culture to culture. It has been estimated that while in Western countries and affluent societies only about 20 per cent of mothers breast-feed their infants, in developing countries with non-European mores, breast-feeding is a near universal practice. Economic, social and medical factors contribute to these variations.

Breast-feeding begins according to the prevailing custom in the community. In almost all Indian communities, it is traditional to give a little honey to the infant soon after birth. Prelacteal feeds of sweetened water, diluted cow's, goat's or donkey's milk are usually given for the first three or four days. By the third or fourth day, a

[1] P. S. Venkatachalam, *Bulletin of the World Health Organization 26* (1962), 193.
[2] Communication from Dr C. Gopalan to the author in 1969 based on unpublished data.

NUTRITION AND INFANT WELFARE

majority of Indian mothers are able to establish successful breast-feeding of their infants.

Table 52 shows the customs affecting prelacteal feeds.

Table 52
PRELACTEAL FEEDS IN INDIA

Region	Duration	Prelacteal feeding
South India	Soon after birth	Honey
	First 3 days	Sugar water or donkey's milk
West Bengal	Soon after birth	Honey
	First 3 days	Sugar water
Assam and Khasi Hills	Soon after birth	None
		Breast-feeding soon after birth
Uttar Pradesh	Soon after birth	Honey
	First 3 days	Goat's milk
Maharashtra	Soon after birth	Honey
	First 3 days	Various decoctions
Punjab	Soon after birth	Honey
	First 3 days	Diluted boiled cow's milk

While women in Western countries are healthy enough to breast feed their babies at least for the first few months, 'the availability of acceptable and convenient infant feeding formulations and their promotion through advertising has contributed greatly to the trend of a decrease in lactation'. This situation has not proved harmful because in most advanced countries milk and baby food formulas are safe, mothers are educated and environmental sanitation and public hygiene of the community leave little to be desired. In view of this, medical and para-medical personnel apparently do not persuade mothers to nurse their babies. While breast feeding one's infant may be done at home in privacy, the exposure of the breast might be embarrassing to some women. And last, certain fashions in vogue about preserving the female form might discourage breast-feeding. Whatever the reason, the variations in the practice persist in the world.

Mother's milk is unquestionably the best food for the baby. The milk contains, in correct proportions, most of the nutrients necessary for the growth and development of the baby, in an easily digestible form. As the W.H.O. Expert Committee Report puts it,

'Mother's milk in sufficient quantity is probably the best food for infants in the first months of life. Its chemical composition,

223

particularly in terms of proteins, fats and carbohydrates, seems the most appropriate for the needs of infants. Breast-feeding, bringing about a close relationship between mother and infant, seems also to be beneficial to the physical and mental development of the child; furthermore, by reducing the hazard of infection associated with artificial feeding, it protects the infant's health.'[1]

Fortunately, infants in India, with rare exceptions, are breast-fed. It is a traditional practice among Indian women of all classes. The value of mother's milk in infant feeding has been realized in India for over two thousand years. The ancient Hindu medical classic *Charaka Samhita* emphasizes the soundness of breast-feeding.

Many are the advantages of breast-feeding. It is safe, simple and clean. As a wag put it in a lighthearted vein, it is 'cheap, on tap and the cat can't get at it'. In poor communities where people live in an unhygienic environment, milk from other sources is likely to be contaminated, resulting in bowel infections among infants. It has been found that bowel disorders are less among breast-fed infants than among artificially fed infants in India.

For the infant, breast-feeding is a happy experience. There is apparently a pronounced urge to suck in every infant and breast-feeding amply satisfies this urge. Moreover, the exercise involved in sucking aids in the proper development of the jaws, palate, mouth and cheek muscles.

Breast-feeding is helpful to the mother also. It involves the posterior pituitary hormone, which is concerned with 'letting down' the milk, and stimulates uterine contraction and involution. In addition, the emotional satisfaction referred to earlier really means that breast feeding enables the baby to derive warmth and cosiness from the mother's arms, milk from her breast, security from her presence and the mother-love which forms the pattern of the infant's psyche much as the mother's milk moulds its physique. Successful suckling ensures the psychological happiness of the mother in her knowledge that the baby is contented.

On the question of actual optimal duration of breast-feeding, Platt has summarized the position as follows:

'In deciding on the duration of breast-feeding, an all-important factor must be the diet available to the child after breast-feeding has ceased. There can be no reasonable objection to the cessation of breast-feeding in the second six months of neonatal life, if a

---

[1] *Nutrition in Pregnancy and Lactation*, op. cit., p. 26.

suitable well-balanced diet can be provided, including cow's milk, eggs and other protective foods. For the majority of infants, such diets are not available and the practice of giving some breast milk throughout the second year of life, or even longer, is therefore most commendable. One might almost say, as a challenge, that breast-feeding should be continued until something equally good can be substituted. . . . Some observers mention that in the second or third year of lactation the infant probably gets nothing but comfort from the breast; unfortunately we have only scanty evidence for the view, which I believe to be correct, that a child should continue to get milk from a well-fed mother in the second year or even longer. Clearly more information is needed; in the meantime, I think it is justifiable to recommend that some breast-feeding should continue throughout the second year of life, if suitable alternatives are not available, and that mothers should be specially nourished to enable them to lactate.'[1]

In a word, the controversy whether or not to breast-feed one's baby has not ended. In developing tropical countries where hygienic conditions are near-primitive, the feeding bottle can be devastating to the baby's health. Even in advanced and affluent countries where baby milk formulations cause no harm whatsoever, an intelligent mother should prefer breast feeding to a bottle. The advantages and disadvantages of breast-feeding have been summarized by a recent writer:[2]

Advantages

1. It is the right food in the right proportion.
2. It is cheap.
3. It is simple, readily available and correctly warm.
4. It assists in the healthy regression of the uterus and recovery from child-birth.
5. It contains some antibodies (e.g. against the common cold) and helps to keep various illnesses at bay for longer.
6. It encourages (if all goes well) the bond between mother and child.
7. It is reasonably sterile and tends to far less gastroenteritis.
8. It will mean less soreness around the baby's bottom, even though the faeces are looser.

[1] B. S. Platt, *Infant Feeding Practices – Breast-feeding and Prevention of Infant Malnutrition* (London, 1956), p. 62.
[2] Anthony Smith, *The Body* (London: Allen & Unwin, 1968), p. 199.

H

Disadvantages
1. It is often a struggle to establish. Bottles may be temptingly near at hand.
2. The baby cannot be fed without the mother.
3. Some breasts just do not produce enough at the best of times.
4. Worry, etc., can stop even a good flow.
5. Breast and nipples can be painful.

NUTRITION IN EARLY INFANCY (1–6 MONTHS)

No food is probably required by the newborn during the first 24 to 48 hours of life. During the first two or three days after the baby is born, the breasts do not secrete milk but a yellowish fluid called colostrum. Colostrum is good for the baby and will take care of its first hunger. Though the amount of colostrum available at each feed is small, the act of sucking during these days promotes the flow of milk and soon the breasts start secreting milk.

In some parts of India there is a belief that colostrum or the first milk has remained in the breasts during the nine months of pregnancy and is therefore harmful. In some Indian communities the colostrum is avoided and a little donkey's milk or water with sugar, or a little diluted cow's milk is given to the newborn. If the water or animal's milk are not clean, the community exposes the helpless infant to infection on the very first day. These mothers have to be educated that colostrum is not only harmless but it is richer in body-building nutrients than natural milk and it is possible that it may provide valuable materials lacking in milk and needed for the protection of the baby against infection.

Practices regarding the time of commencement of breast-feeding

Table 53
START OF BREAST-FEEDING

	Per cent of Mothers	
Start of breast-feeding	*Greater Bombay*	*Rural Pondicherry*
First Day	0·8	30·6
Second Day	9·9	7·1
Third Day	66·0	56·1
Fourth Day	18·4	1·0
Fifth Day	2·7	5·1
Sixth Day	1·4	0·1
Seventh and above	0·8	—

vary considerably. Table 53 presents some data on the start of breast-feeding in Greater Bombay[1] and rural Pondicherry.[2]

During the first three days of life, the infant loses about eight ounces of weight due partly to loss of water from the body and partly because of starvation due to the supply of breast milk not having been properly established. Artificial feeding to correct this in healthy children is undesirable as it may result in the failure of breast-feeding. If artificial feeding is resorted to at this stage (granting that the artificial feeding is done under hygienic conditions) the infant may subsequently prefer the easier flow of bottle feeding to the vigorous sucking necessary to the establishment of an adequate supply of breast milk.

Once breast-feeding has been established satisfactorily, many mothers are able to train the baby to regular feeding times. A baby regularly fed and receiving a sufficient amount of breast milk needs little else to keep him healthy for the first four months of life. (Thereafter, the baby needs increased amounts of certain nutrients not available in breast milk but necessary in building strong bones and sound teeth. It is here, in the fifth or the sixth month that nutritional troubles begin for many babies in India.)

There are few early lactation difficulties even amongst very poorly nourished mothers, and only very weak and premature infants may fail to suck enough for their requirements. In general, breast-fed infants show steady and satisfactory gains in weight during the first four to six months of life. Extensive studies among undernourished women have indicated[3] that despite their poor dietary intake and low nutritional status, the lactation performance of these women is surprisingly satisfactory. It was found that the output of milk in these poor mothers was of the order of 400–600 ml daily and the milk was of satisfactory quality at least with regards to proximate principles. The concentration of vitamins and minerals in the milk, however, was low. The growth rate and nutritional status of infants in poor communities were, therefore, relatively satisfactory during this period.

Though breast-feeding at regular intervals – four hours apart – is desirable and many mothers are able to establish such a schedule, it

[1] The unpublished data were obtained by S. P. Jain in the course of a survey on post partum amenorrhoea conducted by the Demographic Training and Research Centre, Bombay, in 1965.

[2] B. M. Ghosh, 'Feeding Habits of Infants and Children in South India', *Indian Journal of Medical Research*, September 1966.

[3] C. Gopalan, *Bulletin of the World Health Organization*, 26 (1962), 205.

is quite common in India to put the infant on the breast at any time of the day or even night without any regularity. This is rather undesirable because a great majority of mothers in India have to cook, take care of other children and run the home besides looking after the baby. However, no ill effects have been observed as a result of this practice. Quite possibly, on some occasions, the infant merely sucks the breasts without getting any milk and such sucking acts only as a comfort. The infant gets milk only when the 'let-down' reflex functions, perhaps ensuring certain spacing between feeds.

As we are considering here the first six months of the infant's life, it may be pointed out that all the evidence in India and other developing countries shows that the growth and development of infants up to the age of four months are extremely satisfactory even in areas and communities where undernutrition and malnutrition are believed to be extensive. It is at the fourth month when the infant begins to outgrow the average mother's supply of breast milk and when some addition to the infant's diet becomes essential that in a vast majority of cases difficulties arising out of malnutrition begin, though they do not become obvious for a few more months. Here the simple answer is that the mother should continue to breast-feed her baby but give him, in addition, some supplementary nutrition. If only Indian mothers could give their infants at this stage a few drops of fish liver oil, gradually increasing to half a teaspoonful per day, and an ounce or two of fresh orange juice or its equivalent, the baby could thrive. But both ignorance and poverty prevent the average mother from giving her baby these supplementary nutrients. In many advanced countries, infants are given free cod liver oil and orange juice but, unfortunately, in the developing countries there is as yet neither nutrition education of the mother nor free distribution of these necessary supplementary foods for the growing baby.

NUTRITION IN LATE INFANCY (7–12 MONTHS)

In India, among the poor sections of the population, malnutrition of the infant is more the rule than the exception from the sixth to the twelfth month. As observed earlier, mothers continue to breast-feed their infants into the second and sometimes even the third year. Studies on the lactation performance of Indian nursing mothers reveal that up to six months after delivery there is generally a steady rise in the output of milk. Subsequently, the output gradually diminishes, though cases are not wanting where women have produced an abundant amount of milk even as late as eighteen months after delivery. However, if the average baby is to grow and develop, some supplementary feeding is absolutely essential from about the sixth month, if not a little earlier.[1]

As for the breast milk itself, there is little evidence to show that there is any appreciable deterioration in the quality of milk during the second half of the first year or even after more prolonged breast-feeding. It has been found that the protein level of cow's milk is not influenced by an excess or deficiency of protein in the diet of the animal. The normal chemical composition of milk is maintained under widely differing dietetic conditions. In the case of women, it is not definitely established whether malnourished women whose diet is often exceedingly deficient in protein can produce breast milk which has more or less normal protein content for long periods. It is possible that there is some mechanism of adaptation. However, there is sufficient evidence to show that malnutrition during lactation is associated with a declining output of milk, particularly if breast-feeding is prolonged. In a poor country like India, one of the reasons for prolonged breast-feeding is the difficulty of providing alternate protein of good quality, which is so necessary for the growth and survival of the infant.

While breast milk may form the main or sole food of infants in the first six months of life, there is no doubt that in the second half of the year and later it can only be an important supplement to other foods. Based on Calcutta experience, Orkney points out: 'Breast milk alone does not satisfy the nutritional needs of the child (infant) after six months in this area of low income and maternal undernourishment. The wholly breast-fed infant fails to gain weight satisfactorily, his nutrition and health progressively deteriorate, until finally he succumbs to infection generally of the respiratory or digestive tract.'[2]

Thus, after the sixth month early signs of malnutrition set in, though full-fledged nutritional deficiency diseases like Kwashiorkor, Marasmus and Vitamin A deficiency are generally to be seen only beyond the first year. The onset of malnutrition in late infancy is revealed by the flattening of the growth curves in this period and the occurrence of mild signs of nutritional deficiency. Longitudinal studies of growth and development of infants and children of the poor communities in and around Hyderabad, Andhra Pradesh have

---

[1] P. S. Venkatachalam and L. M. Rebello, *Nutrition for Mother and Child* (New Delhi: Indian Council of Medical Research, 1962), passim.

[2] J. M. Orkney, 'The Influence of Feeding on Infant Mortality', *Indian Medical Gazette*, 1966, pp. 81, 150.

provided ample proof that in the great majority of poor children, signs of malnutrition set in during the latter half of the infants' first year of life.[1]

Though severe forms of malnutrition are generally seen in children only between the first and third years of age, it cannot be denied that malnutrition does contribute significantly to mortality even in late infancy by undermining ressitance to various infections.

There is some evidence to establish a direct connection between malnutrition and gastro-intestinal disorders, for one of the major causes of mortality in late infancy is gastro-intestinal disorders, especially diarrhoea. Nearly 25 per cent of deaths in infants between six months and one year in Madras State in 1961 were attributable to diarrhoea. (See Table 54.) It has now been established that malnutrition may, by itself, produce non-specific diarrhoea, over which infection may be subsequently superadded. There is enough evidence on the basis of epidemiological and experimental studies to incriminate malnutrition as a significant factor responsible for the high incidence of diarrhoea in late infancy and early childhood in poor communities.

Malnutrition is also responsible for certain respiratory infections. Studies in other parts of the world have revealed that infections in late infancy or early childhood which are usually non-fatal in well-nourished children often prove fatal in undernourished groups. In Nigeria, for instance, mortality through measles was found to be much higher among poor communities than in well-to-do groups.[2] What applies to measles may well apply to other respiratory virus infections also. An analysis of the infant mortality data would show that nearly 38 per cent of the deaths in infants between six months and one year are caused by respiratory disorders and fevers. (See Table 54.)

The mounting evidence of the interrelationship between nutrition and infection would justify the conclusion that control of malnutrition may bring about a substantial reduction in deaths due to infection among infants.

PROTEIN MALNUTRITION IN SOUTH INDIA

In 1955 an important survey on protein malnutrition of children under five years of age in South India was undertaken by the Indian Council of Medical Research at the instance of the World Health

[1] M. C. Swaminathan et al., *Paediatrics I* (1964), 255.
[2] R. G. Henrickse, *Nutrition and Infection* (London: C.I.B.A. Foundation Study Group No. 37, 1967), p. 108.

Table 54
PERCENTAGE DISTRIBUTION OF DEATHS BY DETAILED CAUSES AND BY AGE AT DEATH IN MUNICIPAL TOWNS WITH A POPULATION OF 30,000 AND ABOVE IN MADRAS STATE (1961)

	Infectious Diseases	Fevers	Respiratory Diseases	Alimentary system	Diseases of the liver	Circulatory system	Genito-urinary diseases excluding venereal diseases	Venereal diseases	Diseases of the nervous system	Accidents	Deficiency diseases	Malignant diseases	Congenital debility and malformation premature birth	Wounds and accidents	All other causes	Total
Under 24 hours	—	0·3	9·5	0·1	0·1	0·6	0·6	0·1	4·6	—	0·1	—	72·6	0·3	11·2	100·0
24 hours and under one week	0·2	1·3	5·8	0·6	0·2	0·7	0·7	0·1	7·5	0·2	0·1	—	68·3	0·1	14·2	100·0
One week and under one month	0·5	2·1	7·3	3·4	0·3	0·5	0·6	0·2	19·1	0·2	0·8	0·1	55·3	0·1	9·5	100·0
One month and under 3 months	0·8	4·2	13·5	9·7	0·7	0·5	0·6	—	33·5	—	1·2	—	23·5	0·2	11·6	100·0
Three months and under 6 months	3·5	6·0	30·3	17·5	1·0	0·3	0·6	0·02	14·7	—	2·2	—	6·8	0·2	16·9	100·0
Six months and under one year	3·1	7·0	28·4	22·0	1·6	0·3	0·4	0·1	17·5	—	1·9	—	3·7	0·3	13·7	100·0
Total under one year	1·8	4·1	18·2	11·0	0·8	0·5	0·6	0·1	14·7	0·1	1·2	0·1	33·0	0·2	13·7	100·0

Source: *A Report of the Health Conditions in Madras State* (Madras: Government of Madras, 1961).

231

Organization, under the direction of Dr K. Someswara Rao and others.[1] The children belonged to poor families whose monthly income was less than Rs.100; this income group constitutes about 85 per cent of the population.

The survey investigated infant care, feeding and weaning practices based on both clinical examinations and analysis of the available hospital records. Although infants were usually breast-fed for a long time, the quantity of breast milk was found to be low after six months, at which time supplementary foods were introduced, but these were found invariably inadequate. Weaning resulted in extreme retardation. About 20 per cent of children suffered from diarrhoea. Kwashiorkor and Marasmus were found in 1 and 1·7 per cent of the children at home. The overall findings revealed protein malnutrition of considerable magnitude.

The authors summarize the results of the survey thus:

'It is difficult to estimate exactly the prevalence of protein malnutrition syndrome in the population under survey. On the basis of the census of 1951, the total number of children under the age of 5 years in South India may be estimated at 14·2 million. As 86 per cent of families in the area have incomes of less than Rs. 100 per month, the number of children belonging to the low-income groups must be about 12 million, assuming that the birth rates among different economic groups are equal. Even taking the incidence at its lowest as 1 per cent, it may be concluded that the probable number of frank cases of Kwashiorkor in the region must exceed 120,000 at any given time.

Poverty is undoubtedly the main cause for the situation just described. As has been said, 86 per cent of the families have an income below Rs. 100 per month; this sum even if spent entirely on food, would be inadequate to meet the nutritional requirements of a family.

Customs and traditional practices are the causes of faulty-feeding practices prevalent in the communities surveyed. Inappropriate choice of supplementary foods, avoidance of protein-rich foods, especially when the child is ill, and continued administration of purgatives are only a few examples of such practices. Poverty and ignorance are also responsible for the unhygienic living conditions, the inadequate child care and the indifference to the needs of the child.

[1] K. Someswara Rao et al., 'Protein Malnutrition in South India', *Bulletin of the World Health Organization*, 20, 1959, 603–29.

NUTRITION AND INFANT WELFARE

Infections usually precipitated the frank cases of Kwashiorkor. Nearly 25 per cent of the children examined gave a history of frequent attacks of diarrhoea, while 12 to 18 per cent were suffering from diarrhoea at the time of examination. Frequently a mere attack of fever without any diarrhoea produced changes in the pigmentation of the hair or even oedema. Probably the nutritional status of the children was so marginal that even quite minor infections sometimes resulted in acute clinical deficiency.'[1]

Though such a careful and detailed survey of protein malnutrition of infants and children in other parts of India is not available, these observations may be considered valid for the rest of India from such fragmentary evidence as is available. Though fifteen years have elapsed since the survey was carried out, there is no reason to believe that conditions have improved. If anything, because of the enormous increase in the country's population without any comparable increase in resources, educational and health facilities or the monthly income of poor rural families, the malnutrition of mothers and children in India today must be a little worse.

NUTRITION AS A CONTRACEPTIVE

Better nutrition for infants, toddlers and pre-school children may prove in the long run the best contraceptive. As observed earlier, nutritional inadequacy in quality and quantity is related to infantile diseases. Better nutrition means less incidence of sickness. And less incidence of sickness means greater probability of survival and less probability of death. Less infant and child mortality means greater survival of children under the age of one and between one and five years. A healthy infant and child will live, live longer and grow up into a productive adult.

Therefore, most parents would like to have fewer children if there were an assurance that the children would survive infantile ailments, live to adulthood and possibly support their parents. It is well known that in agrarian and developing societies many parents look upon children as a kind of social insurance for their old age. In the absence of social security and old-age benefits and under the present conditions of high infant and child mortality, parents tend to have many children so that a few may survive. With an effective decline in the infant mortality rate, this situation will cease to exist. Thus, there is no question but that improved infant and child nutrition will provide

[1] 'Protein Malnutrition in South India', *W.H.O. Chronicle* (Geneva), June 1959.

233

in the long run one of the most effective means of lowering the birth rate in the developing countries.[1]

CULTURAL FACTORS AND INFANT WELFARE

While the broad cultural pattern of child care is more or less uniform all over India, there are numerous regional, religious, linguistic and caste variations. The knowledge of mothercraft and child care prevalent in India is the product of various customs and rituals, traditions and taboos. A part of this information is based on empirical knowledge and derived from long experience, but much of it has been so torn and twisted through the centuries that the present-day child care practices among a majority of Indian mothers are seldom beneficial and often harmful.

Though the present discussion is confined to the first year of life, the various customs prevalent in different parts of India, by no means exhaustive, regarding cord hygiene, clothing, bedding, bathing, charms and medicines covering a higher age group (1–5 years) are summarized in Table 55.

The role of parental, particularly maternal, attitudes towards sickness, superstition and medical practitioners in ensuring total infant welfare cannot be overemphasized. A majority of mothers tend to ignore common infantile ailments for a few days in the belief that somehow the baby will regain normal health. If there are no signs of recovery, the average mother is apt to try some household remedies recommended by her mother, mother-in-law or some solicitous but ill-informed neighbour without the benefit of any diagnosis of the exact nature of the infant's illness. Often these remedies not only fail to cure the infant but aggravate the malady. The third and near disastrous step is to consult an astrologer, magician or a village quack who promptly ties a filthy talisman round the neck or wrist of the ailing infant without, needless to add, bringing about any improvement in the infant's condition. In many cases, the last resort is to a medical practitioner, if one is available, and often his only duty is to pronounce the infant dead.

Dr Someswara Rao et al. summarize the situation admirably. They write:

'Although the areas visited were widely scattered, comparatively few differences were observed in the social customs and practices

[1] S. Chandrasekhar, 'Population Growth in Relation to Economic Development'. Paper presented at the Second World Food Congress, The Hague, June 1970.

Table 55
INFANT CARE PRACTICES IN INDIA

Beneficial and Harmless		Harmful		Neutral
Custom	Explanation	Custom	Explanation	
A. Cord Hygiene				
1. Daily application of turmeric paste mixed with hot ghee to the cord stump	Turmeric may have antiseptic value and hot ghee sterilizes it. Easily available and has an occlusive effect	Application of cow dung or black clay on the cord stump	This should be discouraged for chance of infection particularly with tetanus is great	1. Use of sharp bamboo for cutting the cord (steel is considered inauspicious). Harmless if bamboo is sterilized in boiling water
2. The cord is milked before severing it	Possibly a good practice as it may ensure the baby an extra supply of iron	—	—	2. When the cord stump drops out, it is used as a charm around the child's neck to prevent harm befalling him. This superstition must be discouraged
3. Leaving the cord stump unbandaged	According to some, this helps rapid healing	—	But there is possibility of infection	—

235

B. Clothing A dress for the baby is made from old clothes, particularly those belonging to aged relatives	May be soft if it is properly washed and ironed. The superstition behind this custom is that it will confer longevity on the infant	The newborn may be tightly swaddled in a kind of smock from neck down without much room for the movement of arms and legs	The idea behind this clothing is to let the baby struggle, enabling him to grow Not advisable	No clothes – not even nappies or diapers – are prepared before the birth of the baby as it is considered inauspicious
C. Bedding 1. The baby is put next to the mother on the same bed during the lying-in period	This may give the infant warmth and a feeling of security. It satisfies the mother to have her child next to her	Feeding the baby in the lying position	May have an adverse effect, causing *otitis media* due to the milk trickling via the Eustachian tube into the middle ear	—
2. Later on a cradle made of wood, cane or cloth (as a hammock) is used to keep the baby off the floor	The cloth cradle (made out of a sari) is cheap and can be used even by the poor	—	But if the infant is young, he may be suffocated when he turns over	—
D. Bathing 1. The infant is wiped soon after birth and bathed only on the fifth or the tenth day	Some have suggested that the presence of *vernix caseosa* protects the skin and it therefore should not be washed away	Sometimes the infant's bath involves pouring oil into the eyes, ear and nose	This may cause infection and result in lipoid pneumonia	Sometimes incense is used in the room after the baby's bath to prevent the baby catching cold by keeping out the draught
2. Daily bathing with gentle oil massage is common all over India	Desirable custom as it keeps the skin soft and healthy	—	—	—

3. No basinettes are used. The mother sits stretching out her legs on which the baby lies and is then bathed (see illustration)

Since all babies cry when bathed in this position, it may be uncomfortable to the infant

E. *Medicines and Charms*
The infant is never given plain water to drink. Boiled and cooled water is used

Desirable as in most communities protected water supply is lacking

1. Castor oil or decoction of herbs are regularly administered as a purgative

Undesirable as the strong purgative irritates the intestines and may have other toxic effects

2. In some communities a little opium is given to keep the child drowsy to enable the mother to work outdoors

Most undesirable. Infants should not be drugged on any account

3. Branding to cure colics and fits is a common practice in Andhra Pradesh

Counter irritation may be correct in principle but proves traumatic, painful and even fatal

1. The use of kajal or mai to the eyes and tilak or kumkum on the forehead for both beauty and to ward off evil spirits

2. The custom of ear and nose boring is common unless parents are sophisticated

3. The hair is not cut for a long period. The first haircut – mundan – is a religious ceremony

4. Tattooing is not common but is practiced in some communities

Charms may be considered harmless but the mother expects relief from charms and therefore postpones seeking medical aid till it is too late

of the people. The women from the poorer communities usually worked until pregnancy and returned to work within two or three months after delivery. When the mothers were at work, the babies were generally left at home either in the care of a grandmother or, more frequently, in the charge of an older child. The babies were neither washed regularly nor clothed properly. The mother might return twice or thrice during working hours to suckle the baby, but otherwise it was the duty of the older child to feed or pacify the baby whenever it cried. The feeding was usually carried out with absolute disregard of the principles of hygiene.

A sick child did not get any better attention. It was also not unusual to find children suffering from various infections – diarrhoea, extensive dermatitis or even nutritional oedema – being kept at home without proper medical treatment. They were sometimes treated with traditional household medicines or by tying to them a variety of talismans, until the disease reached an advanced state. Except for smallpox vaccination, which was forced on them periodically by the public health department, the children received no other prophylactic inoculations. This apparent neglect on the part of the parents to pay attention to the personal hygiene or the health needs of the children must be attributed chiefly to their ignorance about the proper method of care and upbringing. Poverty and the absence of facilities for medical aid in some villages were also responsible for this state of affairs.'[1]

It has been noted earlier that signs of malnutrition set in after the sixth month of the infant's life when breast milk is found to be inadequate without supplementary foods for the growing infant. This unfortunate situation really need not arise at all, for it is customary among the Hindus to hold the annaprashan (muki bhat in Bengal) ceremony during the sixth or seventh month of life when solid foods are given to the infant. And yet, it is surprising that today, despite this cultural and ritual sanction, Hindu infants, by and large, do not receive solid foods till they are twelve to eighteen months of age.

A word of explanation of this ceremony may not be out of place here. This annaprashan or traditional rice-feeding ceremony of the infant was at one time universally celebrated among all the Hindus. This ceremony is considered one of the samskaras which are ancient Vedic rites marking the transition from one period or stage of life

[1] K. Someswara Rao, et al., 'Protein Malnutrition in South India', *Bulletin of the World Health Organization*, 20, 1959, pp. 613–14.

to another. The ceremony is a family and social function involving all the members and friends of the joint Hindu family and entails considerable expense to the parents. On this occasion the baby is fed mashed boiled rice with cow's milk and sugar by a grandfather or an uncle. Relatives offer presents and blessings on the infant for a long and prosperous life.

This annaprashan ceremony may be regarded as the ancient Hindu method of celebrating the successful completion of the first six months of the infant's life; this may also represent the ancient Hindu knowledge and understanding that some solid foods, besides breast milk, are needed by the infant after his first six months.

This explanation may appear to some as more a patriotic than a scientific interpretation. While it seems certain that many ancient practices were empirically based on what are currently understood as scientific and sound principles, many customs would also appear to be dogmatic and irrational. Besides, it may be equally true that often customs and practices, beneficial in social settings thousands of years earlier, may no longer be valid today, or may have possibly become so modified that only the husk of the ceremonial is adhered to over-looking the beneficial substance of the practice. However, annaprashan was a useful practice and it is a pity that it has become an empty ritual with the infant receiving solid foods only on that day instead of from that day onwards.

THE WAY OUT

From what has been described earlier, it is evident that the fight against infant mortality has to be carried out along the lines of maternal nutrition during pregnancy and lactation in so far as the first six months of infant life are concerned and later by immunization and proper infant feeding through supplementary foods. This is necessary particularly if the infant is weaned before the end of the first year. Here the word 'weaning' is used in an extended sense for it may spread over the time the baby is partially breast-fed until he is put almost entirely on an adult diet. During this period, the baby must receive both breast milk and exogenous foods.

The problem of infant feeding after about the first six months is not so much a lack of availability of specific infant foods as of proper knowledge about the food value of the locally available foods. Mothers are often not aware of the nutritive value of certain inexpensive and easily available foods and some of the foods are so cheap that they do not appeal to them. Eggs and fish are generally taboo in

239

vegetarian families. Food values are quite often lost through improper cooking. Parental education on infant care and nutrition is a vital factor in tackling the problems of infant nutrition.

India has not yet reached the stage of providing ready-made infant foods to supplement breast milk in later infancy and subsequent months. Infant foods are derived from milk and the range includes baby foods consisting of whole powdered milk, evaporated milk and malted cereals, evaporated milk and unmalted cereals, and only cereals. Sugar, iron and Vitamin D are added and the formula is adapted to human milk. The proportions of protein, fats and carbohydrates are adjusted to suit the requirements of the growing infant.

The Committee on Child Care appointed by the Government of India in 1961 considered the supply of baby foods, demanded mainly by the middle and upper classes in urban areas (though they must be made available to the poorer classes in both rural and urban areas as well), to be insufficient. It recommended the following measures:

'(a) Manufacture of humanized milk, bottling of each feed separately and distribution by fast transport.

(b) Better dairying and supply of pasteurized milk for the use of infants in both rural and urban areas.

(c) Consideration of import of foreign milk powder since indigenous milk is inadequate to meet the requirements of local manufacturers, and the committee has been informed that State authorities do not permit the lifting of large quantities of milk till the needs of the local market are met. The import may be considered essential for feeding the children, as import of grain is considered necessary for the feeding of the whole population. At least a careful consideration of the import policy relating to the import of evaporated milk in powder form appears necessary.

(d) As a result of the recent experiments by the Food Technological Laboratories in India, some baby foods have been evolved from ground-nut and other local ingredients. But their manufacture on a commercial scale has been entrusted to private firms. The Committee therefore urges the Government that they should set up special agencies to manufacture baby foods with the assistance of international agencies like the W.H.O., F.A.O. and U.N.I.C.E.F. Practical measures should be devised at an early stage to utilize fully available foreign assistance to manufacture baby foods for children.'[1]

[1] *Draft Report of the Committee on Child Care* (New Delhi: Central Social Welfare Board, Ministry of Education, 1961–62) p. 123.

In regard to supply of fresh milk, the Committee recommended as follows:

'Whilst appreciating the work of the Protein Advisory Committee of W.H.O. and F.A.O., a recent U.N.I.C.E.F. report emphasizes the need of conserving local milk supplies and developing local supplies of fish flour, Vitamin A, oilseeds flour, meat meal and legumes. The Committee stresses the urgent need of adopting a policy where all children under three years of age are given priority for consumption of local milk supply. Whenever necessary, rationing of milk should be encouraged, and in places experiencing milk shortages, the use of whole milk for manufacture of sweets, pastries, ice-creams, etc. may be prohibited and use of whole milk by hotels and restaurants should be rationed and curtailed to bring about a distinct improvement in the supply position of milk for children.'[1]

On the question of supplementary foods, it stressed the need for searching for cheap foods, which may be readily available or manufactured on a massive scale, and recorded as follows:

'Soya beans, fish flour, cotton seeds and several other alternatives can be very extensively developed in India. The Central Food Technological Research Institute in Mysore, and the All India Institute of Hygiene and Public Health, Calcutta, have successfully conducted experiments in the manufacture of peanut milk. The Meals for Millions Association have prepared multipurpose food and Neutrio biscuits which are very rich in protein content and sold at low prices. Skimmed milk is being used, sometimes with vitamins added, for making a very large number of Indian dishes. A number of nutrition surveys have been carried out by the Indian Council of Medical Research. Experiments on the use of soya milk and cow's milk on children between 1–3 years have revealed the higher value of soya milk. The administration of 0·5 oz of calcium lactate with a daily meal has revealed its value to promote the growth improvement of weight and height of children. Koenigsfeld demonstrated in 1948 the utility of a cheap meal consisting of 2 oz sunflower oil and 1 oz wheat flour mixed into a paste, to which are added 2 oz jaggery and 1,000 cc. of buttermilk. The mixture is allowed to boil for 2 minutes. The meal was adequate to bring up healthy children, including toddlers suffering from marasmus.'[2]

[1] Op. cit., p. 127.
[2] Op. cit., p. 124.

It recommended against the use of skimmed milk for infant feeding unless it is strengthened by Vitamin A, since its exclusive use may cause Karatomalacia due to Vitamin A deficiency. It favoured the supply of skimmed milk with cod liver oil before and after weaning in post-natal clinics.

A sound nutrition education programme to improve infant feeding is perhaps the most important step in the fight against infant mortality. The vital role of the general physician and the paediatrician in nutrition education is often overlooked. It is true that the rural poor cannot easily obtain the services of a general physician and the paediatrician is a rare commodity. The total number of paediatricians in the country as a whole, as in all developing countries, is severely limited in relation to the total number of infants and children and their needs, and they are largely confined to major urban hospitals.

And when the paediatrician is available, he is fully occupied with curative medicine; the pressure of work in hospitals leaves little time for preventive paediatrics or for counselling mothers about nutrition, a task which will have to be entrusted largely to maternal and child health nurses. Because the average mother is too illiterate and uneducated to profit by any printed literature, the responsibility of medical workers to find some time to advise the mother what and how to feed the infant is great.

And last, the government should not shirk their responsibility of embarking upon an effective programme of nutrition education of the population, particularly of expectant and nursing mothers.

Chapter VI

POPULATION GROWTH, INFANT MORTALITY AND FAMILY PLANNING

WORLD POPULATION GROWTH

Today the total world population has passed the three and a half billion mark. And what is more, there seem to be no signs that the growth is likely to taper off in the near future. Population has been increasing at a faster rate during the first half of this century, and even more so during the last two decades than ever before in human history.

According to some 'guesstimates', there were probably no more than ten to fifteen million people in the whole world at the end of the Stone Age.[1] At the beginning of the Christian era, the population increased, according to one estimate, to about 250 million.[2] By A.D. 1650, the middle of the seventeenth century, the population doubled and rose to about 500 million.[3] A century later, in 1750, the number rose to about 700 million.

About 1850, a hundred and twenty years ago, the population exceeded the first billion and became 1,091 million. That is, around 1830, the first billion was reached.

At the beginning of this century, the world's numbers rose to a billion and a half. By about 1925, the population had doubled again to two billion. Ten years ago, in 1960, the three billion figure was

[1] For a discussion of an estimate of the world's population in the Stone Age, see S. L. Washburn, 'Thinking About Race', in Earl W. Count (Ed.), *This is Race* (New York: Henry Schuman, 1950), pp. 691–702.

[2] See W. W. Howell, 'Estimating Population Numbers Through Archaeological and Skeletal Remains', in Robert F. Heizer and Sherburne F. Cook (Eds), *The Application of Quantitative Methods in Archaeology* (New York: Viking Fund, 1961).

[3] Weston La Baire in *The Human Animal* (Chicago University Press, 1963), points out that the total population of the entire world in the Middle Ages was considerably under half a billion, a figure reached only in the mid-seventeenth century (p. 141).

reached. And today, 1971, the total world population according to a United Nations' estimate, is about 3·5 billion.

Thus, it took the human species about a million years to multiply to a billion in the 1830s, but it took less than a century to add the second billion, and about thirty years to add the third – an incredible rate of increase in our times. And at the current rate of increase, short of some global holocaust, the world might well have more than seven billion by A.D. 2,000 – only thirty years away and probably in the lifetime of most of us already on this planet.

The reason behind this ascending graph are simple enough. During the first million years of man's evolution, births and deaths must have almost cancelled each other for the environmental hazards to man's existence must have been enormous. Agriculture and domestication of animals are only about eight to ten thousand years old. When one speculates on the countless odds against man's existence from the point of view of modern health science, it is astonishing not so much for the million years taken to multiply to a billion, but that man proved fit and survived at all.

The second billion was easy enough, for Jenner, Pasteur, Lister and Semmelweiss launched the beginnings of the health revolution which was to save man from the micro-organisms that had sent him to his early grave through the centuries.

And this century, which has witnessed the population increase to the third billion, has seen more inventions and discoveries than in all the earlier centuries put together – in agricultural production, industrial development, and overall economic advancement. Man's control over nature and his environment and countless innovations in the health sciences have alleviated suffering, prolonged life, postponed death and increased the expectation of life at birth from about 25 years in 1750 to more than 74 years in advanced countries today.

Table 56, showing the approximate pattern of world population growth from earliest times to the present day, has been assembled from informed conjectures, speculations, estimates of various writers ranging from archaeologists and anthropologists to historians, demographers, statisticians, and United Nations and various national agencies. Give or take a few million, most writers agree on the figures.

Doubtless there are errors of many millions in these figures. The total population for even modern times may not be all correct for several countries do not have reliable periodical censuses nor regular registration of vital occurrences and some who do count their population decennially or maintain registers of vital statistics do not

Table 56
GROWTH OF HUMAN POPULATION FROM 1 MILLION B.C. TO
A.D. 2000
Man enters the cosmic scene – a little over a million years ago

Approximate Period or Year	*Total Population*
c. 1,000,000 B.C.	125,000
300,000	1 million (and the following numbers are in millions)
25,000	5
8000	10
1000	100
A.D. 1	250
1500	300
1650	565
1700	623
1750	728
1800	906
1830	1,000 (first billion or a thousand million)
1850	1,194
1900	1,608
1920	1,811
1925	2,000 (second billion)
1930	2,015
1940	2,249
1950	2,509
1960	3,008 (third billion)
1970 (estimate)	3,500
2000 (projection)	6,000 to 7,000

always have exact figures for a variety of reasons. But these figures nevertheless give a fair picture of the trend of world population growth from prehistoric times to the present day.

It took all the vast stretch of time from the emergence of Cro-Magnon man 30,000 years ago to the beginning of the Christian era for the world's population to reach about 250 million. Again, it took sixteen and a half centuries from A.D. 1 to A.D. 1650 for the world's population to double and become half a billion. But a little more than three centuries later, 1650–1960, the population soared to three billion – a six-fold increase.

No matter how one looks at this phenomenon, there has been not only a great multiplication but the multiplication itself has been at an accelerating rate.

In other words, roughly every time the clock ticks, day and night, there is another hungry mouth to be fed and taken care of. Every day more than 170,000 people are added to the existing population. That is, every year about 130 million babies are born and about 60 million persons of all age groups die, leaving a net addition of some 70 million to the existing population. This is population explosion – par excellence. 'Viewed in the long run perspective,' observes Kingsley Davis, 'the growth of the earth's population has been like a long thin powder fuse that burns slowly and haltingly until it finally reaches the charge and explodes.'[1] Or to give another analogy, Richie Calder writes: 'If we go back a million years to the hominids, or even 250,000 years to the Swanscombe Man and his Missus, the curve of population is like an aircraft taking off: for most of the time it just skims along the time axis; then about A.D. 1600, the undercarriage is raised and it begins to soar; today it is rising almost vertically, more like a rocket off its pad.'[2]

While this world population explosion is a grim reality, there is no such thing as a single *world* population problem. To different nations and regions this population growth poses a problem of varying magnitude. And present-day India is a country where rapid population growth is a real and serious threat to her economic and social advancement. By virtue of her 5,000-year-old unbroken record of culture and civilization, and as a modern major political entity of considerable area and population, her fortunes and prosperity must be of some concern to all in this shrinking, interdependent world of ours.

INDIA'S POPULATION GROWTH

In the world today, India ranks second in population numbers (Communist China tops the list with more than 750 million people) and seventh in land area. That is, with only 2·4 per cent of the world's total land area or about 3 million square kilometres (1·17 million square miles), India has to support 14 per cent of the world's total population and this population enjoys no more than 1·5 per cent of the world income. Although India is only about two-fifths the size of the Continental United States, she shelters more than two and a half times the population of the United States (204 million in 1970).

The growth of India's population from the earliest times to the present, from such evidence as is available, is not unlike the growth of

[1] Kingsley Davis, 'The World Demographic Transition', *The Annals* of the American Academy of Political and Social Science, January 1945, p. 2.

[2] Ritchie Calder, 'Is Malthus Right? The Gloomy Cleric's Gift to Darwin', *The New Scientist* (London) February 17, 1966.

world population over long stretches of time. The population earlier grew very slowly or remained stationary and began to increase rapidly only during the last half a century.

A few attempts have been made to arrive at the population of the Indian subcontinent for various historical periods on the basis of fragmentary recorded army statistics, land revenue records, and the nature of contemporary economy and diaries of foreign travellers visiting India. According to Pran Nath,[1] the Indian subcontinent's population around 300 B.C. was between 100 and 140 million. Kingsley Davis[2] is inclined to accept this figure. This is apparently a very high figure, for the total world population in A.D. 1 is estimated to be around 250 million. If, however, this figure is accepted, the population apparently remained more or less stationary for the next 2,000 years as a result of high death rates cancelling high birth rates. If one may speculate in the absence of any appropriate data, India's population in ancient times might have fluctuated much as the world's population did – very slow increase over long stretches of time and periodical loss of even the little natural increase through widespread famines and epidemics.

In A.D. 1600, the population of the subcontinent, the undivided India, excluding Burma and Ceylon, according to a rough estimate, was about 100–130 million.[3] (The world's population then was probably about 500 million.) During the next two and a half centuries (up to 1850) the numbers, according to several rough estimates, reached about 150 million – a 20-million addition over a period of 250 years – hardly an increase if the estimates are accepted.

High birth rates were probably matched by near-high death rates. Many factors contributed to the latter, among them the wars the European imperialist nations waged against the people of India as well as the wars between Indian rulers for political supremacy. These eighteenth-century wars contributed to extreme political instability, economic disorganization, famines and epidemics, resulting in heavy mortality. According to some contemporary accounts, a traveller came across a flourishing town or decimated countryside as the fortunes of war rose and fell.

However, with the establishment of British rule and the restoration

---

[1] Pran Nath, *A Study in the Economic Conditions of Ancient India* (London: Royal Asiatic Society, 1929).

[2] Kingsley Davis, *The Population of India and Pakistan* (Princeton University Press, 1959).

[3] W. H. Moreland, *India at the Death of Akbar* (London: Macmillan, 1920), p. 71.

of a measure of internal peace in the sense of averted wars, and the setting up of a skeleton of health and medical services, the population began to grow, slowly up to the turn of the twentieth century and rapidly after 1921.

The first and incomplete census of the undivided subcontinent was taken in 1871–72 and 205 million people were counted. In 1881, the second, and relatively complete census for the same area yielded 256 million. Both these census figures represent more approximations

Table 57
GROWTH OF INDIA'S POPULATION: 300 B.C. to 1971 A.D.

Period or census year	Population in millions (adjusted to the present area from 1891)	Increase or decrease in millions	Percentage variation during the preceding decade
300 B.C.[1]	About 100	—	—
1600 A.D.[2]	130	—	—
1750[3]	130	—	—
1847[4]	133	—	—
1881[5]	253	—	—
1891[6]	236·7	—	—
1901	236·3	−0·4	−0·20
1911	252·1	15·8	5·73
1921	251·4	−0·7	−0·31
1931	279·0	27·6	11·01
1941	316·7	37·7	14·22
1951	361·1	44·4	13·31
1961	439·2	78·1	21·50
1964[7] (midyear estimate)	471·6	—	—
1970[8] (midyear estimate)	550	—	—
1971 census	547·3	108·1	24·48

[1] Pran Nath, op. cit. [2] W. H. Moreland, op. cit.
[3] Findlay G. Shirras, *Poverty and Kindred Economic Problems of India* (London, 1931), p. 26.
[4] J. McCulloch, *Descriptive and Statistical Accounts of the British Empire* (London, 1847), p. 18.
[5] *Census of India, 1881*.
[6] Population figures for the period 1891–1961 are taken from *Census of India 1951, Part 1-A* and *Census of India 1961, Paper 1, 1962*. These figures are adjusted to the present area of India.
[7] United Nations *Demographic Yearbook 1965* (New York, 1966).
[8] Registrar-General's (India) estimate, 1969–70.

than exact figures. The third and complete decennial census was taken in 1891 and from this year the series became more reliable. The growth of population from 300 B.C. to 1971 is summarized in Table 57.

As Table 57 reveals, India's population grew by about 9 per cent between 1881 and 1891. But during the next decade, 1891–1901, it declined by about 0·2 per cent. This decline was due to extensive crop failures over nearly half the country covering the then provinces of Bombay, Madras, Central India, Bengal, and the Punjab. In addition to a severe onslaught of plague, the country suffered from cholera and malaria epidemics as well. Some 5 to 6 million people lost their lives. The population situation during the period is described in the Census Report for 1901 as follows:

'In a period which has witnessed two great famines of the century and the appearance of a new and deadly disease (the plague) the wonder is not that the pace at which the population has grown is less than it was during the previous ten years, when the rate of progress was more rapid than usual, but that there should have been any increment at all.'[1]

During the next decade, 1901–11, India was comparatively normal, having recovered from the onslaught of plague and the severe famine of the previous decade. But during the decade 1911–21, while India's economy was affected adversely only a little by the First World War, the world-wide influenza epidemic of 1918–19 took the lives of some twelve to thirteen million Indians. And on the heels of the influenza epidemic came extensive crop failures and these together 'wiped out in a few months practically the whole natural increase in the population for the previous seven years'. The total population in 1921 revealed a decrease of 0·3 per cent. Thus, the period between 1891 and 1921 proved to be one of slow and sporadic growth, reflecting the general unsettled conditions of life.

The year 1921 proved to be a great divide in the history of India's population. From 1921 the fertility and mortality patterns of the population began to vary considerably. Beginning from this decade, the government became better organized and was able to grapple effectively with the problems of drought, floods, and food scarcity. It undertook suitable measures for epidemic control and treatment of common diseases, thereby avoiding calamities on a national scale.

[1] *Census of India, 1901* (New Delhi: Government of India, 1902), p. 84. The census reference to an 'increment' applies to the then undivided India. The actual population figure adjusted to the present area of India shows a decrease. See Table 57.

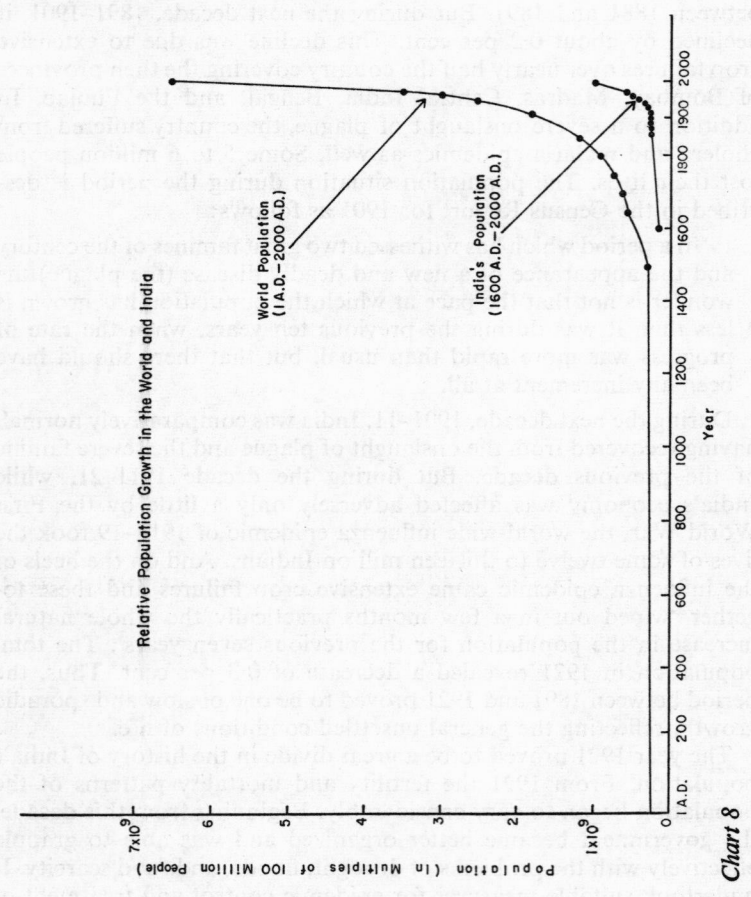

Relative Population Growth in the World and India

World Population (1 A.D.–2000 A.D.)

India's Population (1600 A.D.–2000 A.D.)

Population (in Multiples of 100 Million People)

Year

Chart 8

250

And with the advent of some economic growth and the beginnings of modernization and a relative improvement in medical facilities, mortality rates began to register a steady decline. Just at a time when most Western nations were approaching population stability, India began to embark on what has proved to be an exceedingly rapid expansion. In a sense, after 1921 India's population became quasi-stable with a declining mortality and a stationary or slowly declining fertility resulting in an ever-increasing widening of the demographic gap.

In brief, India's population increased from 236 million in 1891 to 251 million in 1921 – only a 15 million increase in 30 years because of famines, epidemics, and the worldwide influenza epidemic of 1918–19. But during the next thirty years the numbers increased not by another 15 million but by 110 million. And during the succeeding decade, 1951–61, the population increased by 78·1 million. According to an estimate made by the Government of India, the forthcoming 1971 census is expected to reveal more than 550 million. The 1971 Census results announced recently reveal a total of 547,367,926; and this means an addition of more than 108 millions during the last decade 1961–1971.

REASONS FOR GROWTH

What are the factors behind the great increase in numbers during the last half a century?

To begin with, India had a large population and even a small and nominal rate of increase would have yielded an impressive addition decade after decade.

Second, a part of the explanation of the country's population growth is to be found in her formerly relatively high birth rates and recently rapidly declining death rates. These in themselves are products of the nation's age and sex composition. India has a young population, for according to the 1961 Census, 40·2 per cent of the total population was in the 0–14 age group, 47·9 per cent in 15–49, and 11·9 per cent in the 50 and over age groups. Thus, young and more fecund people predominate in the population. If all these young people marry, as they are bound to in view of the universality of the married state of India, the population numbers are bound to increase at an even higher rate than they have in the past.

Third, this well known feature of the universality of the married state in India, documented and recorded in the census reports during the last hundred years, reveals that almost everyone in India, sooner or later, usually sooner, gets married. Marriage is not merely a

251

necessary social institution but a quasi-religious duty. As an individual's economic security or emotional maturity are seldom a prerequisite to marriage and as there is no individual choice, by and large, in obtaining a husband or wife, there is no economic or emotional deterrent to marriage. Thus, bachelors and spinsters are a rare phenomenon in India and nearly every adult male and female in the country participates in reproduction.

Fourth, early marriages are still the rule in India. True, child marriages have virtually disappeared. But though forty years have elapsed since the Child Marriage Restraint Act (the Sarada Act) was passed in 1929 and though the age of consent for girls was raised from 14 to 15 in the Hindu Code in 1956, millions of girls still marry early. Nearly 80 per cent of all teenagers in the rural areas are married and even the latest 1961 enumeration revealed several million boys and girls married below the age of consent (18 for males and 15 for females). It has been estimated that the mean age at marriage of Indian females of all religious and caste groups has increased from 13 to 16 in this century and it is difficult to foresee how many years it will take to raise it to 18 or 20 years.

Fifth, some relief from population pressure was obtained in the past from the traditional, if obscurantist, feature of the Hindu social scene – the social (not legal) ban on widow remarriage. During the last decade, there were some thirty million widows of all ages (including 'virgin widows' who are really widowed child brides) who normally do not marry. Even widowers do not marry widows as a rule. But India is fast changing and, of late, some men, both bachelors and widowers, are coming forward to marry eligible and unencumbered widows. This welcome feature of modernization which negates the traditional custom of banning widow remarriage and withdrawing these women from participating in reproduction contributes its small share to the population problem. In the years to come it is possible that this 'social infertility' may altogether disappear from Indian society.

Sixth, as long as India continues to be predominantly an agrarian economy based on traditional unmechanized subsistence agriculture with only small beginnings of modernization through the so-called Green Revolution, the need for a large rural labour force will continue to exist. This need is largely responsible for the desire for sons which has become through the centuries a fixed social and cultural attitude.

Further, the fact that there are neither old age nor retirement benefits nor any kind of social security for the vast agricultural population bolsters, as we shall discuss later, the strong desire for sons who would grow up and not only support the parents in their old age but survive and succeed to the farmstead.

The seventh factor is the beginnings of the health revolution in India; perhaps the major decisive factor behind the growth of India's population, is the decline in the nation's death rate. The estimated death rate shows a steady decline from 42·6 per 1,000 in 1901 to 14 per 1,000 in 1970. Even more revealing is the decline in the infant mortality rate during the same period and enough has been said already about this earlier. The child and maternal mortality rates have also registered similar decreases during the last half-century. And the last decade has witnessed a greater decline in the overall death rate than in the entire preceding half-century.

This dramatic and definitive decline in the death rate has been brought about by the Government's action in various directions: An increase in the number of medical colleges (from 20 in 1947 to 94 in 1971) and related institutions, and a consequent increase in trained medical and para-medical personnel; D.D.T. spraying for malaria eradication; B.C.G. vaccination for tuberculosis; the services of trained midwives; the spread of a modicum of health education and services in remote areas; American technical aid, particularly in malaria eradication; and the overall assistance of the World Health Organization and the Colombo Plan.

The near-successful attack on such diseases as malaria and tuberculosis has a kind of cumulative effect which has not been adequately studied in the developing countries. For example, malaria not only kills but leaves those victims who do not succumb quite debilitated, unproductive, and an easy prey to numerous infections. Therefore, malaria eradication not only lowers the death rate, but raises the individual's overall resistance to disease, and what is more, increases the birth rate. In response to all this, not only has the general death rate declined but the expectation of life at birth has increased from 23 years in 1931 to 50 in 1970, leading eventually to a rise in the birth rate.

A word of caution is necessary here, for all this should not be construed to mean that a health revolution has swept over India in recent years. But the general picture today is considerably better than that of, say, some 25 years earlier. While it is a common cliché to say that the decline in the death rate is due to modern medicine and vaccine, it is not quite true. This was not so in Europe nor is it true of India today. In both areas, the death rate began to fall long before modern drugs were available. Even today, modern medicines cannot

253

be said to be available in India where there is only one qualified physician per 50,000 rural population, and where the national antibiotic supply is only two tablets of sulpha *per capita* per year (less than a tenth of the dose required to treat a case of dysentery in a population which suffers from multiple attacks of dysentery yearly). The available data on the number of hospital beds, the doctor–population ratio, the total drugs manufactured and imported into India and the percentage of population which does not enjoy any clinical consultation (modern medicine) clearly show that India is yet to experience the modern health revolution.

Without denigrating the role of modern medicine, the fall in the death rate in India must be attributed to far more fundamental measures. They are the new river-valley projects which have brought down the incidence of floods and droughts, compared to uncontrolled conditions of twenty years ago, the extension of the irrigation system and the overall increase in agricultural production as a result of the Green Revolution.

There is also the development of better communications and transportation – railways and bus services – enabling the rapid movement of food and the import of large amounts of food grains from the United States and other friendly countries which have prevented or alleviated such famine conditions as arose in Bihar in 1968–69 and facilitated an overall improvement of general living conditions.

And another factor of considerable importance is governmental and political stability in India. The transfer of political power from Britain to India has been relatively smooth reflecting credit on both sides. And the political evolution during the last nearly quarter century has revealed both the adaptability of Indian political leadership to modern democratic and parliamentary institutions as well as the resilience of the Indian constitution. While sporadic riots and regional revolts have not been wanting, India has been spared the upheavals – both military dictatorships and running civil wars – that some Asian countries have had to endure after their political liberation. This stability is also partly responsible for India's population growth.

And the last contributory factor to the growth of India's population has been the absence of any effective widespread family planning, particularly among the rural population. This will be examined in some detail later in this chapter. But it may be pointed out that despite considerable efforts, particularly during the last five years, family planning has not yet become a part of the marital mores of the more than a hundred million married couples in India.

THE FUTURE GROWTH OF INDIA'S POPULATION

Several official and non-official forecasts and projections of India's population on the basis of various assumptions have been made. The estimates vary according to the assumptions made as well as the base population taken for computation and as such they are not all comparable. This is an area full of pitfalls even for countries where data are relatively reliable and where sophisticated techniques have been adopted. Human reproductive behaviour patterns, being a function of many variables, are not easily predictable. All that can be said is that mortality rates are likely to decline further because death control measures are naturally popular with the people and the Government. While there is no doubt that birth control will receive increasing support from the Government (hoping that a future government is not pro-natalist!), it may not easily permeate all layers of population. But if current levels of fertility and mortality continue and the annual rate of growth hovers around 2·5 per cent, India's population can reach a billion people or a little less, by A.D. 2000. Anything more precise would be more in the nature of a misleading mathematical exercise than a privileged peep into the future.

THE ECONOMIC AND SOCIAL IMPLICATIONS OF POPULATION GROWTH

It is neither possible nor necessary to examine here all the economic and social implications of India's population growth. However, the implications in terms of four major indices of overall development – food supply, educational facilities, job opportunities and the *per capita* income – may be reviewed.

The total food production in India increased from about 50 million tons in 1950–51 to about 96 million tons in 1968–69. While the net availability of food grains increased by 43 per cent between 1951–69, the *per capita* net availability of food grains increased by only 18 per cent for the same period. The reason is, of course, the growth of India's population.

While the minimum requirement of nutritional intake according to the Food and Agricultural Organization is 18 ounces per day, the *per capita* net availability of food grains in 1968 in India was 14·4 ounces. Thus, the average Indian consumes only 82 per cent of the needed calorie requirements. This deficiency falls upon the poorer section of the population and such vulnerable groups as women and children. On the basis of certain regional nutrition surveys it has been

255

estimated that two out of every four persons in India are malnourished while one in every four appears to be underfed. This means that only about 250 million Indians receive adequate nutrition.

Despite the beginnings of the Green Revolution, the problem of food supply has not been solved. On the basis of minimum nutritional needs, it has been estimated that India may have to import about 135 million tons of food grains by 1975–76 for an estimated population of about 603 million. This would mean several things. India will not be able to reach self-sufficiency in food by 1975 (though the political slogan 'No foreign bread' has been the cry for some twenty years) unless she is able to double her efforts in total national agricultural production. This can be done only at the cost of industrial development, which may not be advisable. Therefore, valuable foreign exchange will continue to be spent to cover the importation of food grains and the Indian economy will continue to be more 'extractive' than 'productive'.

As for educational facilities, the picture is almost the same as in food production – considerable progress but poor *per capita* share. The number of universities increased from 16 in 1947 to 72 in 1970 (and the hundreds of liberal arts, science, agricultural, medical, engineering, law, veterinary, and other professional colleges affiliated to these universities have increased proportionately) – an impressive achievement. But thousands of students with the requisite academic credentials continue to find it difficult to secure admission to these colleges. The increased facilities – which means physical plant, libraries, laboratories, and other equipment and trained teachers – simply do not keep pace with the needs of the growing population.

Equally instructive is the position of the labour force. The economic development of any country depends to a large extent on the quantity and quality of the labour force available to carry out various developmental projects. These, in turn, are determined by the country's population size, growth rate, structure, and other characteristics (Chart 9).

India, as noted earlier, has an unfavourable age structure with a large proportion of juvenile population, resulting in a high dependency ratio. Because of this low ratio of adults to children, India's labour force has been increasing at a slower rate as compared to total population increase. Besides, a large proportion of children in the population prevent women from entering the labour force.

While India's labour force in relation to her total population is small, the number of people added each year to it, in absolute terms, is large. And such large absolute additions to the labour force have

Patterns of Growth in Population,
Net Availability and Per Capita Availability of Food Grains: 1951- 6 7
Base: 1950-51 = 100

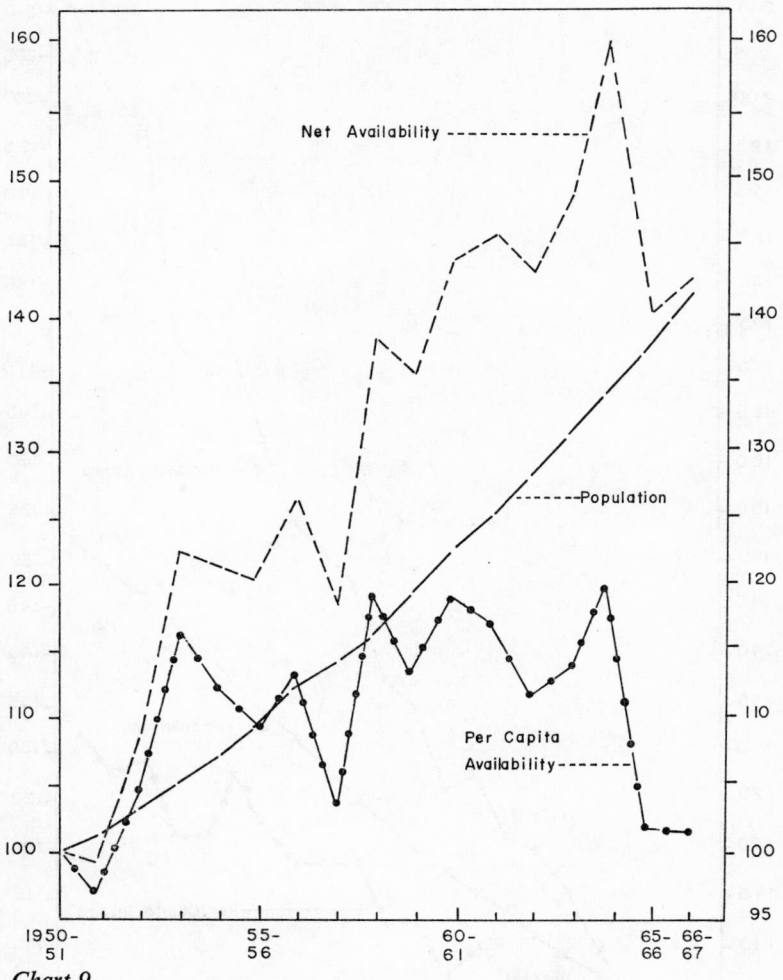

Chart 9

increased the magnitude of the unemployment problem. According
to the Planning Commission, some 23 million people will be added
to the nation's labour force between 1966 and 1971. In view of the

257

I

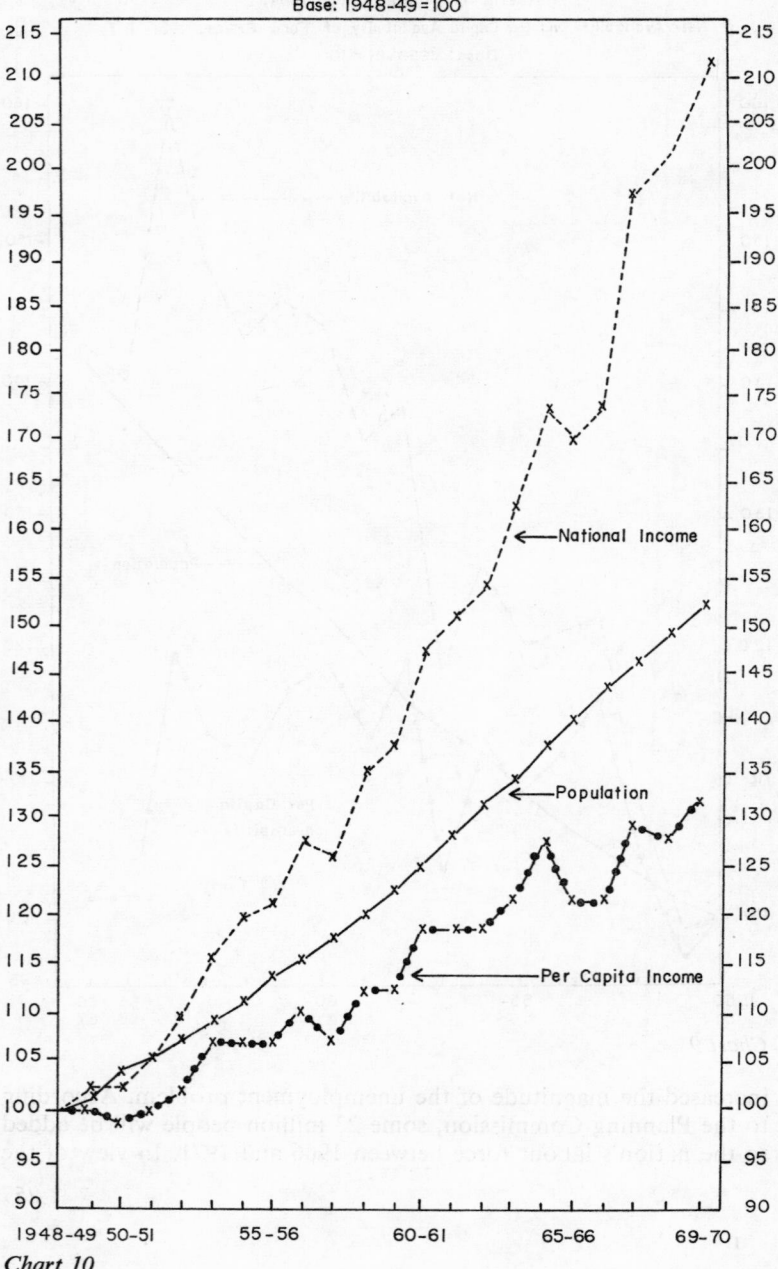

Patterns of Growth in Population
National Income and Per Capita Income: 1949-70
Base: 1948-49=100

← National Income

← Population

← Per Capita Income

Chart 10

already existing backlog of 12 million unemployed persons, India has to find jobs for some 35 million people. The fourth Five Year Plan (1969–74)[1] hopes to build sufficient infrastructure to create about 20 million jobs during the plan period. Judging by the performance of the earlier three five year plans, it is doubtful whether so many jobs will be generated in the current fourth plan. Even if these jobs should materialize, some 15 million adults will continue to remain unemployed and, in the meanwhile, population numbers will continue to soar.

The magnitude of current and prospective unemployment apart, plentiful and cheap labour has impeded the adoption of improved technology in both agricultural and industrial production. As the work is spread among many people, the *per capita* productivity and output are very low. Low wages mean low levels of consumption and poor standards of living. The quality of the labour force, which depends upon such factors as education, skills, health, and energy – which are in short supply – leaves much to be desired. The impoverished population multiplies – flooding the labour market – making labour cheap, unskilled, inefficient, and unproductive. And the circle is complete.

All this is reflected in the national income figures. India's total national income increased from Rs. 86 billion in 1948–49 to Rs. 149 billion in 1967–68 or an increase of 73·25 per cent over a period of about two decades. But the *per capita* income increased during the same period from Rs. 248 to Rs. 297 – a meager 19·76 per cent. Not only is India's *per capita* income today among the lowest in the world, but the rate of increase over two decades of overall national development is remarkably insignificant.

The most important reason for all this is, of course, the growth of India's population. The gains registered in India's national income were absorbed by the growing population to maintain the existing low standard of living, leaving only a small margin for capital formation and investment instead of increasing the *per capita* consumption of badly needed goods and services. A large part of India's national income is utilized for demographic investment (part of it is demographic wastage because of the high infant mortality rate), which is nothing but an unrewarding expenditure to maintain a growing population at a constant standard of living.

Actually, the country's annual needs are of the following order. To provide for the net annual addition of some 13 million, the coun-

[1] *Fourth Five Year Plan: A Draft Outline* (New Delhi: Planning Commission, 1967), passim.

259

try needs, according to an official estimate, resources to the tune of 126,500 schools, 372,500 teachers, 5·9 million housing units, 188 million metres of cloth, 12,545 quintals of food, 4 million jobs, etc.

The implications of the rapid growth of India's population (Chart 10) are more or less the same in every aspect of Indian economic and social life. These are a high percentage of illiteracy, inadequate housing facilities, urban deterioration, rural blight, overcrowding and pollution of a primitive kind, dislocation at individual and group levels, and a general air of distemper and dissatisfaction.

If these are some of the problems posed by India's population growth, their analysis in the light of certain available 'theories' and models become necessary to suggest certain policy measures.

Several studies in many developing countries during the last quarter of a century have shown that there is a significant relationship between large family size and high infant mortality. Infant mortality rates appear to be relatively low for the first, second, and third born and they rise gradually with a rise in parity. Among the average families and particularly among the poor, the chances of survival of the sixth and later births are quite low.

While this trend is established, it does not tell the whole story. A follow-up of case histories will often show that after five or six pregnancies, the weaker mothers tend to be eliminated from the ranks of the child bearers.

Writing more than half a century ago of the then prevailing American conditions, Hibbs pointed out: 'Those parents who bring into the world larger families than their neighbours deem themselves able to rear properly are frequently improvident, with a low standard of life, and, in addition, are often characterized by a lack of intelligence or of sufficient knowledge of the simple laws of hygiene.'[1] In poorer countries and among underprivileged families, infant mortality advances *pari passu* with the size of family, because large families generally cannot avoid the conditions which affect child life adversely.

The estimates of infant mortality rates computed by Jain[2] for the Indian states during 1951–61, range from 109 deaths per 1,000 live births in Madras and Maharashtra to 186 in Uttar Pradesh. Assam, the State having the highest fertility ratio, had an infant mortality

[1] H. H. Hibbs, *Infant Mortality: Its Relation to Social and Industrial Conditions* (New York: Russell Sage Foundation, 1916), p. 44.
[2] S. P. Jain, 'State Growth Rates and Their Components' in Ashish Bose (Ed.), *Patterns of Population Change in India* (Bombay, 1967).

rate of 184, while Madras, the state showing the lowest fertility, had an infant mortality rate of 109. Dr Kleinman[1] has computed correlations between Jain's estimates of births and infant mortality rates (see Table 58). The correlation is small (0·34) but positive, indicating if anything that the higher the birth rate the higher the infant mortality rate.

The reasons behind the association are not clear beyond the assumptions referred to earlier. But one might postulate from a knowledge of the economic development of various states in India that higher levels of development are associated with lower birth and lower infant mortality rates (from relatively better developed states like Madras and Maharashtra to backward Uttar Pradesh), or that higher infant mortality rates are the result of higher birth rates, or that higher infant mortality rates shorten the intervals between births by lessening the period of post-partum lactation amenorrhoea.

This association between high infant mortality rate and large family size is further supported by other evidence. The paediatricians in charge of two children's hospitals in Madras and Delhi have reported to the present writer on the basis of unpublished hospital data (1955–69) that infant mortality rates rise with increase in parity. The

Table 58

ESTIMATES OF BIRTH AND INFANT MORTALITY RATES OF INDIA, 1951–61

| | Jain's estimates (1951–61) of | |
State	Birth rate	Infant mortality rate
Andhra Pradesh	39·7	111
Assam	49·3	184
Bihar	43·4	145
Gujarat	45·7	110
Kerala	38·9	120
Madhya Pradesh	43·2	175
Madras	34·9	109
Maharashtra	42·8	109
Mysore	41·6	120
Orissa	40·4	159
Punjab	44·7	110
Rajasthan	42·7	117
Uttar Pradesh	41·5	186
W. Bengal	42·9	120
All India	41·7	139

[1] David S. Kleinman, 'Fertility Variation and Resources in Rural India'. Unpublished doctoral dissertation, University of Michigan, 1970, p. 186.

261

data, unfortunately, did not include details of the status of the mothers' health, the families' income, and the educational levels of the parents, etc. Some reliable information on this aspect is, however, available from the records of Hospital Barros Luco in Santiago, Chile. Dr Anibal Faundez has published the revealing original data from which Chart 11 has been drawn. In some areas in India, the situation is not dissimilar to the picture presented for Santiago.[1]

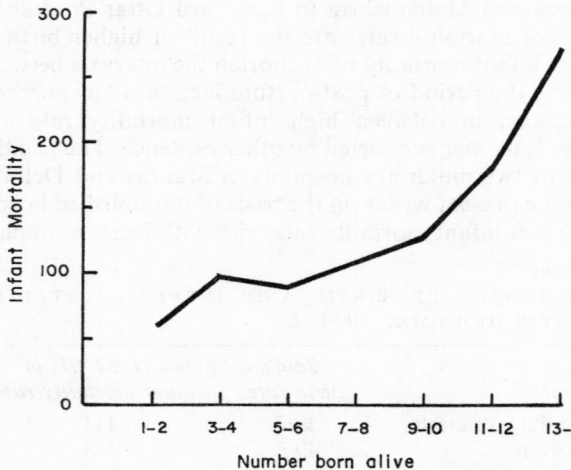

Infant Mortality according to the number born alive to 1300 women in Santiago, Chile(1968)

Chart 11

Effective family-planning programmes resulting in fewer babies per family may eventually lead to a better level of family consumption and living and a lowered infant mortality rate. These parents – and they constitute a majority in agrarian and developing societies – who are anxious for two or three children, preferably sons, who will survive, grow up to productive adulthood, and take care of them in their old age, would like to have five, six, or more children to ensure the survival of at least two or three. If there were some assurance, a kind of guarantee that the first two or three they have would survive to adulthood, there would be less likelihood of parents having say,

[1] See *Revista Chilena de Obstetricia y Ginecologia*, 2, 1969.

six or seven children. A larger number of children involves spreading the available meagre income very thin and the children almost invariably receive a smaller share of food and medical care. This situation often leads to forced neglect, infantile ailments, and even death in the absence of medical care, which the parents may not be able to afford. Fewer children would mean better care, a better share of family resources per child, less morbidity, and greatly lessened mortality. So it can be argued that fewer children per family would mean a lower infant mortality rate, other things remaining more or less the same

And once a community achieves a low infant mortality rate, it is unlikely for couples to have large families. When parents realize that a great majority of infants survive, there is no reason for them to have many children. The norm of the small family becomes an accepted pattern.

While it is not known that couples have a particular number of children as a result of any reasoning outlined above, it is known that cultural practices affecting family size are derived from such cumulative family and community considerations. Therefore, it seems reasonable to assume that family planning resulting in fewer children per family who would receive better care, will lead to less infant mortality; and the lower infant mortality rate will lead to the evolution of the small family.

Rapid population growth is manifestly central to the economic and social development of many countries, particularly the developing ones like India. The major problem before most developing countries dedicated to rapid advancement and a welfare state is the relation between the magnitude of the population problem in general and economic development as part of overall national development. A nation apparently has to choose between population growth and economic development. The overall relationship between such factors as levels of fertility and mortality, huge additions to population, levels of production and consumption, family planning and small family size can be examined in terms of the two schools of thought and their models – the neo-Malthusian and the Humanitarian (Charts 12 and 13).

The neo-Malthusian school assumes that high levels of fertility and mortality and low levels of production and consumption are the major characteristics of a developing economy. The population grows very slowly and the *per capita* income and consumption are low. Modern health-promoting devices and death control technology are imported into this poor economy and they effectively reduce the

263

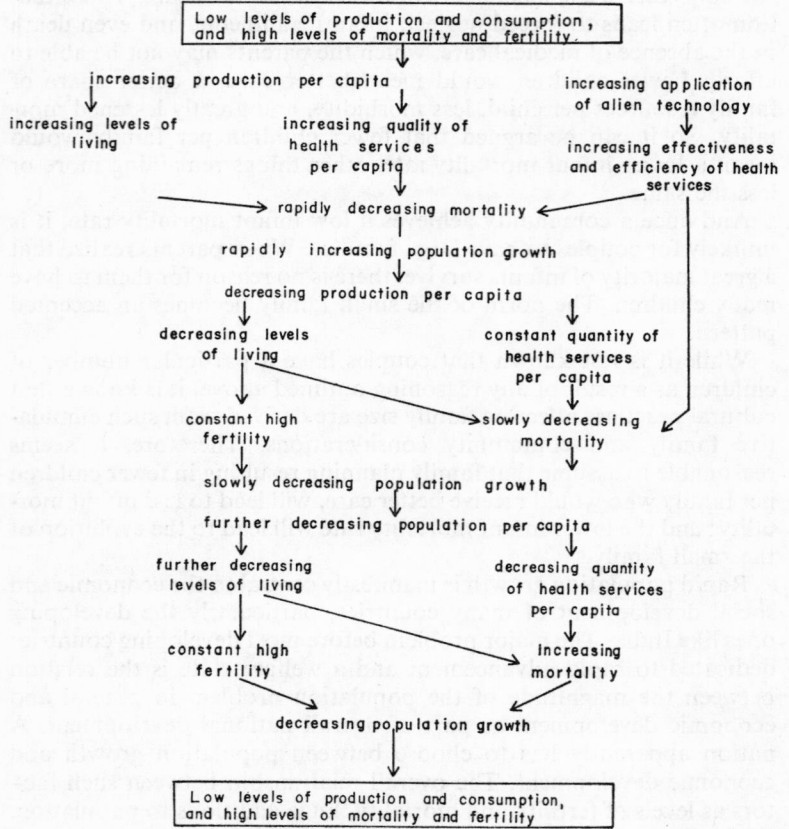

Chart 12

high death rate and particularly the infant mortality, leaving the birth rate untouched, resulting in a high rate of population growth which hampers the process of rapid economic growth. For whatever increase in national income that may be generated is swallowed by the new addition to the population without any perceptible rise in *per capita* consumption.

In other words, the indigenous pattern of high fertility behaviour is

264

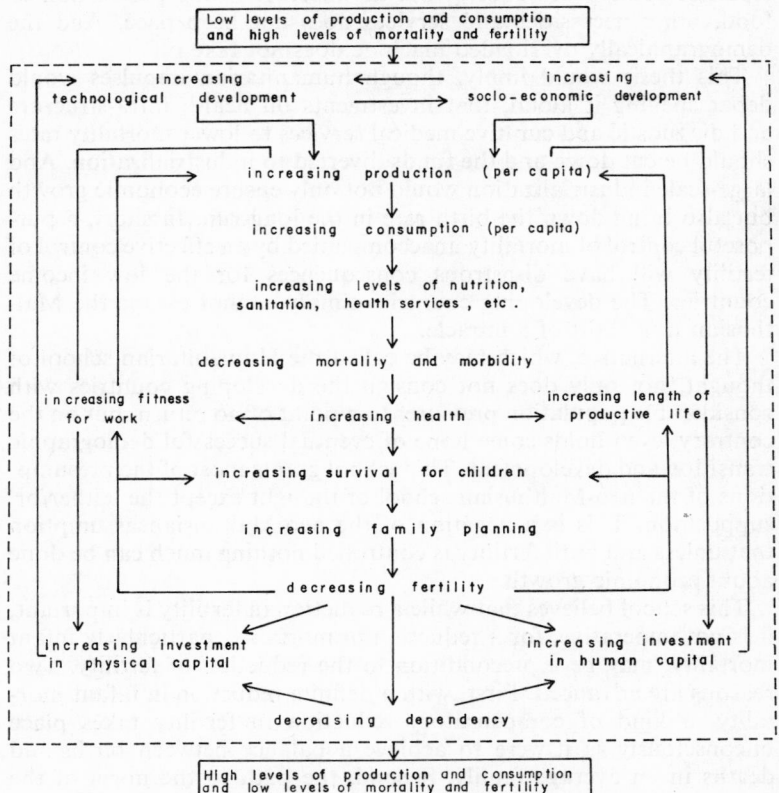

Chart 13

the villain of the piece. How do we transform a low income, under-developed economy with low levels of production and consumption and high levels of mortality and fertility into a growing economy of high levels of production and consumption and declining levels of fertility and mortality? It is readily conceded that in countries such as India, Ceylon, Pakistan and other developing countries the technology of health and hygiene, pesticides and wonder drugs can be more rapidly transmitted than the technology of large-scale industrialization and economic growth or the techniques of contracep-

265

tion? The consequence is that population increases rapidly as a result of some death control but the increase in the production of food, other necessities and services does not keep pace. And the demographically overloaded machine does not take off.

This thesis would imply, though humanitarian impulses would debar spelling it aloud, that investments on health infra-structure and diagnostic and curative medical services to lower mortality rates should be cut down and the funds diverted to industrialization. And large-scale industrialization would not only ensure economic growth but also bring down the birth rate in the long run. In short, a purposeful control of mortality unaccompanied by an effective control of fertility will have disastrous consequences for the low income countries. The developing countries simply cannot escape the Malthusian trap short of a miracle.

The alternative, which may be called the Humanitarian school of thought, not only does not consign the developing countries with considerable population pressures to a point of no return, but on the contrary, even holds some hope of eventual successful demographic transition and development. This school grants most of the presumptions of the neo-Malthusian school of thought except the 'either/or' supposition. This is a negation of the neo-Malthusian assumption that unless and until fertility is controlled nothing much can be done about economic growth.

This school believes that while a reduction in fertility is important, it is not imperative, for a reduction in mortality, particularly infant mortality, may be a precondition to the reduction of fertility. Two reasons are advanced. First, with a definite reduction in infant mortality, a kind of compensatory reduction in fertility takes place unconsciously as it were to achieve a balance between births and deaths in an average family. Second, the path to the norm of the small family may lie through parental certainty about the probability of survival of their children. That is, when there is less uncertainty about the survival of two or three children to adulthood, the desired family size may be reduced. Then actual fertility will equal desired fertility.

In a country like India with traditionally high infant mortality rates, the parents' desire for children, especially sons, acts as we have seen as a barrier to bringing down the family size. Thus, while the population explosion in the developing countries is the product of many factors, and most significantly the general fall in the death rate, *a further decline* in the death rate, particularly the infant mortality rate, may help in slowing down population growth due to certain cultural attitudes. This may sound paradoxical, but this is a possible process.[1]

The basic assumption here is that demographic cause and effect is not a single-plane phenomenon because several causes and effects are going on at various levels at the same time. An effective reduction of mortality need not wait till fertility is controlled. The increasing production of goods and services, at least food supply and health services, need not await the curtailing of the rate of population growth, because small instalments of all desirable processes will in the nature of things happen simultaneously and not one at a time or one after another in some kind of preordained sequence.

The question as to which theory is applicable to the available economic and demographic data is difficult to answer for both theories are partially valid since the development position is really never stagnant for more than a brief period. Nor is there any relevant recorded experience for which any pertinent conclusions can be drawn. There is, of course, the demographic transition theory based on the historical pattern of European population growth and stabilization. The theory assumes that a country's population during the premodernization period maintains its balance by matching its high birth rate by its equally high death rate. As a result of the modernization process, it is assumed the mortality rate suddenly declines without a corresponding change in the fertility rate. This widens the demographic gap resulting in rapid population growth. Then with gradual industrialization, the birth rate declines, approaching once again a balance with the low death rate.

While this phenomenon was largely true of European experience, this does not apply to present day developing countries, for the economic and demographic data of these countries do not fall into the European pattern. In fact, the theory's empirical accuracy and its predictive value may be questioned. There are notable differences between the contemporary developing countries and the European countries before the advent of the industrial revolution. Even though densities in these developing nations are higher, the mortality rates have declined more rapidly than they did in Western Europe during the nineteenth century. The developing countries of today have

[1] Harald Fredericksen, 'Determinants and Consequences of Mortality and Fertility Trends', *Public Health Reports, Vol. 81*, No. 8, August 1966. The present writer is indebted to Dr Fredericksen for some of the material, including the models, which is drawn from the latter's personal communications and since published in *Science*, November 14, 1969. See also David M. Heer and Dean O. Smith, 'Mortality Level, Desired Family Size, and Population Increase', *Demography, Vol. 5*, No. 1, 1968.

adopted health technology and modernization processes more rapidly than the European countries adopted whatever was available then during the period of demographic transition. Besides, a few countries have experienced differential declines in their birth rates. For example, 'it took only 12 years for Poland and Czechoslovakia to undergo changes in birth rates which took almost 70 years for France before World War II'.[1] And the experience of the Soviet Union and, more recently, Greece and Communist China do not support the transition theory. Hence the neo-Malthusian school, while basically sound, does not offer all needed answers on which to base a population policy to promote low birth and death rates and a high rate of economic growth for the newly developing countries.

By virtue of certain basic cultural, demographic, and historical differences between the contemporary developed and under-developed countries, it would be difficult to say whether the present day under-developed countries would recapitulate the 'demographic transition' experience as they undergo the process of industrialization and modernization.

What is more, time is a crucial factor; India, with a population of 550 million, adding annually some 13 million to her existing population, cannot just wait and let time take its course while a desirable balance between births and deaths is leisurely evolved. Hence, the need to invest resources on efforts to lower infant mortality rates without considering the impact of such action on immediate population growth or its cost-benefit analysis.

As far as India's population situation is concerned, the explanation offered by both schools of thought appears to be valid up to a point. The solution, therefore, lies in drawing from the cumulative experience on which both schools of thought are based. The inter-relationship between mortality, fertility, production and consumption, and overall stabilized population and marked economic growth has a kind of interdependence that cannot be explained solely by Western demographic experience. In simple terms, the relationship between fertility decline and economic growth has always been in some measure a chicken-and-egg affair. One presupposes the other.

Hence the attempt to solve India's current and continuing population crisis should follow both approaches of reducing mortality and fertility at the same time. An acceptable solution to India's population problem is not merely the achievement of a low rate of population growth which can be obtained by having high birth and death rates.

[1] United Nations, *Population Growth and the Standard of Living in Under-developed Countries* (New York, 1954), p. 8.

To the present writer the only rational and long-range solution is to ensure simultaneously low birth rates and low death rates. There will be severe competition for limited funds and resources but this attack must be mounted, if necessary with foreign aid. Such an unconventional and 'uneconomic' approach will guarantee maximum dividends from investment on the development of human resources. Hitherto the approach has been a conventional one – spending more on birth control than on death control because of the common belief that even normal death control would lead to increasing investment in birth control. But while birth control is most essential, family planning ends will also be achieved by controlling the death rate, particularly the infant mortality rate.

TACKLING THE HIGH BIRTH RATE

It is against this background of the relationship between infant mortality, population growth and overall development that India's current efforts to tackle her population problem and reduce her high birth rate must be examined before a policy to fight infant mortality is presented.

The Government of India and its thoughtful citizens have been aware of the problems posed by the rapid growth of India's population during the last decade and a half, but the adverse economic circumstances faced by the country in 1965–66 resulting in the Bihar famine brought home to them for the first time after political freedom, as nothing had done in the past, the disturbing nature of India's population explosion. In 1967, the Government of India embarked on a crash programme with the objective of reducing the birth rate from the then 41 per thousand to 25 – if not 20 – per thousand as expeditiously as possible. Although a policy of population control had been in force for the last few years (in fact, the policy as such was outlined in the first Five-Year Plan draft outline in 1951 at the instance of Prime Minister Jawaharlal Nehru), it was only after the new government headed by Prime Minister Indira Gandhi came in February 1967 that a vigorous, new, anti-natalist policy was formulated and an all-out campaign begun to halve the nation's birth rate by 1975–76, if possible.

MASS COMMUNICATION

This population policy has to be made effective within the framework of an open society with centuries-old customs and traditions. India today is the largest democracy in the world, but an overwhelming

269

majority of the people are illiterate (about 70 per cent), are small-scale farmers (nearly 80 per cent), and live in some 564,000 far-flung villages; some 14 major languages with centuries of literature and about 200 dialects are in use. The cultural levels of the population vary all the way from a Nobel Prize winner to a preliterate tribal peasant. What is more, according to the constitution, health and family planning are responsibilities of the states, as distinguished from the central or federal government. Since the efficiency of the administrative machinery of the various state governments is not uniform, there are considerable differences in the achievement of family planning targets.

The major problem before the government is to reach the country's married couples and convince them of the need for small families. During the last 20 years, the government, the universities and other academic bodies have conducted some 30 surveys of attitudes of parents among rural and urban populations, comprising various caste, religious, cultural, and income groups.[1] A summary of these random and other samplings shows that about 70 per cent of wives and about 66 per cent of husbands among couples with at least three children are in favour of family planning for economic and health reasons. And for cultural reasons, those couples with one or two sons are more highly motivated than couples with only daughters. It may be assumed, then, that a majority of Indian couples is in favour, at least in principle, of family planning. Of the 105 million married couples in the country today, living together and leading a normal conjugal life, about 90 million couples are in the reproductive age group, and these are the target couples who must be brought to accept the small family norm.

These target couples are distributed over 18 states, 11 Union territories, 326 administrative districts, some 2,690 towns and cities, and 564,258 villages. In each of these 18 states (except four Hindi-speaking states), a different language is spoken and each can be considered by virtue of its cultural autonomy and intense regional loyalties, almost a country in itself. Indeed, if the State of Uttar Pradesh were to join the United Nations, with its population of about 90 million, it would be the seventh largest member.

India's towns and cities are well knit and it is not difficult to reach their inhabitants. They have government hospitals and clinics, schools, and colleges; they are served by railroads and many are connected by airways. Literacy rates are high, newspapers and

---

[1] L. G. Reeder and G. B. Krishnamurti, 'Family Planning in Rural India: A Problem in Social Change', *Social Problems*, Autumn 1964, pp. 212–13.

periodicals are read avidly and people listen to All-India Radio. But the family planning communications programme nevertheless has to take into account wide differences in culture, religion, custom, and tradition. To carry it through, a media section has been set up in the Ministry of Health and Family Planning. That is, in each of the state offices of All-India Radio, a family planning unit has been set up to tailor the programme to the state's needs. The basic approach has been to present, besides interviews, dialogues, plays, and skits, only a few simple messages, in a few words, repeated in the same form in all possible media. An example of this approach is the use of the happy faces of the 'family of four' with the slogan 'Two or three children – enough' or 'If you have two, that will do' and the Red Triangle to identify the programme and the location of family planning facilities. This simple message is being propagated through motion pictures, on the radio, through a family planning song, in the press, on billboards, posters, cinema slides, on the sides of buses, railroads, etc.

But the villages pose a problem and they have not been neglected. It is the 60 million rural farm couples, illiterate and poor, who need family planning most. Talks, group discussions, and Bhajans (religious musical discourses) on family planning have been promoted. In many rural areas, puppets mime the family planning message, and even an elephant or two with family planning messages printed on their sides amble through the villages attracting crowds and considerable attention. But although radio should be the most effective instrument of our propaganda, the community radio sets presented to about a fourth of the village Panchayats are frequently out of order. Despite these difficulties, countless villages receive visits from peripatetic clinics and many large villages have organized sterilization camps where vasectomies and even tubectomies are performed on those men or women who desire a permanent method of conception control.

Though India is the second largest film-producing country in the world, commercial films deal primarily with mythologies and religious subjects and very few full-length movies are devoted to family planning. But the Government of India, by offering attractive cash prizes to professional and amateur movie-makers, has brought into existence many movies of varying lengths on family planning. The Government of India itself has produced movies that deal with the subject in most of the regional languages and released them through the country's 6,000 cinema halls, but all movies reach only about 20 per cent of the country's total population.

271

As for television, only one experimental station in New Delhi with a 30-mile radius is functioning now. Fortunately, Prime Minister Indira Gandhi, who once held the portfolio of Information and Broadcasting, knows the subject and is in favour of developing T.V. stations all over the country; for the educational value of T.V. for an illiterate country like India cannot be overemphasized, but some consider T.V. a luxury for a poor country. In spite of these difficulties, audio-visual methods are found most rewarding.

THE RED TRIANGLE – SYMBOL OF FAMILY PLANNING

As part of the tremendous mass education effort, it was decided to use throughout the country a symbol that would stand for family planning. A search was undertaken for a symbol that would be both simple and striking, different from any other symbol, easy to draw even when artists or materials might not be available, and above all easy to identify and refer to, like the world famous Red Cross. After examining and testing many symbols, the solid Red Triangle was chosen. The equilateral bright Red Triangle, pointing downwards (symbolically bringing down the birth rate) seemed to meet all the requirements and already in the few years that it has been in use has become well known.

The symbol's importance in illiterate rural India need not be overemphasized. Prominently displayed on all family-planning clinics, on posters in the larger towns and cities, on the back of buses and other means of mass transit, and as a shoulder badge for family-planning workers, it has already become what it was intended to be, an indicator of where to find family-planning help, services, and supplies, and a constant reminder of the country's determination to win the population battle. (The Red Triangle has been sent to various other countries and international agencies in the hope that it might become an international symbol for family planning in a world where population control is the most serious issue of the day.)

METHODS OF FAMILY PLANNING

Perhaps the most difficult problem before low-income and technologically backward countries like India is the choice of a contraceptive that is acceptable under poor living conditions, particularly in the depressed rural areas where privacy, running water, electricity, any knowledge of reproductive physiology, and most important, motivation, are more or less absent. Besides, in India's vast heterogeneous population no single method, however good, can be suitable to all. Hence 'the cafeteria approach' that has been adopted in India. That is, theoretically all the scientifically approved contraceptives are available to the people in the Government Family-Planning Clinics, but for mass consumption only four methods are now advocated and made available.

The first of these is sterilization – vasectomy for fathers or tubectomy for mothers. Vasectomy, the simple operation on the male, which the present writer popularized nearly twenty years ago in Madras State, has now caught on. Sterilization has become popular enough that today when the husband is unwilling or disinclined for any reason, the wife is often willing to undergo tubectomy. A decade ago, tubectomy was largely a post-partum operation and considered a relatively major operation needing at least a week's hospitalization. Today, simple techniques have been devised and the woman needs no more than a day or two of hospitalization. All services for both vasectomy and tubectomy are free – the surgeon's fee, the hospital and drugs and, in addition, a few rupees (from 25 to 50) are given to the patient to offset the loss of wages, transportation, or incidental expenses, though this small amount has assumed the nature of an incentive. In addition, those government (federal and state) and industrial employees who undergo sterilization can avail themselves of leave of up to five days without loss of pay. In fact, in large industrial establishments like the Tatas and others, workers who are willing to undergo vasectomy after the third child are offered an incentive of Rs. 250 and a few days leave with pay. Up to the end of 1970, nearly 7 million persons have been sterilized. About 90 per cent of these sterilizations are vasectomies and the rest tubectomies.

The second widespread method is the I.U.D. (intra-uterine contraceptive device) or the loop, introduced in 1965. By the end of 1970, nearly 4 million loops have been inserted. But the method has not proved very popular as it has led to excessive bleeding in about 10 per cent of the cases, as well as involuntary expulsion in about 6 per cent. Some wives have complained of a kind of psychological discomfort necessitating the removal of the loop. While the loop in principle is a simple, single-motivational and reversible method, the existing designs are apparently not entirely suitable for the Indian women. Research to devise a better loop with a more acceptable material and a better design is underway in India and other parts of the world. All the needed loops are manufactured in India in a government-owned factory.

The third contraceptive method that is advocated is the condom or

273

the sheath. The total requirement is well above 300 million pieces per annum and the indigenous production totalled about 100 million. The rest were imported from abroad, involving scarce foreign exchange. From 1968 to 1969, India obtained about 200 million sheaths as part of American aid to India's Family Planning Programme. Now that a government-owned factory – the Hindusthan Latex Limited in Trivandrum – set up in 1966 with technical assistance from Japan and the United States of America has gone into full production, India has become nearly self-sufficient in the supply of sheaths.

But apart from production, there is also a marketing problem. Since a majority of India's population live in far-flung village communities without any rapid means of transportation or communication, the distribution mechanism for any important commodity poses serious problems. What is more, a demand has to be created first and supplies provided. Of course, all hospitals, clinics, and family welfare centres carry all supplies and distribute them free. Another somewhat unconventional distribution channel is through postmen, school teachers, and members of co-operative societies; they receive the condoms free and in turn sell them at a nominal rate of 5 paise (less than a cent or a penny) for three pieces, keeping the proceeds as commission. Thus, it is hoped that a large number of people who otherwise would not go to the family-Planning centres are reached.

Besides this distribution system, a new system of mass distribution was devised using such commercial houses as Union Carbide India, Western India Match Company, Lipton India, Hindustan Lever, Brooke Bond India, and the Imperial Tobacco Company, India. These large companies have an estimated 400,000 sales outlets penetrating into rural markets. Here the condoms are sold at the rate of 15 paise (less than 2 cents) for three pieces, of which 8 paise go for the remuneration of the distributor. This is the first time the Government has ever undertaken the distribution in this manner of any commodity, much less a contraceptive.

The latest contraceptive method made available on a limited basis is the pill. The Ministry of Health and Family Planning was opposed to its introduction till 1968 when a decision in its favour on a pilot basis was taken. Since the pill was not manufactured till then in India, the import cost in hard currency was a matter of some concern. But with some generous assistance from U.S.A.I.D., it has been made possible to embark on a pilot project in which about 100,000 highly motivated urban wives are to be put on the pill under medical supervision. But so far, due to difficulties of training physicians on the pros and cons of prescribing the pill, only about 50,000 women are involved. The controversies in the medical and popular press in the West on the possible adverse reactions of the pill have not made the implementation of the Indian pill programme any easier. It is hoped that the pill will prove successful and its use will be extended. And recently two American pharmaceutical companies (Searle and Wyeth Laboratories) have set up plants in Bombay to manufacture the pill with Indian raw material. This is expected to cut the cost of the pill considerably.

CLINICS AND HOSPITALS

All these family-planning methods and the necessary supplies and advice are available in both urban and rural centres besides some mobile units. In 1970, there were 3,687 urban family-planning clinics; 1,022 run by state governments, 368 by local bodies, 371 by voluntary organizations, and 1,926 by other urban institutions doing family planning work. More important, there were in the same year 41,151 family-planning centres in rural areas, including 4,812 main rural family-planning centres, 28,912 sub-centres, and 7,427 other rural medical and para-medical institutions. Besides these, some 862 mobile units for inserting I.U.D.s and performing sterilizations were functioning.

The Central Government has taken the necessary steps to provide male and female doctors for these centres. So far, about 15,000 doctors have been trained in various family planning methods to work in these centres and nearly 125,000 para-medical personnel have been trained to assist the doctors. But the paucity of doctors, particularly women doctors trained in family planning and willing to work in rural areas, continues to be an acute problem. In fact, India, like all developing countries, is faced with the perennial problem of finding trained workers at all levels, whether nurses, health educators, or health visitors. But by distribution of scholarships to medical students who opt to work in family planning and special emoluments for doctors working in rural hardship posts, India hopes to meet this difficulty. But for some strange reason, general physicians and gynaecologists and obstetricians working in family planning have not found the specialization prestigious. In administering this vast programme in India, the present writer has seen that many doctors prefer to work in such exciting fields as heart surgery rather than in the unexciting task of inserting I.U.D.s or performing tubectomies and vasectomies. Perhaps there is a great need to create a specialized

275

department of what might be called Population Medicine, which thoughtful medical men and women would consider as important as, if not more important than, any other branch of medicine.

MEDICAL EDUCATION

Those who graduated from medical colleges 15 to 20 years ago, even after the emergence of India as a free nation, and who are now found in responsible medical positions, have little knowledge of contraceptive methods, much less of population dynamics. The simple reason is the absence of family planning as a subject in medical curriculum. Since family-planning work is carried out primarily by the medical profession, it is essential to involve all the medical practitioners to ensure the success of the family-planning programme. The medical colleges of the country have a very important role in this involvement of the medical practitioners. The medical students of today must be taught in such a manner that when they come out of the colleges they are fully informed about the population problem, the various clinical answers to the problem at the personal and family level; and are deeply motivated to help successfully implement the programme in their daily professional life. Hence, the decision in 1967 to direct the deans and principals of all medical colleges to include courses on population dynamics and family planning in the Departments of Obstetrics and Gynaecology and the Departments of Social and Preventive Medicine, for all the medical students during their undergraduate training. Equally important is the recent attempt to establish rural family-planning internships lasting from a few months to a year. This kind of internship of learning by doing in the rural area is probably more important than the routine internship in a city general hospital.

PRIVATE MEDICAL PRACTITIONERS

Till 1967, family planning work was confined to doctors on the government's payroll. Some 35,000 private medical practitioners who naturally charge a fee for advice, supplies, and services were not brought into the government programme. The result was a latent hostility on their part. Since the middle of 1967, however, these private doctors have been successfully brought into the national programme on the basis of a mutually-agreed payment.

A great majority of allopathic doctors live in towns and cities and cater to the needs of about 25 per cent of the country's population.

Apart from some peripatetic clinics and a weekly or a fortnightly visit of a government doctor to a cluster of villages, the average villager by and large receives neither prompt nor adequate medical help. But the practitioners of ancient indigenous systems of Indian medicine – Ayurveda, Siddha and Unani – live in and cater to the simple medical needs of the village population.

There are many and conflicting views on the relevance and role of these practitioners in dealing with the health and medical problems of modern India. While a discussion of this topic is outside the scope of this book, it may be pointed out that allopathic doctors dismiss them as quacks, for Indian indigenous medicine stopped developing after the tenth century when the country lost her political stability as a result of the first of a succession of foreign invasions. That is, the Ayurveda system of medicine is today where allopathic medicine stood about the tenth or eleventh century in Europe. The opposite and patriotic view contends that it is indigenous and cheap and not devoid of value and validity and will prove equal to the task given sufficient patronage.

In the Government's concern to reach anyone in the country who needs family planning, efforts have been made to involve this group at least to the extent of influencing public opinion. Knowing that the rural population does consult these Vaidyas and Hakims, the government has sought their co-operation. The emphasis is on the importance of these practitioners directing the patients who consult them to the family-planning clinics and doing all they can to convince those who come to them of the importance of the small family both for individual and the national well-being.

Besides these, the Government has sought the support of such diverse groups as women's organizations, trained social workers, foreign Christian missionary hospitals and doctors, business and industrial leaders, industrial labour organizations, the army of civil servants of all ranks in various ministries and government departments, various religious organizations, Panchayati Raj and other rural elected agencies, municipalities and other local government bodies, and the Gandhian Sarvodaya workers in the rural areas. These efforts have given family planning real national support from a wide spectrum of voluntary agencies.

FAVOURABLE FACTORS

What factors – political, economic, social and religious – favour India's current efforts to reduce her birth rate? The foremost factor is

277

the Government's awareness that rapid population growth is the nation's number one problem, ranking with the question of modernizing India's agriculture and food production. Indeed, food production and family planning are simply the two sides of the coin of national economic and social development. Awareness of this fact has led to the creation of the largest official family-planning programme of its kind in the world.

Fortunately, India does not have to wage any new battles to make family planning acceptable or respectable. India and other newly emergent countries are reaping the benefits of early and pioneering battles fought by Annie Besant, Charles Bradlaugh, and Marie Stopes in England and Margaret Sanger in the United States of America. Free India under the leadership of Jawaharlal Nehru formulated an anti-natalist population policy. And the present Prime Minister, Mrs Indira Gandhi, is the chairman of the Federal Cabinet Committee on Family Planning.

To implement the Government's policy during the First Five-Year Plan (1951–56), a small sum of Rs. 3 million was appropriated for family planning. But the Health Ministry's energies in popularizing the rhythm method (the only method that W.H.O. would approve for India in terms of assistance, thanks to its Catholic member states who obviously knew what was good for non-Catholic Hindu India) were so misspent that only Rs. 1·5 million was actually used over the five years and only 147 family planning clinics were set up.[1] During the Second Five-Year Plan (1956–61), Rs. 22 million were spent and the number of clinics increased to 4,165. The Third Five-Year Plan (1961–66) witnessed the introduction of all methods of family planning, except the pill, disseminated through the extension education approach and increased the financial outlay to Rs. 270 million. There was a plan holiday between 1966–68. For the Fourth Five-Year Plan (1969–74) begun in 1969 and currently being implemented, a sum of Rs. 3,150 million ($420 million) or 1·2 per cent of the total Plan outlay has been allocated.

Under today's programme, there is one primary health centre for

[1] The Registrar-General and Census Commissioner for India (1951) writes: 'If we recall the fact that, only recently, the World Health Organization felt compelled to avoid even considering this subject [contraception], we must count it a fortunate circumstance that the religious faith of most of our people [Hinduism] is not bound up with this taboo. It is therefore, easier for us – while affirming due respect for religion, morality, and the integrity of family life – to insist that the question whether contraception is good or bad for the people shall be considered in the light of uninhibited reason.' *Census of India, 1951, Vol. 1, Part 1-A: Report* (New Delhi: Government of India, 1953), p. 211.

80,000 of rural population and one urban centre for 50,000 population. And the number of family planning centres will increase, it is hoped, to about 11,168 by the end of the Fourth Plan in 1974, if all the schemes envisaged in the Plan are actually implemented.

As almost all the world's religions – from Animism to Zoroastrianism – are represented in India's population, the religious attitude to family planning is important. Fortunately, there is no objection on religious grounds as such to family planning in India today. As Professor Sarvepalli Radhakrishnan, distinguished philosopher and India's former President, points out, 'The Hindu dharma gives us a programme of rules and regulations and permits their constant change. The rules of dharma are the mortal flesh of immortal ideas and so are mutable.'[1] Social flexibility has always been an essential characteristic of the Hindu code of ethics.

Neither do the Muslims, the largest religious minority group in India, nor such other religious groups as Sikhs, Buddhists, Jains, or Protestant Christians or Parsees, oppose the official family planning programme. Even the old opposition from the Indian Catholic minority is now diminished. Thousands of Indian Catholics not only practise family planning, but have undergone sterilization.

During the last four years, international assistance, support, and sympathy for the programme have increased. Aid, large and small, is coming from the United States (nearly $40 million), Sweden, Japan, Norway, and Denmark; Canada, and a few other countries might soon join the list of those giving aid to India for this vital programme. Several foreign agencies have also helped, the largest aid coming from the Ford Foundation. This foreign assistance covers a wide variety of programmes – provision of technical experts, commodities and supplies, and training for family-planning personnel both in India and abroad. A random listing includes audio-visual equipment, paper, printing and mailing units, films, condoms, oral contraceptives, raw materials, training, and research facilities.

UNFAVOURABLE FACTORS

However, there are some unfavourable factors with which India has to contend. Perhaps the most distressing of these is the injection of communal and religious bias into the programme. While the government has made every effort to keep it truly national, above and beyond party and religious and caste politics, certain parties with

[1] Radhakrishnan, *Religion and Society* (London: Allen & Unwin, 1959), p. 108.

religious and caste affiliations and overtones have attacked the programme on the ground that its actual implementation is changing the
ratio among the existing religious groups. The argument frequently
voiced by the Jan Sangh, the rightist Hindu party, contends that considerably more Hindus than Muslims (in relation to their respective
total populations) are being sterilized. And secondly, since Hindus
are bound by the monogamic law while Muslims are permitted to
have four wives according to their law (shariat), the total population
of the Hindus is likely to dwindle while that of the Muslims is likely
to increase rapidly. The nation's secular law of monogamy applies to
all religious groups except the Muslims who are permitted to follow
in this matter their religious law. (The Hindu *religion*, incidentally,
does not insist on monogamy.) Since numbers matter in a democracy
and since many vote on the basis of religious (and caste and even sub-
caste) loyalties, the present family-planning programme might eventually change the entire complexion of the Indian (Hindu) nation. So
runs the argument.

The reply is that Muslims, Christians (both Protestant and Catholic) and other minority religious communities are all coming to the
Government clinics and that the communal ratio and the religious
composition of the Indian population show no signs of changing.
The available evidence reveals that these Hindu extremist fears are
groundless and that educated and motivated husbands and wives resort to family planning while the very poor, the ignorant, and the
unmotivated do not, among all religious groups.

In fairness to the Hindu point of view, it must be conceded that
there is force in the argument that in a secular democracy the Muslim
minority community alone should not be permitted plurality of wives,
no matter what the Islamic religion says. When even avowedly
Islamic countries like Turkey, the United Arab Republic and Pakistan have given up polygamy, there is no reason why Indian Muslims
should not give up their right to more than one wife, particularly
when in practice 95 per cent of Indian Muslims have only one. But
the demand for this belated social reform must come from the
Muslims, especially the Muslim women.

The political aspect of family planning in India has proved interesting by virtue of India's cultural diversity and the peculiar
nature of her polity.

At least one political party, the D.M.K. (Dravida Munnetra
Kazhagam, the present ruling party in Madras State) has officially
raised the question of family planning leading to loss of seats in the
Parliament. Members to the Rajya Sabha (the Upper House of the

Indian Parliament) are elected by the state legislators, who in turn are elected by the eligible voters (adult universal franchise) in the state. The number of state legislators (M.L.A.s) and consequently the number of members of the Upper House of the Parliament (M.P.s) they elect are determined by the state's total population. The contention of Madras State is that their zealous implementation of the Family-Planning Programme has led to the loss of two seats for Madras State in Parliament, whereas some other states, like Uttar Pradesh, which, failing to implement family planning, have increased their populations and gained more seats in Parliament. (Perhaps the problem can be solved by following the American practice of electing a uniform number of senators to the Parliament from each state irrespective of the state's population.)

Another serious difficulty is the want of an efficient, modernized and national welfare-oriented administrative machinery. The present bureaucracy owes its existence to the British who, as foreign rulers, were understandably interested in maintaining law and order and collecting revenues. It must be remembered that the British created a civil service in India from nothing and, judged by the standards of the day, it was very competent. Most of the officials were British. Secondly, the rules and regulations that were created perhaps more to rule than to administer a vast country were conceived in the late eighteenth century and the efficiency of the civil servant was judged by the degree of mastery of those rules.

Any objective student of British rule in India will readily grant many benefits of the British raj but the civil service (90 per cent Indian) left behind in 1947 when the country became free can hardly be counted as one by anyone with inside knowledge of Indian administrative machinery. The trouble has not been so much with people as with rules. Anyone who masters a set of these outmoded rules is considered a competent civil servant. As for the rules, they largely reflect what may be called 'a flat earth mentality'.

The late Prime Minister Jawaharlal Nehru said many harsh things about this 'creaking', 'slow moving', 'red-tape minded', 'delaying bureaucracy' with its countless pettifogging rules. Recently Prime Minister Indira Gandhi criticized what she called 'the feudal outlook of officials', 'Officials seem to feel that they are masters whom the people must obey.' She wanted 'greater devolution of real responsibility and the power for decision-making and implementation, and less of hierarchy'. She asked for 'performance-oriented financial controls rather than the finance officer wielding the veto, a rational utilization of technical personnel and greater sympathy in dealing

281

with staff problems'.[1] Several serious, but by and large unsuccessful, attempts at reform have been made during the last twenty-four years.[2] Recently, the Administrative Reforms Commission set up by the Government of India issued a series of reports of recommendations – by and large drafted by the civil servants. The recommendations are neither radical nor are they likely to be implemented in full. A cynical view might be that a parliament is unlikely to pass a bill abolishing itself.

A careful student of the present Indian Administrative Service is inclined to agree with Nehru that it is manned largely by men who have been trained to be proficient in old and outdated methods, unsuited to the needs of a modern industrializing economy in a changing world. What India and other developing countries need is a band of dedicated civil servants who are trained to examine issues competently and quickly and take serious and responsible decisions that would ensure the nation's progress.

In addition, in the family planning programme particularly, a generalist is at a great disadvantage because he is innocent of basic knowledge on such subjects as demography, vital statistics, sociology, gynaecology and obstetrics; the need for technical experts in Health and Family Planning Ministry is obvious. To this difficulty is added a general ignorance of conditions in advanced countries. Under the British rule, the prospective Indian civil servant had a year or two of probation and training in British universities. This is no longer true and the present civil servant has little opportunity to learn anything beyond what India has to offer by way of training. However, there are exceptions to every situation and the family-planning programme is being implemented to the greatest possible extent.

There is also some cultural resistance to family planning among certain communities, particularly in rural areas. As observed already the traditional desire of Hindu parents for sons is strong. A couple with two sons, for instance, is highly motivated in favour of family planning, but a couple with five daughters would like to try again for a son. This desire for sons is in part a religious attitude but, basically, it corresponds to an economic need, for with farming completely unmechanized, a villager needs sons as workers on his farm. Moreover, since daughters are eventually absorbed into the household of their husbands, only sons can be relied on for support and security in

[1] *The Hindu* (Madras) May 31, 1971.
[2] See Paul H. Appleby, *Public Administration in India: Report of a Survey* (New Delhi: Government of India, 1953). Also his *Public Administration for a Welfare State* (Bombay: Asia Publishing House, 1961).

old age. The village couple with two or three children but only one son is often reluctant to practise family planning on the grounds that, given the high rate of child mortality as pointed out already, their son might not survive the critical first five years. This very real problem argues the need for the intensive programme now being launched in India to combat malnutrition (the basis of most child mortality) among pre-school-age children. In this group, malnutrition is a qualitative as well as a quantitative problem and calls for a reduction in nutrient deficiencies through food fortification (wheat, rice, and salt), low-cost formulated foods, and large-scale child feeding programs. As discussed earlier, nearly 70 per cent of the childhood malnutrition could be eliminated by the limitation of families to three children.

While there are no religious objections as such to family planning, there is always the weight of custom and tradition, apathy and inertia. Here again, the difficulty appears to be cultural but the roots are also economic. Poverty and low income lead to malnutrition and undernutrition, which in turn lead to apathy and inertia. It is amazing that India's rural labour force is able to do as much work as it does in the light of the protein deficiency of their meagre, unbalanced diet.

However, a few enlightened Government leaders and an awakened public are constantly endeavouring to bring about change through a multipronged effort to modernize Indian society, an adequate discussion of which is outside the scope of this book. Despite an apparent resistance to change, the cake of custom is gradually being broken, the weight of caste is slowly lessening and, in the process of engineered social change, obscurantism is on its way out.

LIBERALIZATION OF ABORTION

These are the major features of India's current programme to cut down her birth rate. Another step which recently reached the statute book is the bill to liberalize abortion. The provisions regarding abortion in the Indian Penal Code were enacted about a century ago, in keeping with the British law on the subject. Abortion was made a crime for which the mother as well as the abortionist could be punished in all cases except where it had to be induced in order to save the mother's life. But, unfortunately, usually neither the average doctor nor the mother is aware of the law that permits therapeutic abortion with the result that very few abortions have been carried out in government or private hospitals. Therefore, the law has been observed in the breach in a very large number of cases in rural and urban

283

areas all over India for a variety of reasons. And the number of induced abortions has been estimated at about five million a year. Whatever may be the moral and ethical feelings professed by some sections of society on the question of induced abortion, it is an undeniable fact that large numbers of Indian mothers are prepared to risk their lives in an illegal abortion rather than carry that particular child to term. Furthermore, it is revealed that a great majority of these mothers are married women. So the major objective of the bill to liberalize abortion is to prevent the mutilation or death of women seeking abortion in the hands of back-street abortionists working under unhygienic conditions. The bill is more a death-control than a birth-control measure.

'The Medical Termination of Pregnancy Bill' was introduced in the Upper House (the Rajya Sabha) of the Indian Parliament in 1970 by the present writer and has been referred to the Joint Select Committee of its two Houses. It came back to the Parliament in 1971 and was passed by both Houses of Parliament.

The main argument in India against liberalizing abortion is that the strain on the existing medical services would be too great. But a recent breakthrough in the Soviet Union which has been widely adopted in Europe and America makes this argument invalid. Soviet scientists have prepared an aborting device on the suction principle which is virtually harmless and does not need special surgical supervision. Moreover, the entire operation takes no more than a few minutes and does not require more than a day or two of hospitalization.[1]

RAISING THE AGE OF CONSENT

A proposal which will help reduce the country's total fertility is to raise the age of consent for girls and boys. As noted earlier, early marriages are common in India. The minimum age at marriage for girls, fixed at 14 by the Child Marriage Restraint Act of 1929, was raised to 15 in 1957 as part of the revision of the Hindu code involving a revision of the Hindu personal law.

As responsible and disciplined children are raised in homes where parents are mature and responsible citizens themselves, the Government hopes to raise the age of consent to 18 for girls and 20 for boys.

[1] See S. Chandrasekhar, 'The Role of Abortion in Population Control', *The Statesman*, New Delhi, June 9, 1966. Also 'Should We Legalize Abortion in India?', *Population Review*, July 1966; and 'Abortion in India' in Robert E. Hall (Ed.), *Abortion in a Changing World* (New York: Columbia University Press, 1970), pp. 243–50.

Raising the minimum age of marriage is inherently desirable to improve the social climate in India, quite apart from its beneficent effects on population growth.

It has been established that either as a result of being generally more mature or because of greater opportunities for education and training and chances of gainful employment, or a combination of these, girls marrying at a later age favour and adopt family planning measures much more readily. Marrying at a slightly higher age cuts down the reproductive span and some recent studies show that if the minimum age at marriage for females were fixed at 20 years, the reduction in total fertility would range from 12 to 25 per cent. Fertility is affected by a number of biological and institutional factors of which the age at marriage is an important one. In any case, there is no doubt that, by marrying a few years later, after they have had the opportunity to at least complete their high-school education and obtain some gainful employment, young women will be better equipped to embark upon marriage and parenthood with a greater degree of mature responsibility.

The age at which young men marry has been slowly going up to 20 and 21 years, particularly in urban areas, due to possibilities of extended education, economic necessity, housing shortage, and other factors. However, in rural areas, the concept of later marriage has not spread. If the villages are provided with some new vocational high schools for girls with emphasis on home economics, hygiene and mother craft, the girls could be kept busy, and this might help to postpone marriage by a few years. Once the necessary social climate is created and rural parents are convinced of the gains of education and benefit of later marriages, legislation on this subject can be successfully enforced.

ROLE AND STATUS OF WOMEN

And last, the impact of the role and status of women (or, to put it differently, women's emancipation or the lack of it) on India's population problem has for some strange reason received little attention in demographic discussions. Perhaps the want of a precise definition of 'emancipation' and the difficulty in measuring the impact in any exact quantitative terms may be the reason.

The subject embraces a variety of such questions as the legal and political status of women, the differing roles of the two sexes in the home and in society, and the existing general attitudes toward women, the family and children, separation, divorce, family size and family planning. India's present demographic dilemma might not be what it is today were it not for the relatively backward position which the majority of Indian women occupy in the social economy. To repeat, such social attitudes and institutions as early marriage have a very definite impact on population growth. Besides early marriage, the near-universality of marriages, the inauspicious nature of infertility and the unwanted barren woman, the desire for male children, the social ban on widow remarriage, the lack of economic independence for single women, the want of prolonged education, training, and professional careers for women in general, the unhappy plight of the widow, divorced and separated women – all have a direct effect on family size and population growth.

It is obvious that the emancipation of women in the full political, legal, social, and particularly economic sense, can basically alter the magnitude of India's population problem. A Woman's economic freedom is perhaps more important than other freedoms. Today, with the exception of a small minority, women are economically dependent on men. Through the ages, the concept that the Hindu woman should be dependent upon her father until marriage, her husband during his lifetime and her son when a widow, has been firmly entrenched in Indian cultural mores. Even today while a thin segment of the educated and enlightened women at the top enter the professions, and a large number at the base do some unskilled but gainful labour, the large segment of middle-class women do not enter the labour force at all. It is often this want of economic freedom that chains the average woman to motherhood throughout her reproductive period.

The Indian institutional and social bias against women is revealed in the fact that the expectation of life at birth for females is lower than for males, while in all the advanced countries the reverse is the case. and in India, it may be recalled, the infant mortality rate is higher for female than for male babies.

Purposeful education and consequent economic freedom will enable women to decide when and whom they will marry, whether they will be homemakers or career women or both, how many children they will choose to bear and rear and when they will have them. Then almost all the children will be wanted ones. This will be both the cause and consequence of the biological emancipation of the women of India.

ACHIEVEMENTS SO FAR

What has been described so far reveals that India is on the right path toward national development. The government and the people by and large have realized the desirability and the need for small families. While aspiration is one thing and achievement another, India has begun to move towards achieving the set targets. Obviously, today's population policy cannot yield full results at once, but it is encouraging to note that a perceptive beginning of the decline in the birth rate is already visible in certain areas where there are dedicated doctors and para-medical personnel, ready supplies, good incentives, excellent administrative machinery, and satisfactory public relations.

What is the effect of all the family planning work done so far on the nation's birth rate? This may be answered in more than one way. A sterilization normally averts 1·5 births over a decade and about 2·1 births over a period of 15 years. The number of births prevented per each loop insertion is approximately half a birth. One who uses a conventional contraceptive like the sheath prevents 0·125 birth per year of use.

As noted earlier, so far some 8 million persons have been sterilized. On the above supposition, about eleven million births have been prevented. Another way to look at it is that since a majority of sterilizations are done on parents (father or mother) with three children and since most of these come from a socio-economic group which normally has 6·2 children, each sterilization has possibly prevented the arrival of some 3 children who otherwise would have been born in the next six to ten years. This would mean that these sterilizations have prevented the arrival of more than 20 million children. But since some sterilizations have been performed on an unknown number of parents of more than three children, a reduction of some magnitude must be effected. So a figure of 10 to 12 million may be accepted. Besides, nearly 4 million women have accepted the loop. Of course, the number of women who have removed the loop or experienced unconscious expulsion is not known. Anyway, the loops may account for the prevention of some 2 million babies. And last, while it is difficult to estimate the number of husbands who use the condom or the sheath, a figure of about 2 million may be accepted on the basis of the sales of the condom and an assumed pattern of frequency of use. All these methods jointly have perhaps prevented the birth of more than 15 million babies. There is no doubt that there is a distinct downward trend in the birth rate. With continued and dedicated endeavour, particularly with the co-operation of the medical profession and the voluntary agencies, the number of parents practising family planning should increase from year to year till the norm of the small family becomes a reality among all classes of the

287

population. At this rate, it should be possible to make a real dent in the nation's birth rate by 1975–76.

Family planning must not be a mere Government programme, particularly a Central Government programme, imposed from the top and reaching down gradually to the grass roots. It must eventually, within a decade or so, become a people's programme as it is in the advanced countries where the enlightened self-interest of parents prevails and where the government does not have to advise citizens how many children they should have.

AREAS OF DARKNESS

An overall review of the entire family planning work in India reveals that there are still three large areas where greater knowledge is urgently needed – in the fields of motivation, communication, and perfecting an ideal contraceptive suitable for an impoverished population. High-powered inter-disciplinary research is necessary to find quick and convincing solutions to these apparently simple but baffling problems.

The first is motivation. The familiar dilemma before India and other developing countries is that whereas population control is needed not only to increase but also to check the threatened decline in the already poor living standards of her people, the successful practice of family-planning methods requires a far higher general living standard than is the case. How does one motivate a couple to want family planning in a free society without any coercion or compulsion? The question sounds easy, but a real workable answer has been elusive. How does one explain to the average couple in a country like India that a large family is incompatible with a higher standard of living? How does one convince them that the simplest way out of family poverty is to have less children? If one wants to provide a better home, more and better food, clothing, educational and medical facilities, then it is obvious that, other things being equal, a couple should not have more than one or two children. The logic of reduced rations looks so simple and so commonsensical. But trying to convince any slum or pavement dweller that he should postpone marriage or when married not have too many children will receive an extremely adverse response. Every citizen, no matter what his plight, feels he has an inherent right to produce children even when he can barely support himself. Obviously, talking about the world's population explosion or India's population problem and the shortages of resources is irrelevant. But even the problem of poverty at the most basic individual or family level does not seem to help.

Perhaps incentives can play some part. But no serious and scientific study of the role of incentives has been made in the area of family planning. Then there is the question of money incentive versus service incentive. Some students think any incentive is a bribe. Is it?[1] Though anthropologists and psychologists have not adequately examined these questions so far, they need careful study and an adequate answer must be found.

The second problem is that of communication. In the ordinary sense, communication in India is extremely inadequate; all the existing channels of mass media do not reach more than 25 per cent of the total population. Predominant illiteracy is a barrier to the effectiveness of the printed word and the radio is beyond the purchasing power of most people in the rural areas. Even the cinema, which is so popular in urban India as an escape mechanism, has not become a permanent feature of rural life. All this, of course, is only a problem of resources and technology.

The question of communication in the more fundamental sense of transferring a body of knowledge from one person to another is even more difficult, particularly in nations with polyglot populations. Neither a language nor a vocabulary has been perfected to convey the family-planning message effectively to the man least equipped mentally to receive the message. Diverse linguistic groups belonging to the same nationality live crowded in one city but mentally in splendid isolation from each other. And yet all these groups must be reached quickly and effectively with the family-planning message.

And the third and last problem is the desperate need for an ideal contraceptive. From the Egyptian papyrus and the Hindu Ayurveda have come recipes to control conception. In our own day, we have methods galore – from Mahatma Gandhi's, 'Abstain unless you want children' through the current conventional contraceptives,

---

[1] E. Cahn writes: 'One of the major malpractices of our era consists in the "engineering of consent". Sometimes this is effected simply by exploiting the condition of necessitous men, as in certain Indian states where thousands of consents to sexual sterilization have been purchased by offering a trivial bounty to the members of a destitute caste.' 'The Lawyer as Scientist and Scoundrel: Reflection on Francis Bacon's Quadricentennial', *New York University Law Review XXXVI*, 1961.

It is unfortunate that the author has managed to commit three mistakes in this single comment, for the Government of India, dedicated to a welfare state, can hardly be accused of a malpractice; sexual sterilization implies castration which is not the case; and last, sterilization is not confined to any particular caste.

K

down to the suggestion of introducing an effective anti-fertility agent in the drinking water supply which would sterilize and then rationing an antidote, providing each family with one or two children.

Almost all the research on contraceptives, whether they are biological, chemical, or mechanical is carried on in the West. (Only in surgical methods is India carrying out family planning research.) And the Western scientists have in their mind, by and large, the problems posed in advanced countries. While human physiology is the same the world over, the conditions under which the human being functions vary enormously between countries and between city and village, and region and region within the same country.

In the West, even in relatively poor communities, bathrooms, running hot and cold water, privacy, electricity, a drug store or a chemist's shop, a clinical consultation, the availability of a doctor or a nurse, a modicum of literacy and some elementary knowledge of human reproduction – are more or less taken for granted. But this is not so in India and many other developing countries, where these amenities are enjoyed by only a small minority. Hence, the need for a contraceptive – an ideal one from the point of view of these difficult and deprived conditions. The new contraceptive of the future should be really simple (easy to understand and use), cheap (no more than a few pennies), reliable (should prevent conception) with no side effects (immediate and long range) and, above all, be acceptable to the cultural milieu of the people.

CONCLUSION

The Green Revolution is wonderful. But in itself, apart from the food supply, it will not solve the problems posed by excessive fertility. Man does not live by bread alone but by other goods and services as well. The battle against hunger may be won but the war against poverty lost. Hence the need to wage war on two fronts: increasing the production of food and other commodities and services and, equally important, promoting family planning so that there are no more than two or three babies in every family.

Man, despite all his unique gifts, has often throughout history worked at cross purposes. He has tended to plunder the planet which supports him and destroy the environment that sustains him.

Man's quarrel with Nature is an old and perennial one. Perhaps it goes back to the Biblical command to 'be fruitful and multiply and fill the earth and subdue it; and have dominion over . . . every living thing'. Armed with this injunction, and now further armed with the powerful tools of modern technology, man has multiplied as never before and asserted his supremacy by reckless destruction and senseless slaughter.

Now two questions must be raised and answered.

First, what can be done to repair the damage and restore normal ecological balance between man and his fellow beings, between man and his total biological environment?

Second, what can be done to avert future disaster?

First, we must give up the belief that man is the monarch of all he surveys and the rest of creation exists only for his pleasure and profit, that all other forms of life are somehow at his mercy, to be hunted or harnessed, conquered or crushed. Man must realize that he is just one member, albeit the most important, of Nature's large and interdependent fellowship of all living organisms, and that only by learning to live in humility and harmony with all else that lives and breathes can he ensure his own survival.

Second, we must put a ceiling to family size and control world population growth. If the world population is not stabilized at some manageable and reasonable figure, disaster is in store for all in this fast-shrinking and interdependent world – disease and hunger for the developing world and social chaos and political turmoil in the developed world. We must take an inventory of our resources in the light of present and possible future technology and see what this finite planet can support at an agreed desirable level of living – not the privileged minority – but all including the majority of the underprivileged.

And last, there is no need for alarm or pessimism. While time is running out in many parts of the world, there is still hope for peaceful change. History bears witness to the fact that man, when threatened, is capable of extraordinary endeavour. Now that man's very survival is at stake, let us hope he will control his numbers, stop polluting his environment, and finally learn to live at peace with his fellow beings. Let us hope man will endure.

Chapter VII

THE FIGHT AGAINST INFANT MORTALITY AND FOR THE SMALL FAMILY NORM

MORE AND BETTER STATISTICS

To sum up, a policy, whether in the field of economics or health, demography or medicine, presupposes an adequate knowledge of facts relevant to the subject. In the realm of public health and preventive and social medicine, it is not easy to obtain facts. They are not obvious to the naked eye and the necessary statistics can only be obtained through a complex, expensive and official organization where the reporting and recording are obligatory. And a government cannot embark on a policy of lowering the death rate of a community in an effective manner unless they have reliable knowledge of the causes that are responsible for the high death rate.

Lord Keynes once observed that there is nothing a government hates more than to be well informed, for it makes the process of arriving at decisions much more complicated and difficult. Public administration in our country can be defined as the 'easy' art of reaching decisions on insufficient evidence. We must so change this situation that every major decision of our Government is reached after a scrutiny of the available body of objective, scientific and unimpeachable data.

The need for complete reorganization and streamlining of the present inadequate, inefficient and archaic system of vital registration is being met in some measure by the new Act (which went into effect in April 1970) demanding compulsory vital registration all over the country. The country needs well-trained and efficient personnel to staff a well-organized national network of rural and urban vital registration offices.

Vital statistics are usually a by-product of social services. If a citizen could not admit his child into a free, tax-supported government school unless he could produce a birth certificate, there would be a demand on the part of every parent for a birth certificate. But in

India there are no social services comparable to those in the West and nobody cares to inform the authorities of vital occurrences because the citizen gets nothing in return. No citizen anywhere has any great love for vital statistics for their own sake.

The fact that the financial implications involved in streamlining our registration system are enormous does not in any way lessen the great importance of adequate vital registration. Sampling studies, no matter how excellently designed, are no substitute for complete vital registration in a country of the size and variegated pattern of life of India.

In the case of infant mortality the need for adequate and authentic vital statistics – the number of infants born, the number of infants who die before reaching their first year and the causes of their death with all the attendant information – cannot be over-emphasized. The minimum information necessary in this connection has been discussed at some length in the first and second chapters and hence there is no need to repeat it here. In a word, without this basic and precise knowledge, no sound policy can be formulated to attack the present infant mortality situation in India.

CONCEPTION

In India almost every pregnancy is a natural corollary of the married state, and for the most part pregnancies are accidents and not products of design. Babies arrive by chance and not by choice. For a pregnancy to occur under ideal conditions, the wife should first undergo a general medical examination to decide whether she is fit to become a mother. Such fitness can be considered from several points of view – primarily physical, emotional and mental health, and secondarily economic and social conditions. It is possible, though we have no direct evidence, that a large number of pregnancies that occur in India every year are undesirable in the sense that they are ill-advised from the point of view of the mother's health. The mother may be anaemic or weak, may suffer from some reproductive disorder or deformity, may have too large a family already to have enough energy and leisure to cope with another baby, and last the strain on the slender family purse may be considerable. The problems here are the absence of limitation of family size and lack of spacing of children. If every pregnancy could occur under conditions that satisfy *all* the relevant factors, the infant mortality rate could be reduced to a very low and nominal figure – say 10 or 15 per 1,000 live births. If family planning were practised by every couple, this end

293

could be much more easily achieved. If children can be spaced, say three years apart, the mother can successfully cope with the children and their necessary demands. Further, family planning must become efficient enough to limit the number of children to no more than three under normal, present-day circumstances. This would put an end to the present improvident maternity and lower not only infant mortality but also maternal mortality. We have sufficient evidence to show that infant mortality is greater among families of improvident births where children arrive too often and too close to one another.

As a matter of policy, we have already seen that this question is receiving considerable attention in the country both at the governmental and the private family level. The Government of India and several state governments (particularly Madras, Maharashtra and the Punjab), it must be said to their credit, have taken a progressive stand on the subject of intensive family planning.

Soon after Independence, the nation's medical and public health services were integrated. This meant considerable improvement in the maternal and the child health services since comprehensive services covering both preventive and curative aspects could now be offered by the same institution.

During the Second Five-Year Plan period (1956–61) the maternal and child health programme in the rural areas was integrated with the community health programme of the primary health centres. The medical officer, the health visitor and the auxiliary nurse mid-wife of the primary health centre now look after mothers' and children's special services such as antenatal care, delivery service, post-natal and general child care. They also look after vaccination and control of communicable diseases, take blood smears in cases of fever in connection with the malaria eradication programme, help in domiciliary treatment of tubercular cases and attend to the programme of health and nutrition education. Thus the staff is overburdened with manifold duties. In the urban areas, the number of maternity and women's and children's hospitals has steadily increased. Where it was not possible to have separate hospitals, additional wards for women and children have been earmarked in the general hospitals. Maternity homes and maternal and child health centres for attending to normal deliveries have been set up.

Under the Government of India's massive programme of popularizing family planning the state governments are offering the necessary advice and medical services and supplies and have built up a close network of adequately staffed family welfare planning centres

294

and sub-centres in the rural areas around the primary health centres. A primary health centre covers roughly 80,000 population in the rural areas. One family welfare planning centre and sometimes more than one is required for each extension block. Three sub-centres in a primary health centre are planned under the health programme and another three to six with finances provided by the Family-Planning Programme so as to provide one sub-centre for every 10,000 population. In the urban areas, one family welfare planning centre has been set up for every 50,000 population. In 1970, about 5,000 major family-planning centres with about 20,000 sub-centres were functioning in the rural areas of the country. There were over 1,600 centres in the urban areas. When the Third Five-Year Plan began in 1964, the family-planning programme was integrated with the maternal and child health programme. All maternity hospitals offer sterilization and intra-uterine contraceptive device insertion services. All maternal and child health institutions distribute conventional contraceptives.

In the course of daily routine in the clinic and during home visits maternal and child health personnel render follow-up services to couples who are practising family planning, and talk about family planning to others who are not yet doing so. They also motivate couples to adopt a suitable method for planning their children and offer the necessary services for the purpose. In the antenatal period, the mothers are told about puerperal sterilization. If they wish to adopt the method, delivery is arranged in a hospital and a tubectomy performed. For others, the subject is discussed in the post-natal period and suitable contraceptive methods are made available. With this integration family planning has been given a new slant. It does not merely mean limitation of the family size or spacing of children, but also implies taking adequate care of the health of the family and particularly of the living children. It is realized that a couple is much more likely to practise contraception if they are convinced that the children they already have will be well looked after and their proper health care ensured to enable them to survive the health hazards and accidents of early life.

The maternal and child health (M.C.H.) centres and family-planning clinics, therefore, attend to immunization and nutritional programmes also. The children, who come with the mothers to the clinics or to the centres, are attended to and given the necessary child health services. It is hoped that the large network of institutions for maternity and child welfare and family planning work will develop both the activities in an integrated manner.

295

ORGANIZATIONAL SET UP

Ministries of Health and Local Self Government between them organize maternal and child health services. Teaching medical colleges are run by the Ministry of Health. There are 94 such colleges which are located in state capitals or in big district headquarters with separate maternity and children's hospitals or combined women's and children's hospitals nearby. They may have from 50 to 300 beds. They provide medical care and run antenatal, post-natal and child welfare clinics and other speciality clinics such as cardiology, tuberculosis, child guidance, etc. They have better standards of staff and facilities and provide better patient care than the ordinary general hospitals. Obstetricians and paediatricians of the college may provide consultations to neighbouring district hospitals.

At district headquarter towns, there is usually a separate maternity and children's hospital or fairly well-developed maternity units attached to the general hospitals. They provide institutional care and hold antenatal, post-natal, child welfare and family planning clinics. The obstetricians and paediatricians of the district hospital are expected to offer consultations to smaller hospitals and primary health centres at regular intervals.

In municipal towns, municipalities run maternity homes for normal deliveries, and maternal and child health centres offer antenatal, post-natal and child welfare clinic services and assistance in domiciliary delivery. In some instances, the maternal and child health centres may keep four to six beds for normal deliveries. A few municipal corporations run maternity and children's hospitals and even medical colleges.

Rural India has been divided into 5,223 national extension-service blocks, each with one primary health centre. This centre offers maternity and child health services. Out of six hospital beds in the centre, two are allotted for maternity cases. The centre conducts weekly antenatal and child welfare clinics and arranges home visits. A block is further subdivided into sub-centres, each serving 10,000 population, with one midwife/auxiliary nurse-midwife for maternal and child health and family planning services and a basic health worker for other preventive and public health services. The training of midwives *per se* has been discontinued. They are being replaced by auxiliary nurse-midwives, who are basically maternity and child health workers. In their training 15 months are devoted to midwifery and only 9 months to elementary nursing. The health visitor/public health nurse is the key person in so far as maternal and child health

296

services are concerned. She helps the medical officer in the bedside nursing of inpatients and in organizing and conducting maternal and child health clinics. She conducts the mothercraft and mother's health education classes. She and the medical officer visit the sub-centres weekly or bi-weekly, when antenatal and child welfare clinics are arranged by the sub-centre midwife. The latter makes regular home visits, gives assistance in home deliveries, and imparts education to mothers in matters of health and nutrition.

Over and above the primary health centres, there are a number of dispensaries which may only treat outpatients or may have four to six beds. They also render midwifery services. Then there are voluntary organizations which run maternity hospitals, maternity homes, maternal and child health centres and specialized services both in the urban and rural areas.

In keeping with the policy of democratic decentralization, the administrative control of the primary health centres and maternal and child health centres rests with the local authorities, the zilla parishads and the panchayats, while the technical control is vested in the Health Department. With this organization for maternal and child health services in the urban and the rural areas, a substantial impact has been made on the problems of maternal and child health care.

In addition to about 5,000 primary health centres and 20,000 sub-centres in the rural areas, as already mentioned, there were a little over 6,000 maternity and child health (M.C.H.) centres in March 1967. In the urban areas, there were 1,211 M.C.H. centres, 581 maternity homes, 502 maternity hospitals, 1,142 maternity wards in the general hospitals, 32 children's hospitals, and 307 children's wards in the general hospitals. Taken altogether, there were over 45,000 maternity beds and 8,600 children's beds.

Considering the dimensions of the country, the provision is far from adequate: still the achievement has been substantial. Against an estimated maternal mortality rate of 20–25 per 1,000 births during the 1930s, the rate is estimated to be 6 per thousand in 1970. The main causes of maternal death are anaemia, toxaemias, haemorrhages, obstetric shock and sepsis. There has been a corresponding improvement in infant care, which is responsible for the observed reduction in infant mortality, but the effort is not large enough to bring it down to the level of the advanced countries.

The advanced countries are now grappling with the hard core of the problems involved in the reduction of infant mortality. They have come to a stage where a major break-through in medical research is needed. For instance, the causative agents involved in post-natal asphyxia and atelectasis, which make significant contributions to infant mortality, have not yet been identified. Their association with prematurity is an observed fact, but causes are not known. A large proportion of infant deaths is due to immaturity but additional diagnostic information is lacking. Congenital malformations arise from a number of causes, most of which have not been identified or properly understood. Some of them, which have been implicated, are infectious diseases, drugs and radiation. The problems of gene mutation and prevention of undesirable mutations are not fully understood.

On the side of environmental causes, lack of therapeutics for certain viruses and development of microbial strains resistant to antibiotics are hampering further progress. The provision of good water, food, housing and relief from over-crowding require alleviation of poverty, health education and public housing, which are being attended to in developmental planning. In regard to accidents, crib deaths are being investigated to obtain aetiological leads.

All these advances are bound to help the developing countries too. But their problems are more basic and are concerned with social and external environmental factors which hamper rapid progress in India. We shall now examine these basic difficulties.

ANTENATAL SUPERVISION

Antenatal care in general has two primary objectives. They are, first, to conserve the health of the expectant mother in pregnancy, labour, and during the lying-in period, and secondly, to enable her to produce a healthy child with the highest possible potentiality of developing into a healthy adult.

In the words of a British study on the general problems of maternity: 'The aim of the antenatal movement is to make contact with each expectant mother as early as possible in pregnancy and keep her under regular supervision, viz. monthly during the first four months, then fortnightly until the eighth month, and thereafter weekly until confinement.'[1]

In view of these objectives, the antenatal clinics in the advanced countries have been designed to provide certain specific services. These are to remove the anxiety and fear of the expectant mother, especially when she is a primigravida, to diagnose and treat any early complications, to increase the proportion of normal deliveries, to lower the maternal morbidity and mortality rates, and last to reduce

[1] *Maternity in Great Britain* (London: Oxford University Press, 1948), p. 29.

the incidence of premature births, stillbirths, perinatal and neonatal deaths. The antenatal services as provided in some advanced countries have covered a wide field. The expectant mothers are advised in clinics set up by local authorities, general practitioner clinics and homes by visiting health visitors and midwives. As a result, these twin objectives of antenatal care have been achieved to a large degree in the United States, Australia, New Zealand, and in some countries of Western Europe. Their success is demonstrated in the striking reduction in overall maternal and infant mortality rates.

As early as 1951, Dr B. C. Das Gupta, in a report that is still relevant, brought out that in India prematurity and immaturity are outstanding causes of infant mortality in the neonatal period and that the state of health of the mother during pregnancy and her economic, social and nutritional condition play an important part in the incidence of premature births. His recommendations for reducing prematurity and immaturity are quoted below at some length:

'1. *Measures to lessen the incidence of premature births*

(a) *Pre-natal clinics*: In order to allow every expectant mother the benefit of pre-natal care, a larger number of pre-natal clinics are necessary. These should be situated at suitable distance to serve certain areas and thus be easily accessible to all.

They should be staffed by medical women and a sufficient number of health visitors, to allow for the follow-up, and education of every expectant mother attending the clinic.

Laboratory facilities should exist for full pathological examinations, so as to allow for early diagnosis and treatment of complications particularly of anaemia.

Apart from the medical care available which should include giving of liver and/or iron according to blood picture, amenities in the way of milk and additional nutrition to supplement what is lacking in the home diet should be arranged for at the clinic.

Lastly, every mother should be made to realize the importance and advantages of early and sustained pre-natal care for herself and her unborn child.

(b) *Pre-natal beds*: A sufficient number of pre-natal beds should be provided in maternity hospitals to allow for observation and treatment of complications which threaten premature labour.

(c) *Improvement in social conditions*: This would include improvement in the economic status of the expectant mother. Her standard of living should be raised, her housing conditions im-

299

proved, and diets so constituted as to be balanced, to contain the requisite amount of protective foods and to provide sufficient caloric value.

2. *Measures to lower the incidence of deaths in premature infants*
    (a) *Intra-natal care:* This can be obtained by the provision during labour of a skilled obstetrician, an expert physician, a paediatrician and specialized nursing facilities required to aid the survival of the newly-born premature and immature infant.
    (b) *Post-natal care:* Reduction of neonatal mortality can only be effected by expert and trained care during the early neonatal period. In the majority of mothers this can only be possible by hospitalization, where such care would be available. Delivery in the house would allow the infant very little chance of survival, for in addition to unsuitable home conditions, there is lack of intelligent care from the mother or relatives.

Follow-up of cases showed that in over 75 per cent of them, the housing conditions were poor and standard of living low. Such help as can be given by paid personnel for home confinements is of no use, as the knowledge of births is not available early enough. Registration of the births within the first 36 hours is not compulsory, as it should be, and hence the early care so very necessary to tide the infant over the first few days is absent. In the inquiry, it was observed that 60 per cent of the infants who succumbed in the neonatal period did so in the first week of life. Having passed this critical period, they had a better chance of survival. Thus the necessity for delivery in an institution, where there is a better prospect of saving the infant.

Maternity institutions should, therefore, arrange to have the following:

(a) A separate staff of nurses, specially trained in the care and management of the premature infant, so as to be at hand for every premature birth.
(b) A separate premature-baby ward away from the general lying-in ward suitably equipped and heated for the isolation and care of the premature infant.

From the facts which have emerged from this inquiry, it can be judged that neonatal mortality is the chief factor responsible for swelling the infant mortality rate and that it is entirely preventible. It is, therefore, incumbent on Government and local authorities to consider this question seriously and adopt the measures suggested above for enlarging and improving the present maternity service.

It is important that every expectant mother should receive expert care during the entire period of pregnancy so as to safeguard her and her infant, and thus help to save many precious lives. This would result in lowering the present infant mortality rate which is far in excess of that of many countries.'[1]

Some of these suggestions have been implemented. Antenatal services have been greatly strengthened as a result of integration of M.C.H. work with the total health services. Expectant mothers are encouraged to register as early as possible at the weekly or bi-weekly antenatal clinics organized by the different agencies already mentioned. The clinics carry out routine health check-ups and specialized examinations if necessary, and give health and nutrition education. It is estimated that in the urban areas 90 per cent of the mothers avail themselves of these services, but in the rural areas, where about 80 per cent of expectant mothers live, only a small percentage of the mothers take advantage of these services. They are requested to register in the first trimester but a majority of those that do report late in the second or third trimester. They do not feel the need for any antenatal consultation or supervision. They take it for granted that their condition is 'natural' and that such discomforts as they may have are the necessary 'price' of their condition. It is estimated that in the rural areas, an antenatal mother pays an average of 2·5 to 3 visits to antenatal clinics. During the routine home visits, the mothers registered at the antenatal clinics are followed up to check on whether the advice given to them is practised and to assist them in making necessary preparations for the home confinement which is usual in the rural areas. They also contact those who fail to attend the clinics with a view to arousing their interest in them. The domiciliary services are generally confined within a radius of 2 to 3 kilometres from the maternal and child welfare centres for want of transportation facilities.

The needs are simple but not easy to meet. Expectant mothers should be medically examined and in normal cases home delivery by a trained midwife arranged for. Should the examination reveal possibilities of complications, the mother-to-be must be referred to a hospital, where necessary arrangements for confinement with competent obstetrical care can be made.

[1] B. C. Das Gupta, *Report of the Inquiry into the Bearing of Premature and Immature Births on Infant Mortality in Bombay 1946–48* (New Delhi: Indian Council of Medical Research, 1951).

NATAL SERVICES

The question of confinement poses, for our purposes, only two problems – the place of confinement and the nature of trained assistance during confinement.

Should the confinement be conducted in hospital or in the home? In the West, hospital confinement is generally the rule and home confinement the exception. In the United States of America in 1965, for example, more than 98 per cent of white babies and nearly 85 per cent of Negro babies were delivered in hospital. In rural regions, however, home confinements constitute the majority. In India, home confinement is the common practice and while there are no figures, a calculated guess would put these at 80 per cent of all deliveries. There is no reason why home confinements cannot be comfortable and safe, *so long as the delivery is a normal one and the mother has received the domiciliary services.* The home has certain advantages such as the availability of domestic help, little or no expense, and a sense of security arising out of familiar surroundings and being in touch with the routine of a running home. On the other hand, certain familiar factors in the average home, as pointed out in the previous chapter, militate against home confinement. These are the overcrowding and the attendant noise of a large family, lack of aseptic conditions and complete rest for the mother.

Institutional confinements overcome these difficulties and when the labour is expected to be abnormal the question of confinement at home does not arise at all.

In the urban areas, institutional deliveries are becoming more and more popular. There are cities where nearly 90 per cent of the deliveries occur in maternity hospitals. Maternity beds are concentrated in urban areas. Out of a total of 45,000, nearly 38,000 beds are in towns. Even then the demand is not fully met. In several maternity hospitals, normal cases are discharged within 48 hours of delivery to make room for others.

In the rural areas, home delivery is the rule. The demand on hospital beds is generally limited to abnormal cases requiring skilled attention by a doctor. In normal cases, the maternal and child health personnel visit the mothers in their homes during the last weeks of pregnancy, make preparations for the confinement and assist at the time of delivery. If these services can be intensified with improved efficiency, a considerable saving of life can be effected. It is not possible in the foreseeable future to provide institutional beds to take care of some twenty-one million births every year. Nor is it advisable that the limited resources of buildings, equipment and medical personnel should be diverted for this purpose.

The second and perhaps more important question is the provision of medical help to conduct the confinement. While difficult cases should receive the most skilled obstetrical care, ordinary confinements can be conducted successfully by the general physician and often by a trained midwife alone. It is here that the country is faced with an intractable problem – the dai.

THE DAI

The dai, our untrained, indigenous midwife, poses a serious problem in any plan to reorganize maternal and child welfare services. The best course would be to stop her from carrying on her traditional task. But this is easier said than done and before she can be stopped, better alternative services must be provided.

It is physically impossible for the midwife/auxiliary nurse-midwife to provide skilled assistance in all normal births, especially now that they have become multipurpose workers. The proportion of deliveries they are able to attend varies from 20 to 50 per cent in the different parts of the country. The rest are attended to by the traditional birth attendant, the dai, who practises midwifery as a hereditary profession.

There are three alternatives open to the authorities: (1) to leave the dai as she is; (2) to register and train her; and (3) to replace her by a trained midwife. We cannot of course leave her as she is, for her ignorant, superstitious and unclean ways have all along been a danger to the community. The second alternative must be attempted for it is inexpensive. It is rather difficult to train a middle-aged woman who is set in her ways. Moreover the midwives are generally restricted to poor women belonging to the underprivileged barber caste.

But, realizing the inevitability of dais in the present circumstances, the Government of India has launched a programme of training them in the primary health centres and maternal and child health centres where they live and practise midwifery. The training is spread over six months and is given by the health visitors and auxiliary nurse-midwives with greater emphasis on practical demonstrations. Monetary inducement is offered and a midwifery kit, which can be refilled, is presented to them so that they may practise the precepts they have learned. The maternal and child health personnel exercise supervision over their work. About 30,000 dais have been trained and the training programme is proposed to be intensified in the coming years. In a few states, where an adequate number of trainees with the prescribed 7 years of schooling are not forthcoming for auxiliary nurse-midwife courses, young literate women are enrolled for the 'trained dais' course. It lasts for 9 to 12 months and is conducted in maternity hospitals and M.C.H. centres. They are posted as mid-wives/auxiliary nurse-midwives after training. This course will be discontinued in the near future. In a majority of states, nurses are given a course in midwifery and register themselves as midwives also. They are fully competent to work in maternal and child health.

The third alternative should become the only acceptable way in modern India. Midwives should be recruited from the general population without any caste bias and with certain minimum educational qualifications such as a high-school passing certificate. The ideal is to have one trained midwife for five villages or a rural population of about 10,000. We need in this connection an all-India Midwives Act on the lines of the Midwives Act of 1936 in the United Kingdom which will not only eliminate the untrained dai and forbid any untrained midwife to attend childbirth in any capacity, but provide an efficient midwifery service under the supervision of the health officer in urban areas and medical officers in the rural areas.

Many states have legislation requiring the registration of nurses and midwives but enforcement is often indifferent.

POST-NATAL CARE

If prenatal care is important, post-natal care is equally if not more important. Post-natal care, unlike antenatal care, involves not only the mother's own health, but the infant's as well, and the mother's ability to take care of the infant.

Post-natal clinics are organized only in the teaching hospitals and larger maternity hospitals. Generally post-natal clinics are combined with child welfare clinics. Attendance of mothers is not satisfactory. They do not report back to clinics unless they experience major illness. Maternal and child health field personnel give post-natal health supervision to the extent possible during home visits.

The foremost requisite here is that the Government and the community set up infant welfare centres where the mother can receive advice, assurance and some instruction to protect the infant from neonatal infection due to poor sanitary and hygienic environment. The mother also needs to be taught antiseptic routine to guard the infant from all too familiar infections.

The second problem most mothers are confronted with at this

stage of infant development is that of feeding, which is discussed in some detail in an earlier chapter. However, to summarize, the question is whether the infant should be breast-fed or bottle-fed. In all cultures breast-feeding is natural and preferred to artificial feeding, so long as the mother's milk has not dried up for health or psychological reasons and breast-feeding is possible. If the infant can obtain the necessary amount of nutrition through the mother's milk, half the battle is won. Mother's milk at the early stages need not be supplemented and the question of cleanliness and purity does not arise. Should the mother's milk fail or should the mother be unable to breast-feed adequately for any reason, bottle feeding has to be resorted to. In India bottle-fed babies are exposed to numerous difficulties. Most mothers do not realize the imperative need for cleanliness and infantile summer diarrhoea in India has frequently been traced to the ubiquitous fly and its contact with the bottle or teat. Sterilization, or even careful washing with soap and hot water of bottles and teats, is not an accepted procedure in most homes. The difficulty is one of both ignorance and poverty – ignorance of the need for cleanliness, and poverty which renders the purchase of the necessary equipment for artificial feeding beyond the power of the mother and her family.

Even today, pasteurization of milk is undertaken in only a few cities in India and the cost of such milk is prohibitive. It can be asserted that nearly 90 per cent of the mothers who resort to artificial feeding have to use unpasteurized milk, often adulterated, and too expensive for most mothers to be able to afford an adequate supply of it for their infants. If a community can provide clean milk to infants (and if possible even free meals to nursing mothers), its infant mortality rate could easily be reduced. But the role of the Infant Milk Depot, providing pasteurized milk free or at nominal cost, in effectively lowering the infant mortality rate, as it has in European countries, has not yet been appreciated in India.

The practice of prolonged breast-feeding without the introduction of supplementary feeding is another serious problem. The growth curve of an average Indian infant compares favourably with that of the better nourished infants in developed countries up to 6 to 8 months of age, but thereafter the curve shows a plateau, if not a fall. At this stage Indian infants develop signs of undernourishment and malnutrition, which may develop to severe degrees of Marasmus and Kwashiorkor. Indian mothers are averse to early introduction of solids, because of the belief that the baby is incapable of digesting solids before he cuts his teeth. Even where supplementary foods are introduced, they are generally limited to starchy gruel. The maternal and child health workers, therefore, lay emphasis on nutritional education with reference to infant feeding, early introduction of solids and whatever suitable protein-rich weaning foods may be locally available. Child welfare clinics demonstrate cooking of different types of high protein weaning foods which have been evolved by the Nutrition Research Laboratories.

In addition, direct nutrition services are also offered on a limited scale. Skim milk donated by U.N.I.C.E.F. is distributed to mothers and children by some maternal and child health centres, primary health centres and maternity and children's hospitals. During the last five years, 1965–70, on an average more than a million mothers and children received milk daily under this programme. A nation-wide Applied Nutrition Programme was launched in 1963 with international assistance. It is a co-ordinated approach for solving nutrition problems by increased production of protective foods, nutrition education of mothers and children and popularizing nutritious diets through supplementary feeding programmes. The programme is in operation in 250 community development blocks. Another 1,500 blocks are proposed to be covered during the current Fourth Five-Year Plan period, 1969–74.

VACCINATION

As for vaccination, there is a law on the statute books in India requiring compulsory vaccination of all infants against smallpox. Most city corporations and municipalities try to enforce this and a majority of villages also attempt to provide this service.

Maternal and child health personnel either vaccinate infants themselves or get it done by the sanitary inspectors/basic health workers, who are responsible for this work.

But even today millions of infants escape primary vaccination in the remote villages. The country launched a National Smallpox Eradication Programme and nearly 69·5 million primary vaccinations were done from 1962 to February 1967. During 1966, 13·4 million primary vaccinations were done. Considering that over 20 million births take place every year, there is a big gap to be filled. The position regarding revaccination is even more unsatisfactory.

The extent of non-vaccination can be estimated by the incidence of regular smallpox attacks amounting to a minor epidemic every summer. It is sad to contemplate that, while the United Kingdom has made vaccination a voluntary matter, and years go by in Scandinavia without a single attack of smallpox, we in India should still be endeavouring in vain to vaccinate all our infants.

OTHER IMMUNIZATIONS

The Government of India has prescribed a schedule of immunizations for the guidance of the child welfare clinics. This includes B.C.G. vaccination, smallpox vaccination, Diphtheria–Pertussis–Tetanus (D.P.T.) and Trevalent Poliomyelitis and cholera, if indicated. A national B.C.G. vaccination programme has been carried out from the year 1951. Vaccination of the newborn was introduced early in the year 1958 and so far 0·65 million have been vaccinated. Many large maternity hospitals have now introduced the practice of the nurse in the maternity ward giving the B.C.G. vaccination to the infant. The Triple (D.P.T.) vaccination is offered in larger towns and cities by the child welfare clinics. The administration of repeat doses is presenting a problem; hardly 50 per cent of the children who take the first dose turn up for the second and a much smaller percentage for the third. Owing to the fact that the vaccine is not produced in India and has to be imported, immunization against poliomyelitis is given only in areas where there has been sporadic outbreaks of the disease.

MOTHERCRAFT

Mothers need to be taught about infant care. In Indian homes, knowledge about bearing and rearing children is derived from a fund of folklore, traditionally handed down from mother to daughter. While there is no doubt that the folklore contains profound knowledge and robust common sense based on centuries of human experience, there are areas where this knowledge is at glaring variance with the scientific verdict. These areas cover infant feeding, clothing and treatment of common ailments. We need to educate every mother in the latest scientific findings about the most desirable methods of rearing infants to ensure their proper physical and emotional development.

Mothers in human society, unlike those in the animal kingdom, do not have any instinctive knowledge about infant care. Our knowledge is derived from accumulated experience. The only way of disseminating correct knowledge is through demonstration and the printed word. Demonstration implies clinics and doctors which mean in turn considerable expenditure, and the printed word means literacy and the reading habit, both of which are rather rare in our country. Some kind of school for young mothers is one of India's pressing needs. These schools could provide instruction in mothercraft on the soundest lines in keeping with the cultural traditions and needs of the community and country.

Above all, infant welfare and survival depend on what Sir James Spence calls the 'mother's ability to cope with life'. It is true that a happy and stable family life must have as its basis three essential conditions – adequate housing, a reasonable income and a competent mother. But of these the most essential condition is the competent mother. It is the mother and the home that are infinitely more important than all the infant welfare institutions and the medical personnel. Sir James Spence et al. in their survey of *A Thousand Families in Newcastle upon Tyne* write:

> 'In the study of these families and in attempting to correlate their environments with the health of the children, there emerged one dominating factor – the capacity of the mother. If she failed, her children suffered. If she coped with life skilfully and pluckily, she was a safeguard of their health. In spite of lapses and failures, the mother stands out as the cornerstone of the family structure, and our experience confirms that in all sections of society she remains the chief guardian of child welfare, a fact which is sometimes in danger of being forgotten. A family with a good mother can withstand a feckless or even a vicious father but rarely can a family survive if the mother fails.'[1]

It is difficult to define this 'capacity of the mother'. Any attempt at definition can be more negative than positive. At one end of the scale we have stupid, ignorant and incapable mothers (some of whom are emotionally unfit to be mothers at all) and at the other end are those mothers who organize and run a home and bring up children with care, love and wisdom. In such happy homes where sickness is rare and infant mortality absent, the entire credit goes to the mother. The role of the mother in ensuring a happy and healthy family cannot be overestimated. And the point is that this 'maternal capacity' is neither instinctive nor hereditary. It is largely teachable.

The problem is made more complicated by the low level of nutrition and environmental sanitation of the community. It has been estimated that almost half of the admissions in children's hospitals are infants. The maternal and child health organization finds that in spite of the fact that problems of early childhood demand prompt care, it is the most difficult group to reach. The experience is that

---

[1] James Spence, et al., *A Thousand Families in Newcastle upon Tyne* (London: Oxford University Press, 1954), p. 120.

children are brought to the child welfare clinics only when they are sick and in need of urgent medical care. Much has to be done to educate mothers in the act of child care and mothercraft.

PAEDIATRIC SERVICES

In India, obstetricians have been looking after the newborn but now this responsibility has been passed on to the paediatricians in the teaching hospitals and other larger hospitals. Special intensive care units for premature and sick newborns are being organized in children's hospitals. However, the available facilities hardly touch the fringe of the problem. There are just over 8,000 paediatric beds in the different children's hospitals and wards of general hospitals. They are located in the larger hospitals of towns and cities. In other hospitals children are admitted in the general wards. Recently paediatric surgical units have been developed in a few medical college hospitals. The development of a special paediatric unit in all district hospitals to begin with is emphasized. Provision for paediatric consultations for the smaller hospitals and primary health centres is made by arranging visits of the district paediatricians at regular intervals.

The inclusion of paediatrics in the medical curriculum is a recent feature. Infant diseases constitute a new field and the specialists in it are few. There is a pressing need for medical colleges to give greater emphasis to children's diseases and turn out more and competent paediatricians. While specialization is necessary, the future general practitioner must be taught and trained much more about childhood diseases, for often a family summons first a general practitioner when an infant becomes ill. In other words, the family doctor must also be a competent paediatrician, if possible.

EVOLUTION OF POLICY

From the beginning, the Government was aware of the need not only to modernize maternal and children's health services but extend them to areas where they were absent. As early as 1946 the Health Survey and Development Committee gave considerable attention to this question in their report submitted to the Government.[1]

The late Prime Minister Jawaharlal Nehru in his address to the International Study Conference on Child Welfare held in New Delhi in December, 1952, said:

[1] *Report of the Health Survey and Development Committee* (New Delhi: Government of India Press, 1946), 4 vols.

'In three or four days' time we are going to consider the five-year plan of this country. . . . Of course, there is a little chapter here and there on child welfare too, probably lost among the numerous other chapters dealing with all kinds of industrial, agricultural and other subjects, which are no doubt important. But somehow the fact that ultimately everything depends on the human factor gets rather lost (I am talking of my own country; I would not presume to say that of others), in our thinking of plans and schemes of national development, in terms of factories, mines and general schemes. It is all very important and you must have them, but ultimately, of course, it is the human being that counts and if the human being counts, well, he counts much more as a child than as a grown up. So, therefore, child welfare . . . should really be considered as of paramount importance in the states' plans.'[1]

The Planning Commission in their First Five-Year Plan observed:

'Maternity and child health is a service that is kept in the forefront in the planning of health programmes. The protection of the health of the expectant mother and her child is of the utmost importance for building a sound and healthy nation. The maternal mortality of India is very high and is estimated at 20 per thousand live births. Maternal morbidity is also very high, being nearly 20 times the mortality. The infant mortality rate is of the order of 127 per thousand live births. The corresponding rates in progressive countries are very low and have been achieved by concentrated effort on the improvement of the health of the mother and child.

The lack of trained personnel like women doctors, health visitors, midwives, dais, etc., and of institutional facilities for training them add to the handicaps to provide an efficient service. The growth of maternity and child health work has been mainly through voluntary efforts and Governments and local authorities have taken it up only recently. Maternal and child health services should form an integral part of the general health services. Many of the states have developed the service in varying degrees – Madras, Uttar Pradesh, Bombay and West Bengal leading. It is essential to have on the staff of each Director of Health Services a specially trained woman medical officer. At present it is understood that only 9 states have got such organization at the headquarters of the States. In a very few states, women doctors are employed in

[1] Government of India press release dated December 12, 1952, as quoted in the Indian press.

both urban and rural areas. The pattern of organization for urban and rural areas may be considered separately.

While it is desirable to develop community centres which can cater to the needs of all members of a family and the whole community, such a development may not be possible except gradually. We have, therefore, to develop the ordinary type of maternity and child health centres. An adequate number of such centres properly equipped and staffed should be provided in all the urban health organizations. One centre with a minimum staff of one health visitor, 2 midwives, a peon and a part-time sweeper to serve a population of 10,000 is recommended. In addition, there should be a woman doctor preferably with post-graduate training in maternity and child health to be in charge of these centres. There is ordinarily overcrowding in practically all the maternity hospitals and the number of maternity beds should be increased to double its present strength in order to accommodate more delivery cases and to give post-natal care for a longer period. Ten per cent of the maternity beds should be reserved for antenatal cases. It is also essential to reserve for children at least 10 per cent of the beds where there is no separate children's hospital with an adequate number of beds. Antenatal and post-natal clinics should form an essential feature of all hospitals with maternity beds. Provision should be made for day nurseries to look after infants and children of working mothers with the help of voluntary organizations or under the provisions of the Indian Factories Act. Private nursing homes established by doctors should be licensed.

In rural areas the present trend is to provide integrated curative and preventive health services and to organize them on the basis of health centres of different grades. There should be a unit for 10,000 to 12,000 population for efficient service. This will yield a total of 300 to 400 births a year. The maternity and child health staff in such a centre should be two midwives. A number of such primary centres would come under a higher unit for the Thana or Taluka. Here the staff for maternity and child health work should be a woman doctor and two health visitors. Their main functions would be training of dais, supervision of midwives and dais, care of maternity cases needing hospitalization and conducting the clinics in the different peripheral units. One of the important activities of health units in intensive development areas like the community projects is the provision of adequate maternity and child health services, both in the primary centres and at the headquarters of the project areas in the secondary centres.

311

All doctors engaged in maternity and child health work should have training in this branch of preventive medicine for a period of at least three months, and must have done a house job in an obstetrics department for at least six months. The practical training should cover both rural and urban fields. The period of field training will vary according to the total period the course covers. The department of maternity and child health of the All-India Institute of Hygiene and Public Health in Calcutta is to be expanded as a Centre for Post-graduate training for maternity and child health doctors and for public health nurses with the aid of U.N.I.C.E.F. Rural and urban training fields for nurses and midwives in the Delhi area and paediatric training centres in Madras, Bombay and Patna (Hyderabad is also under consideration) are being developed by the Government with W.H.O. and U.N.I.C.E.F. assistance.

Voluntary organizations have played an important role in the past. They were responsible for starting the training of dais, midwives and health visitors. Voluntary bodies have also been responsible for the establishment and maintenance of a large number of maternity and child health centres. But the responsibility for providing such services rests upon the Government. The activities of the voluntary bodies should supplement the functions of the Government. The Government should have power of supervision and control to ensure that health activities of voluntary organizations are maintained at a satisfactory level and they should extend the fullest support to these organizations. The provision made by the various states for maternity and child health work is Rs. 1.35 crores and by the centre Rs. 53.48 lakhs.'[1]

The Second Five-Year Plan gave similar attention to the problem. They observed:

'During the Second Five-Year Plan it is intended to provide for larger hospital accommodation and to improve the services in hospitals, including staff, accommodation, equipment, and supplies. For this purpose the plan provides about Rs. 40 crores. It is estimated that in 1951 there were 8,600 medical institutions in the country with about 113,000 beds; in 1955–56 the number of institutions is estimated to be about 10,000 with about 125,000 beds. These figures represent an increase during the first plan of 16 per cent in institutions and of 10 per cent in beds. At the

[1] *The First Five-Year Plan* (New Delhi: Planning Commission, 1953), pp. 509–11.

end of the second plan the number of institutions is likely to be about 12,600 and the number of beds about 155,000 so that the increase expected is about 26 per cent in institutions and about 24 per cent in hospital beds.

The provision of rural medical and health care is the central problem in health planning. The object is to be achieved through the setting up of "health units" in national extension and community projects. These units perform a variety of services and in their work curative and preventive aspects are integrated. During the first plan, in all 725 health units are expected to be set up. According to the tentative plans which have been drawn up and are now under consideration, it is proposed to establish over 3,000 health units in community project, national extension and other areas. State governments also propose to convert 131 of the existing dispensaries into primary health units and to set up a number of secondary health units.

The key to the extension of health services and their efficient operation is the availability of trained personnel in all categories. Training programmes have, however, to be linked with employment opportunities which are likely to become available. At the end of 1950 there were about 59,300 registered medical practitioners. The number had increased by the end of 1954 to about 67,000. It is estimated that by the end of the first plan there will be about 70,000 registered medical practitioners. At the rate of one doctor for every 5,000 population at the end of the second plan about 80,000 doctors will be needed. Allowing for supervisory posts, the number of doctors needed will be about 90,000. That is to say, each year 4,000 more doctors are required. The number of medical colleges has increased from 30 in 1950–51 to 40 in 1955–56 and the number of annual admissions from 2,500 to about 3,500 providing, at present, for a net annual turnout of about 2,000 doctors. State plans provide for the expansion of about 28 medical colleges and attached hospitals. The Central Government will assist the setting up of six new medical colleges and the establishment of full-time teaching units and of Preventive Medicine and Psychiatric Departments in medical colleges. Provision has also been made for completing the All-India Institute of Medical Sciences and upgrading certain departments of medical colleges for post-graduate training and research.

Shortages in personnel other than doctors have been more marked and are likely to persist longer than in the case of doctors. At the end of 1954 the numbers registered in different categories in the states were 20,793 nurses, 24,290 midwives, 756 health visitors, 4,468 dais and 946 nurse-dais. As norms to aim at there should be one hospital bed for 1,000 population, one nurse and one midwife for every 5,000 population and one health visitor and one sanitary inspector for 20,000 population. For ancillary categories of personnel, figures in the last column in the table [59] below are still somewhat distant. They illustrate, however, the character of the present shortages and the need for accelerated and sustained action if even elementary services are to reach the mass of the people in any adequate degree.

Table 59
NUMBER OF HEALTH PERSONNEL IN THE THREE FIVE-YEAR PLANS

	1950–51	*1955–56*	*1960–61*	*Number needed*
Doctors	59,000	70,000	80,000	90,000
Nurses (including auxiliary nurse-midwives)	17,000	22,000	31,000	80,000
Midwives	18,000	26,000	32,000	80,000
Health visitors	600	800	2,500	20,000
Nurse-dais and dais	4,000	6,000	41,000	80,000
Health assistants and Sanitary inspectors	3,500	4,000	7,000	20,000

During the second plan, an attempt is being made to achieve substantial advance in the provision of training facilities for different classes of personnel. Arrangements are being made for the training of nurses, midwives, pharmacists, sanitary inspectors and other technicians at medical colleges and at the larger hospitals which are not in use as teaching hospitals. There are at present six dental colleges in the country and they need to be more adequately staffed, equipped and housed. It is proposed to establish four new dental colleges and expand two existing colleges. The plan provides about Rs. 40 crores for various training programmes. . . .

Maternal and child health programmes are proposed to be integrated with the primary health unit services. The plans of states provide for the setting up of about 2,100 maternity and child health centres. At present paediatrics is the weakest link in the maternal and child health services. It is therefore proposed to start four regional training centres in paediatrics to give adequate training for medical as well as associated personnel in preventive and curative paediatrics. These centres will be associated with a number of properly staffed and equipped maternal and child health centres and will offer paediatric care in an area around the training centre.'[1]

On the subject of maternal and child health, the Third Plan observed:

'At the end of the Second Plan there were nearly 4,500 maternity and child welfare centres, each serving a population varying between 10,000 and 25,000. One third of these centres are located in urban areas. As a result of improvements in maternity care effected during the first two Plans, the maternal mortality rate which was as high as 20 per thousand live births in 1938 is now estimated to have come down to 12·4 per thousand live births. There has also been a general reduction in the incidence of severe cases of anaemia in areas where antenatal services are well established and there has been a steady decrease in the infant mortality rate. During the Second Plan, maternity and child welfare services became an integral part of the overall health services in rural areas. Maternity and Child Welfare Bureaux have been established in most of the states. Steps were also taken during the Second Plan to improve training in paediatrics.

Facilities for the teaching of paediatrics in medical colleges have been expanded in recent years. Maternity and child welfare services provided by the primary health centres are supplemented by services provided by the welfare extension projects and by voluntary organizations.

During the Third Plan it is proposed to link up the maternity and child health services associated with the primary health units with extended facilities in referral and district hospitals. Short orientation courses will be arranged at these hospitals for personnel engaged in maternity and child health work.'[2]

In regard to training of ancillary personnel, the Third Five-Year Plan pointed out:

'Although since the beginning of the First Plan, steps have been taken to expand training facilities for nurses and other ancillary personnel, shortages have continued to be acute. The relevant statistics of the progress made and the targets for the Third Plan

[1] *Second Five-Year Plan: A Draft Outline* (New Delhi: Planning Commission, 1956), pp. 151–3, 155–6.
[2] *The Third Five-Year Plan* (New Delhi: The Planning Commission, 1961), p. 666.

are set out in [Table 60]. The problem is proposed to be dealt with in the Third Plan along the following lines.

1. *Nurses.* To improve the condition of service for nurses and to attract larger numbers of women to this profession it is proposed that in each state, there should be a special Nursing Service and a Nurse Superintendent should advise and assist the Director of Health Services. It is also proposed that competent and experienced Nursing Sisters should be appointed in hospitals.

2. *Auxiliary nurse midwives.* Auxiliary nurse midwives go through a two-year course of training. The aim is that they should eventually replace midwives in primary health units and elsewhere. Training facilities are being considerably stepped up in the Third Plan.

3. *Health visitors.* The Plan as at present formulated envisages increase in the number of training institutions for health visitors from 30 to 50, the annual intake rising from 650 to 850. Considering the existing shortage of health visitors and the important role assigned to them in the rural health services, the training facilities need to be augmented to a much greater extent. It is suggested that the present training programmes in the States should be reviewed at an early date in relation to health visitors as well as other women workers required for implementing the rural health programme.

4. *Dais.* Child births in rural areas are attended to mostly by dias. They, however, lack training. The general object is to give to dais a measure of reorientation and training to enable them to render better service in the villages. Provision for such training is being made in the Plan.'[1]

The relevant figures regarding progress in the First and the Second Plans and the physical targets for the Third Plan are given in Table 60.

The Fourth Five-Year Plan does not go into the subject of maternal and child health but confines its attention to the education and training of manpower – doctors, nurses and other para-medical personnel – to meet the nation's requirements for the plan period. Their plans for training are as follows:

'*Medical Personnel.* Expansion in admissions and turnout of doctors during the Third Plan period, the three subsequent years

---

[1] *Third Five-Year Plan* (New Delhi: The Planning Commission, 1961), p. 663.

Table 60
ACHIEVEMENTS AND TARGETS

Categories/unit	1950–51	1955–56	1960–61	1965–66
Doctors	56,000	65,000	70,000	81,000
Nurses	15,000	18,500	27,000	45,000
Auxiliary nurse-midwives				
and midwives	8,000	12,780	19,900	48,500
Health visitors	521	800	1,500	3,500
Nurse-dais/dais	1,800	6,400	11,500	40,000
Sanitary inspectors	3,500	4,000	6,000	19,200

The above figures give the number practising or in service.

and as planned for the last year of the Fourth Plan are shown in [Table 61].

By the end of the Fourth Plan, the number of medical colleges is expected to increase to 103, with an admission capacity of 13,000. To meet the requirement of teachers in medical colleges, specialists and research workers, existing facilities for post-graduate education will be expanded.

The stock of doctors increased from an estimated 70,000 in 1960–61 to 86,000 in 1965–66 and to 102,000 in 1968–69. It is estimated that it will increase to 138,000 in 1973–74. The doctor–population ratio in 1968–69 was approximately 1:5,200. It is

Table 61
ADMISSION AND TURNOUT OF MEDICAL
GRADUATES

			(Numbers)
Year	Colleges	Annual Admission	Annual Turnout
(1)	(2)	(3)	(4)
1961	66	7,008	4,068
1962	71	7,348	3,992
1963	79	9,667	4,179
1964	81	10,227	4,415
1965	87	10,520	5,135
1966	89	11,079	6,159
1967	91	11,106	7,407
1968	93	11,500*	9,080*
1973	103	13,000*	10,300*

* Provisional estimates.

317

expected that by the end of the Fourth Plan a doctor-population ratio of 1:4,300 will be reached and five years later of 1:3,700.

The training of nurses and para-medical personnel takes less time and adjustments of supply and demand can be made within a shorter span of time. The programme of expansion of facilities for the training of nurses and para-medical personnel will be related broadly to the requirements of these categories of personnel in connection with medical, public health and family planning programmes. The expected increase in their number is [shown in Table 62].'[1]

Table 62
STOCK OF PARA-MEDICAL PERSONNEL

				(Numbers)
St. No. (0)	Category (1)	1965–66 (2)	1968–69 (Anticipated) (3)	1973–74 (Targets) (4)
1	Nurses	45,000	61,000	88,000
2	Auxiliary nurse-midwives	22,000	34,000	54,000
3	Health/Sanitary inspectors	18,000	20,000	32,000
4	Pharmacists	48,000	51,000	66,000
5	Radiographers	700	1,300	11,300
6	Laboratory technicians	2,000	3,200	8,600

As for further plans to promote family planning, the Planning Commission has allocated Rs. 3,150 million to be spent during the five-year period of the Fourth Plan. In the words of the Fourth Five-Year Plan:

'Family Planning finds its place in the Plan as a programme of the highest priority. Its crucial importance is reflected in the widespread public interest that has been aroused no less than in the magnitude of the effort, organization and finance which Government is devoting to the programme.

The estimated population in 1968 (on October 1) was 527 million. The increase in population from 365 million in 1951 to 445 million in 1961 and 527 million in 1968 has been the result of a sharp fall in mortality rate without any significant change in the fertility rate. The birth rate appears to have remained unchanged around 41 per thousand population during the greater part of the

[1] *Fourth Five-Year Plan: 1969–74* (New Delhi: Planning Commission, 1970), pp. 367–8.

past two decades up to 1965–66. Recent surveys carried out by the Registrar-General and the National Sample Survey Organization appear to indicate that the birth rate has come down to 39 per thousand population for the country as a whole, the rate being somewhat higher in rural areas. The population growth rate is estimated to be 2·5 per cent per annum. In order to make economic development yield tangible benefits for the ordinary people, it is necessary that the birth rate be brought down substantially as early as possible. It is proposed to aim at its reduction from 39 per thousand to 25 per thousand population within the next 10–12 years. In order to achieve this, a concrete programme has been drawn up for creating facilities for the married population during their reproductive period by bringing about (1) group acceptance of the small-sized family, (2) personal knowledge about family-planning methods, and (3) ready availability of supplies and services.

Keeping in view the aim to reduce the birth rate to about 32 per thousand population by 1973–74 from the present 39, it is proposed to step up the target of sterilization and I.U.C.D. insertions and to widen the acceptance of oral and injectible contraceptives. The use of conventional contraceptives will also be stepped up so as to cover 3·24 million persons in 1969–70 and 10 million persons by 1973–74. As a result of these measures, 28 million couples are likely to be protected by 1973–74. The births expected to be prevented will aggregate to 18 million for the Plan period.

Arrangements will be made for training 10,000 medical and 150,000 para-medical personnel. In the research programmes, emphasis will be laid on the bio-medical aspect. New centres for reproductive biology and human reproduction will be established and orientation-cum-training courses in these subjects for teachers of medical colleges will be arranged. Demographic and communication studies will be used for efficient implementation of the programme. Its cost under various conditions will be analysed. Fertility surveys combined with K.A.P. studies (knowledge, attitude and practice) will be carried out to evaluate the ultimate and intermediate objectives of the programme.

The programme of family planning is likely to be more effective and acceptable if maternity and child health services are integrated with family planning. This has now been done. The scheme of immunization of infants and pre-school children with D.P.T.,

319

immunization of expectant mothers against tetanus, prophylaxis against nutritional anaemia for mothers and children and a nutritional programme for control of blindness caused by Vitamin A deficiency among children will be implemented through family welfare planning centres. Family planning will be effectively integrated with the general health services of primary health centres and sub-centres.'[1]

FINANCIAL OUTLAY (1951–71)

As has already been explained, maternal and child health services

Table 63

FINANCIAL OUTLAYS IN THE FOUR FIVE-YEAR PLANS

Plan	Total public sector (in millions) Rs.	Health plans outlay (in millions) Rs.	Health outlay as percentage of total plan
First Plan	23,600	1,400	5·8
Second Plan	46,000	2,250	4·9
Third Plan	82,000	3,450	4·2
Fourth Plan	159,020	11,550	13·0

Table 64

BREAKDOWN OF FINANCIAL OUTLAYS FOR HEALTH AND FAMILY PLANNING IN THE FOUR FIVE-YEAR PLANS

Group	(Rs. in millions)			
	First Plan (1951–56)	Second Plan (1956–61)	Third Plan (1961–66)	Fourth Plan (1969–74)
Hospitals and dispensaries, Public Health centres	250	360	617	⎫
Medical education, Training and research	216	360	563	⎪
Control of communicable diseases	231	640	705	⎬ 4,350
Other schemes including indigenous system of medicine	206	100	210	⎭
Family planning	7	30	270	3,150
Water supply and sanitation	490	760	1,053	4,050
Total	1,400	2,250	3,418	11,550

[1] *Fourth Five-Year Plan: 1969–74* (New Delhi: Planning Commission, 1970), pp. 391–4.

form an integral part of the total health services for the community. Control of communicable diseases has a direct impact on the maternal and child health services. Environmental sanitation and water supply programmes provide a more healthy environment for the growth of the child. Further, maternal and child health services are spread over other sectors like education, social welfare, labour welfare, community development, etc. Then again, there is a large number of voluntary organizations which carry out a variety of services, most of which are assisted by grants in aid by the central and state governments. It is, therefore, not possible to separate the financial outlay on the maternal and child health programme. An increasing amount has been provided for health plans, though their percentage to total plan outlay has been diminishing to some extent, as will be seen from the figures in Table 63. The distribution of the above health outlay is shown in Table 64.

CONCLUSION

All these suggestions for preventive, diagnostic and curative services appear so important and sound that one wonders why they have not been implemented in full in a country which is advancing in so many directions. The answer is lack of resources – financial, administrative, and technical. It is true that our country cannot afford all the necessary social services in the present stage of economic development. When funds are limited, the question of priorities naturally arises. But it needs no elaborate argument to prove that infant and maternal services should receive the topmost priority, and their expansion to cover the entire relevant population should take precedence over anything else in the disbursement of public funds. We might close down our embassies and consulates abroad without any great loss but we dare not cut down funds for the health, medical and social services necessary for infants and mothers. It is a poor policy to neglect mothers, and the infants who are the future citizens. Human resources constitute the most powerful factor in the prosperity of a nation. Both the health and character of a nation depend primarily upon its mothers. And the welfare of the nation in a real sense depends on the attention and care bestowed on the most defenceless and vulnerable section of our population – the mother and her infant.

Actually, the problem facing India on this question is not in any way unique and there is no need for pessimism. Every one of the modern advanced countries from Australia and New Zealand to

Scandinavia and the United States has faced somewhat similar problems, only about fifty years earlier. They have stumbled, pioneered, and progressed and a vast knowledge of their experience is available to us. The necessary scientific knowledge in social and medical spheres to achieve an infant mortality rate of fifteen or less is available today, but the major difficulty seems to be in bringing the available knowledge to every parent in the world and in removing the cultural obstacles in the path of accepting this knowledge. While scientific or social revolutions are not wrought overnight, we have today the requisite technical means to disseminate needed knowledge at all cultural levels through modern mass media. There is the problem of devising simple and inexpensive means of mass communication whereby needed knowledge can be rapidly transmitted to those who need it.

Our efforts should be directed to the ideal of reducing the present inordinate infant mortality rate of about 100 per 1,000 live births to something like fifteen. This may appear too ambitious in our present stage of socio-economic development, but this should be our target in the next ten or twenty years. The nation's children are too precious to be wasted by premature death or preventible disease.

In conclusion, the world should devote a little more attention to the care and welfare of children. All the available knowledge must be harnessed to reduce infant and childhood mortality rates to the lowest possible level. The quality of a culture and civilization may well be judged by how effectively it prevents the needless suffering and death of innocent children.

Further, there is a great need for mounting a campaign to qualify the right to reproduce. While the right to marry and to have children may be considered basic biological rights, society has found it necessary to stipulate the minimum age at marriage, whom one can marry in terms of consanguinity, etc. One further step is needed: the constitutional or legal right to have an unlimited number of children must be questioned and should not be taken for granted any longer.

The fundamental biological obligations of all married couples of the future should include:

1. Limiting their family size to two or three children, spacing the arrival of these children and not under any circumstances producing unwanted children. (The fourth child must be considered an unwanted child by society.)
2. Not producing children in response to political demands, religious injunctions, or cultural compulsions.

3. Not producing children whose physical and mental endowment would be defective or less than normal (assuming the knowledge of such a possibility is available to parents).
4. No couple need assume that the small family norm is applicable only to the poor and the underprivileged and they are exempt by virtue of intellectual superiority, wealth, or physical stamina. Those couples determined to have more than two or three children should adopt homeless children who are already in this world.

Appendix 1

DECLARATION OF THE RIGHTS OF THE CHILD[1]

Preamble

Whereas the people of the United Nations have, in the Charter, reaffirmed their faith in fundamental human rights, and in the dignity and worth of the human person, and have determined to promote social progress and better standards of life in larger freedom.

Whereas the United Nations has, in the Universal Declaration of Human Rights, proclaimed that every one is entitled to all the rights and freedoms set forth therein, without distinction of any kind, such as race, colour, sex, language, religion, political or other opinion, national or social origin, property, birth or other status.

Whereas the child by reason, of his physical and mental immaturity, needs special safeguards and care, including appropriate legal protection before as well as after birth.

Whereas the need for such special safeguards has been stated in the Geneva Declaration of the Rights of the Child of 1924, and recognized in the Universal Declaration of Human Rights and in the statutes of specialized agencies and international organizations concerned with the welfare of children.

Whereas the mankind owes to the child the best it has to give,

Now therefore,

The General Assembly

Proclaims this Declaration of the Rights of the child to the end that he may have a happy childhood and enjoy for his own good and for the good of society the rights and freedoms herein set forth, and calls upon parents, upon voluntary organizations, local authorities and national governments to recognize these rights and strive for

[1] Adopted by the General Assembly of the United Nations in 1959.

their observance by legislative and by other measures progressively taken in accordance with the following principles:

Principle 1
The child shall enjoy all the rights set fourth in this Declaration. All children, without any exception whatsoever, shall be entitled to these rights, without distinction or discrimination on account of race, colour, sex, language, political or other opinion, national or social origin, property birth or other status, whether of himself or of his family.

Principle 2
The child shall enjoy special protection, and shall be given opportunities and facilities by law and by other means, to enable him to develop physically, mentally, morally, spiritually and socially in a healthy and normal manner and in conditions of freedom and dignity. In the enactment of laws for this purpose the best interests of the child shall be the paramount consideration.

Principle 3
The child shall be entitled from his birth to a name and a nationality.

Principle 4
The child shall enjoy the benefits of special security. He shall be entitled to grow and develop in health; to this end special care and protection shall be provided both to him and to his mother, including adequate pre-natal and post-natal care. The child shall have the right to adequate nutrition, housing, recreation and medical services.

Principle 5
The child who is physically, mentally or socially handicapped shall be given the special treatment, education and care required by his particular condition.

Principle 6
The child, for the full and harmonious development of his personality, needs love and understanding. He shall, wherever possible, grow up in the care and under the responsibility of his parents, and in any case in an atmosphere of affection and of moral and material security; a child of tender year shall not, save in exceptional circumstances, be separated from his mother. Society and the public authorities shall have the duty to extend particular care to children without a family

325

and to those without adequate means of support. Payment of state and other assistance toward the maintenance of children of large families is desirable.

Principle 7
The child is entitled to receive education, which shall be free and compulsory, at least in the elementary stages. He shall be given an education which will promote his general culture, and enable him on a basis of equal opportunity to develop his abilities, his individual judgment, and his sense of moral and social responsibility, and to become a useful member of society.

The best interests of the child shall be the guiding principle of those responsible for his education and guidance; that responsibility lies in the first place with his Parents.

The child shall have full opportunity for play and recreation, which should be directed to the same purpose as education; society and the public authorities shall endeavour to promote the enjoyment of this right.

Principle 8
The child shall in all circumstances be among the first to receive protection and relief.

Principle 9
The child shall be protected against all forms of neglect, cruelty and exploitation. He shall not be the subject of traffic, in any form.

The child shall not be admitted to employment before an appropriate minimum age; he shall in no case be caused or permitted to engage in any education or employment which would prejudice his health or education, or interfere with his physical, mental or moral development.

Principle 10
The child shall be protected from practices which may foster racial, religious and any other form of discrimination. He shall be brought up in a spirit of understanding, tolerance, friendship among peoples, peace and universal brotherhood and in full consciousness that his energy and talents should be devoted to the service of his fellow men.

Appendix 2

THE REGISTRATION OF BIRTHS AND DEATHS ACT, 1968

(As introduced in the Rajya Sabha)

A

BILL

to provide for the regulation of registration of births and deaths and for matters connected therewith.

BE it enacted by Parliament in the Eighteenth Year of the Republic of India as follows:

CHAPTER I

PRELIMINARY

1. (1) This Act may be called the Registration of Births and Deaths Act, 1967.

(2) It extends to the whole of India.

(3) It shall come into force in a State on such date as the Central Government may, by notification in the *Official Gazette*, appoint:

Provided that different dates may be appointed for different parts of a State.

2. (1) In this Act, unless the context otherwise requires,

(a) 'birth' means live birth or stillbirth;

(b) 'death' means the permanent disappearance of all evidence of life at any time after live birth has taken place;

(c) 'foetal death' means absence of all evidence of life prior to the complete expulsion or extraction from its mother of a product of conception irrespective of the duration of pregnancy;

(d) 'live birth' means the complete expulsion or extraction from its mother of a product of conception, irrespective of the duration of pregnancy, which, after such expulsion or extraction, breathes or shows any other

327

evidence of life, and each product of such birth is considered live born;

(e) 'prescribed' means prescribed by rules made under this Act;

(f) 'State Government', in relation to a Union territory, means the Administrator thereof;

(g) 'still birth' means foetal death where a product of conception has attained at least the prescribed period of gestation.

(2) Any reference in this Act to any law which is not in force in any area shall, in relation to that area, be construed as a reference to the corresponding law, if any, in force in that area.

CHAPTER II

REGISTRATION-ESTABLISHMENT

3. (1) The Central Government may, by notification in the *Official Gazette*, appoint a person to be known as the Registrar General, India.

(2) The Central Government may also appoint such other officers with such designations as it thinks fit for the purpose of discharging, under the superintendence and direction of the Registrar General, such functions of the Registrar General under this Act as he may, from time to time, authorize them to discharge.

(3) The Registrar General may issue general directions regarding registration of births and deaths in the territories to which this Act extends, and shall take steps to co-ordinate and unify the activities of Chief Registrars in the matter of registration of births and deaths and submit to the Central Government an annual report on the working of this Act in the said territories.

4. (1) The State Government may, by notification in the *Official Gazette*, appoint a Chief Registrar for the State.

(2) The State Government may also appoint such other officers with such designations as it thinks for the purpose of discharging, under the superintendence and direction of the Chief Registrar, such of his functions as he may, from time to time, authorize them to discharge.

(3) The Chief Registrar shall be the chief executive authority in the State for carrying into execution the provisions of this Act and the rules and orders made there-under subject to the directions, if any, given by the State Government.

(4) The Chief Registrar shall take steps, by the issue of suitable instructions or otherwise, to co-ordinate, unify and supervise the work of registration in the State for securing an efficient system of registration and shall prepare and submit to the State Government, in such manner and at such intervals as may be prescribed, a report on the working of this Act in the State along with the statistical report referred to in Sub-section (2) of Section 19.

5. The State Government may, by notification in the *Official Gazette*, divide the territory within the state into such registration divisions as it may think fit and prescribe different rules for different registration divisions.

6. (1) The State Government may appoint a District Registrar for each revenue district and such number of Additional District Registrars as it thinks fit who shall, subject to the general control and direction of the District Registrar, discharge such functions of the District Registrar as the District Registrar may, from time to time, authorize them to discharge.

(2) The District Registrar shall superintend, subject to the direction of the Chief Registrar, the registration of births and deaths in the district and shall be responsible for carrying into execution in the district the provisions of this Act and the orders of the Chief Registrar issued from time to time for the purposes of this Act.

7. (1) The State Government may appoint a Registrar for each local area comprising the area within the jurisdiction of a municipality, panchayat or other local authority or any other area or a combination of any two or more of them:

Provided that the State Government may appoint in the case of a municipality, panchayat or other local authority, any officer or other employee thereof as a Registrar.

(2) Every Registrar shall, without fee or reward, enter in the register maintained for the purpose all information given to him under Section 8 or Section 9 and shall also take steps to inform himself carefully of every birth and of every death which takes place in his jurisdiction and to ascertain and register the particulars required to be registered.

(3) Every Registrar shall have an office in the local area for which he is appointed.

(4) Every Registrar shall attend his office for the purpose of registering births and deaths on such days and at such hours as the Chief Registrar may direct and shall cause to be placed in some conspicuous place on or near the outer door of the office of the Registrar a board bearing, in the local language, his name with the

329

addition of Registrar of Births and Deaths for the local area for which he is appointed, and the days and hours of his attendance.

(5) The Registrar may, with the prior approval of the Chief Registrar, appoint Sub-Registrars and assign to them any or all of his powers and duties in relation to specified areas within his jurisdiction.

CHAPTER III

REGISTRATION OF BIRTHS AND DEATHS

8. (1) It shall be the duty of the persons specified below to give or cause to be given, either orally or in writing, according to the best of their knowledge and belief, within such time as may be prescribed, information to the Registrar of the several particulars required to be entered in the forms prescribed by the State Government under Sub-section (1) of Section 16,

> (a) in respect of births and deaths in a house, whether residential or non-residential, not being any place referred to in clauses (b) to (e), the head of the house, or in case more than one household live in the house, the head of the household, the head being the person, who is so recognized by the house or the household, and if he is not present in the house at any time during the period within which the birth or death has to be reported, the nearest relative of the head present in the house, and in the absence of any such person, the oldest adult male person present therein during the said period;
>
> (b) in respect of births and deaths in a hospital, health centre, maternity or nursing home or other like institution, the medical officer in charge or any person authorized by him in this behalf;
>
> (c) in respect of births and deaths in a jail, the jailor in charge;
>
> (d) in respect of births and deaths in a choultry, chattram, hostel, dharmasala, boarding-house, lodging-house, tavern, barrack, toddy shop or place of public resort the person in charge, thereof;
>
> (e) in respect of any new-born child or dead body found deserted in a public place, the headman or other corresponding officer of the village in the case of a village

and the officer in charge of the local police station elsewhere:

Provided that any person who finds such child or dead body, or in whose charge such child or dead body may be placed, shall notify such fact to the headman or officer aforesaid;

(f) in any other place, such person as may be prescribed.

(2) Notwithstanding anything contained in Sub-section (1), the State Government, having regard to the conditions obtaining in a registration division, may by order require that for such period as may be specified in the order, any person specified by the State Government by designation in this behalf shall give or cause to be given information regarding births and deaths in a house referred to in Clause (a) of Sub-section (1) instead of the persons specified in that clause.

9. In the case of births and deaths in a plantation, the superintendent of the plantation shall give or cause to be given to the Registrar the information referred to in Section 8:

Provided that the persons referred to in Clauses (a) to (f) of Sub-section (1) of Section 8 shall furnish the necessary particulars to the superintendent of the plantation.

Explanation: In this section, the expression 'plantation' means any land not less than four hectares in extent which is being prepared for the production of or actually produces tea, coffee, pepper, rubber, cardamom, cinchona or such other products as the State Government may by notification in the *Official Gazette*, specify and the expression 'superintendent of the plantation' means the person having the charge or supervision of the labourers and work in the plantation, whether called a manager, superintendent or by any other name.

10. (1) It shall be the duty of:

    (i) the midwife or any other medical or health attendant at a birth or death;

    (ii) the sweeper in a municipality, panchayat or other local authority;

    (iii) the keeper or the owner of a place set apart for the disposal of dead bodies or any person required by a local authority to be present at such place, or

    (iv) any other person whom the state government may specify in this behalf by his designation,

to notify every birth or death or both at which he or she attended or was present, or which occurred in

331

such areas as may be prescribed, to the Registrar within such time and in such manner as may be prescribed.

(2) In any area, the State Government, having regard to the facilities available therein in this behalf, may require that a certificate as to the cause of death shall be obtained by the Registrar from such person and in such form as may be prescribed.

(3) Where the State Government has required under subsection (2) that a certificate as to the cause of death shall be obtained, in the event of the death of any person who, during his last illness, was attended by a medical practitioner, the medical practitioner shall, after the death of that person, forthwith, issue, without charging any fee, to the person required under this Act to give information concerning the death, a certificate in the prescribed form stating to the best of his knowledge and belief the cause of death; and the certificate shall be received and delivered by such person to the Registrar at the time of giving information concerning the death as required by this Act.

11. Every person who has orally given to the Registrar any information required under this Act shall write in the register maintained in this behalf, his name, description and place of abode, and, if he cannot write, shall put his thumb mark in the register against his name, description and place of abode, the particulars being in such a case entered by the Registrar.

12. The Registrar shall, as soon as the registration of a birth or death has been completed, give, free of charge, to the person who gives information under Section 8 or Section 9 an extract of the prescribed particulars under his hand from the register relating to such birth or death.

13. (1) Any birth or death of which information is given to the Registrar after the expiry of the period specified therefor, but within thirty days of its occurrence, shall be registered on payment of such late fee as may be prescribed.

(2) Any birth or death, of which delayed information is given to the Registrar after thirty days but within one year of its occurrence, shall be registered only with the written permission of the prescribed authority and on payment of the prescribed fee and the production of an affidavit made before a notary public or any other officer authorized in this behalf by the State Government.

(3) Any birth or death which was not registered within one year of its occurrence, shall be registered only on an order made by a magistrate of the first class or a Presidency Magistrate after verifying

the correctness of the birth or death and on payment of the prescribed fee.

(4) The provisions of this section shall be without prejudice to any action that may be taken against a person for failure on his part to register any birth or death within the time specified therefor and any such birth or death may be registered during the pendency of any such action.

14. Where the birth of any child has been registered without a name, the parent or guardian of such child shall within the prescribed period give information regarding the name of the child to the Registrar either orally or in writing and thereupon the Registrar shall enter such name in the register and initial and date the entry.

15. If it is proved to the satisfaction of the Registrar that any entry of a birth or death in any register kept by him under this Act is erroneous in form or substance, or has been fraudulently or improperly made, he may, subject to such rules as may be made by the State Government with respect to the conditions on which and the circumstances in which such entries may be corrected or cancelled, correct the error or cancel the entry by suitable entry in the margin, without any alteration of the original entry, and shall sign the marginal entry and add thereto the date of the correction or cancellation.

CHAPTER IV

MAINTENANCE OF RECORDS AND STATISTICS

16. (1) Every Registrar shall keep in the prescribed form a register of births and deaths for the registration area or any part thereof in relation to which he exercises jurisdiction.

(2) The Chief Registrar shall cause to be printed and supplied a sufficient number of register books for making entries of births and deaths according to such forms and instructions as may, from time to time, be prescribed; and a copy of such forms in the local language shall be posted in some conspicuous place on or near the outer door of the office of every Registrar.

17. (1) Subject to any rules made in this behalf by the State Government, including rules relating to the payment of fees and postal charges, any person may:

    (a) cause a search to be made by the Registrar for any entry in a register of births and deaths; and

    (b) obtain an extract from such register relating to any birth or death:

333

Provided that no extract relating to any death, issued to any person, shall disclose the particulars regarding the cause of death as entered in the register.

(2) All extracts given under this section shall be certified by the Registrar or any other officer authorized by the State Government to give such extracts as provided in section 76 of the Indian Evidence Act, 1872, and shall be admissible in evidence for the purpose of proving the birth or death to which the entry relates.

18. The registration offices shall be inspected and the registers kept therein shall be examined in such manner and by such authority as may be specified by the District Registrar.

19. (1) Every Registrar shall send to the Chief Registrar or to any officer specified by him, at such intervals and in such form as may be prescribed, a return regarding the entries of births and deaths in the register kept by such Registrar.

(2) The Chief Registrar shall cause the information in the returns furnished by the Registrars to be compiled and shall publish for the information of the public a statistical report on the registered births and deaths during the year at such intervals and in such form as may be prescribed.

CHAPTER V

MISCELLANEOUS

20. (1) The Registrar General shall, subject to such rules as may be made by the Central Government in this behalf, cause to be registered information as to births and deaths of citizens of India outside India received by him under the rules relating to the registration of such citizens at Indian Consulates made under the Citizenship Act, 1955, and every such registration shall also be deemed to have been duly made under this Act.

(2) In the case of any child born outside India in respect of whom information has not been received as provided in Sub-section (1), if the parents of the child return to India with a view to settling therein, they may, at any time within sixty days from the date of the arrival of the child in India, get the birth of the child registered under this Act in the same manner as if the child was born in India and the provisions of Section 13 shall apply to the birth of such child after the expiry of the period of sixty days aforesaid.

21. The Registrar may either orally or in writing require any per-

son to furnish any information within his knowledge in connection with a birth or death in the locality within which such person resides and that person shall be bound to comply with such requisition.

22. The central government may give such directions to any state government as may appear to be necessary for carrying into execution in the state any of the provisions of this Act or of any rule or order made thereunder.

23. (1) Any person who:

(a) fails without reasonable cause to give any information which it is his duty to give under any of the provisions of Sections 8 and 9; or

(b) gives or causes to be given, for the purpose of being inserted in any register of births and deaths, any information which he knows or believes to be false regarding any of the particulars required to be known and registered; or

(c) refuses to write his name, description and place of abode or to put his thumb mark in the register as required by Section 11, shall be punishable with fine which may extend to fifty rupees.

(2) Any Registrar or Sub-Registrar who neglects or refuses, without reasonable cause, to register any birth or death occurring in his jurisdiction or to submit any returns as required by Sub-section (1) of section 19 shall be punishable with fine which extend to twenty-five rupees.

(3) Any medical practitioner who neglects or refuses to issue a certificate under Sub-section (3) of Section 10 and any person who neglects or refuses to deliver such certificate shall be punishable with fine which may extend to fifty rupees.

(4) Any person who, without reasonable cause, contravenes any provision of this Act for the contravention of which no penalty is provided for in this Section shall be punishable with fine which may extend to ten rupees.

(5) Notwithstanding anything contained in the Code of Criminal Procedure, 1898, an offence under this Section shall be tried summarily by a magistrate.

24. (1) Subject to such conditions as may be prescribed, any officer authorized by the Chief Registrar by a general or special order in this behalf may, either before or after the institution of criminal proceedings under this Act, accept from the person who has committed or is reasonably suspected of having committed an offence

335

under this Act, by way of composition of such offence a sum of money not exceeding fifty rupees.

(2) On the payment of such sum of money, such person shall be discharged and no further proceedings shall be taken against him in respect of such offence.

25. No prosecution for an offence punishable under this Act shall be instituted except by an officer authorized by the Chief Registrar by general or special order in this behalf.

26. All Registrars and Sub-Registrars shall, while acting or purporting to act in pursuance of the provisions of this Act or any rule or order made thereunder, be deemed to be public servants within the meaning of Section 21 of the Indian Penal Code.

27. The State Government may, by notification in the *Official Gazette*, direct that any power exercisable by it under this Act (except the power to make rules under Section 30) or the rules made thereunder shall, subject to such conditions, if any, as may be specified in the direction, be exercisable also by such officer or authority subordinate to the State Government as may be specified in the direction.

28. (1) No suit, prosecution or other legal proceeding shall lie against the government, the Registrar General, any Registrar, or any person exercising any power or performing any duty under this Act for anything which is in good faith done or intended to be done in pursuance of this Act or any rule or order made thereunder.

(2) No suit or other legal proceeding shall lie against the Government for any damage caused or likely to be caused by anything which is in good faith done or intended to be done in pursuance of this Act or any rule or order made thereunder.

29. Nothing in this Act shall be construed to be in derogation of the provisions of the Births, Deaths and Marriages Registration Act, 1886.

30. (1) The State Government may, with the approval of the Central Government, by notification in the *Official Gazette*, make rules to carry out the purposes of this Act.

(2) In particular, and without prejudice to the generality of the foregoing provision, such rules may provide for:

(a) the forms of registers of births and deaths required to be kept under this Act;

(b) the period within which and the form and the manner in which information should be given to the Registrar under Section 8;

(c) the period within which and the manner in which births and deaths shall be notified under Sub-section (1) of Section 10;

(d) the person from whom and the form in which a certificate as to cause of death shall be obtained;

(e) the particulars of which extract may be given under Section 12;

(f) the authority which may grant permission for registration of a birth or death under Sub-section (2) of Section 13;

(g) the fees payable for registration made under section 13;

(h) the submission of reports by the Chief Registrar under Sub-section (4) of Section 4;

(i) the search of birth and death registers and the fees payable for such search and for the grant of extracts from the registers;

(j) the forms in which and the intervals at which the returns and the statistical report under Section 19 shall be furnished and published;

(k) the custody, production and transfer of the registers and other records kept by Registrars;

(l) the correction of errors and the cancellation of entries in the register of births and deaths;

(m) any other matter which has to be, or may be, prescribed.

31. (1) Subject to the provisions of Section 29, as from the coming into force of this Act in any State or part thereof, so much of any law in force therein as relates to the matter covered by this Act shall stand repealed in such State or part, as the case may be.

(2) Notwithstanding such repeal, anything done or any action taken (including any instruction or direction issued, any regulation or rule or order made) under any such law shall, in so far as such thing or action is not inconsistent with the provisions of this Act, be deemed to have been done or taken under the provisions aforesaid, as if they were in force when such thing was done or such action was taken, and shall continue in force accordingly until superseded by anything done or any action taken under this Act.

32. If any difficulty arises in giving effect in a State to the provisions of this Act in their application to any area, the State government may, with the approval of the Central Government, by order

make such provisions or give such directions not inconsistent with the provisions of this Act as appears to the State Government to be necessary or expedient for removing the difficulty.

Provided that no order shall be made under this section in relation to any area in a State after the expiration of two years from the date on which this Act comes into force in that area.

STATEMENT OF OBJECTS AND REASONS

At present only a few States like Assam, Madras, Kerala and West Bengal have separate legislation in regard to registration of births and deaths, while others have only enabling provisions in this behalf in the Municipal Act, Panchayat Act, Chowkidar Manual or Land Revenue Manual so that the matter is governed by executive orders or bye-laws setting out legal registration procedure. Such a situation, by its very nature, leads to diversity in practices and inefficiency of performance. Various national committees and experts, who gave attention to the problem, have strongly recommended the need for a Central legislation to regulate registration of births and deaths in the country.

The Central Government needs adequate and accurate country-wide registration data for purposes of national planning, organizing public health and medical activities and developing family planning programmes. Population is one of the most dynamic factors in the present economy of the country but it is here that information on trends furnished by the registration data is very defective and un-reliable. The national interest requires an acceptable level of per-formance by the States and technical uniformity of the methods and standards used in the collection and compilation of data throughout the country. The Government, therefore, consider that in order to develop a sound and unified system of registration in the country, Central legislation is necessary on the subject.

The Bill seeks to give legal status to the existing officials in the registration machinery, who are drawn from different Departments to look after the registration work in addition to their other normal duties and to bind them in a registration hierarchy with the Registrar General, India, at the Centre and Chief Registrar at the State, run-ning through District Registrars to the village and town Registrars at the periphery. The provisions of the Bill are built closely around the current registration practices, where experience of their working in several States has shown them to be practicable and efficient. They unify the existing legal and administrative provisions. They are

338

broad enough to permit State variation in operational details as demanded by the particular characteristics of their respective ad-
ministrations but are specific enough to ensure development of the
system so as to secure a minimum of uniformity and comparability in
coverage and efficiency. The Bill lays down specific principles, general
lines of action and channels of authority but execution is left with the
States, and accordingly details of implementation are relegated to
rules to be made by the State Governments with the approval of the
Central Government so as to secure a minimum uniformity. The
Bill also empowers the Central Government to issue directions to
State Governments for implementing the provisions of the Bill when
enacted.

FINANCIAL MEMORANDUM

Chapter II of the Bill gives the details of registration-establishment
at the Centre and at State, district, municipal and village levels. This
establishment already exists, although the specific designations used
in the Bill may not be current. The Bill gives a legal status to the
various officials in the registration machinery who at present attend
to the registration work in addition to their other normal duties. The
machinery will thus consist of officials of various Departments
associated with registration work. The Bill binds them in a registration hierarchy with the Registrar General, India, at the centre and
Chief Registrar at the State, running through District Registrars to
the village and town registrars at the periphery. No extra expenditure
on account of staff or otherwise will be needed so far as the office of
the Registrar General, India, is concerned. In the case of Union
Territories, which have no separate Consolidated Fund namely,
Delhi, Andaman and Nicobar Islands; Laccadive, Minicoy and
Amindive Islands and Dadra and Nagar Haveli, there will be no
expenditure on Chief Registrars, District Registrars and Registrars,
since the duties and responsibilities of these offices will devolve on
regular officers of the various departments of the territories already in
position.

A recurring annual expenditure estimated at Rs 10,000 may,
however, be incurred on printing of the registers and statistical reports
referred to in clauses 16(2) and 19(2) of the Bill in respect of the
Union territories mentioned above.

MEMORANDUM REGARDING DELEGATED LEGISLATION

Clause 20 of the Bill empowers the Central Government to make

339

rules for the registration of information as to births and deaths of citizens abroad received by the Registrar General under the Citizenship Act, 1955. The matters to be provided for by rules are merely of an administrative or procedural nature.

Clause 30 of the Bill empowers the State Government in regard to all other matters to make rules, but only with the approval of the Central Government. The matters in respect of which rules may be so made relate, *inter alia*, to the forms of registers of births and deaths, the period within which and the manner in which information is to be given or notified, the authority who may grant permission for delayed registration and the fees payable for delayed registration, the search of registers of births and deaths and grant of extracts on payment of fees, the period of gestation for classifying a foetal death as a still birth and the conditions subject to which an offence against the Act may be compounded. These are matters of form, procedure or detail.

The delegation of legislative power is, therefore, of a normal character.

Appendix 3
POPULATION OF INDIA ACCORDING TO 1951 AND 1961 CENSUSES AND ESTIMATED POPULATION FOR 1971

Sl. No.	State/Union Territory	1951*	1961*	1971†
1.	Andhra Pradesh	31,115,259	35,983,447	43,920,000
2.	Assam	8,830,732	11,872,772	15,994,000
3.	Bihar	38,783,778	46,455,610	58,762,000
4.	Gujarat	16,262,657	20,633,350	27,093,000
5.	Haryana	X	X	10,302,000
6.	Jammu and Kashmir	3,253,852	3,560,976	4,088,000
7.	Kerala	13,549,118	16,903,715	21,701,000
8.	Madhya Pradesh	26,071,637	32,372,408	41,490,000
9.	Madras (Tamil Nadu)	30,119,047	33,686,953	40,034,000
10.	Maharashtra	32,002,564	39,553,718	51,000,000
11.	Mysore	19,401,956	23,586,772	29,832,000
12.	Orissa	14,645,946	17,548,846	21,992,000
13.	Punjab	16,134,890	20,306,812	15,111,000‡
14.	Rajasthan	15,970,774	20,155,602	26,822,000
15.	Uttar Pradesh	63,215,742	73,746,401	92,378,000
16.	West Bengal	26,302,386	34,926,279	45,801,000
17.	Nagaland	212,975	369,200	Y
18.	Andaman and Nicobar Is.	30,971	63,548	Y
19.	Chandigarh	X	X	Y
20.	Dadar and Nagar Haveli	41,532	57,963	Y
21.	Delhi	1,744,072	2,658,612	4,376,000
22.	Goa, Daman and Diu	637,591	626,978	—
23.	Himachal Pradesh	1,109,466	1,351,144	3,690,000‡
24.	Laccadive, Minicoy and Amindive Islands	21,035	24,108	Y
25.	Manipur	577,635	780,037	Y
26.	N.E. Frontier Agency	—	336,558	Y
27.	Pondicherry	317,253	369,079	Y
28.	Tripura	639,029	1,142,005	Y
29.	Sikkim	137,725	162,189	Y
30.	Other areas			5,236,000
	India	361,129,622	439,235,082	559,622,000

* *Census of India 1961, Paper No. 1 of 1962* (New Delhi: Government of India Press, 1962), p. 8.

† Estimated by the Expert Committee on Population Projection – Registrar General, Govt. of India, 1967.

X: Included in the Punjab.   Y: Included in other areas.

‡ Reorganized states.

341

Appendix 4
REGISTERED BIRTH RATES, DEATH RATES AND INFANT MORTALITY RATES IN INDIA: 1901–70[1]

Years	Birth rate per mille	Death rate per mille	Infant mortality rate per mille
1901	34·6	29·6	202
1902	39·4	31·5	213
1903	39·0	34·6	227
1904	40·9	32·5	204
1905	39·1	35·2	226
1906	37·8	33·8	225
1907	37·7	36·2	216
1908	37·8	37·3	243
1909	36·7	29·8	202
1910	39·5	31·9	212
1911	38·6	32·3	205
1912	39·0	29·6	208
1913	39·3	28·5	195
1914	39·6	29·7	212
1915	37·8	29·3	202
1916	27·1	28·5	195
1917	39·3	32·0	205
1918	35·4	—	267
1919	30·2	35·5	224
1920	33·0	30·6	195
1921	32·0	31·0	198
1922	31·9	24·0	175
1923	35·1	24·8	176
1924	34·5	28·1	189
1925	33·7	24·2	174
1926	34·8	25·9	189

[1] Registration throughout is officially stated to be incomplete. This is also true of the present states of the Indian Union. Comparability of these annual rates is adversely affected by different degrees of reliability. Registration has been deteriorating gradually. Secondly, there is the question of the validity of comparing the three parts of the time series – the period before 1921 relating to a scattered growing area, the period 1921–46 relating to the former provinces of British India, and the period since 1947 relating to the registration area of the Indian Republic, that is, British provinces minus Pakistan and plus Native States. Until 1946, the registration area comprised the British Provinces in undivided India excluding the Native States. For 1948 and subsequent years, the figures are taken for the Indian Union as reconstituted after partition into India and Pakistan.

342

Years	Birth rate per mille	Death rate per mille	Infant mortality rate per mille
1927	35·3	23·8	167
1928	36·8	24·1	173
1929	35·5	24·2	178
1930	36·0	26·9	181
1931	34·3	24·9	179
1932	33·7	21·6	169
1933	35·5	22·4	171
1934	33·7	24·9	187
1935	34·9	23·6	164
1936	35·4	22·6	162
1937	34·5	22·4	162
1938	34·1	24·3	167
1939	33·6	22·2	156
1940	32·0	21·1	160
1941	32·1	21·8	158
1942	29·8	21·3	163
1943	25·9	23·6	165
1944	25·4	24·1	169
1945	28·2	21·5	152
1946	29·2	19·0	137
1947	26·6	19·7	146
1948	25·2	17·0	130
1949	26·4	15·8	123
1950	24·9	16·1	127
1951	24·9	14·4	123
1952	25·4	13·8	116
1953	24·8	13·0	118
1954	24·4	12·5	109
1955	27·0	11·7	100
1956	23·1	10·6	106
1957	22·5	11·5	103
1958	23·0	11·9	102
1959	23·6	9·9	88
1960	21·2	9·7	89
1961	23·1	10·1	83
1962	22·9	9·7	81
1963	22·6	9·6	78
1964 Ad-	41·0	17·0	126
1965 justed	41·0	17·2	124
1966 rates	41·0	16·0	
1967	40·0	16·0	113 (5-year average)
1968	39·0	16·0	
1969	39·0	14·5	
1970	39·0	14·0	

343

Appendix 5

RELIGIOUS COMPOSITION OF INDIA'S POPULATION

(According to the 1951 and 1961 Censuses)

Community	Total number (in millions, 1951)	Percentage	Total number (in millions, 1961)	Percentage
Hindus	303·6	84·98	366·5	83·50
Muslims	35·4	9·91	46·9	10·70
Christians	8·4	2·35	10·7	2·44
Sikhs	6·2	1·74	7·8	1·79
Buddhists	0·2	0·05	3·3	0·74
Jains	1·6	0·45	2·0	0·46
Others	1·8	0·52	1·6	0·37
All communities	357·2	100·00	438·8	100·00

Source: *Census of India 1961, Vol. I*, Part II–C(i) Social and Cultural Tables (New Delhi: Government of India Press, 1965), pp. 482–3.

Note: The total population of India according to 1951 and 1961 censuses are 361·1 million and 439·2 million, respectively. Community-wise break up for 3·9 million in 1951 and 0·4 million in 1961 is not available.

Appendix 6
INFANT MORTALITY RATES IN
SELECTED COUNTRIES: 1900–68

Year	Denmark	Norway	Sweden	Australia	New Zealand
1900	130	—	94	—	—
1901	136	91	—	104	—
1902	114	74	—	107	—
1903	114	78	—	111	—
1904	113	75	—	89	—
1905	120	82	—	89	—
1906	111	69	81	83	62
1907	108	66	77	81	89
1908	124	75	85	78	68
1909	99	70	72	72	62
1910	101	67	75	75	68
1911	105	65	72	69	56
1912	94	67	71	72	51
1913	92	64	70	72	59
1914	99	68	73	72	51
1915	93	67	76	68	50
1916	101	64	70	70	51
1917	99	64	65	56	48
1918	76	63	65	59	48
1919	91	62	70	69	45
1920	91	58	65	69	49
1921	77	54	64	66	48
1922	82	55	63	53	42
1923	85	50	56	61	44
1924	84	50	60	57	40
1925	80	50	56	53	40
1926	84	48	56	54	40
1927	84	51	60	55	39
1928	81	49	59	53	36
1929	83	54	59	52	34
1930	82	46	60	47	35
1931	81	46	57	42	32
1932	72	47	51	41	31
1933	68	48	50	40	32
1934	64	39	47	44	32
1935	71	44	46	40	32
1936	67	42	43	41	31
1937	66	42	45	38	31
1938	59	37	43	38	36

345

Year	Denmark	Norway	Sweden	Australia	New Zealand
1939	58	37	40	38	31
1940	50	39	39	38	30
1941	55	43	57	40	30
1942	47	36	29	40	29
1943	45	35	29	36	31
1944	48	37	31	31	30
1945	48	36	30	29	28
1946	46	35	27	29	26
1947	40	35	25	29	29
1948	35	30	23	28	22
1949	34	28	23	25	24
1950	31	28	20	25	23
1951	29	26	21	25	23
1952	29	24	20	24	22
1953	27	23	19	23	20
1954	27	22	19	23	20
1955	25	21	18	22	20
1956	25	21	17	22	20
1957	23	21	18	21	24
1958	22	20	16	21	23
1959	23	19	17	22	24
1960	22	19	17	20	23
1961	22	18	16	20	23
1962	20	18	15	20	20
1963	19	17	15	20	20
1964	19	17	14	19	19
1965	20	18	12	19	20
1966	17	15	13	18	18
1967	16	15	13	18	18
1968	16	14	13	18	19

Appendix 7

INFANT MORTALITY RATE BY AGE AND SEX IN SELECTED COUNTRIES (FOR LATEST AVAILABLE YEARS)

Country (1)	Year (2)	Sex (3)	Age						Age Both sexes					
			Under 1 day (4)	1-6 days (5)	7-27 days (6)	28 days to 5 months (7)	6-11 months (8)	Under 1 year (9)	Under 1 day (10)	1-6 days (11)	7-27 days (12)	28 days to 5 months (13)	6-11 months (14)	Under 1 year (15)
Africa:														
Kenya	1965	M			28·8		6·8	35·6			27·9		6·3	34·2
		F			26·9		5·7	32·6						
South Africa:														
(i) Asiatic population	1962	M	6·9	15·6	7·3	20·5	15·4	65·7	6·7	13·7	6·6	18·8	14·9	60·7
		F	6·5	11·8	5·8	17·2	14·5	55·7						
(ii) Coloured population	1962	M	6·7	18·0	14·2	47·9	37·7	124·5	6·4	16·4	13·1	47·7	37·5	121·1
		F	6·1	14·9	12·0	47·5	37·3	117·8						
(iii) White population	1962	M	8·0	10·3	2·6	6·4	2·8	30·0	7·1	9·0	2·5	5·8	3·0	27·3
		F	6·1	7·6	2·3	5·1	3·1	24·3						
South West Africa:														
(i) Coloured population	1962	M	1·5	19·1	11·8	51·5	25·0	108·8	3·8	12·2	8·4	48·2	25·2	97·9
		F	6·4	4·8	4·8	44·7	25·5	86·1						
(ii) White population	1962	M	14·5	2·9	1·9	10·6	—	29·9	9·0	7·0	1·5	9·5	2·0	28·9
		F	3·1	11·4	1·0	8·3	4·1	27·9						
United Arab Republic	1964	M	0·8	9·3	13·6	45·1	45·0	113·8	0·8	7·9	12·8	47·1	48·7	117·3
		F	0·7	6·4	11·9	49·2	52·8	121·1						

Country (1)	Year (2)	Sex (3)	Age						Age Both sexes					
			Under 1 day (4)	1–6 days (5)	7–27 days (6)	28 days to 5 months (7)	6–11 months (8)	Under 1 year (9)	Under 1 day (10)	1–6 days (11)	7–27 days (12)	28 days to 5 months (13)	6–11 months (14)	Under 1 year (15)
North America:														
Canada	1966	M	10·3	5·9	2·0	5·8	1·9	25·8	9·4	4·9	1·7	5·2	1·7	23·1
		F	8·5	4·0	1·5	4·7	1·6	20·2						
Mexico	1966	M	3·4	13·3	9·7	25·7	16·1	68·0	2·9	11·5	8·8	24·1	15·6	62·9
		F	2·5	9·6	7·8	22·4	15·1	57·4						
United States	1966	M	11·2	6·5	1·8	5·5	1·7	26·6	9·9	5·6	1·6	4·9	1·6	23·7
		F	8·6	4·7	1·5	4·3	1·5	20·6						
South America:														
Argentina	1964	M	5·5	10·0	8·6	22·2	9·6	55·9	5·0	8·5	7·8	20·7	9·4	51·5
		F	4·5	7·0	7·0	19·2	9·2	46·9						
Chile	1965	M	12·4	14·3	14·8	54·3	18·3	114·2	11·2	12·8	13·7	51·2	18·2	107·1
		F	10·0	11·3	12·4	48·0	18·0	99·8						
Columbia	1966	M	10·6	13·2	13·6	27·9	22·0	87·3	9·4	11·5	12·3	25·6	21·2	80·0
		F	8·2	9·8	11·0	23·3	20·3	72·5						
Ecuador	1965	M	4·5	14·6	20·3	33·7	26·9	99·9	4·0	12·5	18·8	31·6	26·1	93·0
		F	3·5	10·3	17·3	29·5	25·2	85·8						
Venezuela	1965	M	—	31·8	—	10·2	9·9	51·9	—	28·0	—	9·7	10·0	47·7
		F	—	24·0	—	9·1	10·2	43·3						
Asia:														
Burma	1963	M	10·3	26·6	18·0	58·3	18·4	131·7	9·8	23·7	16·2	53·3	18·7	121·8
		F	9·2	20·7	14·3	48·2	19·1	111·6						

	Year	Sex											
Ceylon	1963	M	26·9		10·4	15·0	8·4	60·8	23·8	9·6	14·2	8·2	55·8
		F	20·6		8·8	13·4	7·9	50·7					
China (Taiwan)	1966	M	5·1		4·6	7·8	5·5	22·9	4·5	4·2	7·4	5·5	21·7
		F	3·7		3·7	6·8	5·3	19·6					
India	1964	M	20·3		15·7	19·3	18·1	74·7	19·0	14·8	19·3	18·5	72·8
		F	17·6		13·9	19·3	18·9	70·7					
Israel	1966	M	6·5	7·6	2·5	7·0	2·8	26·5	5·7	2·2	7·4	3·2	25·3
		F	4·8	5·8	1·8	7·8	3·7	24·1	6·7				
Japan	1965	M	2·7	6·7	3·8	5·0	2·5	20·7	2·4	3·5	4·6	2·3	18·5
		F	2·0	4·9	3·2	4·1	2·1	16·2	5·8				
Philippines	1965	M	10·5	17·3	12·3	20·4	19·8	80·4	9·5	11·2	18·3	18·7	72·9
		F	8·4	12·7	10·0	16·0	17·4	64·6	15·1				
Singapore	1966	M	4·9	10·8	3·0	5·7	3·6	28·3	4·5	3·1	5·4	3·6	25·8
		F	4·2	7·1	3·1	5·1	3·5	23·1	9·0				
Thailand	1964	M	1·1	3·6	6·2	22·4	7·6	41·8	1·0	5·5	19·9	7·3	37·8
		F	0·9	2·8	4·8	17·2	6·9	33·5	3·2				
Europe: Austria	1966	M	13·3	8·1	2·3	5·1	3·1	32·1	11·6	2·2	4·7	2·8	28·1
		F	9·7	5·4	2·0	4·4	2·4	23·9	6·8				
Belgium	1965	M	8·6	6·7	2·3	6·3	2·1	26·1	8·0	2·1	5·5	2·1	23·7
		F	7·3	5·1	1·9	4·7	2·1	21·2	5·9				
Bulgaria	1966	M	1·3	8·4	5·5	14·3	4·6	34·9	1·8	5·2	13·8	4·2	32·2
		F	1·3	6·1	4·8	13·2	3·8	29·3	7·3				
Czechoslovakia	1965	M	10·3	6·4	2·8	6·8	2·3	28·6	9·0	2·6	6·1	2·2	25·5
		F	7·6	4·8	2·3	5·3	2·1	22·2	5·6				
Denmark	1965	M	5·3	10·1	1·9	3·3	1·3	21·9	4·6	1·5	2·7	1·3	18·7
		F	3·8	7·1	1·1	2·1	1·3	15·4	8·7				
Finland	1965	M	6·7	7·4	1·6	2·8	1·7	20·2	5·9	1·3	2·6	1·4	17·6
		F	5·1	5·3	1·0	2·4	1·1	14·9	6·4				

Country (1)	Year (2)	Sex (3)	Age						Age Both sexes					
			Under 1 day (4)	1-6 days (5)	7-27 days (6)	28 days to 5 months (7)	6-11 months (8)	Under 1 year (9)	Under 1 day (10)	1-6 days (11)	7-27 days (12)	28 days to 5 months (13)	6-11 months (14)	Under 1 year (15)
France	1965	M	2·4	7·9	2·7	5·0	2·3	20·4						
		F	1·6	5·9	2·2	4·0	2·1	15·8	2·0	6·9	2·5	4·5	2·2	18·7
Germany:														
(i) Eastern Germany	1965	M	8·6	5·8	2·3	7·6	3·3	27·7						
		F	6·7	4·4	1·7	6·1	2·6	21·6	7·7	5·1	2·0	6·9	3·0	24·8
(ii) Federal Republic of Germany	1965	M	10·1	8·6	1·9	4·0	2·1	26·6						
		F	8·0	6·4	1·7	3·0	1·9	21·0	9·1	7·5	1·8	3·5	2·0	23·9
Hungary	1966	M	15·3	11·7	4·2	7·6	3·0	41·8						
		F	12·5	9·1	3·6	6·8	2·6	34·7	13·9	10·4	3·9	7·2	2·8	38·4
Italy	1965	M	9·7	10·0	5·6	10·1	4·4	39·9						
		F	7·4	6·9	4·7	8·4	4·4	31·9	8·6	8·5	5·2	9·3	4·4	36·0
Netherlands	1966	M	4·8	6·2	1·8	2·5	1·5	16·8						
		F	3·8	4·4	1·4	1·9	1·2	12·5	4·3	5·3	1·6	2·2	1·3	14·7
Norway	1965	M	4·7	7·5	1·5	3·4	1·6	18·6						
		F	3·5	5·4	1·3	3·2	1·6	14·9	4·1	6·5	1·4	3·3	1·7	16·8
Poland	1965	M	7·3	8·2	7·5	18·6	5·2	46·9						
		F	5·8	6·1	5·9	14·2	4·1	36·2	6·6	7·2	6·7	16·5	4·7	41·7
Portugal	1966	M	9·1	9·6	10·1	28·0	13·7	70·5						
		F	7·0	7·9	6·7	23·4	13·5	58·4	8·1	8·2	9·0	25·8	13·6	64·7
Spain	1962	M	10·5	—	—	35·6	—	46·0						
		F	8·2	—	—	28·7	—	36·9	9·4	11·2		15·3	5·8	41·6

Country	Year	Sex												
Sweden	1966	M	4·8	5·7	1·5	1·7	0·8	14·5	4·0	4·9	1·3	1·5	0·8	12·6
		F	3·3	4·0	1·2	1·3	0·7	10·5						
Switzerland	1965	M	9·0	5·1	1·4	2·6	1·6	19·8	8·0	4·5	1·3	2·4	1·6	17·8
		F	6·9	3·9	1·1	2·2	1·6	15·8						
United Kingdom: England and Wales	1966	M	7·3	5·3	1·9	5·1	1·8	21·4	6·5	4·6	1·7	4·5	1·6	19·0
		F	5·7	3·8	1·6	3·9	1·4	16·5						
Northern Ireland	1966	M	9·1	5·9	2·7	6·8	2·3	26·8	9·1	5·6	2·3	5·9	2·6	25·6
		F	9·1	5·2	1·9	5·0	3·0	24·2						
Scotland	1966	M	8·5	6·4	2·2	6·4	2·3	25·8	7·9	5·4	1·9	5·9	2·0	23·2
		F	7·3	4·4	1·6	5·4	1·8	20·4						
Yugoslavia	1965	M	7·4	12·4	12·6	29·2	12·2	74·4	6·5	11·5	12·4	28·9	12·5	71·8
		F	5·6	10·0	12·1	28·6	12·8	69·0						
Oceania: Australia	1966	M	7·4	5·8	1·5	3·8	1·8	20·3	6·8	5·0	1·4	3·4	1·6	18·2
		F	6·1	4·1	1·3	3·0	1·4	15·9						
New Zealand	1966	M	6·9	4·9	1·4	4·9	2·4	20·5	6·0	3·9	1·7	4·1	2·4	17·7
		F	4·9	2·8	1·4	3·2	2·4	14·7						

Source: *Demographic Year Book*, 1967.

351

Appendix 8

INDIA–AREA, POPULATION AND LITERACY (1971 CENSUS)

States and Union Territories in order of population rank in 1971 with 1961 rank in parentheses		Population in 1971	Percentage to total population	Area in square kilometres	Literacy rate in 1971
Uttar Pradesh	(1)	88,299,453	16·14	294,366	21·64
Bihar	(2)	56,387,296	10·31	174,008	19·97
Maharashtra	(3)	50,295,081	9·20	307,269	39·06
West Bengal	(5)	44,440,095	8·12	87,676	33·05
Andhra Pradesh	(4)	43,394,951	7·93	275,244	24·56
Madhya Pradesh	(7)	41,449,729	7·58	443,459	22·03
Tamil Nadu	(6)	41,103,125	7·51	129,966	39·39
Mysore	(8)	29,224,046	5·34	191,757	31·47
Gujarat	(9)	26,660,929	4·87	187,091	35·70
Rajasthan	(10)	25,724,142	4·70	342,267	18·79
Orissa	(11)	21,934,827	4·01	155,860	26·12
Kerala	(12)	21,280,397	3·89	38,869	60·16
Assam	(14)	14,857,314	2·72	121,973	28·74
Punjab	(13)	13,472,972	2·46	50,376	33·39
Haryana	(15)	9,971,165	1·82	44,056	26·69
Jammu and Kashmir	(16)	4,615,176	0·84	222,870	18·30
Delhi	(18)	4,044,338	0·74	1,483	56·65
Himachal Pradesh	(17)	3,424,332	0·63	55,658	31·32
Tripura	(19)	1,556,822	0·29	10,451	30·87
Manipur	(20)	1,069,555	0·20	22,346	32·80
Meghalaya	(21)	983,336	0·18	(included in Assam)	28·41
Goa, Daman & Diu	(22)	857,180	0·16	3,733	44·53
Nagaland	(23)	515,561	0·10	16,488	27·33
Pondicherry	(24)	471,347	0·09	473	43·36
N.E.F.A.	(25)	444,744	0·08	81,426	9·34
Chandigarh	(26)	256,979	0·05	115	61·24
Andaman and Nicobar Islands	(27)	115,090	0·02	8,293	43·48
Dadar and Nagar Haveli	(28)	74,165	0·01	489	14·86
Laccadive, Minicoi and Amindivi Islands	(29)	31,798	0·01	28	43·44
India (Total)		546,955,945		3,268,090	29·35

The above provisional total of 546,955,945 was announced by the Registrar-General of India on April 3, 1971. Later, according to the revised figures for the 1971 Census, India's population on April 1, 1971 was 547,367,926. That is, 411,981 persons or 0.08 per cent more had to be added. The reason for the revision was the delay in some distant areas filing late returns.

SELECT BIBLIOGRAPHY

I INFANT MORTALITY

ABHAYARATNE, O. E. R., 'The Influence of Malaria on Infant Mortality in Ceylon', *Ceylon Journal of Medical Science*, 8(2), 1950.

ABHAYARATNE, O. E. R., 'Infant Mortality in Ceylon', *Ceylon Medical Journal*, 4, 129–50, 1958.

ABRAMSON, J. H., 'Infant Mortality in Africa', *Israel Journal of Medical Sciences*, January–February 1967.

ACHAR, S. T., *Child Care in India and Neighbouring Countries* (Madras: Macmillan, 1959).

AHVENAINEN, E. K., 'Study of Causes of Neonatal Deaths', *Journal of Paediatrics*, December 1959.

ALEXANDER, CHESTER, 'Infant Mortality and Longevity', *Social Research*, New York, Summer 1953.

ALEXANDER, E. M. *Some Possible Approaches to the Care of the Child from 1–6* (Geneva: W.H.O., 1956).

ALFORD, C. A., et al., 'A Correlative Immunologic, Microbiologic and Clinical Approach to the Diagnosis of Acute and Chronic Infections in Newborn Infants', *New England Journal of Medicine*, August 1967.

ALLAN, T. M., 'British Stillbirths and First-Week Deaths, 1950–57', *British Journal of Preventive and Social Medicine*, January 1960.

ALTENDERPER, MARION E. and CROWTHER, BEATRICE, 'Relationship between Infant Mortality and Socio-economic Factors in Urban Areas', *Public Health Reports*, March 18, 1949.

ANDERSON, ODIN, W., 'Infant Mortality and Patterns of Living', *The Child*, April 1953.

ANDERSON, W. J. R., et al. 'Epidemiology of Still Births and Infant Deaths due to Congenital Malformation', *Lancet*, June 1958.

Annual Report of the Public Health Commissioner with the Government of India, New Delhi: Government of India Press; for various years, 1920–48.

Annual Report of the Director General of Health Services, New Delhi: Government of India; for various years, 1948–69.

M

353

Annual Report on Sanitary Measures in India, London: H.M.S.O.; for various years, 1901–20.

APTEKAR, HERBERT, *Anjea: Infanticide, Abortion and Contraception in Savage Society* (New York: Goodwin, 1931).

ARMSTRONG, ANNE, 'Infant Mortality – Some Possible Determinants', *Canadian Journal of Public Health*, June 1966.

ASHBY, H. P., *Infant Mortality* (London: Cambridge University Press, 1926).

Assignment Children (Paris: U.N. Children's Fund, 1966).

AYKROYD, W. R., 'Infantile Mortality in the Beri-Beri Area of the Madras Presidency', *Indian Journal of Medical Research*, October 1941.

BABBAR, G. S., 'Neonatal Mortality in First Stage of Labour', *Indian Journal of Surgery*, 25: 216, March 1963.

BAGCHI, K., 'The Use of Vegetable Protein in Supplementary Feeding of Infants and Children on Protein-Deficient Diets', *Report on Seminar on Protein Malnutrition in Children*, Hyderabad, January 1963.

BAI, B. MUKTHA, 'Infant Mortality in India', *Indian Medical Gazette*, June 1939.

BAIRD, DUGALD, 'Variations in Reproductive Pattern According to Social Class', *The Lancet*, July 13, 1946.

BAIRD, DUGALD, 'Social Class and Foetal Mortality', *The Lancet*, October 11, 1947.

BAIRD, DUGALD, 'Social Factors in Obstetrics', *The Lancet*, June 25, 1949.

BAIRD, DUGALD, 'The Future of Obstetrics', *The Transactions of Edinburgh Obstetrical Society*, 1952–53.

BAIRD, DUGALD, 'The Prevention of Prematurity', *Proceedings of the Royal Society of Medicine*, October 1953.

BAIRD, DUGALD, 'Environmental and Obstetrical Factors in Prematurity, with Special Reference to Experience in Aberdeen', *Bulletin of the World Health Organization*, 26: 291–5, 1962.

BAIRD, D. and SCOTT, E. M., 'Intelligence and Childbearing', *The Eugenics Review*, 45, 1953.

BAJPAI, P. C., KUTTY, D., RAJAGOPALAN, K. C. and WAHAL, K. M., 'Observations on Perinatal Mortality', *Indian Paediatrics*, March 1966.

BALFOUR, MARGARET, 'Early Infant Mortality in India with Special Reference to Premature Birth', *Indian Medical Gazette*, Calcutta, November, 1930.

BALFOUR, MARGARET I. and TALPADE, S. K., 'The Influence of Diet on Pregnancy in India', *Indian Medical Gazette*, Calcutta, 67, 1932.

BANKS, LESLIE A., 'Enquiry into Sudden Death in Infancy', *Canadian Journal of Public Health*, July 1966.

BASAK, K. C., 'Infant Mortality in British India', *Indian Journal of Paediatrics*, 5, 1939.

BEHAR, M., 'Death and Disease in Infants and Toddlers of Pre-industrial Countries', *American Journal of Public Health and Nation's Health*, July 1964.

BENJAMIN, B., *Social and Economic Factors Affecting Mortality* (The Hague: Mouton & Co., 1966).

BENNETT, H., 'Exposure of Infants in Ancient Rome', *Classical Journal*, *Vol. 18*, March 1923.

BERG, ALAN D., 'Malnutrition and National Development', *Foreign Affairs*, New York, October 1967.

BERGMAN, ABRAHAM B., et al. (Eds), *Proceedings of the Second International Conference on Causes of Sudden Death in Infants* (Seattle: University of Washington Press, 1970).

BHARGAVA, V., GHOSH, S. and BHARGAVA, S. K., 'Survival Rate, Growth and Development Pattern of Low-Birth-Weight Babies in First Year of Life', *Indian Paediatrics*, 6: 226, April 1969.

BHINDER, P. K., 'Impressions on Infant Feeding in Different Parts of India', *Alumni Association Bulletin*, Calcutta: All-India Institute of Hygiene and Public Health, October 1965.

BHOWMICK, A. C., 'Maternal and Perinatal Mortality', *Alumni Association Bulletin*, Calcutta: All-India Institute of Hygiene and Public Health, April 1960.

BLACKER, C. P., 'Maternity and Child Welfare Work and the Population Problem', *Eugenics Review*, July 1939.

BLAGG, HELEN M., *Statistical Analysis of Infant Mortality and Its Causes in the United Kingdom* (London: P. S. King, 1910).

BOSE, K. C., 'Infantile Mortality: Its Cause and Prevention', *The Proceedings of the Second All-India Sanitary Conference held at Madras, 1912*, Simla: Government Central Press, 1913.

BOUND, J. P., et al., 'Classification and Causes of Perinatal Mortality', I and II, *British Medical Journal*, November 24, 1956 and December 11, 1956.

BOURGEOIS-PICHAT, J., 'De la measure de la mortalité infantile', *Population*, Paris, January–March 1946.

BOURGEOIS-PICHAT, J., 'Analyse de la mortalité infantile', *Revue de l'institut international de statistique*, 18, 1950.

BOURGEOIS-PICHAT, J., 'De la measure de la mortalité infantile', *Population*, Paris, April–June 1951.

BOURGEOIS-PICHAT, J., 'De la measure mortalité infantile (II) Le causes de deces', *Population*, Paris, July–September 1951.

BOWDEN, D. H., et al., 'Observations on Neonatal Mortality', *Canadian Medical Association Journal*, December 15, 1956.

BRADY, SYLVIA, *Patterns of Mothering, Maternal Influence During Infancy* (New York: International University Press, 1956).

BREND, WILLIAM A., *Health and the State* (London: Constable, 1917).

BREND, WILLIAM A., *The Relative Importance of Pre-natal and Post-natal Conditions as Causes of Infant Mortality* (London: H.M.S.O., 1918).

BRITISH MEDICAL ASSOCIATION, 'National Inquiry into Perinatal Mortality', *British Medical Journal*, March 1, 1958.

BRITISH RED CROSS SOCIETY, *Maternal and Child Welfare Manual*, revised

355

by Susan M. Tracy and Arshiball P. Norman (London: Cox & Wyman, 1963).

BROOKE, E. M., 'Causes of Perinatal Mortality; Report of a Study of 4,429 Cases', *Monthly Bulletin of the Ministry of Health*, London, October 20, 1961.

BROWN, MARJORIE THELMA, *Care of the Child* (Karachi: Ministry of Health, Rehabilitation and Works, 1963).

BROWN, R. E. and SANDHU, T. S., 'An Autopsy Survey of Perinatal Deaths in Uganda', *Tropical and Geographical Medicine*, Haarlem, December 1966.

BUNDESEN, HERMAN N., et al., 'Progress in Reduction of Needless Neonatal Deaths', *Journal of the American Medical Association*, March 15, 1952.

BURGESS, A. and DEAN, R. F. A. (Eds), *International Conference on Malnutrition and Food Habits, Cuernavaca* (London: Tavistock, 1962).

BURLINGHAM, DOROTHY and FREUD, ANNA, *Infants Without Families* (London: Allen & Unwin, 1943).

BURNS, C. M., *Infant and Maternal Mortality in Relation to Size of Family and Rapidity of Breeding* (Durham: University, 1942).

BUTLER, N. R., 'Causes and Prevention of Perinatal Mortality', *W.H.O. Chronicle*, February 1967.

BUTLER, N. R., *The Causes and Prevention of Perinatal Mortality in the European Region* (Geneva: W.H.O., 1966).

BUTLER, N. R., *Perinatal Mortality* (Geneva: W.H.O., 1964).

BUTLER, N. R. and ALBERMAN, E. D., *Perinatal Problems: Second Report of the 1958 British Perinatal Mortality Survey* (Edinburgh: Livingstone, 1969).

BUTLER, N. R. and BONHAM, D. G., *Perinatal Mortality*, The First Report of the 1958 British Perinatal Mortality Survey (Edinburgh: Livingstone, 1963).

CAFFIN, S. W., 'Infantile Mortality Rates', *Population Studies*, July 1952.

CARPENTER, R. G. and SHADDICK, C. W., 'Role of Infection, Suffocation and Bottle-Feeding in Cot Death', *British Journal of Preventive and Social Medicine*, 19: 1–7, 1965.

CARTER, C. O., 'Congenital Malformations', *Eugenics Review*, July 1951.

CHAKRABORTY, B., 'Sixteen-Year Trend in the Regional Mortality in India 1947–63', *Indian Journal of Public Health*, April 1967.

CHAKRABORTY, P. N., 'Trend of Infant Mortality in Chetla Area', *Indian Journal of Public Health*, October 1962.

CHAKRABORTY, P. N., 'Study of Differential Infant Mortality Among the Residents of Bustees and Non-Bustees in Chetla Area', *Alumni Association Bulletin*, Calcutta: All India Institute of Hygiene and Public Health, April 1963.

CHAN, H. and WATERLOW, J. C., 'The Protein Requirement of Infants at the Age of About One Year', *Bulletin of the World Health Organization*, 33, 1965.

CHANDRASEKHAR, S., *Census and Statistics in India* (Chidambaram: Annamalai University, 1948).

CHANDRASEKHAR, S., 'Some Observations on Infant Mortality in India 1901–51', *Eugenics Review*, January 1955.

CHANDRASEKHAR, S., 'Infant Mortality in India, 1901–51', *Proceedings of the World Population Conference, Rome, 1954, Vol. I*, New York: United Nations, 1955.

CHANDRASEKHAR, S., 'Our Vital Statistics; Infant Welfare and Survival', *The Hindu*, Madras, September 3, 1955.

CHANDRASEKHAR, S., *Infant Mortality in India 1901–1955* (London: Allen & Unwin, 1959).

CHANDRASEKHAR, S., 'Infant Mortality in Madras City', *Population Review*, January and July 1965; also *Proceedings of the World Population Conference, Belgrade, 1965, Vol. 2*, pp. 406–09. New York: United Nations, 1966.

CHANDRASEKHAR, S., 'Control of Mortality in India', *Medical Science and Service*, 4: 14–16, September 1967.

CHANDRASEKHARA, M. R., et al., 'Development of Infant Foods Based on Soyabean', *Journal of Food Science and Technology*, 3, 1966.

CHASE, H. C., 'Perinatal and Infant Mortality in the United States and Six West European Countries', *American Journal of Public Health and Nation's Health*, 57, 1967.

CHASE, H. C., *International Comparison of Perinatal and Infant Mortality; The United States and Six West European Countries* (Washington: National Center for Health Statistics, Series 3, No. 6, March 1967).

CHIPMAN, SIDNEY, S., et al. *Research Methodology and Needs in Perinatal Studies* (Springfield: Charles C. Thomas, 1966).

CLARK, F. LEGROS, *The Feeding of Pre-School Children* (London: National Societies of Children's Nurseries, 1951).

COLLINS, SELWYN D., *Illness among Infants with Comparative Mortality Data* (Washington D.C.: U.S. Public Health Service, 1948).

COLLINS, S. DEWITT, KATHARINE, S. TRANTHAM and LEHMANN, JOSEPHINE L., *Illness and Mortality Among Infants During the First Year of Life* (Washington, D.C.: U.S. Government Printing Office, 1955).

COLLIS, W. R. F., et al., *Modern Methods of Infant Management: Before, During and After Birth* (London: William Heinemann Medical Books, 1948).

COOKE, H. R., *Repression of Female Infanticide in the Bombay Presidency* (Bombay, 1875).

COOKE, ROBERT E. (Ed.), *The Biologic Basis of Pediatric Practice* (New York: McGraw Hill, 1968), 2 vols.

CRAIG, W. S. M., et al., *Care of the Newly Born Infant* (Edinburgh: Livingstone, 1966).

CRAVIOTO, J., et al., 'Motor and Adaptive Development of Premature Infants from a Preindustrial Setting During the First Year of Life', *Biologia Neonatorum*, 77, 1967.

CREW, F. A. E., *Measurement of Public Health; Essays on Social Medicine* (London: Oliver & Boyd, 1948).

357

CROSSE, M. V., *The Premature Baby* (London: Churchill, 1949).

CRUIKSHANK, J. N., *The Causes of Neonatal Death* (London: Medical Research Council, Stationery Office, 1930).

CURTIS, THOMAS B., 'Infant Mortality' in Buck, Albert H. (Ed.), *A Treatise on Public Hygiene and Public Health, Vol. 2* (London: Sampson Low, 1879).

CZERMAK, HANS and HANSLUWKA, HARALD, 'Infant Mortality in Australia', *British Journal of Preventive and Social Medicine*, October 1962.

DALY, C., et al., 'Social and Biological Factors in Infant Mortality: III. The Effect of Mother's Age and Parity on Social Class Differences in Infant Mortality', *The Lancet*, February 26, 1955.

DAS, KEDARNATH and MAHALANOBIS, P. C., 'A Preliminary Note on the Rates of Maternal Deaths and Stillbirths in Calcutta', *Sankhya*, 1933.

DAS GUPTA, B. C., *Report of Inquiry into the Bearing of Premature and Immature Births on Infant Mortality in Bombay 1946-48* (New Delhi: Indian Council of Medical Research, 1951).

DAVID, M., *Study of Infants Deprived of Maternal Care in the First Three Months of Life*, 1958.

DUTTA, A., 'Plea for Preventive Paediatrics', *Journal of Christian Medical Association of India*, May 1964.

DATTA BANIK, N. D., KRISHNA R., MANE, S. I. S., and LILA RAI, 'Longitudinal Study of Morbidity and Mortality Pattern in Children in Delhi during the First Two Years of Life', *Indian Journal of Medical Research* May 1967.

DATTA BANIK, N. D., KRISHNA, R., MANE, S. I. S., andLILA RAI, 'Longitudinal Study of Morbidity and Mortality Pattern in Children Under the Age of Five Years in an Urban Community', *Indian Journal of Medical Research*, May 1969.

DAYAL, R. S., PRASAD, R., and MATHUR, G. P., 'Morbidity and Mortality Data', *Indian Journal of Child Health*, December 1962.

DEKABAN, A. S., et al., 'Correlation of Fetal Wastage and Condition of of Offspring during Gestation, and Circumstances of Delivery in 4,156 Pregnancies', *American Journal of Obstetrics and Gynecology*, February 1962.

DEL MUNDO, F., *Public Health Aspects of Low Birth Weight: A Survey of Hospital-born Prematures in the Philippines*, 1960.

DEBODE, J. V., 'Rate of Infant Mortality Adjusted to a Rapidly Changing Birth-rate', *Health News*, New York State Department of Public Health, 1944.

Deprivation of Maternal Care: A Reassessment of its Effects (Geneva: W.H.O., 1962).

DERASARI, ATULA J., 'Infant Feeding: Nurses' Role in Educating Mothers', *The Nursing Journal of India*, February 1969.

DE SILVA, C. C., FERNANDO, P. V. D., and GUNARATNA, C. D. H., *The Research for a Prematurity Level in Colombo, Ceylon* (Geneva: W.H.O., 1960).

DE SILVA, D. M., 'Public Health and Sanitation Measures as Factors Affecting Mortality Trends in Ceylon', *Proceedings of The World Population Conference, Rome, 1954* (New York: United Nations, 1955).

D'HAVRINCOURT, HUBERT, 'Precious Lives', *World Health*, December 1967.

DICEY, E., 'Infanticide Amongst Poor of England', *Nation, Vol. 1*, 270.

DICKINSON, F. G., and WALKER, E. L., *Infant Deaths and Stillbirths in Leading Nations* (Chicago: American Medical Association, Bureau of Medical Economic Research, 1950).

DOGRAMACI, I. and RAY, J. D., 'Severe Infantile Malnutrition and Its Management', *The Turkish Journal of Paediatrics*, November–December 1958.

DONNELLY, J. F., 'Infant Mortality and Morbidity in Relation to Certain Maternal Factors', *North Carolina Medical Journal*, March 1956.

DORN, HAROLD F., 'Some Problems for Research in Mortality and Morbidity', *Public Health Reports*, January 1956.

DOUGHTY, J. H., 'Neonatal Mortality in British Columbia', *Canadian Journal of Public Health*, January 1957.

DOUGLAS, J. W. B., 'Social Class Differences in Health and Survival during the First Two Years of Life; Results of a National Survey', *Population Studies*, July 1951.

DOUGLAS, J. W. B., 'Health and Survival of Infants during the First Two Years of Life', *The Lancet*, September 8, 1951.

DUBLIN, LOUIS I. and SPIEGELMAN, MORTIMER, *The Facts of Life from Birth to Death* (New York: Macmillan, 1951).

DUNHAM, ETHEL C., *Deaths of Premature Infants in the United States* (Washington D.C.: U.S. Children's Bureau, 1947).

DUNHAM, ETHEL C., *Premature Birth as a World Health Problem* (Geneva: W.H.O., 1960).

DUNHAM, ETHEL C., *Problems Relating to Collection of Vital Statistics on Prematurity* (Geneva: W.H.O., 1950).

DYKES, R. M., *Illness in Infancy: A Comparative Study of Infant Sickness and Infant Mortality in Luton* (Luton: Leagrave Press, 1950).

EASTMAN, N. J., 'The Effect of the Interval between Births on Maternal and Foetal Outlook', *American Journal of Obstetrics and Gynecology*, April 1944.

EASTMAN, P. R., 'Infant Mortality in Relation to Month of Birth', *Journal of American Public Health Association*, September 1945.

EBRAHIM, G. J. and D'SA, A., 'Prematurity in Dar-es-Salaam', *Journal of Tropical Paediatrics and African Child Health*, 12, 1966.

EDGE, P. GRANVILLE, 'Infant Mortality in B.W.I.', *Transactions of the Royal Society of Tropical Medicine and Hygiene, Vol. 38*, No. 2.

The Effects of Labour on the Foetus and the Newborn: Report of a W.H.O. Scientific Group (Geneva: W.H.O., 1957).

EHRENFEST, H., *Birth Injuries of the Child* (London: Appleton, 1922).

359

ELDERTON, E. M., 'On the Relative Value of the Factors which Influence Infant Welfare', *Annals of Eugenics,* October 1925.

ELIOT, M. M., 'Deaths Around Birth – the National Score', *Journal of the American Medical Association,* June 1958.

EL-KAMMASH, MAJDI M., 'Stockwell's Infant Mortality Index for Measuring Economic Development – A Comment', *Milbank Memorial Fund Quarterly.* January 1962.

ELLIS, RICHARD W. B. (Ed.), *Child Health and Development* (London: Churchill, 1947).

ERHARDT, CARL L., et al., 'Influence of Weight and Gestation on Perinatal and Neonatal Mortality by Ethnic Group', *American Journal of Public Health and the Nation's Health,* November 1964.

ERICKSEN, E. GORDON, 'Concubinage and Infanticide in the Negroid West Indies – Observations on Population Control and the Hypothesis of Social Choice'. Paper presented before the Mid-West Sociological Society, Des Moines, Iowa, 1957, mimeographed.

ERICKSEN, E. GORDON, *Infanticide in a Disorganized Society: A Study in Fringe Demography* (Lawrence: University of Kansas, 1959).

'Evolution of Infant Mortality from the Beginning of the Century in Selected Countries', *Epidemiological and Vital Statistics Report,* W.H.O., 7, 1954.

Expert Committee on Maternity Care: First Report; A Preliminary Survey, (Geneva: W.H.O., 1952).

FAMINE ENQUIRY COMMISSION: *Report on Bengal* (New Delhi: Government of India Press, 1945).

FELDSTEIN, M. S., et al., 'Analysis of Factors Affecting Perinatal Mortality; A Multivariate Statistical Approach', *British Journal of Preventive and Social Medicine,* 19: 128–34, 1965.

FERGUSON, W. F., 'Perinatal Mortality in Multiple Gestations; A Review of Perinatal Deaths from 1,609 Multiple Gestations', *Obstetrics and Gynaecology,* 23, 1964.

FIAWOO, CHARITY, *Health and Diet of the African Child* (London: Longmans Green, 1949).

FILER, L. J., JR, and MARTINEZ, G. A., 'Intake of Selected Nutrients by Infants in the United States; An Evaluation of 4,000 Representative Six-months-olds', *Clinical Paediatrics,* 3, 1964.

'Foetal Mortality, 1945–1963', *Epidemiological and Vital Statistics Report,* W.H.O., 19 (6), 1966.

FOX, A. R., 'A Survey of Fetal and Neonatal Loss', *Journal of the American Osteopathic Association,* January 1962.

FRENCH, J. G., 'Relationship of Morbidity to the Feeding Patterns of Navajo Children from Birth through Twenty-four Months', *American Journal of Clinical Nutrition,* 20, 1967.

FREW, R. S., *Diseases in Childhood* (London: Macmillan, 1936).

FULOP, T., 'Considerations Concerning Investigations of the Problems of Infant Mortality', *Sante Publique,* Bucharest, 8, 1966.

GARCIA, ARROYA, M. L., 'Analysis of Mortality Statistics of Infants and Children in Ecuador', *Journal of the American Medical Women's Association,* August 1958.

GAMBLE, DAVID P., 'Infant Mortality Rates in a Sierra Leone Urban Community', *Journal of Tropical Medicine and Hygiene,* August 1961.

GARBER, C. M., 'Eskimo Infanticide', *Science Monthly,* February 1947.

GARDINER, E. M., and YERUSHALMY, J., 'Familial Susceptibility to Still-births and Neonatal Deaths', *American Journal of Hygiene,* July 1939.

GARDINER, C. E., 'Maori Infant Mortality', *New Zealand Medical Journal,* June 1959.

GEERTINGER, PREBERN, *Sudden Death in Infancy* (Springfield, Illinois: Thomas, 1966).

GESELL, ARNOLD LUCIUS, *Feeding Behaviour of Infants: A Paediatric Approach to the Mental Hygiene of Early Life* (Philadelphia: Lippincott, 1937).

GESELL, ARNOLD LUCIUS, *Infant Development: The Embryology of Early Human Behaviour* (London: Hamish Hamilton, 1952).

GESELL, ARNOLD, et al., *The First Five Years of Life; A Guide to the Study of Pre-School Child* (London: Methuen, 1947).

GHOSH, LEILA, et al., *Inquiry into Vital Loss up to One Year as Recorded by Seven Maternity and Child Welfare Centres in Calcutta* (Calcutta: Government of India Press, 1942).

GHOSH, S., 'Study of Childhood Mortality', *Indian Journal of Child Health,* May 1961.

GHOSH, S., and DAGA, S., 'Comparison of Gestational Age and Weight as Standards of Prematurity', *Journal of Pediatrics,* 71, 1967.

GIBBENS, JOHN, *The Care of Young Babies* (London: Churchill, 1955).

GINZBERG, ELI, *The Nation's Children* (New York: Columbia University Press, 1960).

GODDARD, R. F., LELAND, S. J. and COBB, J. C., 'Aspects de Salud Publica de la Mortalidad Infantil', *Boletin de la Oficiana Sanataria Panamericana,* 51, 1961.

GORDON, J. E., et al., 'Causes of Death at Different Ages by Sex and by Season in a Rural Population of Punjab 1957–59', *Indian Journal of Medical Research,* September 1965.

GRAHAM, STANLEY and SHANKS, ROBERT A., *Notes on Infant Feeding* (Edinburgh: Livingstone, 1954).

GREAT BRITAIN, *Enquiry into Sudden Death in Infancy* (Report on Public Health and Medical Subjects, 113) (London: H.M.S.O., 1965).

GREAT BRITAIN, ENGLAND AND WALES, GENERAL REGISTER OFFICE, *Social and Biological Factors in Infant Mortality* by J. A. Heady and M. A. Haasman (London: H.M.S.O., 1959).

GRISWOLD, D. M. and CAVANAGH, D., 'Prematurity – The Epidemiologic Profile of the "High Risk" Mother', *American Journal of Obstetrics and Gynecology,* 96, 1966.

GRUNDY, FRED and LEWIS-FANING, E. (Ed.), *Morbidity and Mortality in the*

First Year of Life; A Field Enquiry in Fifteen Areas of England and Wales (London: Eugenics Society, 1957).

GULATI, P. N., 'Mortality Rate and Causes of Deaths among Children below Five Years', *Indian Journal of Paediatrics*, August 1967.

GUPTA, J. P., 'Infant Mortality; Some Socio-economic Determinants', *Licentiate*, March 1963.

GUPTA, S., 'Mortality in Children in South India', *Archives of Child Health*, December–February 1966–67.

GURALNICK, LILLIAN and WINTER, EDWARD D., 'Note on Cohort Infant Mortality Rates', *Public Health Reports*, August 1965.

HALER, D., 'Cot Deaths', *Medical Gynaecology and Sociology*, 2, 1967.

HAMMOND, ESMAT I., 'Studies in Fetal and Infant Mortality', *American Journal of Public Health and Nation's Health*, August 1965.

HARFOUCHE, J. K., *Infant Health in Lebanon* (Beirut: Khayats, 1965).

HAYMAN, C. R. and KESTER, F. E., 'A Study of Infant Mortality in Alaska', *North-West Medicine*, July 1957.

HEADY, J. A., et al., 'Social and Biological Factors in Infant Mortality: II. Variation of Mortality and Mother's Age and Parity', *Lancet*, February 19, 1955.

HEADY, J. A., et al., 'Social and Biological Factors in Infant Mortality: IV. The Independent Effects of Social Class, Region, the Mother's Age and Her Parity', *Lancet*, March 5, 1955.

HEADY, J. A. and HEASMAN, M. A., *Social and Biological Factors in Infant Mortality* (London: H.M.S.O., 1959).

HEALTH INFORMATION FOUNDATION, 'The Diminishing Hazards of Infancy', *Progress in Health Services*, March 1957.

HERRMAN, C., 'Infant Mortality and the Survival of the Fittest', *Scientific Monthly*, January 1926.

HIBBS, JR, H. H., *Infant Mortality* (New York, 1916).

HOBART, R. T., *Infanticide Manual for the Guidance of the North-West Frontier Police* (Allahabad, 1876).

HOLLEND, E. L., *The Causation of Foetal Death* (London: H.M.S.O., 1922).

HOLZER JERSY 'The Evolution of Infant Mortality in Poland', *World Population Conference, Belgrade, 1965* (New York: United Nations, 1966).

HOWARTH, WILLIAM J., 'The Influence of Feeding on the Mortality of Infants', *The Lancet, Vol. D*, 1965.

HOWE, G. M. (Ed.), *National Atlas of Disease Mortality in the United Kingdom* (London: Nelson, 1969).

HUNT, ELEANOR P. and CHENOWETH, ALICE D., 'Recent Trends in Infant Mortality in the United States', *American Journal of Public Health and Nation's Health*, February 1961.

HUNT, ELEANOR P. and GOLDSTEIN, STANLEY M., *Trends in Infant and Childhood Mortality in 1961* (Washington, D.C.: U.S. Children's Bureau Series, 1964).

HUNT, ELEANOR P. and MOORE, RUTH R., *Perinatal, Infant and Maternal*

Mortality 1954 (Washington, D.C.: U.S. Department of Health Education and Welfare, 1957).

HURLOCK, E. B., *Child Development* (New York: McGraw-Hill, 1964).

HUTTON, M. M., 'Study of Perinatal Deaths as a Means of Improving Perinatal Mortality and Morbidity', *Obstetrics and Gynaecology*, 24, 1964.

IGHODARO, IRENE, *Baby's First Year* (London: Collins, 1966).

ILLINGWORTH, R. S. and ILLINGWORTH, CYNTHIA, *Babies and Young Children: Feeding, Management and Care* (London: Churchill, 1960).

INDIA, REGISTRAR GENERAL, *Registration of Births and Deaths in India* (New Delhi: Ministry of Home Affairs, 1968).

INDIA, REGISTRAR GENERAL, *Vital Statistics of India, Since 1958* (Delhi: Manager of Publications, 1960).

INDIAN RESEARCH FUND ASSOCIATION MATERNITY AND CHILD WELFARE ADVISORY COMMITTEE, *Memorandum on the Conduct of an Enquiry into Infant Mortality* (New Delhi: 1949).

'Infant and Child Mortality in Selected Countries, 1951–1962', *Epidemiological and Vital Statistics Report* (Geneva: W.H.O., Vol. 17, No. 11, 1964).

Infant and Perinatal Mortality in Denmark (Washington, D.C.: U.S. Department of Health, Education and Welfare, 1967).

Infant and Perinatal Mortality in England and Wales (Washington, D.C.: U.S. Department of Health, Education and Welfare, 1968).

Infant and Perinatal Mortality in Scotland (Washington, D.C.: U.S. Department of Health, Education and Welfare, 1966).

Infant and Perinatal Mortality in the United States (Washington, D.C.: U.S. Department of Health, Education and Welfare, 1965).

Infant Care (Washington, D.C.: Children's Bureau Publication, 1955).

Infant, Foetal, and Maternal Mortality – United States – 1963 (Washington, D.C.: U.S. Department of Health, Education and Welfare, 1966).

Infant Loss in the Netherlands (Washington, D.C.: U.S. Department of Health, Education and Welfare, 1968).

'Infant Mortality – An Appraisal of World Situation for the Decade 1949–58' *Indian Medical Journal*, August 1963.

'Infant Mortality During the War Period', *League of Nations Monthly Bulletin*, September 1945.

'Infant Mortality in the United States and Abroad', *Statistical Bulletin* (New York: Metropolitan Life Insurance Company), 48, 1967.

'Infant Mortality, 1901–1958', *Epidemiological and Vital Statistics Report*, W.H.O., 13, 1960.

'Infant Mortality (Five Latest Available Years)', *Epidemiological and Vital Statistics Report*, W.H.O., 19, 1966.

'Infant Mortality Interaction with Fertility and Effect on Population Growth and Economic Development', *Current Medical Practice*, 7, February 1963.

Infant Mortality Problems in Norway (Washington, D.C.: U.S. Department of Health, Education and Welfare, 1967).

363

'Infant Mortality – Sources and Coverage Data for Research Work in Child Health', *Indian Medical Journal*, 57, May 1962.

Infant Mortality Trends – United States and Each State, 1930–1964 (Washington, D.C.: U.S. Department of Health, Education and Welfare, 1965).

Infant, Neonatal and Perinatal Mortality and Stillbirths, Ontario, 1925–1960 (Toronto: Department of Medical Statistics, 1963).

Infants at Risk: An Historical and International Comparison (London: Office of Health Economics, 1964).

Infantile Mortality: Report on the Special Committee Appointed to Inquire into the Systems Adopted in Different Countries for the Registration of Births Including Stillbirths and Deaths with Reference to Infantile Mortality (London: Royal Statistical Society, 1912).

INTERNATIONAL CLASSIFICATION OF DISEASES; Preparation of Eighth Revision, *Causes of Perinatal Morbidity and Mortality*, W.H.O., 1965.

INTERNATIONAL CLASSIFICATION OF DISEASES; Preparation of Eighth Revision, *XV, Certain Causes of Perinatal Morbidity and Mortality*, W.H.O., 1964.

International Comparison of Perinatal and Infant Mortality: The United States and Six West European Countries (Washington, D.C.: U.S. Department of Health, Education and Welfare, 1967).

JACKSON, E. B., *Transactions of the First Conference on Problems of Early Infancy* (New York: Josiah Macy, Jr, Foundation, 1947).

JACKSON, EDITH B. and GENEVIEVE TRAINHAM (Eds), *Conference on Problems of Infancy and Childhood* (New York: Josiah Macy, Jr, Foundation, 1950).

JACKSON, Q. M., *A Handbook of Paediatrics for Nurses in General Training* (London: Lewis, 1952).

JAIN, S. P., 'Mortality Trends in India', *Proceedings of the World Population Conference, 1954* (New York: United Nations, 1955).

JAIN, V. C., 'Some Social Components of Infant Mortality in India', *Indian Journal of Paediatrics*, February 1968.

JAMES, L. S., 'Scientific Basis for Current Perinatal Care', *Archives of Disease in Childhood*, 42, 1967.

JAYANT, K., 'Birth Weight and Some Other Factors in Relation to Infant Survival; A Study of an Indian Sample', *Annals of Human Genetics*, March 1964.

JEGER, LENA M. (Ed.), *Illegitimate Children and Their Parents* (London: National Council for the Unmarried Mother and Child, 1951).

JELIFFE, D. B., 'Approaches to Village Level Infant Feeding: Breast Feeding', *Journal of Tropical Paediatrics*, September 1967.

JELLIFFE, D. B., *Child Health in the Tropics: A Practical Handbook for Medical and Para-medical Personnel* (London: Arnold, 1968).

JELIFFE, D. B., *Infant Nutrition in the Sub-Tropics and Tropics* (Geneva: W.H.O., 1968).

JELIFFE, D. B., *Child Nutrition in Developing Countries* (Washington, D.C.: Agency for International Development, 1969).

JHA, SAROJ S., 'Stillbirths in the City of Bombay', *British Journal of Social and Preventive Medicine*, October 1961.

JHIRAD, J., *Report on an Investigation into the Causes of Maternal Mortality in the City of Bombay* (New Delhi: Government of India Press, 1941).

JOHNSON, GWENDOLYN Z., 'Public Health Activities as Factors in Levels and Trends of Mortality and Morbidity in Developing Countries', *Proceedings of the World Population Conference, Belgrade, 1965* (New York: United Nations, 1966).

Joint Study with United Nations Statistical Services on Wastage of Human Life (Geneva: W.H.O., 1949).

JOLLY, H. R., *Diseases of Children* (Oxford: Blackwell Scientific Publications, 1968).

KAERN, T., 'Perinatal Mortality; An Analysis of Perinatal Deaths in Copenhagen, 1949–52', *Danish Medical Bulletin*, March 1956.

KAERN, T., 'Perinatal Mortality', *Acta Obstetricia et Gynecologica Scandinavica*, Stockholm, 1960.

KALLNER, G., *Neonatal Mortality in Israel* (Geneva: W.H.O., 1958).

KANNISTO, VAIN O., 'The Value of Certain Refinements of the Infant Mortality Rate', *Bulletin of the World Health Organization*, 16: 763–82, 1957.

KANNISTO, V. and PASCUA, M., 'Study of the Influence of the Decline in Mortality on Growth of Population', *Epidemiological and Vital Statistics Report*, 5, 1962.

KARAMCHANDANI, P. V., 'Advanced Medical Views, Perinatal Deaths', *Maharashtra Medical Journal*, June 1961.

KATHJU, M., *Memorandum on Female Infanticide with a Minute by Sir D. F. McLeod on the Suppression of Infanticide* (Lahore, 1874).

KENDALL, N., 'Neonatal Mortality in Philadelphia', *Transactions and Studies of the College of Physicians of Philadelphia*, August 1958.

KHAMIS, SALEM H., 'A Report on a Pilot Infant Mortality Survey of Rural Lebanon', *Bulletin de l'Institut International de Statistique*, 36: 60–70, 1958.

KHAN, M. K. H. and SIDDIQUI, M. Z., 'Mortality Among Children Born in Families of Various Economic Groups Living in Certain Areas of the City of Lahore', *Proceedings of the Pakistan Statistical Association*, 9: 13–14, 1960–61.

KNOEDEL, J. and VAN DE WALLE, E., 'Breast Feeding, Fertility and Infant Mortality: Analysis of Some Early German Data', *Population Studies*, September 1967.

KNOX, G. and MACKINTOSH, J., 'Post-neonatal Infant Mortality in Birmingham Between 1947 and 1956', *British Journal of Preventive and Social Medicine*, July 1958.

KOLAH, P. J., et al., 'Congenital Malformations and Perinatal Mortality in Bombay', *American Journal of Obstetrics and Gynecology*, February 1967.

365

KROTKI, KAROL J., 'A Correction to Infant Mortality', *Sudan Notes and Records, Vol. 42*, 1961.

KURUP, R. S., 'Recent Mortality Trends in the E.C.A.F.E. Region', *Population Review*, January 1964.

LAL, R. B. and SEAL, S. C., *General Health Survey, Singhur Health Centre, 1944* (Calcutta: Government of India Press, 1949).

LANCASTER, H. O., 'Infant Mortality in Australia', *Medical Journal of Australia*, July 21, 1956.

LANKESTER, A., *Lecture on the Responsibility of Man in Matters Relating to Maternity* (At the Maternity and Child Welfare Exhibition held in Delhi, February 1920), (Simla: Government Of India Press, 1924).

LEAGUE OF NATIONS HEALTH ORGANIZATION, *Memorandum Relating to the Inquiries into the Causes and Prevention of Stillbirths and Mortality during the First Year of Life: Austria, France, Germany, Great Britain, Italy, Netherlands, Norway* (Geneva, 1930).

LESI, F. E. A., 'The Incidence of Prematurity in Lagos, Nigeria', *West African Medical Journal*, 16, 1967.

LEVIN, SIMON S., *A Philosophy of Infant Feeding* (Springfield, Illinois: Thomas, 1963).

LIBERATI, FABRIZO, 'Infant Mortality in Italy According to the Profession of the Father', *World Population Conference, Belgrade, 1965*, New York: United Nations, 1966.

LINDER, F. E. and GROVE, R. D., *Vital Rates in the United States, 1900–40* (Washington, D.C.: Government Printing Office, 1943).

LINSKY, ARNOLD S., *Infant Mortality Trends in the State of Washington, 1917–1959* (Seattle: Washington State Department of Health, Research and Program Evaluation Division, 1963).

LOGAN, W. P. D., 'The Measurement of Infant Mortality', *Population Bulletin of the United Nations*, October 1953.

'Low Birth Weight and Intelligence', *British Medical Journal*, 2, 1964.

LOWE, C. R. and RECORD, R. G., 'Risk of Stillbirth in Twin Pregnancy Related to Sex and Maternal Age – An Analysis of 90,386 Twin Materni-ties', *British Journal of Social Medicine*, January 1951.

LUCEY, J. F., 'Hazards to the Newborn Infants from Drugs Administered to the Mother', *Paediatric Clinics of North America*, May 1961.

MADISON, E. K., 'Perinatal Mortality; Causes and Control', *Journal of the National Medical Association*, July 1958.

MALLIK, S. N., 'On the Causation of the High Mortality Among Children and Mothers in India', *Journal of State Medicine*, 36, 1928.

Malnutrition and Disease (Geneva: W.H.O., 1962).

MANCHANDA, S. S. and SACHDEV, K. K., 'Morbidity and Mortality in Children in Northern India', *Indian Journal of Paediatrics*, October 1962.

MANNHEIMER, E., 'Mortality of Breast Fed and Bottle Fed Infants: A Comparative Study', *Acta Genetica et Statistica Medica*, Basel, 5: 134–63, 1955.

MARAVIGLIA, MARIA NYDIA, 'Infant Mortality Trends in Latin America',

World Population Conference, Belgrade, 1965 (New York: United Nations, 1966).

MARTINEZ, P. D., et al., 'Mortalidad de la Ninez en Mexico', *Boletin de la Oficiana Sanataria Panamericana*, 47, 1959.

MASSEY, ARTHUR (Ed.), *Modern Trends in Public Health* (London: Butterworth, 1949).

Maternal and Child Health (With particular reference to integration into the General Health Services), (New Delhi: W.H.O. Regional Office for South East Asia, 1967).

Maternal and Child Health in the U.S.S.R. (Geneva: W.H.O., 1962).

Maternal and Newborn Nutrition Studies at Philadelphia Lying-in Hospital (New York: Milbank Memorial Fund, 1958).

Maternal Mortality in Childbirth: A Summary of the Investigation Conducted Under the Indian Research Fund Association, 1925–27 (New Delhi: Government of India Press, 1928).

Maternal Nutrition and Child Health (Washington, D.C.: National Research Council, 1950).

Maternity in Great Britain (London: Oxford University Press, 1948).

MATHEN, K. K. and POTI, S. J., 'An Adjustment for the Effect of Changing Birth Rates on Infant Mortality Rates', *Sankhya*, June 1954.

MATHEW, N. T. and PANT, PITAMBER, *Report on the Present Statistical Organization in Provinces and States* (New Delhi, 1949).

MATHIESSEN, P. C., *Infant Mortality in Denmark 1931–1960* (Copenhagen: Statistical Department, 1965).

MAURER, ROSE, *Child Care in the Soviet Union* (New York: The National Council of American–Soviet Friendship, 1950).

MAYER, ALBERT J. and MARKS, RICHARD V., 'Differentials in Infant Mortality by Race, Economic Level and Cause of Death for Detroit, 1940–50', *Human Biology*, 1952.

MAYO, KATHERINE, *Mother India* (New York: Blue Ribbon Books, 1930).

MCCARRISON, ROBERT, *Nutrition and National Health* (London: Faber & Faber, 1936).

MCCARTY, R., et al., 'A Quinquennial Study of Infant Mortality, Omaha–Douglas County, Nebraska, 1880–1960', *Nebraska State Medical Journal*, July 1964.

MCCLEARY, G. F., *Infant Mortality and Infant Milk Depots* (London: 1905).

MCCLEARY, G. F., *The Early History of the Infant Welfare Movement* (London: Lewis, 1933).

MCCLEARY, G. F., *The Maternity and Child Welfare Movement* (London: P. S. King, 1935).

MCCLEARY, G. F., *The Development of British Maternity and Child Welfare Services* (London: National Association of Maternity and Child Welfare Centres and for the Prevention of Infant Mortality, 1945).

MCCOY, R. S., 'Perinatal Mortality', *Medical Journal of Malaya*, Singapore, September 1958.

367

McKEOWN, THOMAS and GIBSON, J. R., 'Observations on all Births (23,970) in Birmingham, 1947: IV. Premature Births', *British Medical Journal*, September 1951.

McKEOWN, THOMAS and GIBSON, J. R., 'Observations on All Births (23,970) in Birmingham, 1947', *British Journal of Social Medicine*, October 1951.

McKEOWN, T. and LOWE, C. R., 'The Sex Ratio of Stillbirths related to Causes and Duration of Gestation', *Human Biology*, February 1951.

McKEOWN, T. and LOWE, C. R., 'Sex Ratio of Stillbirths related to Birth Weight', *British Journal of Social Medicine*, October 1951.

McLAREN, D. S., 'A Study of the Factors Underlying the Special Incidence of Keratomalacia in Oriya Children in the Phulbani and Ganjam Districts of Orissa, India', *Journal of Tropical Paediatrics*, 1956, 2, 135.

McMAHAN, C. A., 'Lower Limit of the Infant Mortality Rate in the United States', *Milbank Memorial Fund Quarterly*, October 1959.

McNIEL, CHARLES, 'Child Health in Holland, England and Scotland: Sixty Years of progress', *British Medical Journal*, April 4, 1942.

McNIEL, CHARLES, 'Infantile Mortality; The Clinical Aspect', *Journal of the Royal Sanitary Institute*, 67, 1947.

MEDICAL SOCIETY FOR THE COUNTY, SPECIAL COMMITTEE ON INFANT MORTALITY *Proceedings 1951–1952* (New York, 1952).

MEDYANIK, R. V., 'Measures to Reduce Infant Mortality in the Ukranian Soviet Socialist Republic', *Proceedings of the World Population Conference, Belgrade*, New York: United Nations, 1966.

MEERDINK, J. and RAMACHANDRAN, K. V., 'Infant Mortality According to Social Status in Greater Bombay', *Journal of the Indian Medical Association*, May 1, 1962.

MEHDI, Z., NAIDU, P. M. and GOPALRAO, V., 'Incidence and Causes of Perinatal Mortality in Hyderabad, Andhra Pradesh, India', *Indian Journal of Medical Research*, September 1961.

MEDHI, Z. and NAIDU, P. M., 'Peri-natal Mortality: A Statistical Survey from Hyderabad', *Journal of Obstetrics and Gynaecology of India*, December 1961.

Memorandum on the Conduct of an Enquiry into Infant Mortality (Delhi: Indian Research Fund Association, 1949).

Memorandum Related to the Enquiries into the Causes and Prevention of Stillbirths and Mortality during the First Year of Life (Geneva: League of Nations Health Organization, 1930).

MENON, K. M. K., 'Perinatal Mortality in India', *Journal of International Federation of Gynaecologists and Obstetricians*, 1, 1963.

METHORST, H. W., 'Research on Income, Nationality and Infant Mortality in Holland', In Pitt-Rivers, W.H.L.F. (Ed.), *Problems of Population: Proceedings of the International Union for the Scientific Investigation of Population Problem*, London, 1932.

MEYER, ERNEST C., *Infant Mortality in New York City* (New York, 1921).

Midwives: A Survey of Recent Legislation (Geneva: W.H.O., 1954).

MILBANK MEMORIAL FUND, *The Promotion of Maternal and Newborn Health; Papers Presented at the 1954 Conference of the Fund*, New York, 1955.

MILBANK MEMORIAL FUND, *Trends and Differentials in Mortality*, New York, 1956.

MILLER, F. J. W., 'Classification of Deaths in Infancy', *The Lancet*, September 5, 1942.

MILLER, F. J. W., 'The Mortality of Birth', *The Medical Officer*, May 15, 1954.

MILLIN, GILBERT W., 'Foetal Life Tables; A Means of Establishing Perinatal Rates or Risk', *Journal of the American Medical Association*, April 1962.

MINKOWSKI, A., *Public Health Aspects of Low Birth Weight; Comments on Prematurity Criteria* (Geneva: W.H.O., 1960).

MITCHELL, HELEN S., et al., *Nutrition in Health and Disease* (Philadelphia: Lippincott, 1963).

MITRA, K. N., et al., 'A Study of Recent Trends in Infantile Mortality Rates in Calcutta by Longitudinal Survey', *Sankhya*, Part 2, 1951.

MITRA, S., 'Infant Mortality and its Relation to Normal and Abnormal Conditions of Pregnancy and Labour', *Indian Journal of Paediatrics*, October 1934.

MONCRIEFF, ALAN, *Infant Feeding* (London: Edward Arnold, 1948).

MONCRIEFF, ALAN, *Child Health and the State* (London: Oxford University Press, 1953).

Monthly Vital Statistics Report: Annual Summary for the United States, 1966 Births, Deaths, Marriages and Divorces (Washington, D.C.: U.S. Department of Health, Education and Welfare, 1967).

MORDECAI, J., 'Analysis of Autopsies on Infants at the Sassoon Hospital, Poona', *Indian Journal of Child Health*, September 1960.

MORIYAMA, I. M., 'Present Status of Definition of Perinatal Mortality in the United States', *Canadian Journal of Public Health*, February 1959.

MORIYAMA, I. M., 'Recent Change in Infant Mortality Trend', *Public Health Reports*, 75: May 1960.

MORIYAMA, I. M., 'Infant Mortality in Certain Countries of Low Mortality', *Proceedings of the World Population Conference, Belgrade, 1965* (New York: United Nations, Vol. 2, 1965).

MORIYAMA, I. M., 'Present Status of Infant Mortality Problem in the United States', *American Journal of Public Health and Nation's Health*, April 1966.

MORRIS, J. N. and HEADY, J. A., 'Social and Biological Factors in Infant Mortality: Objects and Methods', *The Lancet*, February 12, 1955.

MORRIS, J. N., HEADY, J. A. and DALY, C., 'Social and Biological Factors in Infant Mortality: *V*. Mortality in Relation to Father's Occupation, 1911–50', *The Lancet*, March 12, 1955.

MORRIS, J. N., HEADY, J. A. and DALY, C., 'Social and Biological Factors in Infant Mortality – England and Wales, 1949–50', *Proceedings of the*

World Population Conference, 1954 (New York: United Nations, 1955).

MUDALIAR, A. L., *The Causes of Antenatal, Natal and Neonatal Mortality of Infants with Specific Reference to South India* (Madras: University of Madras, 1928).

MUNDO, F. D., 'Infant Mortality – A Challenge', *Journal of the Indian Paediatric Society*, January 1962.

MUTHUSUBRAMANIAN, A., 'Infant Mortality and Population Growth', *Indian Journal of Social Work*, April 1962.

MYER, E. C., *Infant Mortality in New York City: A Study of the Results Accomplished by Infant Life-Saving Agencies, 1885–1920* (New York: Rockefeller Foundation, International Health Board, 1921.

MYSORE STATUTES: *Act No. 3 of 1918: An Act to Make Provision for the Registration of Births and Deaths in Rural Tracts* (Bangalore, 1918).

NAG, ANIL CHANDRA, 'A Study in the Area Distribution of Infantile Mortality in Calcutta during 1905–35', *Sankhya*, December 1942.

NAIR, N. S. and NAYAR, T. C. V., 'Pre-natal Mortality in Calicut, Kerala', *Journal of Obstetrics and Gynaecology of India*, August 1965.

NAMBOZE, J. M., 'General Infections in the Newborn with Special Reference to East Africa', *Journal of Tropical Medicine and Hygiene*, 67, 1964.

National Conference on Infantile Mortality: Proceedings of a Conference held in London in 1906 (London: P. S. King, 1907).

'Neonatal Aspects of Infant Mortality', *Statistical Bulletin*, New York. Metropolitan Life Insurance Company, 48, 1967.

Neonatal Deaths due to Infection: Report of a Sub-Committee of the Scientific Advisory Committee (Edinburgh: Department of Health for Scotland, 1947).

Neonatal Mortality and Morbidity: Report by a Joint Committee of the Royal College of Obstetricians and Gynaecologists and the British Paediatric Association (London: H.M.S.O., 1949).

NESBIT, R. E. L., *Perinatal Loss in Modern Obstetrics* (Philadelphia: Davis, 1957).

NESBITT, R. E. L., JR, SCHLESINGER, E. R. and SHAPIRO, S., 'Role of Preventive Medicine in Reduction of Infant and Perinatal Mortality', *Public Health Reports*, August 1966.

NEWCOMBE, HOWARD B., 'Risk of Fetal Death to Mothers of Different A.B.O. and R.H. Blood Types', *American Journal of Human Genetics*, December 1963.

NEWMAN, GEORGE, *Health and Social Evolution*, Hailey Stewart Lecture, London, 1931.

NEWMAN, GEORGE, *Infant Mortality* (London: Methuen, 1906).

NEWSON, JOHN and ELIZABETH, *Infant Care in an Urban Community* (London: Allen & Unwin, 1963).

NEWSHOLME, ARTHUR, *The Last Thirty Years in Public Health* (London: Allen & Unwin, 1936).

THE NEW YORK ACADEMY OF MEDICINE, *Infant and Maternal Care in New York City* (New York: Columbia University Press, 1952).

NEW ZEALAND, *Report on Vital Statistics*, Wellington (for various years).

Nutrition: Report of a Seminar (New Delhi: Lady Irwin College, 1968).

Nutrition and Healthy Growth (Washington, D.C.: U.S. Children's Bureau, 1955).

Nutrition and Infection: Report of a W.H.O. Expert Committee (Geneva: W.H.O., 1965).

Nutrition in Pregnancy and Lactation: Report of a W.H.O. Committee (Geneva: W.H.O., 1965).

'An Object Lesson in Infant Mortality', *Statistical Bulletin*, New York. Metropolitan Life Insurance Company, October 1938.

OFFICE OF HEALTH ECONOMICS (LONDON), *Infants at Risk: An Historical and International Comparison* (London, 1964).

OKASAKI, AYANORI, 'Infant Mortality in Japan', *Courier* (Centre International de l'Enfance), March 1953.

ONABAMIRO, SANYA DOJO, *Why Our Children Die: The Causes and Suggestions for Prevention of Infant Mortality in West Africa* (London: Methuen, 1949).

OOMEN, H. A. P. C., 'Infant Malnutrition in Indonesia', *Bulletin of the World Health Organization*, 9, 1953.

OOMEN, H. A. P. C. and MALCOLM, S. H., *Nutrition and the Papuan Child: A Study in Human Welfare* (Noumea, New Caledonia: South Pacific Commission, 1958).

OPPENHEIMER, ELLA, 'Population Changes and Perinatal Mortality', *American Journal of Public Health*, February 1961.

O'REILLY, M. J. J. and WHILEY, M. K., 'Cot Deaths in Brisbane, 1962–1966', *Medical Journal of Australia*, 2, 1967.

ORISSA: *Report on Vital Statistics and Fertility* (Census of India, 1961, Vol. XII: Orissa, Pt I-B) (Delhi: Manager of Publications, 1969).

ORKNEY, JEAN M., 'Maternity and Child Welfare', *The Journal of the Association of Medical Women in India*, November 1932.

ORKNEY, JEAN M., 'The Influence of Feeding on Infant Mortality', *Indian Medical Gazette*, August 1946.

ORR, JOHN B., *Food, Health and Income* (London: Macmillan, 1937).

PAN AMERICAN SANITARY BUREAU, *Child Mortality in the Americas: Facts and Figures* (Washington D.C. 1957).

PARPIA, H. A. B., *India – Infant and Weaning Foods* (W.H.O. 1966).

PARPIA, H. A. B., *A Note on Pre-cooked Protein Food Formulation Suitable for Feeding Weaned Infants and Young Children* (W.H.O.: U.N.I.C.E.F. 1965).

PARPIA, H. A. B., *Production of Infant Food Based on Peanut Flour* (W.H.O.: U.N.I.C.E.F. 1965).

PASCUA, M., 'Natality, Mortality and Infant Mortality in 1949', *Epidemiological and Vital Statistics Report*, 3, 1950.

PASCUA, M., 'Natality, Mortality and Infant Mortality in 1950', *Epidemiological and Vital Statistics Report*, 4, 1951.

PASCUA, M., 'Natality, General Mortality and Infant Neonatal Mortality in 1951', *Epidemiological and Vital Statistics Report*, 5, 1952.

371

PASCUA, M., 'Natality, Mortality and Infant Mortality in 1951', *Epidemiological and Vital Statistics Report*, 5, 1952.

PASCUA, M., 'Brief Summary of Recent Mortality Trends in Areas of Higher Death Rates', *Proceedings of the World Population Conference, 1954*, New York: United Nations, 1955.

PASSAMORE, R., *Nutritional Diseases of India* (Calcutta: Dhar, 1948).

PATNAIK, K. C. and SARMA, A. S. R., 'Changing Trends in Mortality and Morbidity in India', *Indian Journal of Medical Research*, November 1967.

PATWARDHAN, V. N. 'Nutrition in India', *Indian Journal of Medical Services*, Bombay, 1962.

PATWARDHAN, V. N. and KAMEL, W. W., *Studies on Vitamin A Deficiency in Infants and Young Children in Jordan* (W.H.O., 1967).

PEARSON, H. E. and ANDERSON, G. V., 'Perinatal Deaths Associated with Bacteroides Infections', *Obstetrics and Gynaecology*, 30, 1967.

Paediatrics in General Practice (Hyderabad: College of General Practitioners, 1967).

PELLER, SIGISMUND, *Der Geburtstod* (Vienna: Franz Denticke, 1936).

PELLER, SIGISMUND, 'Mortality, Past and Future', *Population Studies*, March 1948.

PELLER, SIGISMUND, 'Proper Delineation of the Neonatal Period in Perinatal Mortality', *American Journal of Public Health and Nation's Health*, July 1965.

PERITZ, E., 'Infant Mortality in Israel 1960–61 – A Study Based on Matched Birth and Death', *World Population Conference, Belgrade, 1965*, New York: United Nations, 1966.

PETERSON, D. and SMITH, J. F., *Modern Methods of Feeding in Infancy and Childhood* (London: Constable, 1947).

PHADKE, M. V., 'Causes of Infant Mortality and Morbidity', *Journal of Indian Paediatric Society*, October 1962.

PHELPS E. B. 'The World-wide Efforts to Diminish Infant Mortality in its Present Status and its Possibilities', *Transactions of the Fiftieth International Congress of Hygiene and Demography* (Washington, D.C.: 1912).

PIMPARKAR, S. V., 'Trends in the Registered Infant Mortality Rates in the Union Territory of Delhi', *Punjab Medical Journal*, April 1965.

PLATT, B. S., *Chinese Methods of Infant Feeding and Nursing* (London, 1938).

POSTHUMA, J. H., *Demography, Perinatal Mortality and Care of the Newborn in the Netherlands* (With Special Reference to Rotterdam), 1956.

POSTHUMA, J. H., 1. *Perinatal Problems in Countries with Reduced Infant Mortality*; 2. *Organization of Services and the Role of Personnel*; 3. *Training of Personnel*; 1953.

POTI, S. JANARDAN and BISWAS, S., 'Study of Child Health During the First Year of Life', *Sankhya* (B), November 1963.

POTTER, EDITH L. and ADAIR, FRED L., *Foetal and Neonatal Death* (Chicago: University of Chicago Press, 1949).

POTTER, E. L., 'Planning Perinatal Mortality Studies', *Obstetrics and Gynaecology*, March 1959.

POWERS, L. E., et al., 'Infant Mortality in Rural Lebanon', *Journal Medical Libunais*, May–September 1955.

Problems of Foetal and Neonatal Mortality (Albany: New York Bureau of Maternal and Child Health, 1950).

Proceedings of the Third All-India Sanitary Conference held at Lucknow, 1914 (Calcutta: Thacker Spink, 1914).

PROVINCE, SALLYANN and LIPTON, ROSE C., *Infants in Institutions: A Comparison of their Development with Family Reared Infants during the First Year of Life* (New York: International University Press, 1962).

Public Health Aspects of Low Birth Weight: Third Report of the Expert Committee on Maternal and Child Health (Geneva: W.H.O., 1961).

PULOP, T., 'Considerations Concerning Investigations of the Problems of Infant Mortality', *Sante Publique: Revue International*, Bucharest, 9: 1967.

RACHMILEWITZ, D. and LOWENTHAL, H., 'Mortality of Prematures in the Negev', *Dapim Refuiim*, 23, 1964.

RADIN, M., 'Exposure of Infants in Roman Law and Practice', *Classical Journal*, March 1925.

RALPH, J. WEDGEWOOD and BENDITT, EARL P. (Eds), *Proceedings: Conference on Causes of Sudden Death in Infants* (Bethesda: National Institute of Child Health and Human Development, 1966).

RAMAIAH, T. J., 'Incidence of Prematurity and Perinatal Mortality; A Statistical Study', *Indian Journal of Public Health*, October 1967.

RAMIAH, T. J. and NARASIMHAN, V. L., 'Birth Weight as a Measure of Prematurity and its Relationship with Certain Maternal Factors', *Indian Journal of Medical Research*, May 1967.

RAO, K. SOMESWARA, et al., 'Protein Malnutrition in South India', *Bulletin of the World Health Organization, 1959, 20*. Also a summary of the same material in *W.H.O. Chronicle*, June 1959.

RAO, P. THIRUMALA (Ed.), *Paediatric Problems in Developing Countries*, Dr S. T. Achar Commemoration Volume (Madras: Orient Longmans, 1970).

RECORD, R. G., et al., 'Foetal and Infant Mortality in Multiple Pregnancy', *The Journal of Obstetrics and Gynaecology of the British Empire*, August 1952.

Report of the Age of Consent Committee, 1928–29 (Calcutta: Government Press, 1929).

Report on Annual Conference on Maternity and Child Welfare (London: National Association for Maternity and Child Welfare, 1952).

Report of the Inter-Departmental Committee on Official Statistics (Simla: Government of India Press, 1946).

Report of the International Conference on the Perinatal and Infant Mortality Problem of the United States (Washington, D.C.: U.S. Department of Health, Education and Welfare, 1966).

Report on Maternity and Child Welfare Work in India by Special Committee (Simla: Central Advisory Board of Health, 1939).

Report of National Sample Survey: Fourteenth Round – July 1958 to June 1959; Eighteenth Round – February 1963 to January 1964 (New Delhi: Cabinet Secretariat, Government of India, 1965).

Report of the Population Data Committee (Simla: Government of India Press, 1945).

Report of the Proceedings of the National Conference of Infantile Mortality (London: P. S. King, 1906).

Report of the Royal Commission on Labour in India (Calcutta: Government Press, 1931).

Report on Seminar on Protein Malnutrition in Children (New Delhi: W.H.O. Regional Office for South East Asia, 1963).

Report: Royal Commission on Agriculture in India (Bombay: Government Central Press, 1928).

RIBBLE, MARGARET, A., *The Rights of Infants; Early Psychological Needs and their Satisfaction* (New York: Columbia University Press, 1953).

ROBINSON, PINCHAS (Ed.), *A Manual of Paediatrics* (Madras: Orient Longmans, 1959).

ROBERTSON, E. J., 'Perinatal Mortality, The Problem and its Definition', *Canadian Journal of Public Health*, August 1959.

ROCHESTER, A., *Infant Mortality* (Washington, D.C.: U.S. Department of Labour, Children's Bureau, 1923).

ROMERO, H. and VILDOSOLA, J., 'Mortalidad Infantil', *Boletin de la Sanatoria Panamericana*, 35, 1953.

ROSE, R. J., *Infant and Foetal Loss in New Zealand* (Wellington: Government Printer, 1964).

ROSENFELD, F., 'La mortalité infantile à Alexandrie', *L'Egypte contemporaine* Cairo, 1939.

ROSS, R. A., 'Some Important Factors in Perinatal Mortality Statistics in a Rural State', *American Journal of Obstetrics and Gynaecology*, February 1, 1964.

ROY, KRISHNA, 'India's Changing Death Rate: A Critique', *Monthly Commentary of Indian Economic Conditions*, May 1965.

ROYAL COLLEGE OF OBSTETRICIANS AND GYNAECOLOGISTS and BRITISH PAEDIATRICS ASSOCIATION, *Neonatal Mortality and Morbidity* (London: H.M.S.O., 1949).

ROYAL COMMISSION ON POPULATION, *Reports of the Biological and Medical Committee: Reproductive Wastage: Abortion, Stillbirth and Infant Mortality* (London: H.M.S.O., 1950).

ROZDON, S., 'Infant Mortality', *The Proceedings of The Third All-India Sanitary Conference held at Lucknow, 1914, Vol. 2* (Calcutta: Thacker Spink, 1914).

SABRY, Z. I., *The Development of Protein Food Mixtures for Infant Feeding in the Middle East* (W.H.O., 1963).

Sample Registration Bulletin; Provisional Statistics (monthly) (New Delhi: Registrar-General, India).

SAND, RENE, *Health and Human Progress* (London: Macmillan, 1936).

SAND, RENE, *The Advance to Social Medicine* (London: Staples Press, 1952).

SANGAR, USHA and RAMA RAO, AMLA, 'Maternal and Child Health Services in Delhi', *Indian Journal of Public Health*, January 1969.

SARKANY, I. and GAYLARDE, C. C., 'Skin Flora of the Newborn', *Lancet*, 1, 1967.

SARMA, VISHNU, 'Congenital Abnormalities of the Foetus and their Association with Genital Tract Malformations in the Mother', *The British Journal of Clinical Practice*, July 1965.

SATUR, D. M. and BHATIA, S., *A Review of Work Done on Infant Mortality* (New Delhi: Indian Council of Medical Research, 1957).

SAVAGE, S., 'Intelligence and Infant Mortality Among Problem Families', *British Medical Journal, Vol. 1*, 1946.

SAXENA, G. B., 'Analysis of Inequalities in Infantile Mortality; A Sample Survey of Rural Uttar Pradesh', *Medical Digest*, March 1962.

SCHLESINGER, EDWARD R. and ALLAWAY, NORMAN C., 'The Combined Effect of Birth Weight and Length of Gestation on Neonatal Mortality Among Single Premature Births', *Paediatrics*, June 1955.

SCHLESINGER, E. R. and NESBITT, R. E. L., JR, 'Public Health Viewpoint: Scope and Perspective (Perinatal Mortality)', *Clinical Obstetrics and Gynaecology*, June 1961.

SCHOENECK, F. J., 'Progress in Reduction of Perinatal Mortalities', *New York State Journal of Medicine*, November 15, 1962.

SCHOENECK, F. J., 'Infectious Factors in Perinatal Mortality', *New York State Journal of Medicine*, November 1964.

SCRIMSHAW, N. S., et al., *Interactions of Nutrition and Infection* (Geneva: W.H.O., 1968).

SCURLETIS, T. D., et al., 'Trends in Infant Mortality in North Carolina, 1933-36', *North Carolina Medical Journal*, August 1966.

SELLERS, A. H., 'Some Further Data on the Causes of Stillbirth in Ontario', *Canadian Journal of Public Health*, January 1954.

SELLWYN, SYDNEY and BAIN, A. D., 'Deaths in Childhood Due to Infection', *British Journal of Preventive and Social Medicine*, 19: 1965.

SEN, A. R., *Vital Statistics in the United Provinces* (Allahabad: Superintendent of Printing, 1948).

SEN GUPTA, N., 'Infant Mortality and Hindu Customs', *Medical Review of Reviews*, 5, 1930.

SEN, MUKHTA, 'Maternity and Child Welfare Work in the Singhur Health Centre', *Mother and Child*, December 1950.

SHAPIRO, S., 'Influence of Birth Weight, Sex and Plurality on Neonatal Loss in The United States', *American Journal of Public Health and the Nation's Health*, September 1954.

SHAPIRO, S., et al., *Infant and Perinatal Mortality in the United States*, National Center for Health Statistics, October 1965.

SHAPIRO, S., SCHLESINGER, E. R. and NESBITT, R. E. L., *Infant, Perinatal, Maternal, and Childhood Mortality in the United States* (Cambridge, Mass.: Harvard University Press, 1968).

375

SHARMA, H. M., *Enquiry into Infant Mortality in the Poonamallee Health Unit Area Under the Director of Public Health* (Madras, 1955).

SHARMA, M. L., 'Infant Mortality in India and its Causes and Prevention', *Indian Medical Journal*, 27, 1933.

SHETH, S. C., 'Perinatal Morbidity and Mortality', *Indian Journal of Child Health*, July 1961.

SHETTY, B. M. V., NAYER, V. and SOKHI, S. K., 'Pre-natal Mortality; A Clinico-Pathological Correlation of Causes among 400 Autopsies', *Journal of Obstetrics and Gynaecology of India*, December 1, 1961.

SHU-CHUNG, S., TI-HSIEN, C. and CHIEH, S., 'Endeavours to Reduce Perinatal Mortality in a Maternity Hospital', *Chinese Medical Journal*, 85, 1966.

SIEGEL, E., et al., 'Post-neonatal Deaths in North Carolina, 1959–1963', *North Carolina Medical Journal*, August 1966.

SINGH, PAUL S., 'A Study of Mortality Rate in Kalavati Saran Hospital', *Indian Journal of Child Health*, November 1959.

SKOGRAND, A. and HARNAES, K., 'Causes of Death in Premature Infants', *Acta Pathologica et Microbiologica Scandinavica*, Copenhagen, 49, 1960.

SMITH, ANTHONY, *The Body* (London: Allen & Unwin, 1968).

SMITH, C. A., *The Physiology of the Newborn Infant* (Springfield, Illinois: Thomas, 1951).

SMITH, C. A., *Shortcomings of Present Definition of Prematurity* (W.H.O., 1960).

SAROJINI, R., 'Pre-natal Mortality in Forceps Operations in King George Hospital, Vishakhapatnam', *Journal of Obstetrics and Gynaecology of India*, December 1961.

SPENCE, J. C. and MILLER, F. J. W., *Report of an Investigation into the Causes of Infantile Mortality in Newcastle upon Tyne During the Year 1939* (Newcastle upon Tyne: Christie & Malcolm, 1941).

SPENCE, JAMES, WALTON, W. S., MILLER, F. J. W. and COURT, S. D. M., *A Thousand Families in Newcastle upon Tyne* (London: Oxford University Press, 1954).

SPICER, C. C. and LIPWORTH, L., *Regional and Social Factors in Infant Mortality* (London: H.M.S.O., 1966).

SPITE, A. J. W., *Malaria Infection of the Placenta and Its Influence of Prematurity in Eastern Nigeria* (W.H.O., 1959).

SPITZ, RENE ARPAD, *The First Year of Life: A Psychosomatic Study of Normal and Deviant Development of Object Relations* (in Collaboration with W. Godfrey Cobliner) (New York: International University Press, 1965).

SPOCK, B. M., *Baby and Child Care* (New York: Pocket Books, 1957).

STEINER, MORRIS and POMERANCE, WILLIAM, 'Studies on Prematurity II. Influence of Fetal Maturity on Fatality Rate', *Paediatrics*, December 1950.

STEVENSON, ALAN C., et al., *Congenital Malformations: Report of a Study of Series of Consecutive Births in 24 Centres* (Geneva: W.H.O., 1966).

376

STEWARD, DAVID B. and SCOTT, EILEEN M., 'The Assessment of Efficiency in Labour: Psychological Factors Related to Labour', *The Transactions of the Edinburgh Obstetrical Society*, 1952–53.

STOLNITZ, G. J., 'Recent Mortality Trends in Latin America, Asia and Africa', *Population Studies*, November 1965.

STONE, EMERSON L., *The New-born Infant: A Manual of Obstetrics and Paediatrics* (Philadelphia: Lea and Febiger, 1946).

STOUMAN, K., 'The Perilous Threshold of Life', *Quarterly Bulletin of the Health Organization*, League of Nations, December 1934.

STOWMAN, K., 'Downward Trend of Infant Mortality Persists', *Epidemiological and Vital Statistics Report*, 1, 1948.

Study Group on Perinatal Mortality, Dublin, 26–30 November, 1956: Report, 1957.

A Study of Maternal, Infant and Neo-natal Mortality in Canada (Ottawa: Dominion Bureau of Statistics, 1942).

SUHRAWADY, H., *Mother and Infant Welfare for India* (Lillooah, 1926).

Summary of Vital and Health Statistics, South East Asia Region (New Delhi: W.H.O. Regional Office for South East Asia, 1966).

SURINDER NATH, 'Infant Mortality', *Licentiate*, December 1959.

SUTHERLAND, IAN, 'The Stillbirth Rate in England and Wales in Relation to Social Influences', *The Lancet*, December 1946.

SUTHERLAND, IAN, *Stillbirths: Their Epidemiology and Social Significance* (London: Oxford University Press, 1949).

SWAMI, A. and MANGOL, S., 'Economic Implications of Infant Mortality', *Journal of Family Welfare*, June 1961.

SWAROOP, SATYA, 'Note on the Probable Effect of a Decrease in Infantile Mortality on the Future Population of India', *Census of India* by M. W. M. Yeatts, Vol. 1 (Simla: Government of India Press, 1943).

SWAROOP, SATYA, *Probable Effect of Decrease in Infantile Mortality on Future Population*, Paper No. 3, Census of India, (New Delhi, 1949).

SYDENSTRICKER, E., *Health and Environment* (New York: McGraw Hill, 1933).

Symposium on Infant Nutrition, New York, 1959 (Chicago: Council on Foods and Nutrition, American Medical Association, 1961).

'Symposium on the Newborn', *Paediatric Clinics of North America*, 13, 1966.

SZARKANY, J., 'Methods of Analysis of Infantile Mortality', *Sante Publique: Revue Internationale* (Bucharest), 7, 1964.

TABACK, MATTHEW, 'Birth Weight and Length of Gestation in Relation to Prematurity', *Journal of American Medical Association*, 32: 793, 1963.

TAKAHASHI, EIJI, 'The Sex Ratio of Neonatal Deaths in Japan', *Human Biology*, May 1954.

TAYLOR, E. STEWART and WALKER, LOUISE C., 'Premature Infant Deaths', *Obstetrics and Gynaecology*, May 1959.

TAYLOR, WALLIS, 'The Changing Pattern of Mortality in England and Wales: Infant Mortality', *British Journal of Preventive and Social Medicine*, January 1954.

377

TAYLOR, W. F., 'On the Methodology of Measuring the Probability of Fetal Death in a Prospective Study', *Human Biology*, May 1964.

The Children's Annual (New Delhi: The Indian Council for Child Welfare, 1967).

The Children in Day Centres (Geneva: W.H.O., 1964).

The Midwife in Maternity Care (Geneva: W.H.O., 1966).

The Effects of Labour on the Foetus and the Newborn (Geneva: W.H.O., 1965).

THIERSCH, S. (Ed.), *Ciba Foundation Symposium on Congenital Malformations* (London, 1960).

THOMAS, R. H., *Report of the Measures by A. Walker and Subsequently by I. P. Willoughby and his Successors for the Suppression of Female Infanticide in the Province of Kathiawar* (Bombay, 1893).

THOMAS, R. H., *Report of the Measures Adopted for the Suppression of Female Infanticide* (Bombay, 1856).

THOMPSON, A. M., 'Human Foetal Growth', *British Journal of Nutrition*, Vol. 5, 1951.

THOMPSON, CHRISTINE J., *Stillbirths and Neonatal Deaths in India: A Preliminary Inquiry* (London: Lewis, 1931).

THOMSON, J., 'Introduction to Prenatal Mortality', *Journal of Indian Medical Profession*, May 1963.

THORBURN, M. J. and CURZEN, P., 'Perinatal Mortality in The University College Hospital of the West Indies, Jamaica', *West Indian Medical Journal*, December 1966.

THORNER, R. M. and WILLIAMS, E. H. JR, 'Neonatal Mortality in Florida: I. Birth Weight, Race and Sex', *Journal of The Florida Medical Association*, May 1956.

THORNER, R. M. and WILLIAMS, E. H. JR, 'Neonatal Mortality in Florida: II. Place of Birth, Attendance by Mid-wife or Physician', *Journal of The Florida Medical Association*, June 1956.

TIRUMURTI, T. S., 'Infantile Mortality and the Present State of Public Health in India', *Science and Culture*, April 1936.

TITMUSS, RICHARD M., *Birth, Poverty and Wealth: A Study of Infant Mortality* (London: Hamish Hamilton, 1943).

TITMUSS, RICHARD M., *Poverty and Population* (London: Macmillan, 1950).

TITMUSS, RICHARD M., *Problems of Social Policy* (London: H.M.S.O., 1950).

TOCK, P. C., 'An Autopsy Survey of Stillbirths and Neonatal Deaths in Singapore', *Journal of Tropical Paediatrics*, 10, 1964.

TOVERUD, KIRSTON, et al., *Maternal Nutrition and Child Health; An Interpretative Review* (Washington, D.C.: National Research Council, National Academy of Sciences, 1950).

Transcript of Report on Conference on Perinatal Mortality Held at the New York Academy of Medicine in 1957 (New York, 1958).

TSURUTA, J., 'Infant Mortality in a Rural Health Centre District and Its

Socio-economic Analysis', *Japanese Journal of Hygiene*, October 1961.

UDANI, P. M., 'Morbidity and Mortality', *Indian Journal of Child Health*, June 1962.

UNITED NATIONS, *Demographic Yearbook* (For the Years 1951, 1957, 1961, 1966, 1967), New York.

UNITED NATIONS, *Handbook of Vital Statistics Methods* (New York, 1955).

UNITED NATIONS, *Foetal, Infant and Early Childhood Mortality, Vol. I: Statistics* (New York, 1954).

UNITED NATIONS, *Foetal, Infant and Early Childhood Mortality, Vol. 2: Biological, Social and Economic Factors* (New York, 1954).

UNITED NATIONS, 'Testing Reliability of Age-Data in Census', *U.N. Population Bulletin*, New York, October 1952.

U.S. CHILDREN'S BUREAU, *Births, Infant Mortality and Maternal Mortality; Graphic Presentation* (Washington, D.C., 1940).

U.S. CHILDREN'S BUREAU. *Infant Care* (Washington, D.C., 1963).

U.S. NATIONAL CENTER FOR HEALTH STATISTICS, *Infant and Perinatal Mortality in England and Wales* (Washington D.C., 1968).

U.S. PUBLIC HEALTH SERVICE, 'Geography of Infant Mortality', *Public Health Reports*, March 1963.

VALAORAS, V. G., 'Refined Rates for Infant and Childhood Mortality', *Population Studies*, December 1950.

VAUGHAN, KATHLEEN OLGA, *The Purdah System and its Effect upon Motherhood* (Cambridge: Heffer, 1928).

VENKATACHALAM, P. and REBELLO, L. M., *Nutrition for Mother and Child* (Hyderabad: Nutrition Research Laboratories, 1962).

VERHOESTRAETE, LOUIS J. and PUFFER, RUTH R., 'Challenge of Fetal Loss, Prematurity and Infant Mortality – A World Review', *Journal of the American Medical Association*, June 1968.

VINCENT, M. and HUGON, J., *Studies on the Premature African Infant* (Geneva: W.H.O., 1960).

VINES, A. P. and DUDLEY, A., 'Perinatal Mortality Survey in Five Hospitals in Papua and New Guinea', *Papua and New Guinea Medical Journal*, 10, 1967.

VINYARD, JOHN H., 'Infant Mortality in Pennsylvania 1954–58', *Public Health Reports*, May 1960.

VISWANATHAN, T. K. and ATHVALE, V. B., 'Morbidity and Mortality in the Neonates', *Indian Paediatrics*, April 1969.

'Vital Statistics: Natality, General Mortality, Infant and Neonatal Mortality (From Third Quarter of 1965 to the Third Quarter of 1966)', *Epidemiological and Vital Statistics Report*, W.H.O., 20, 1967.

'Vital Statistics (Fourth Quarter of 1965 to the Fourth Quarter of 1966); Natality, General Mortality, Infant and Neonatal Mortality', *Epidemiological and Vital Statistics Report*, W.H.O., 20, 1967.

'Vital Statistics: Natality, General Mortality, Infant and Neonatal Mortality, I. 1966–1967', *Epidemiological and Vital Statistics Report*, W.H.O., 20, 1967.

'Vital Statistics: Natality, General Mortality, Infant and Neonatal Mortality (From the Second Quarter of 1966 to the Second Quarter of 1967)', *Epidemiological and Vital Statistics Report*, W.H.O., 20, 1967.

VYAS, K. J., 'Morbidity and Mortality in Children', *Indian Journal of Child Health*, June 1962.

WADIA, E. N., et al., 'Observations on 1,000 Live-Born Infants', *Indian Journal of Child Health*, April 1963.

WANG, SHU-CHEN and LU HSIANG-YUN, *Analysis of Causes of Stillbirths and Neonatal Deaths, Communist China* (Washington, D.C.: U.S. Joint Publication Research Service, July 1962).

WATERS, H. S., 'Neonatal Deaths and Stillbirths in Bombay', *Indian Medical Gazette*, August 1946.

WEBB, J. K. G., et al., 'Protein Malnutrition: Clinical Features and Patho-Physiology' in *Report of Seminar on Protein Malnutrition in Children* (New Delhi: W.H.O. Regional Office, 1968).

WEBSTER, A., 'Factors Affecting Neonatal Mortality', *American Journal of Obstetrics and Gynecology*, February 1957.

WEGMAN, MYRON E., et al., 'Infant Mortality and Infant Feeding in Puerto Rico', *The Puerto Rico Journal of Public Health and Tropical Medicine*, March 1942.

WEGMAN, MYRON E., et al., 'Public Health, Nursing and Medical Social Work', *Paediatrics*, October 1954 and January 1956.

WEGMAN, MYRON E., et al., 'Task of Practitioner in Child Health Protection', *Journal of the Oklahoma State Medical Association*, January 1950.

WENNEN-VAN DER MAY, C. A. M., 'A Longitudinal Study of Children at Igbo-Ora, Nigeria', *Tropical and Geographical Medicine*, 20, 1968.

WESTPHAL, M. C. and JOSHI, G. B., 'The Interrelationship of Birth Weight, Length of Gestation and Neonatal Mortality , *Clinical Obstetrics and Gynaecology*, 7, 1964.

WEST BENGAL, *Report on Vital Statistics*, Census of India 1961, Vol. XVI: West Bengal and Sikkim: Part I–B (Delhi: Manager of Publications, 1967).

WILKERSON, L. R., DONNELLY, J. F. and ABERNATHY, J. A., 'Perinatal Mortality and Premature Births Among Pregnancies complicated by Threatened Abortion', *American Journal of Obstetrics and Gynecology*, 96, 1966.

WINNICOTT, DONALD WOODS, *The Ordinary Devoted Mother and Her Baby; Nine Broadcast Talks* (London: Brock, 1949).

WINNICOTT, DONALD WOODS, *The Child and the Outside World: Studies in Developing Relationships* (London: Tavistock Publications, 1957).

WINSLOW, C. E. A. and HOLLAND, D. F., 'The Influence of Certain Public Health Procedures upon Infant Mortality', *Human Biology*, May 1937.

WISHART, W. DE W. and COCHRANE, E., *Infant Feeding in the Tropics*; with a chapter on the Milch Goat by W. S. Mitchell (London: Longmans Green, 1947).

WISHIK, SAMUEL M. and RYCHECK, RUSSEL R., 'A Formula for Comparison of Perinatal Mortality Rates in Hospitals', *American Journal of Public Health and the Nation's Health,* January 1966.

WOFINDEN, R. C., et al., *An Inquiry into Stillbirths and Neonatal Deaths in Bristol, 1948–50* (Bristol, 1952).

WOLF, GEORGE, *Maternal and Infant Mortality in 1944* (Washington, D.C.: Children's Bureau, 1947).

WOODBURY, R. M., *Infant Mortality and its Causes* (Baltimore: Williams and Wilkins, 1920).

WOODBURY, R. M., *Infant Mortality and Preventive Work in New Zealand* (Washington, D.C.: U.S. Children's Bureau, 1922).

WOODBURY, R. M., 'Relation between Breast and Artificial Feeding and Infant Mortality', *The American Journal of Hygiene,* November 1922.

WOODBURY, R. M., 'Economic Factors in Infant Mortality', *Journal of the American Statistical Association,* June 1924.

WOODBURY, R. M., 'Infant Mortality in the United States', *The Annals of the American Academy of Political and Social Science,* November 1936.

WOOLF, BARNETT, 'Studies on Infant Mortality', *Journal of Hygiene,* 44, 1945.

WOOLF, BARNETT, 'Studies on Infant Mortality', *The British Journal of Social Medicine,* April 1947.

WOOLF, B. and WATERHOUSE, J., 'Studies in Infant Mortality: Influence of Social Conditions in County Boroughs of England and Wales', *Journal of Hygiene,* 44, 1945.

YANKAUER, ALFRED, 'An Approach to the Cultural Base of Infant Mortality in India', *Population Review,* July 1959.

YERUSHALMY, J., et al., 'Studies on Childbirth Mortality', *Public Health Reports,* June and July 1940 and July 1941.

YERUSHALMY, J., et al., 'The 1940 Record of Maternal and Infant Mortality in the United States', *The Child* (Washington), February 1942.

YERUSHALMY, J., 'On the Interval between Successive Births and its Effect on Survival of Infant', *Human Biology,* May 1945.

YERUSHALMY, J., 'The Existence of an Optimum Interval between Births', *Human Fertility,* December 1945.

YERUSHALMY, J., 'The Classification of Newborn Infants by Birth Weight and Gestational Age', *Journal of Paediatrics,* 71, 1967.

YERUSHALMY, J. and BIERMAN, JESSIE M., 'Major Problems in Fetal Mortality', *Obstetrical and Gynaecological Survey,* February 1952.

YUN, D. J., 'Infant and Child Mortality in a Korean Rural Area', *Journal of Paediatrics,* December 1957.

II POPULATION PROBLEMS AND FAMILY PLANNING

AGARWAL, B. L., 'Sample Registration in India', *Population Studies,* November 1969.

BEHRMAN, S. J., CORSA, JR, LESLIE and FREEDMAN RONALD (Eds), *Fertility and Family Planning* (Ann Arbor: University of Michigan Press, 1969).

BERELSON, BERNARD, et al. (Eds), *Family Planning and Population Programs* (Chicago: University of Chicago Press, 1966).

BOSE, ASHISH, *Patterns of Population Change in India: 1951–61* (Bombay: Allied Publishers, 1967).

BOSE, ASHISH, DESAI, P. B. and JAIN, S. P., *Studies in Demography: Essays Presented in Honour of Professor S. Chandrasekhar* (London: Allen & Unwin and Chapel Hill: University of North Carolina Press, 1971).

BORGSTROM, GEORG, *The Hungry Planet* (New York: Macmillan, 1965).

CALLAHAN, DAVID, *Abortion: Law, Choice and Morality* (New York: Macmillan, 1970).

Census of India, 1951, Report, Vol. 1 Part 1A (New Delhi: Government of India Press, 1953).

Census of India, 1951, Estimation of Births and Deaths in India During 1941–50 (New Delhi: Government of India Press, 1954).

Census of India, 1961, Paper No. 1 of 1962 (New Delhi: Government of India Press, 1962).

Census of India, 1961, Vol. 1 Part 1A Levels of Regional Development in India. Part I of the General Report on India (New Delhi: Government of India Press, 1964).

CHANDRASEKHAR, S., 'Prospect of Planned Parenthood in India', *Pacific Affairs*, December 1953.

CHANDRASEKHAR, S., 'Population Growth, Socio-economic Development and Living Standards', *International Labour Review*, July 1954.

CHANDRASEKHAR, S., 'The Family in India', *Marriage and Family Living*, November 1954.

CHANDRASEKHAR, S., *Hungry People and Empty Lands* (London: Allen & Unwin, 1954), third edition.

CHANDRASEKHAR, S., 'Cultural Barriers to Family Planning in Under-developed Countries', *The Rationalist Annual*, December 1955.

CHANDRASEKHAR, S., 'Family Planning in Rural India', *Antioch Review*, Spring 1959.

CHANDRASEKHAR, S., 'A Note on Demographic Statistics in India', *Population Review*, January 1960.

CHANDRASEKHAR, S., *Population and Planned Parenthood in India* (London: Allen & Unwin, 1961), second edition.

CHANDRASEKHAR, S., 'A Billion Indians by 2,000 A.D.', *The New York Times Magazine*, April 4, 1965.

CHANDRASEKHAR, S., 'Should We Legalize Abortion in India', *Population Review*, July 1966.

CHANDRASEKHAR, S., 'Asia's Population Problems', in Guy Wint (Ed.), *Asia: A Handbook* (London: Anthony Bond and New York: Praeger, 1966).

CHANDRASEKHAR, S. (Ed.), *Asia's Population Problems* (London: Allen & Unwin, 1967).

CHANDRASEKHAR, S., 'Population Control Successful in India', *Journal of the American Medical Association*, June 3, 1968.

CHANDRASEKHAR, S., 'India's Population Policy', *Manchester Guardian*, August 15, 1968.

CHANDRASEKHAR, S., 'How India is Tackling her Population Problem', *Foreign Affairs*, October 1968.

CHANDRASEKHAR, S., *India's Population: Fact, Problem and Policy* (Meerut: Meenakshi Prakashan, 1970), second edition.

CHANDRASEKHAR, S. and CHARLES HULTMAN (Eds), *Problems of Economic Development* (Boston: Heath, 1967).

COALE, A. J. and HOOVER, E. M., *Population Growth and Economic Development in Low Income Countries* (Princeton: Princeton University Press, 1958).

DAVIS, KINGSLEY, 'Population Policy: Will Current Programs Succeed?', *Science*, November 10, 1967.

DEMARATH, NICHOLAS J., 'Can India Reduce Its Birth Rate? A Question of Modernization and Governmental Capacity', *Journal of Social Issues*, October 1967.

Demography and Vital Statistics (Census of India 1961, Madras, Part 1B) (Delhi: Manager of Publications, 1965).

DESAI, P. B., *Size and Sex Composition of Population in India: 1901-1961* (New Delhi: Asia Publishing House, 1969).

DRAPER, ELIZABETH, *Birth Control in the Modern World* (Harmondsworth: Penguin Books, 1965).

EHRLICH, PAUL R. and EHRLICH, ANNE, *Population, Resources Environment: Issues in Human Ecology* (San Francisco: Freeman, 1970).

ENKE, STEPHEN, 'The Gains to India from Population Control', *Review of Economics and Statistics*, May 1960.

ETIENNE, GILBERT, *Indian Agriculture, The Science of the Possible* (Berkeley: University of California Press, 1968).

FREDERICKSEN, H., 'Feedbacks in Economic and Demographic Transition', *Science*, November 4, 1969.

GUTTMACHER, A. F., BEST, WINFIELD and JAFFE, FREDERICK S., *Birth Control and Love* (New York: Macmillan, 1969).

HALL, ROBERT (Ed.), *Abortion in a Changing World* (New York: Columbia University Press, 1970) 2 vols.

HARDIN, GARRETT, *Population, Evolution and Birth Control: A Collage of Controversial Ideas* (San Francisco: W. H. Freeman, 1969).

HAUSER, PHILIP M., *World Population Problems* (New York: Foreign Policy Association, 1965).

HEER, DAVID M. and SMITH, DEAN O., 'Mortality Level, Desired Family Size and Population Increase', *Demography. Vol. 5, No. 1, 1968.

HILL, REUBEN, DRIVER EDWIN D. and NAG, MONI, *Needed Social Science Research in Population and Family Planning* (New Delhi: The Ford Foundation, 1968).

383

HIMES, NORMAN E., *Medical History of Contraception* (New York: Gamut Press, 1963).

INDIA, OFFICE OF THE REGISTRAR-GENERAL, *Vital Statistics of India for 1961* (New Delhi, 1964).

INDIA, OFFICE OF THE REGISTRAR-GENERAL, *Report on the Population Projections* (New Delhi, 1968).

INDIA, PLANNING COMMISSION, *The First Five-Year Plan – A Draft Outline* (New Delhi: Government of India, 1951).

INDIA, PLANNING COMMISSION, *The First Five-Year Plan* (New Delhi: Government of India, 1953).

INDIA, PLANNING COMMISSION, *The Second Five-Year Plan* (New Delhi: Government of India, 1956).

INDIA, PLANNING COMMISSION, *Third Five-Year Plan* (New Delhi: Government of India, 1960).

INDIA, PLANNING COMMISSION, *Fourth Five-Year Plan 1969–74* (New Delhi: Government of India, 1970).

KISER, CLYDE V. (Ed.), *Research in Family Planning* (Princeton University Press, 1962).

KOYA, Y., 'A Study of Induced Abortion in Japan', *Milbank Memorial Fund Quarterly*, July 1954.

MCNAMARA, ROBERT S., *Address to the University of Notre Dame* (Washington, D.C.: World Bank, 1968).

MURAMATSU, M. and HARPER P. A. (Eds), *Population Dynamics* (Baltimore: Johns Hopkins Press, 1965).

MYRDAL, GUNNAR, *Asian Drama* (London: Allen Lane, 1968) 3 vols.

NATIONAL ACADEMY OF SCIENCE NATIONAL RESEARCH COUNCIL, *The Growth of World Population* (Washington, D.C., 1963).

Papers Contributed by Indian Authors to the World Population Conference Belgrade, August–September 1965 (New Delhi: Office of the Registrar-General, 1965).

PETERSEN, WILLIAM, *The Politics of Population* (Garden City: Doubleday, 1964).

PETERSEN, WILLIAM, *Population* (New York: Macmillan, 1969).

RAINWATER, LEE, *And the Poor Get Children* (Chicago: Quadrangle Books, 1960).

RAINWATER, LEE, *Family Design, Marital Sexuality, Family Size and Contraception* (Chicago: Aldine, 1965).

RAULET, HARRY M., 'Family Planning and Population Control in Developing Countries', *Demography*, 1970, 7:2.

Report of the Committee to Study the Question of Legalization of Abortion (New Delhi: Ministry of Health and Family Planning, 1967).

ROSSI, ALICE S., 'Social Change and Abortion Law Reform', Paper Presented to the American Orthopsychiatric Association, Chicago, 1968.

SAUVY, ALFRED, *General Theory of Population* (New York: Basic Books, 1970).

384

SCHIEFFELIN, OLIVIA (Ed.), *Muslim Attitudes Toward Family Planning* (New York: The Population Council, 1967).

SHELESNYAK, M. C. (Ed.), *Growth of Population* (New York: Gordon & Breach, 1969).

STOLNITZ, GEORGE J., *An Analysis of the Population of India* (New Delhi: A.I.D. Office, 1967), mimeographed.

STOLNITZ, GEORGE J., *Estimating the Birth Effects of India's Family Planning Targets: A Report on Statistical Methodology and Illustrative Projections, 1968–78* (New Delhi: A.I.D. Office, 1968).

THOMLINSON, RALPH, *Demographic Problems: Controversy over Population Control* (Belmont, California: Dickensen, 1967).

THOMPSON, WARREN S., *Population and Progress in the Far East* (Chicago: University of Chicago Press, 1959).

UNITED NATIONS, *The Determinants and Consequences of Population Trends* (New York: 1953).

UNITED NATIONS, *Report on the Family Planning Program in India* (New York, 1966).

UNITED NATIONS, *Methods of Estimating Basic Demographic Measures from Incomplete Data* (New York, 1967).

UNITED NATIONS, *Evaluation of the Family Planning Programme in India* (New York, 1969).

VOGT, WILLIAM, *People* (New York: William Sloane, 1960).

INDEX OF NAMES

387

INDEX OF SUBJECTS